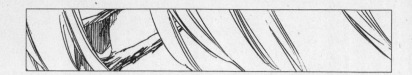

There is no pain as long as I keep my eyes on the balance scale.

BLEACH 70 | FRIEND

Shonen Jump Manga

ALL STARS AND

ユーハバッハ

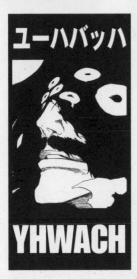

YHWACH

BAZZ-B

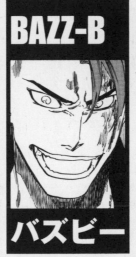

バズビー

ユーグラム・ハッシュヴァルト

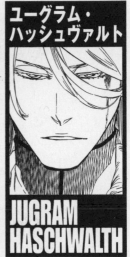

JUGRAM HASCHWALTH

plot

Ichigo Kurosaki meets Soul Reaper Rukia Kuchiki and ends up helping her eradicate Hollows. After developing his powers as a Soul Reaper, Ichigo befriends many humans and Soul Reapers and grows as a person...

As Yhwach absorbs the power of Reio, the three Quincies who survived the Auswahlen appear before Kyoraku. Bazz-B then proposes an alliance in order to defeat Yhwach. Meanwhile, Ichigo and friends join up with Grimmjow, Nel, Riruka and Yukio thanks to Urahara. They then succeed in getting to Reiokyu again, but find that it's been transformed by Yhwach. As they head for Yhwach's castle, Bazz-B reunites with an old friend…

BLEACH

PERNIDA PARNKGJAS

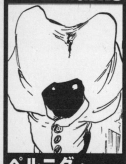

ペルニダ・
パルンカジャス

涅マユリ
クロツチマユリ

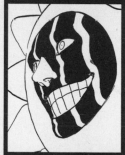

MAYURI
KUROTSUCHI

KENPACHI ZARAKI

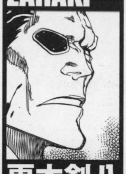

更木剣八
ザラキケンハチ

STORIES

BLEACH70

FRIEND

CONTENTS

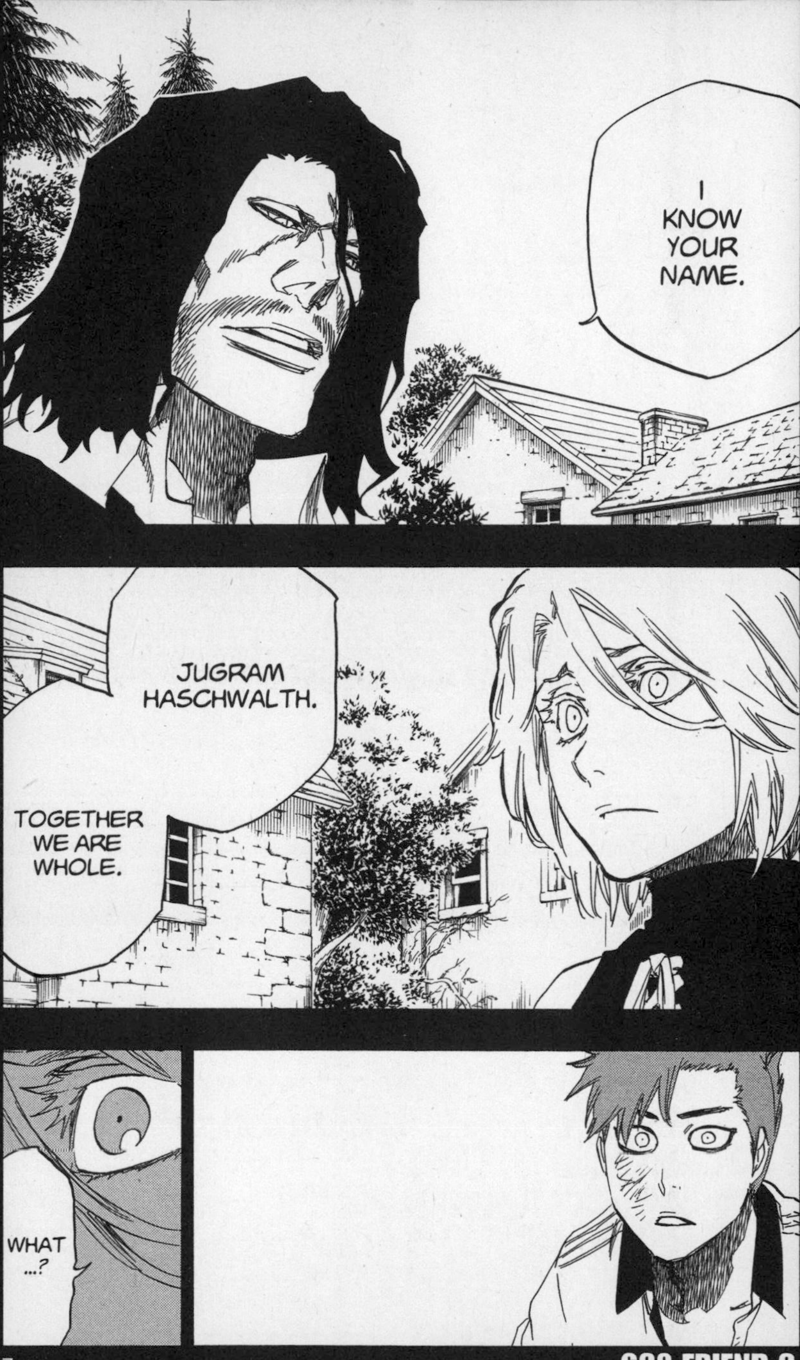
I KNOW YOUR NAME.
JUGRAM HASCHWALTH.
TOGETHER WE ARE WHOLE.
WHAT ...?

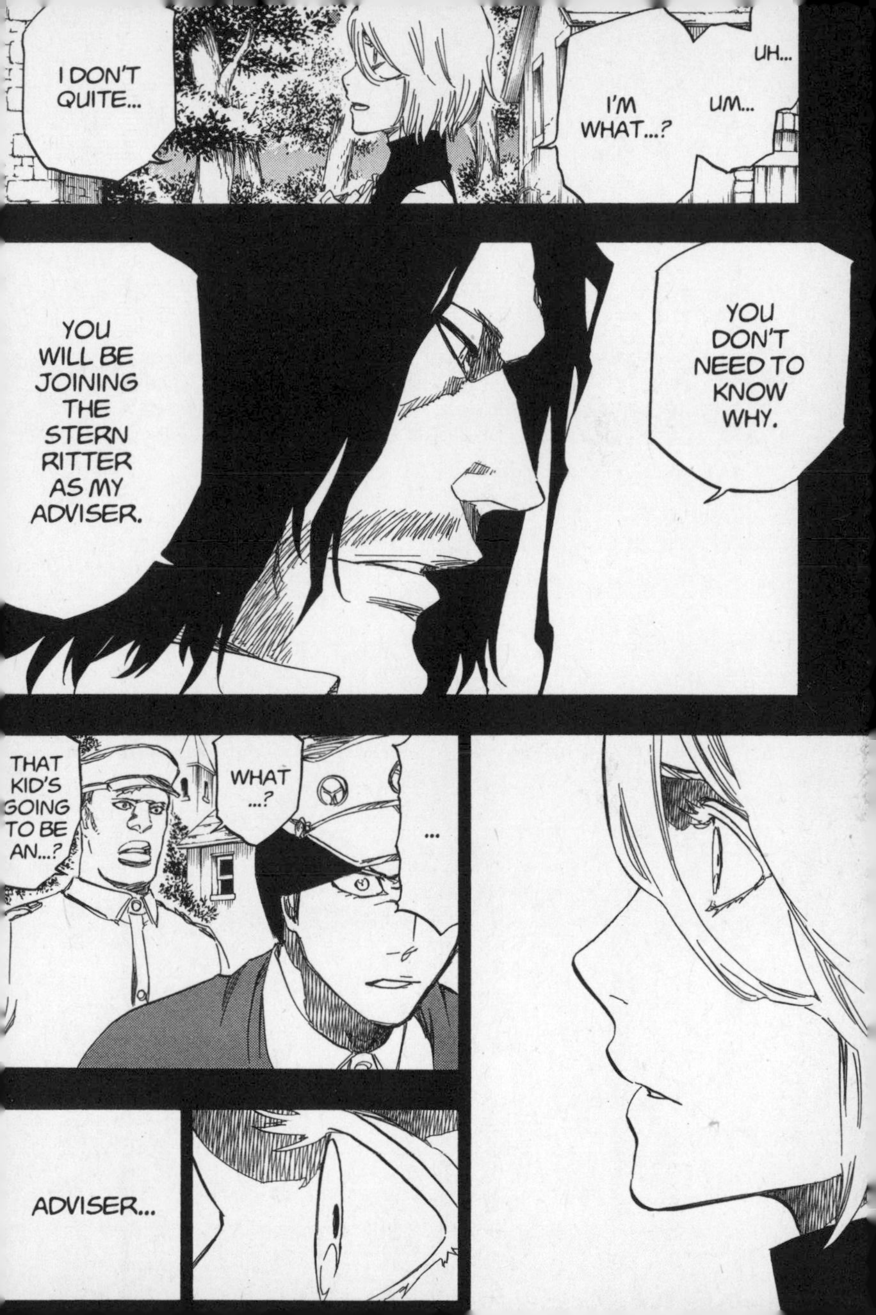

UH...
UM...
I'M WHAT...?
I DON'T QUITE...
YOU DON'T NEED TO KNOW WHY.
YOU WILL BE JOINING THE STERN RITTER AS MY ADVISER.
WHAT ...?
...
THAT KID'S GOING TO BE AN...?
ADVISER...

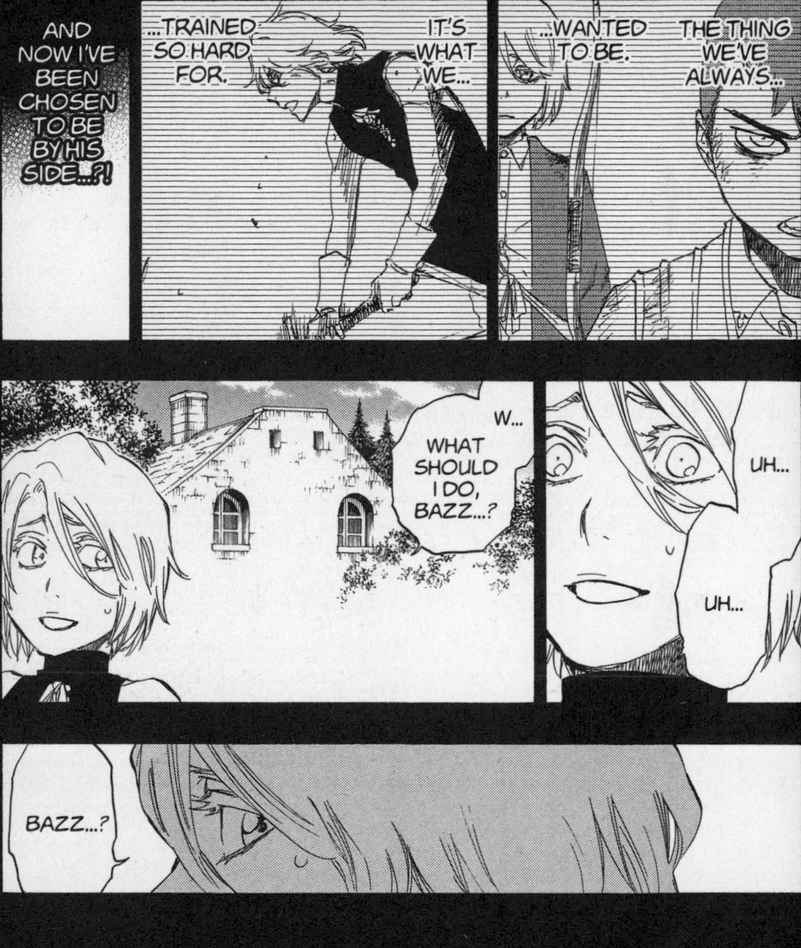
THE THING WE'VE ALWAYS...
...WANTED TO BE.
IT'S WHAT WE...
...TRAINED SO HARD FOR.
AND NOW I'VE BEEN CHOSEN TO BE BY HIS SIDE...?!
UH...
UH...
W...
WHAT SHOULD I DO, BAZZ...?
BAZZ...?

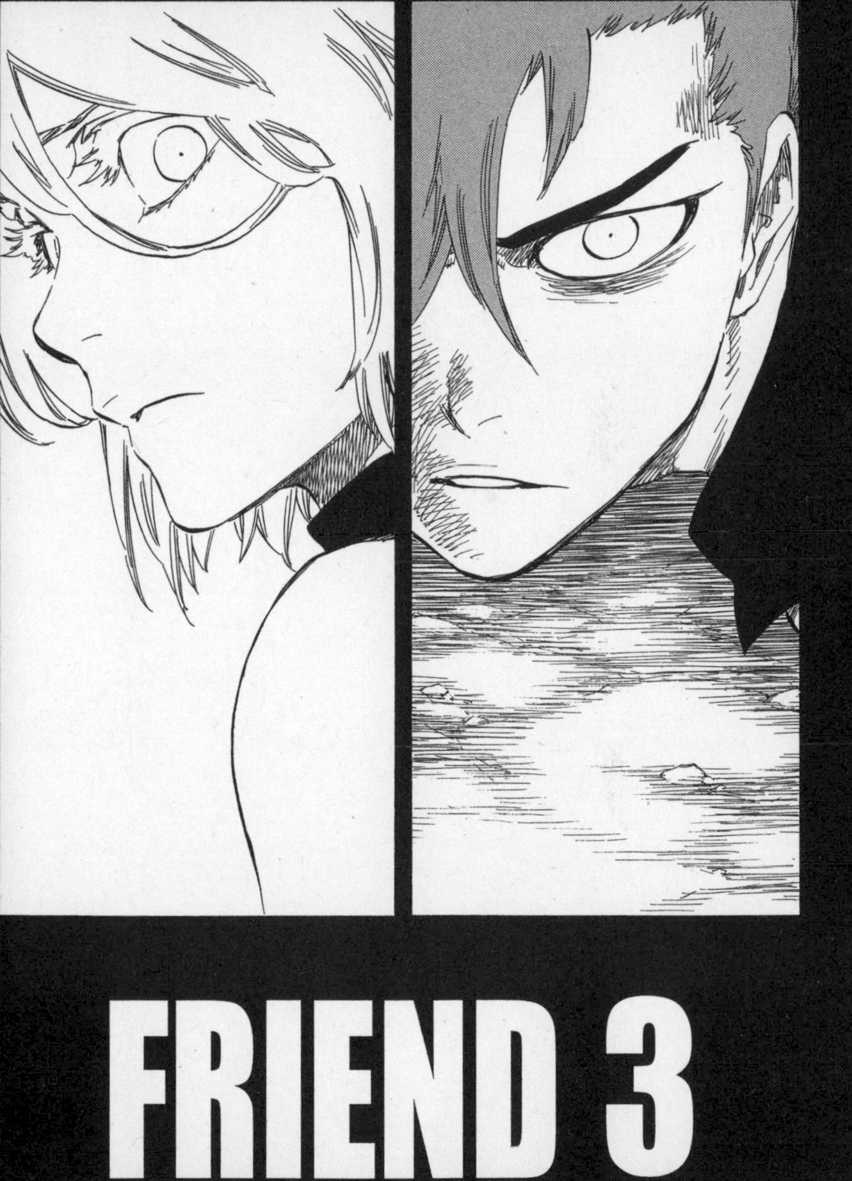

FRIEND 3

READ THIS WAY

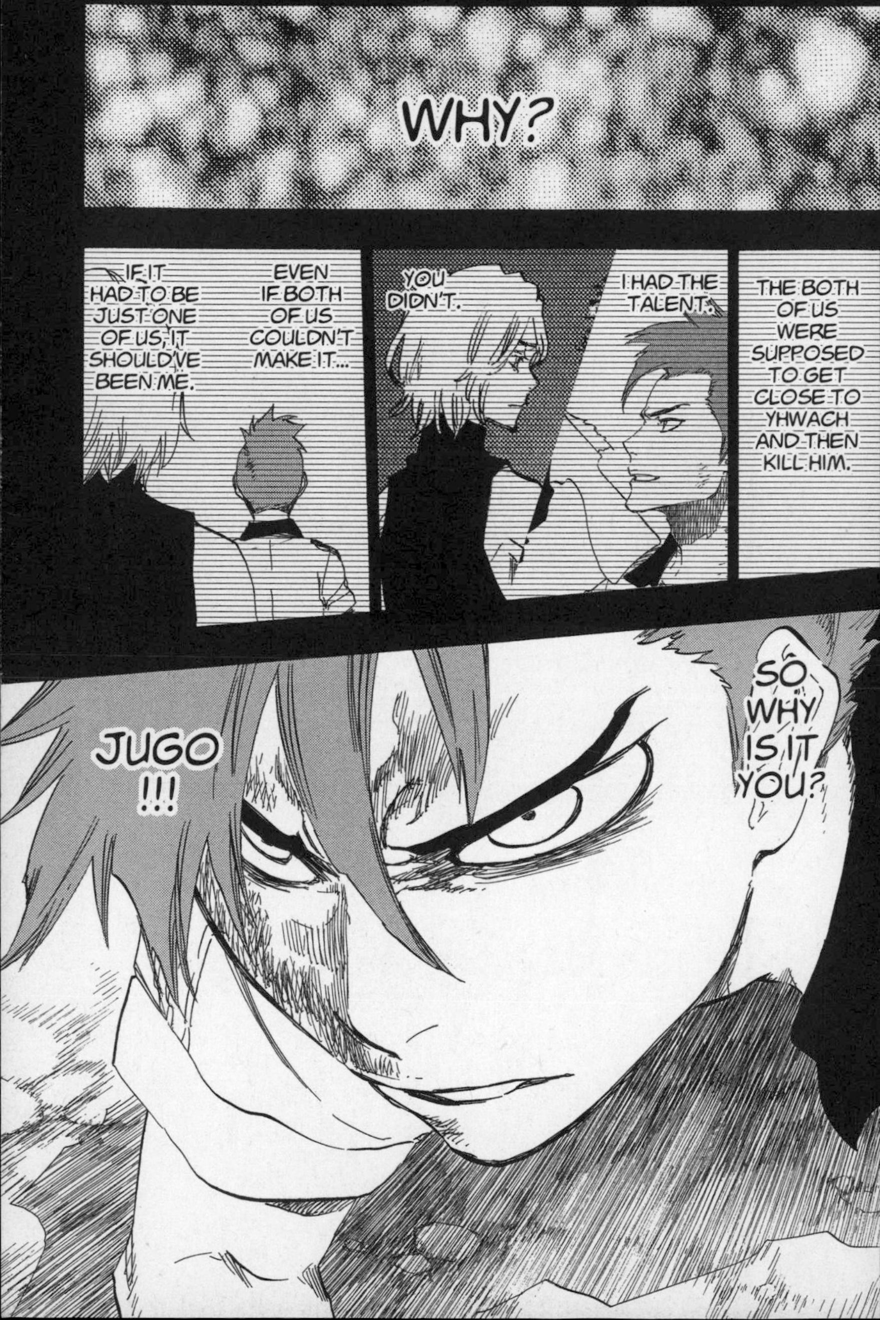
WHY?
THE BOTH OF US WERE SUPPOSED TO GET CLOSE TO YHWACH AND THEN KILL HIM.
I HAD THE TALENT.
YOU DIDN'T.
EVEN IF BOTH OF US COULDN'T MAKE IT...
IF IT HAD TO BE JUST ONE OF US, IT SHOULD'VE BEEN ME.
SO WHY IS IT YOU?
JUGO !!!

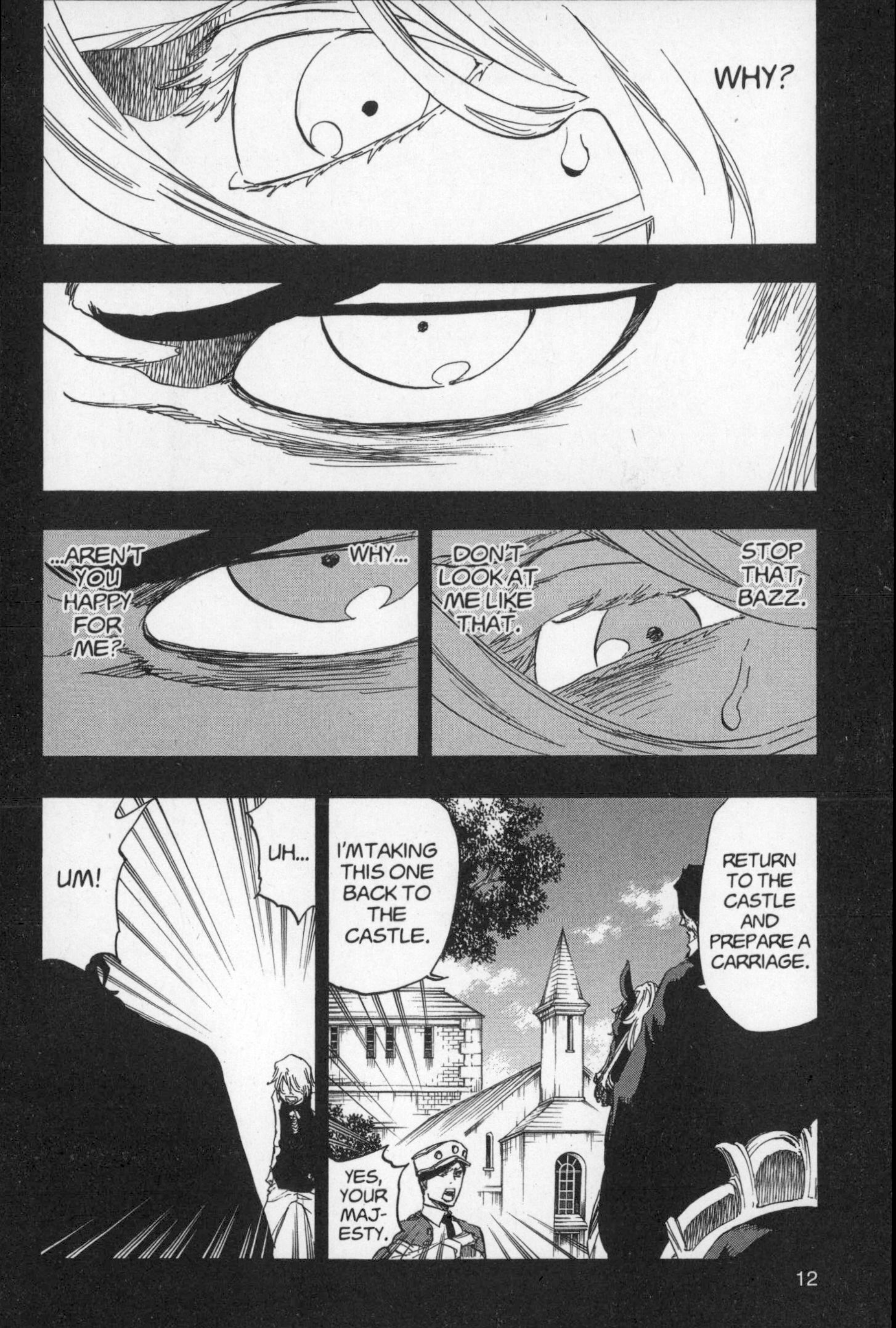
WHY?
STOP THAT, BAZZ.
DON'T LOOK AT ME LIKE THAT.
WHY...
...AREN'T YOU HAPPY FOR ME?
RETURN TO THE CASTLE AND PREPARE A CARRIAGE.
I'MTAKING THIS ONE BACK TO THE CASTLE.
YES, YOUR MAJ-ESTY.
UH...
UM!

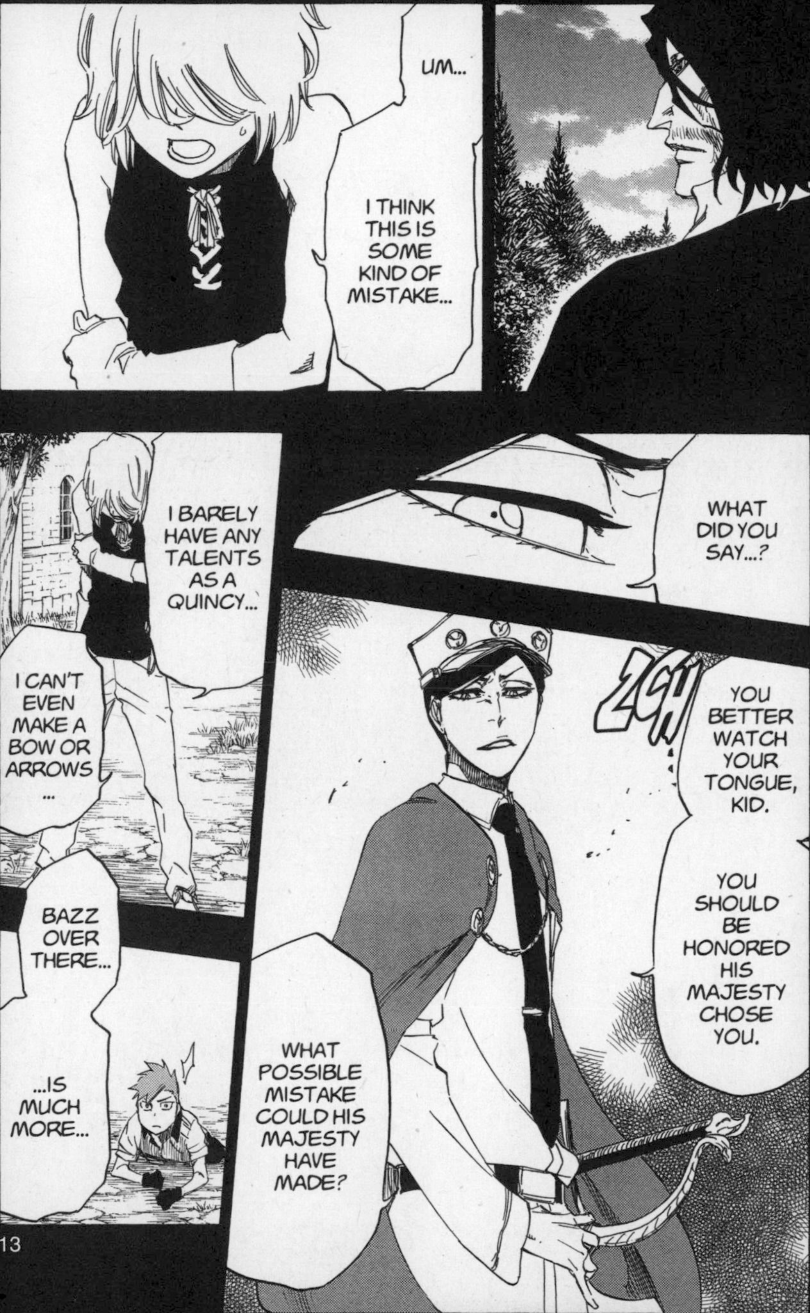
UM...
I THINK THIS IS SOME KIND OF MISTAKE...
WHAT DID YOU SAY...?
YOU BETTER WATCH YOUR TONGUE, KID.
YOU SHOULD BE HONORED HIS MAJESTY CHOSE YOU.
WHAT POSSIBLE MISTAKE COULD HIS MAJESTY HAVE MADE?
I BARELY HAVE ANY TALENTS AS A QUINCY...
I CAN'T EVEN MAKE A BOW OR ARROWS...
BAZZ OVER THERE...
...IS MUCH MORE...

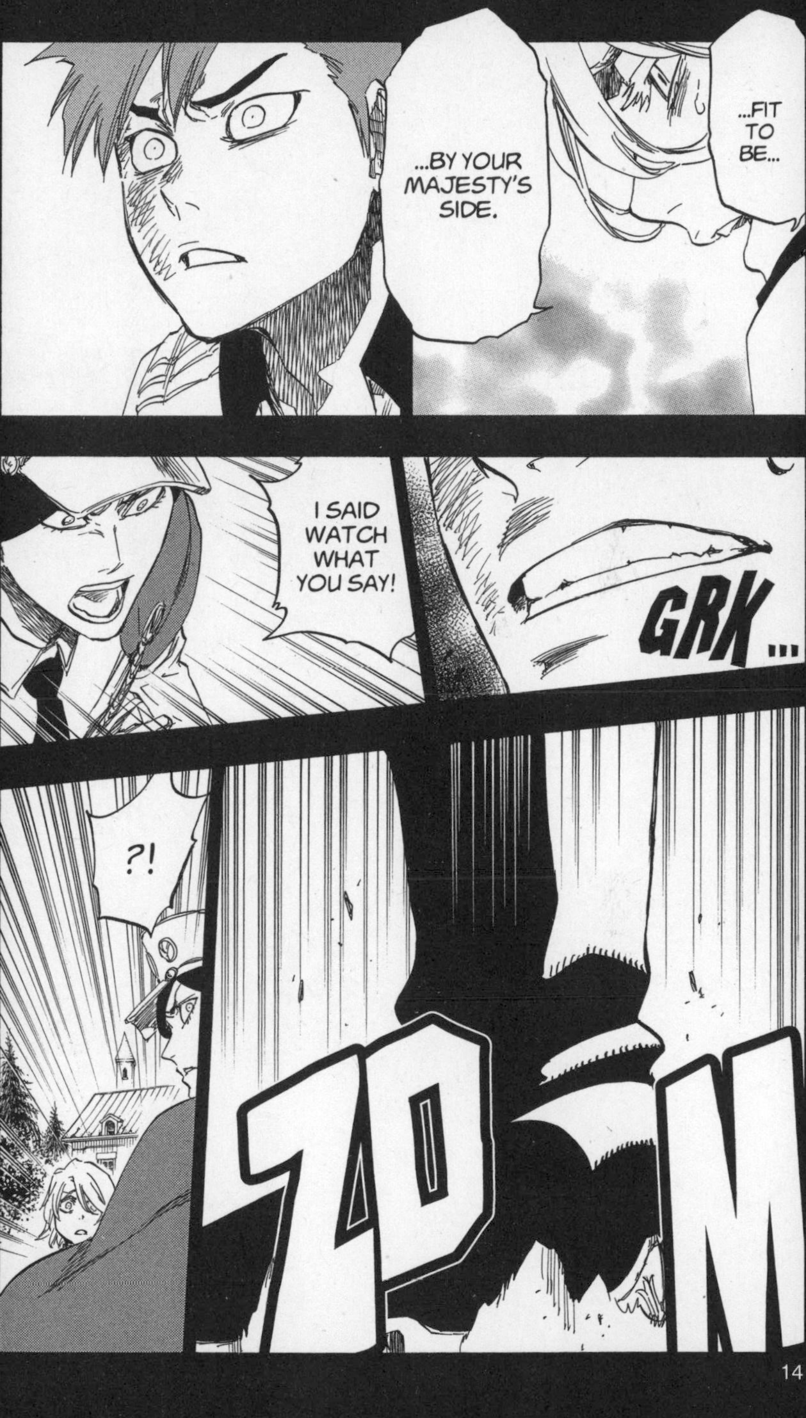
...FIT TO BE...
...BY YOUR MAJESTY'S SIDE.
GRK...
I SAID WATCH WHAT YOU SAY!
ZO M
?!

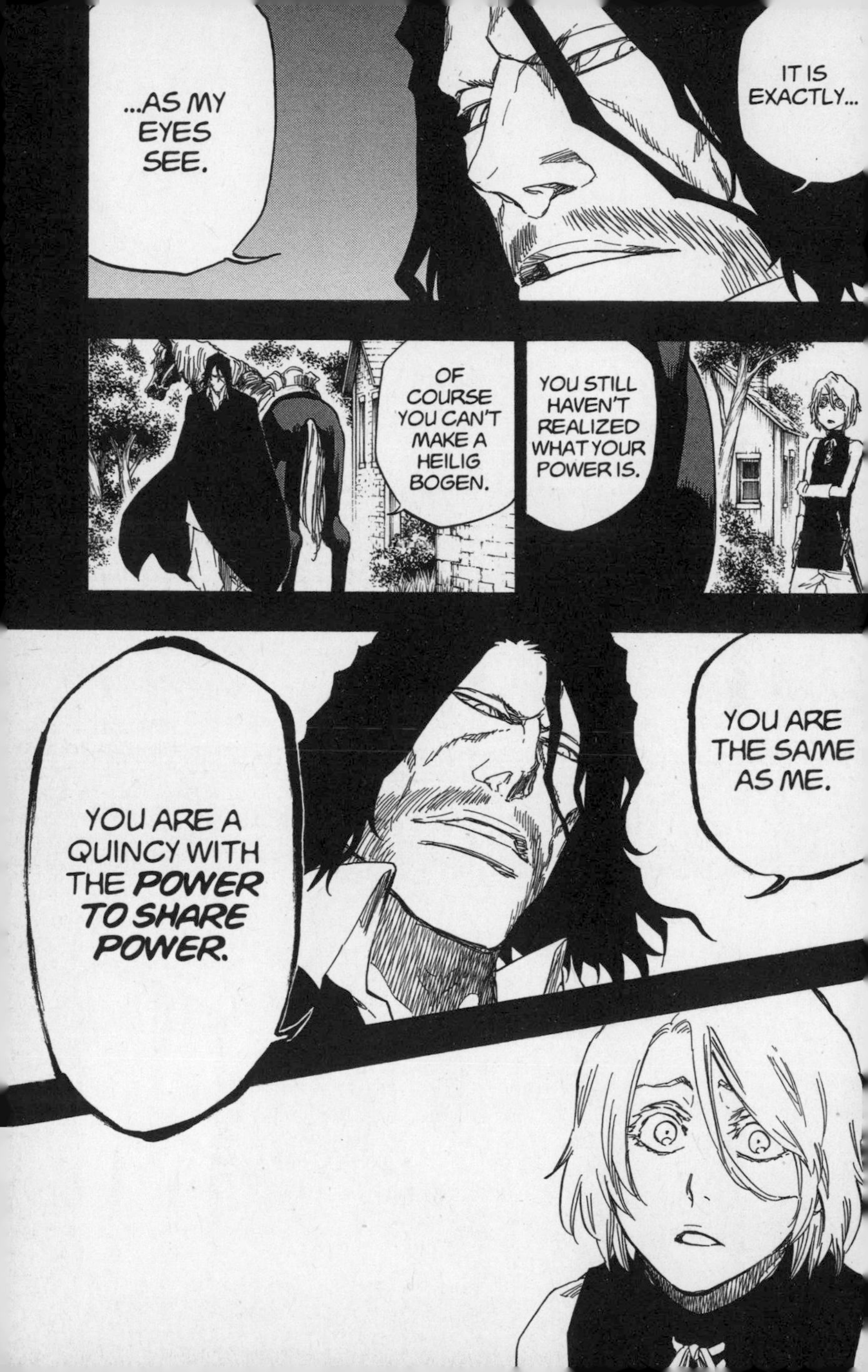
IT IS EXACTLY...
...AS MY EYES SEE.
YOU STILL HAVEN'T REALIZED WHAT YOUR POWER IS.
OF COURSE YOU CAN'T MAKE A HEILIG BOGEN.
YOU ARE THE SAME AS ME.
YOU ARE A QUINCY WITH THE POWER TO SHARE POWER.

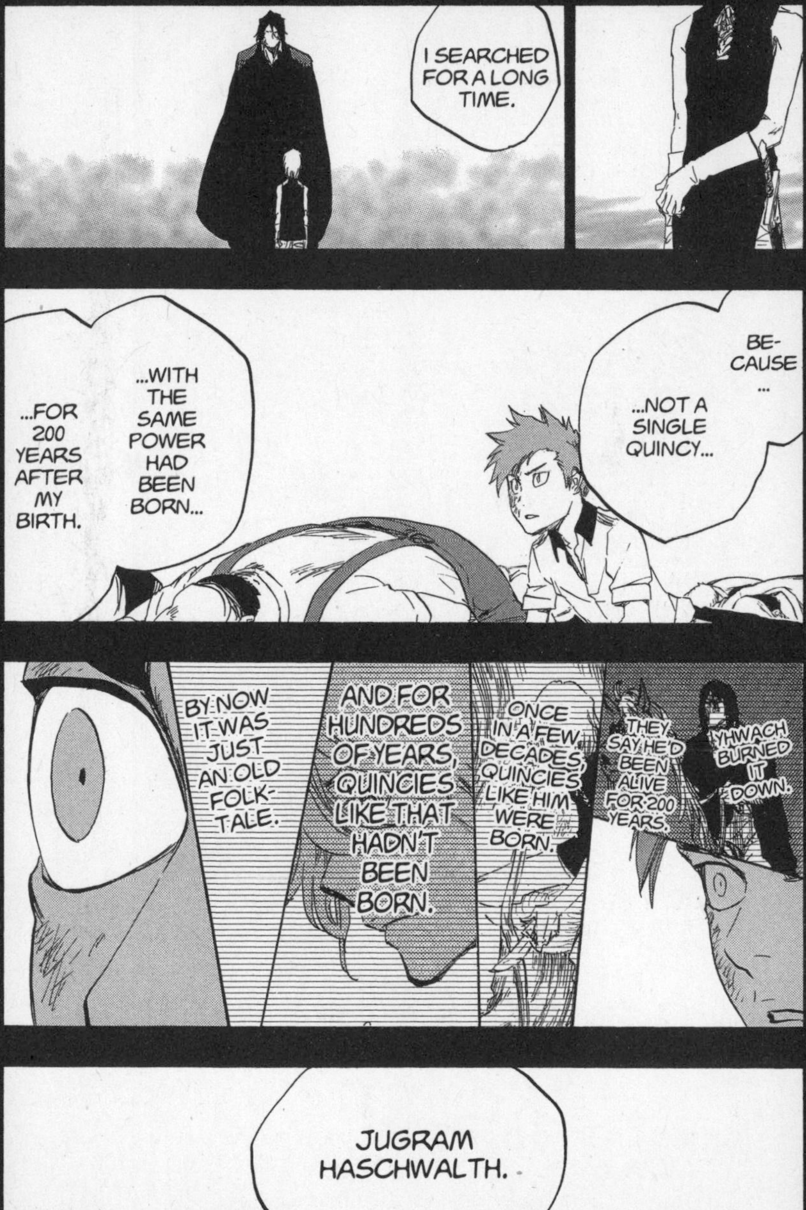
I SEARCHED FOR A LONG TIME.
BE-CAUSE...
...NOT A SINGLE QUINCY...
...WITH THE SAME POWER HAD BEEN BORN...
...FOR 200 YEARS AFTER MY BIRTH.
YHWACH BURNED IT DOWN.
THEY SAY HE'D BEEN ALIVE FOR 200 YEARS.
ONCE IN A FEW DECADES, QUINCIES LIKE HIM WERE BORN.
AND FOR HUNDREDS OF YEARS, QUINCIES LIKE THAT HADN'T BEEN BORN.
BY NOW IT WAS JUST AN OLD FOLK-TALE.
JUGRAM HASCHWALTH.

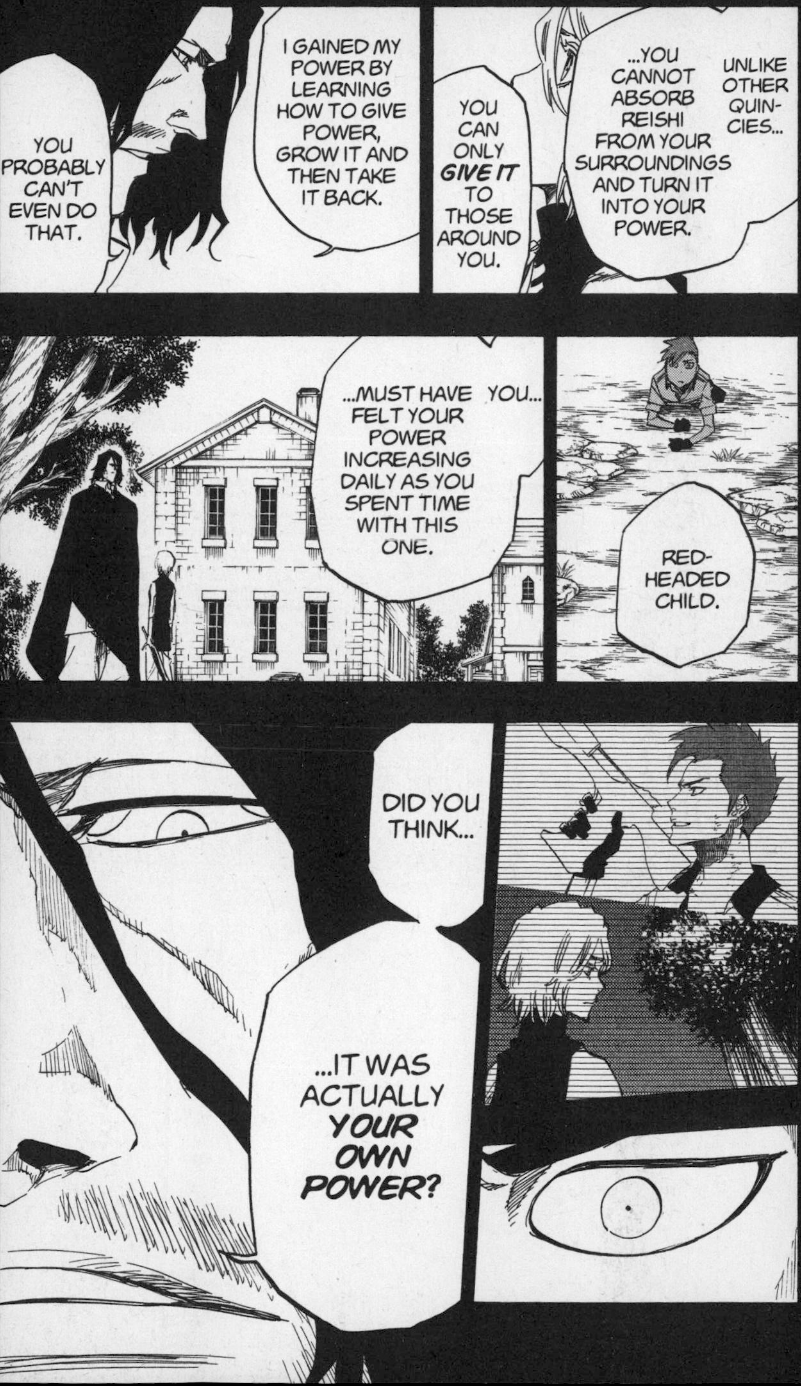
UNLIKE OTHER QUIN-CIES...
...YOU CANNOT ABSORB REISHI FROM YOUR SURROUNDINGS AND TURN IT INTO YOUR POWER.
YOU CAN ONLY ***GIVE IT*** TO THOSE AROUND YOU.
I GAINED MY POWER BY LEARNING HOW TO GIVE POWER, GROW IT AND THEN TAKE IT BACK.
YOU PROBABLY CAN'T EVEN DO THAT.
RED-HEADED CHILD.
YOU...
...MUST HAVE FELT YOUR POWER INCREASING DAILY AS YOU SPENT TIME WITH THIS ONE.
DID YOU THINK...
...IT WAS ACTUALLY ***YOUR OWN POWER?***

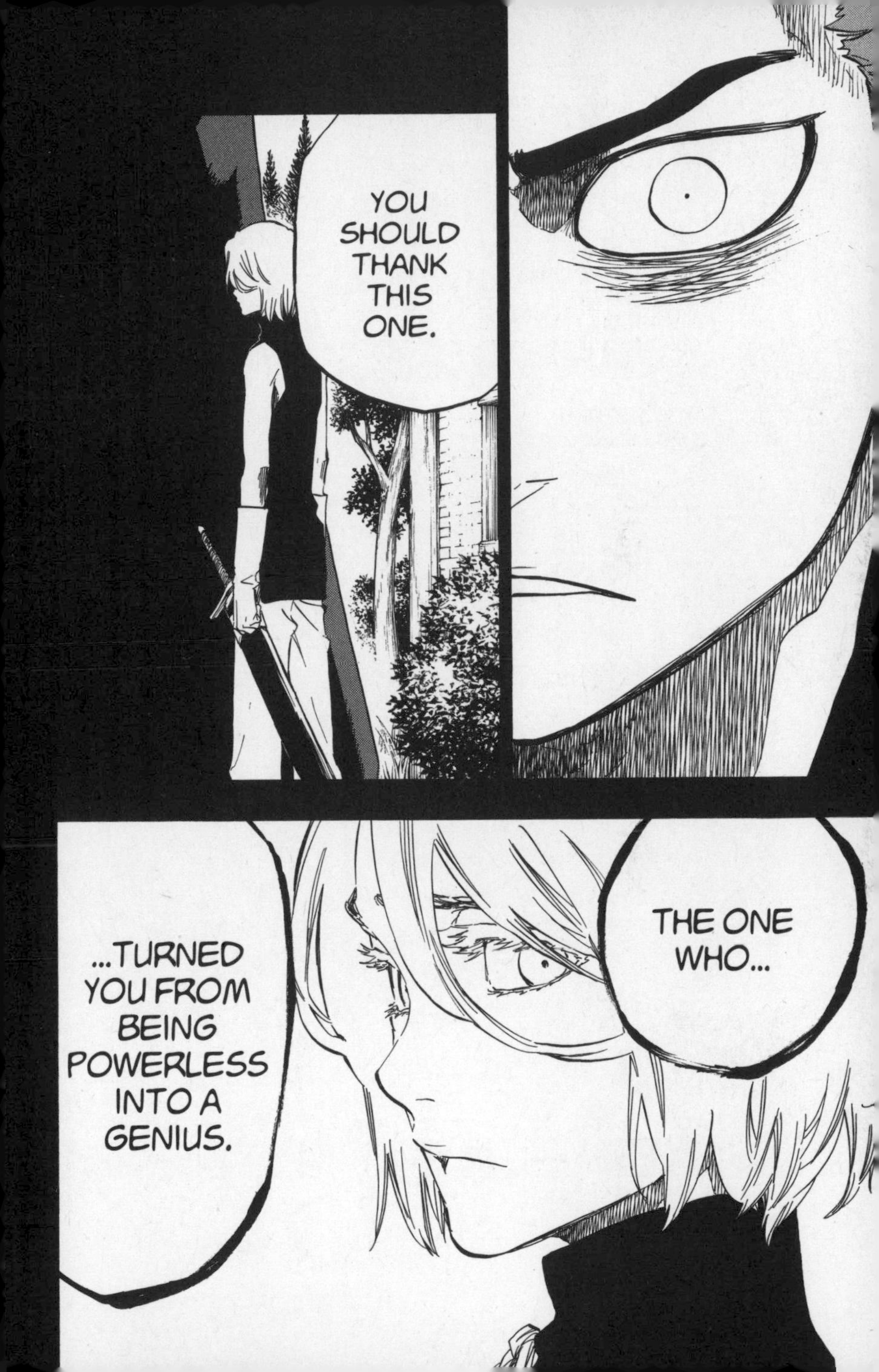
YOU SHOULD THANK THIS ONE.
THE ONE WHO...
...TURNED YOU FROM BEING POWERLESS INTO A GENIUS.

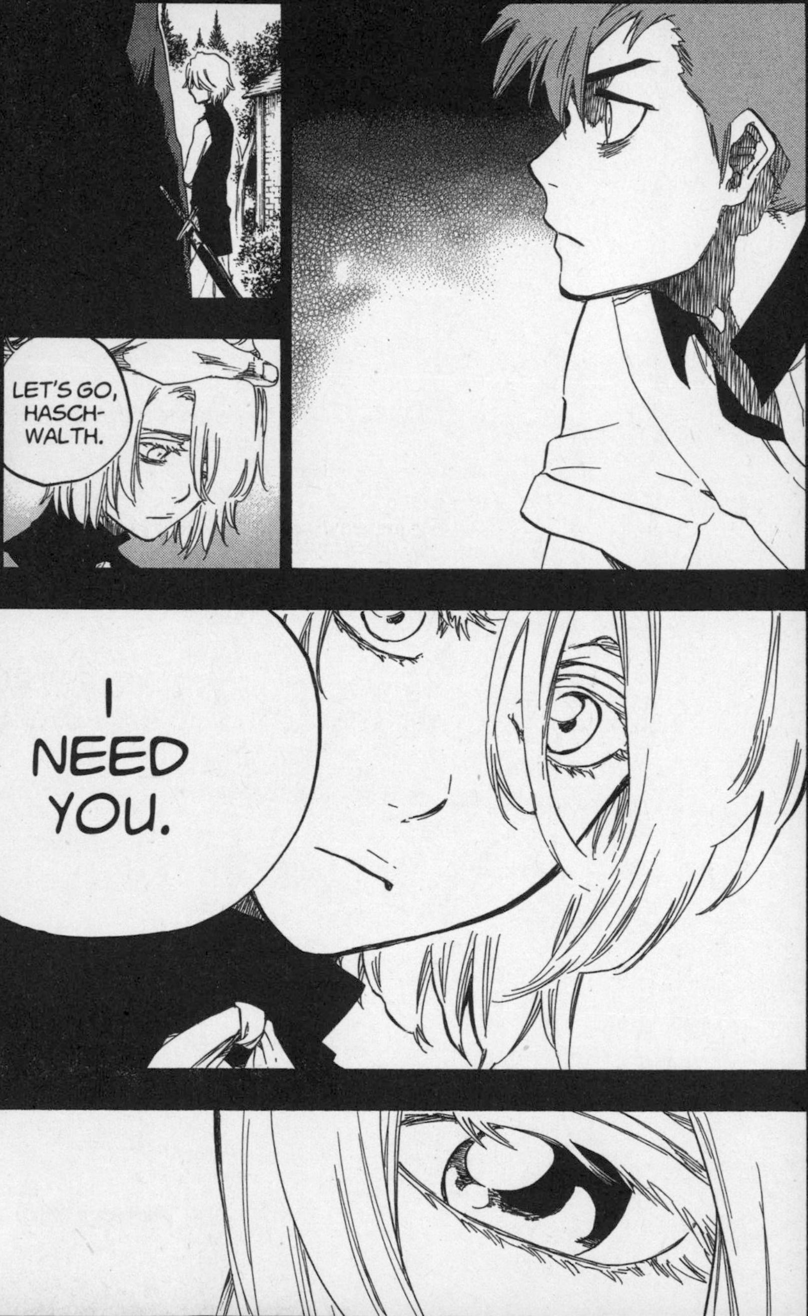

READ THIS WAY
LET'S GO, HASCH-WALTH.
I NEED YOU.

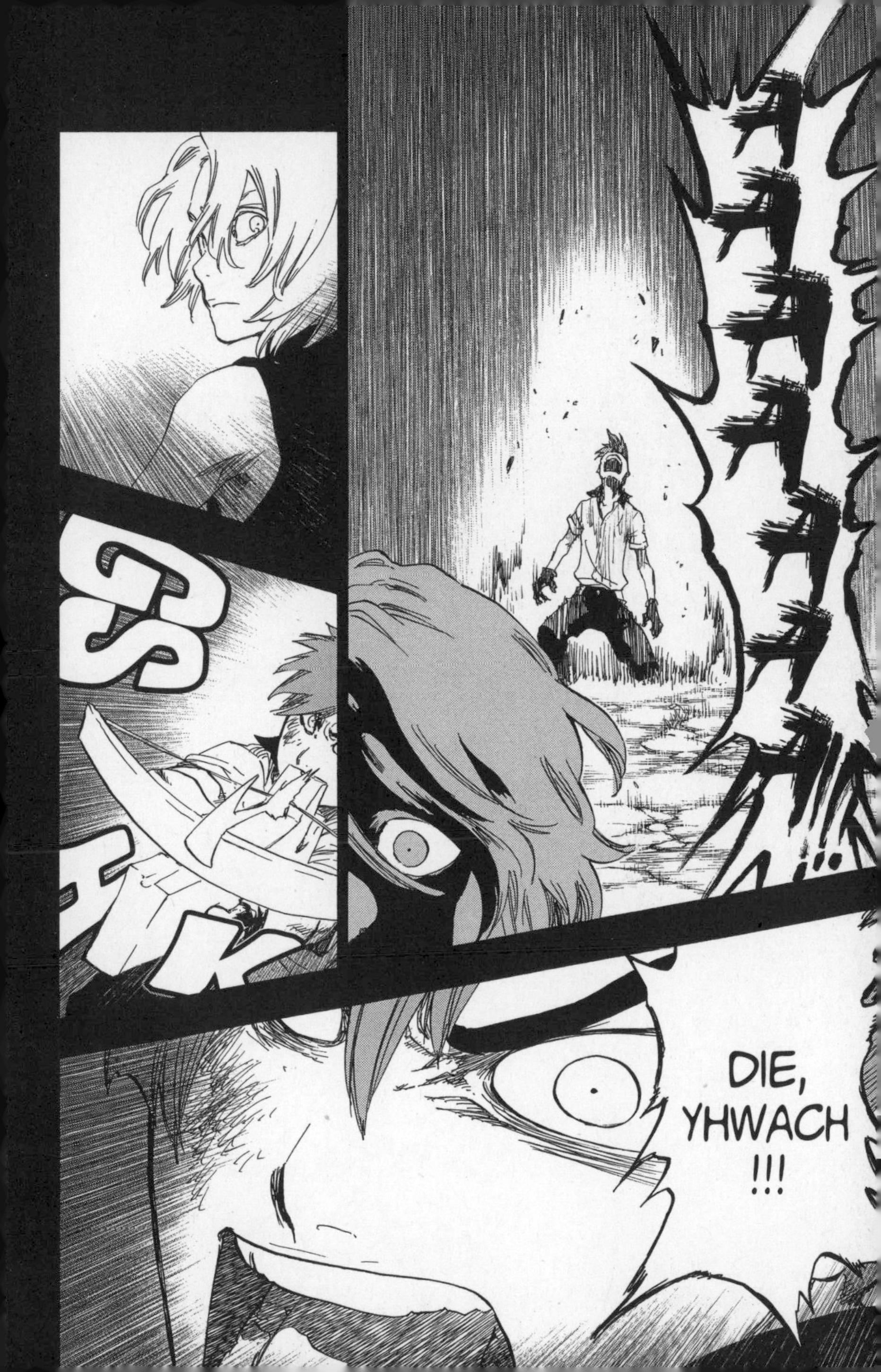
DIE, YHWACH !!!

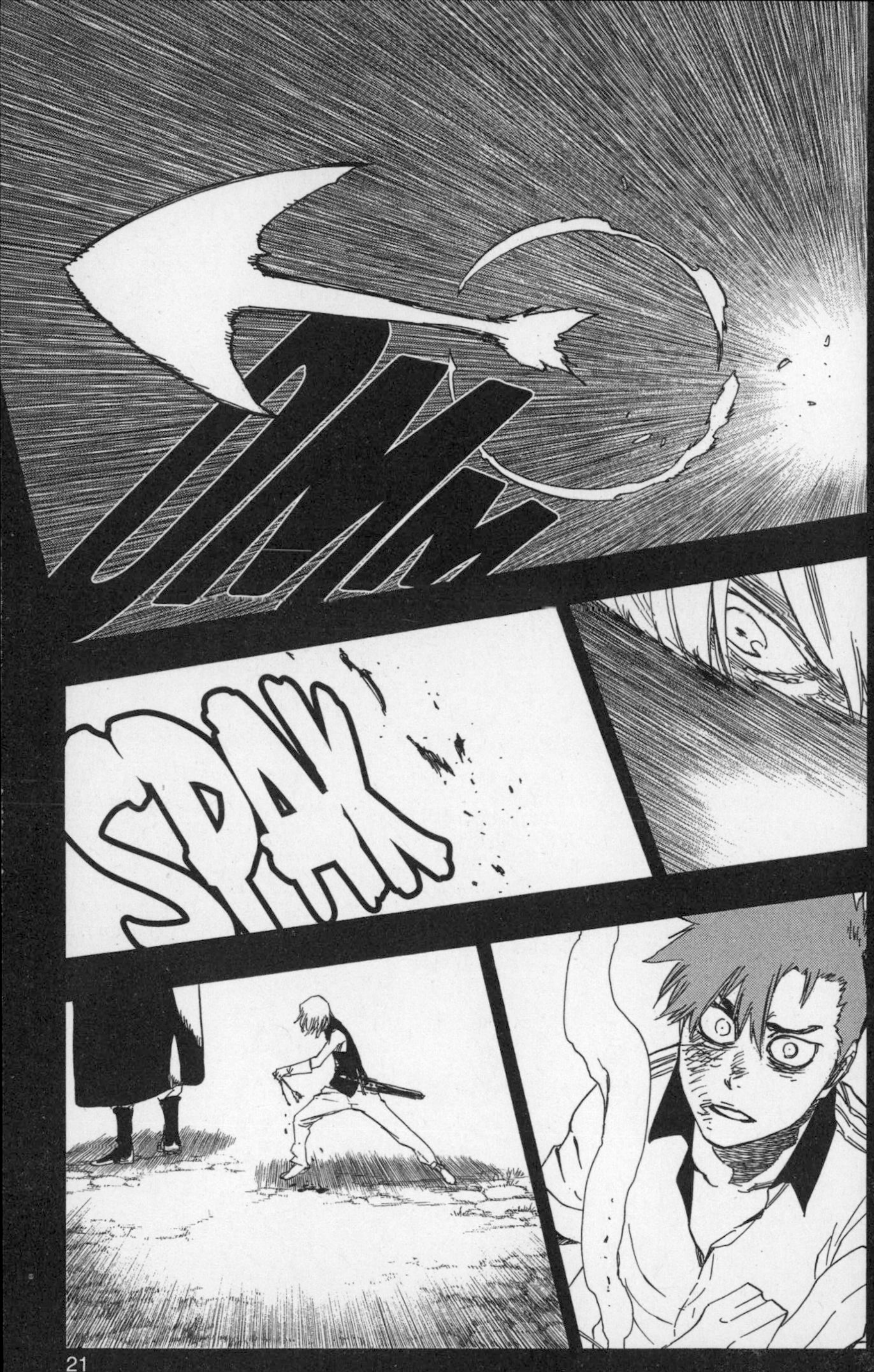
SHNNM
SPAK

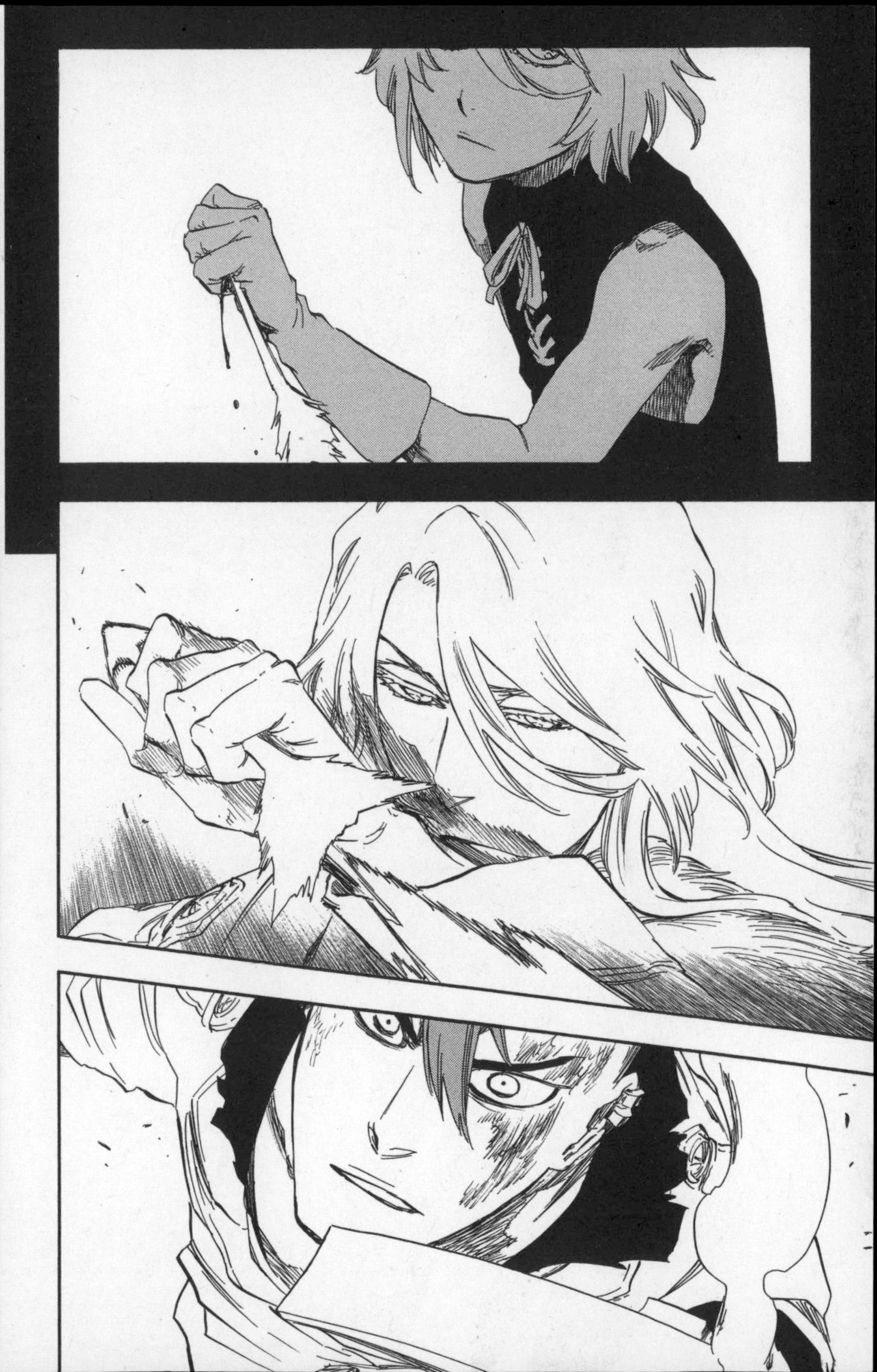

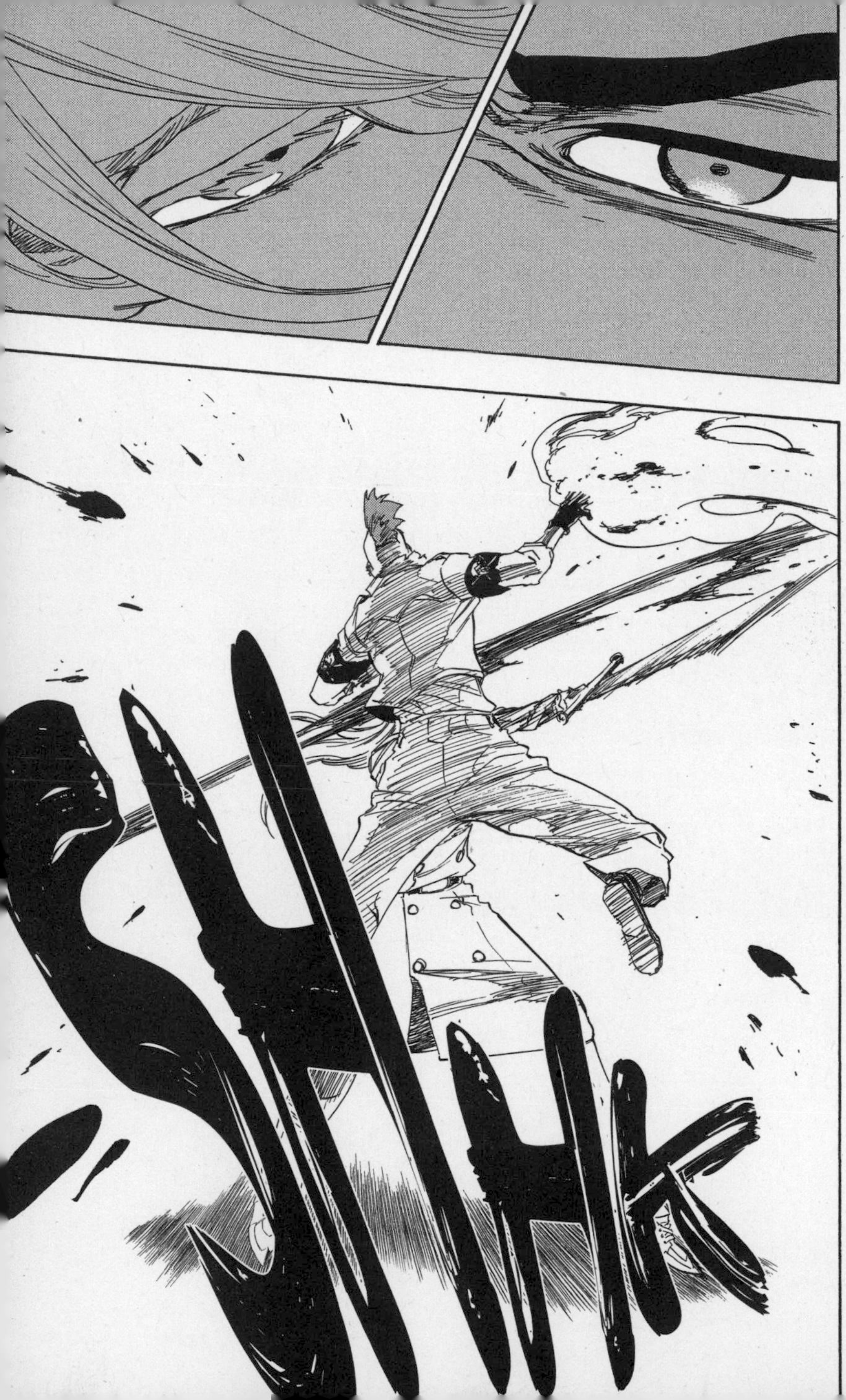
SHHK

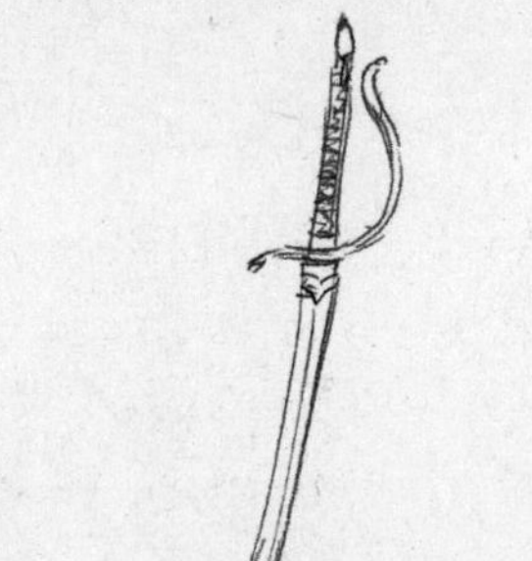

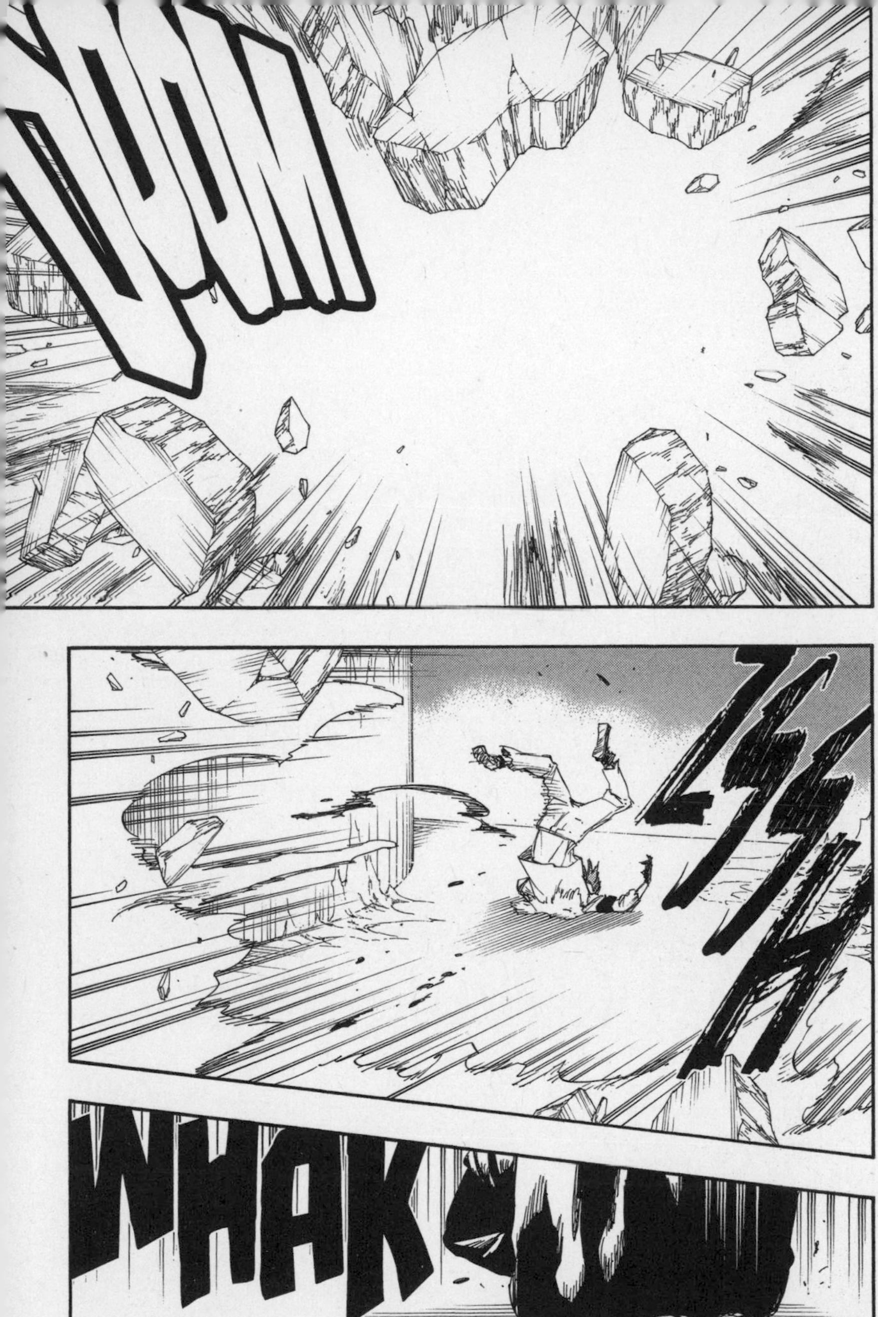
DOOM
ZSSH
WHAK

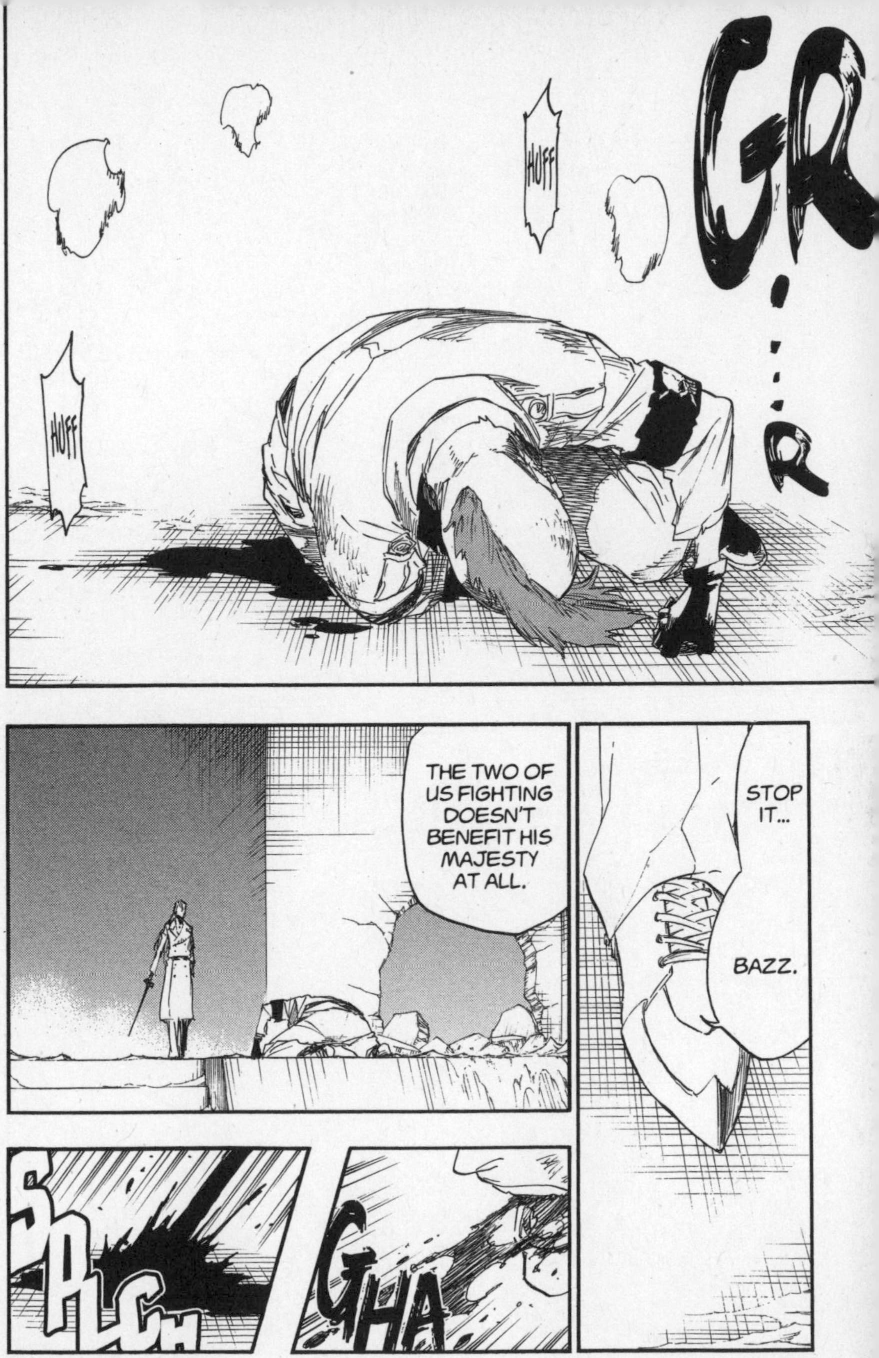
GR...R
HUFF
HUFF
STOP IT...
BAZZ.
THE TWO OF US FIGHTING DOESN'T BENEFIT HIS MAJESTY AT ALL.
GHA
SPLCH

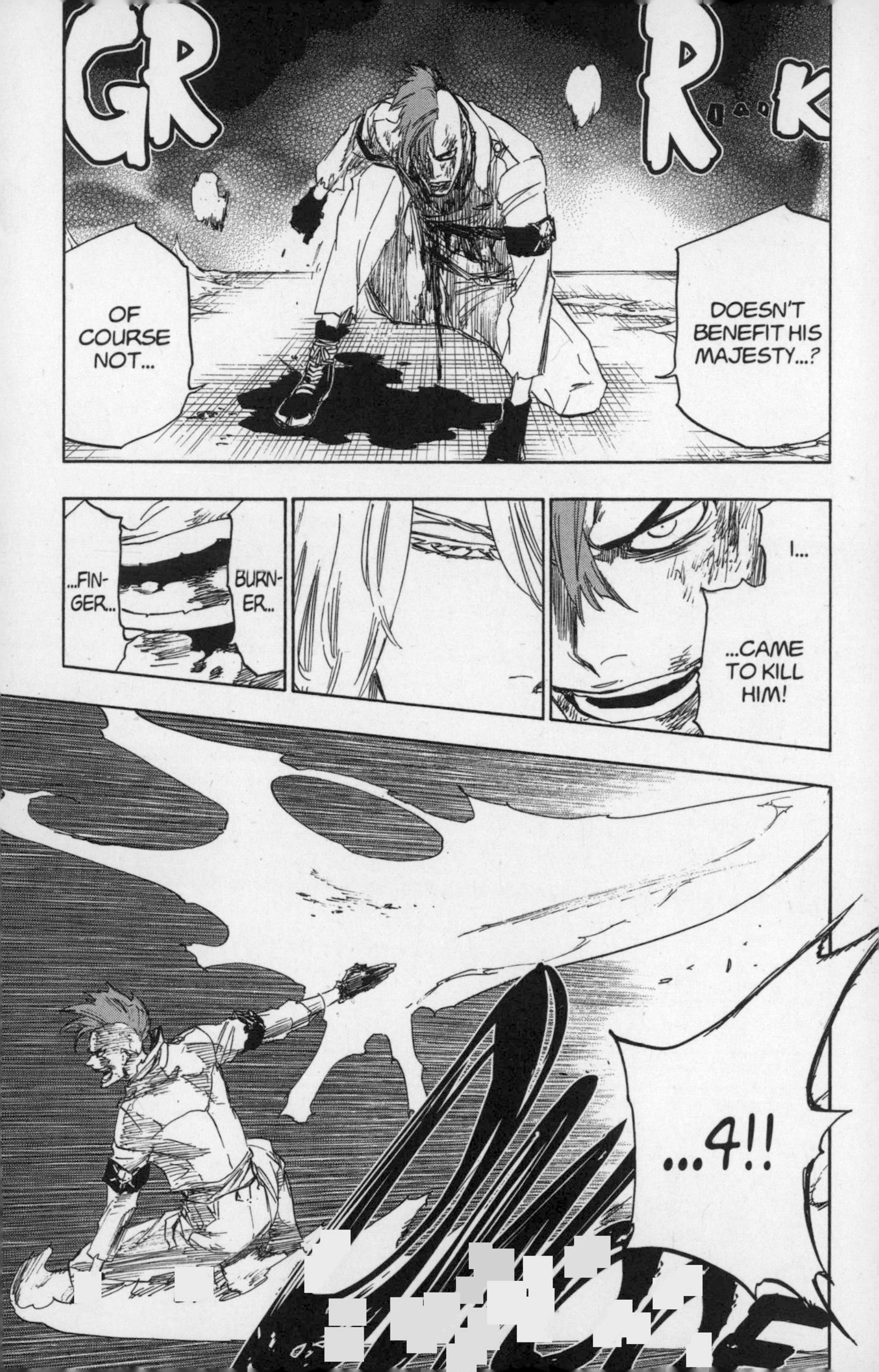
GR
RK
DOESN'T BENEFIT HIS MAJESTY...?
OF COURSE NOT...
I...
...CAME TO KILL HIM!
BURN-ER...
...FIN-GER...
...4!!

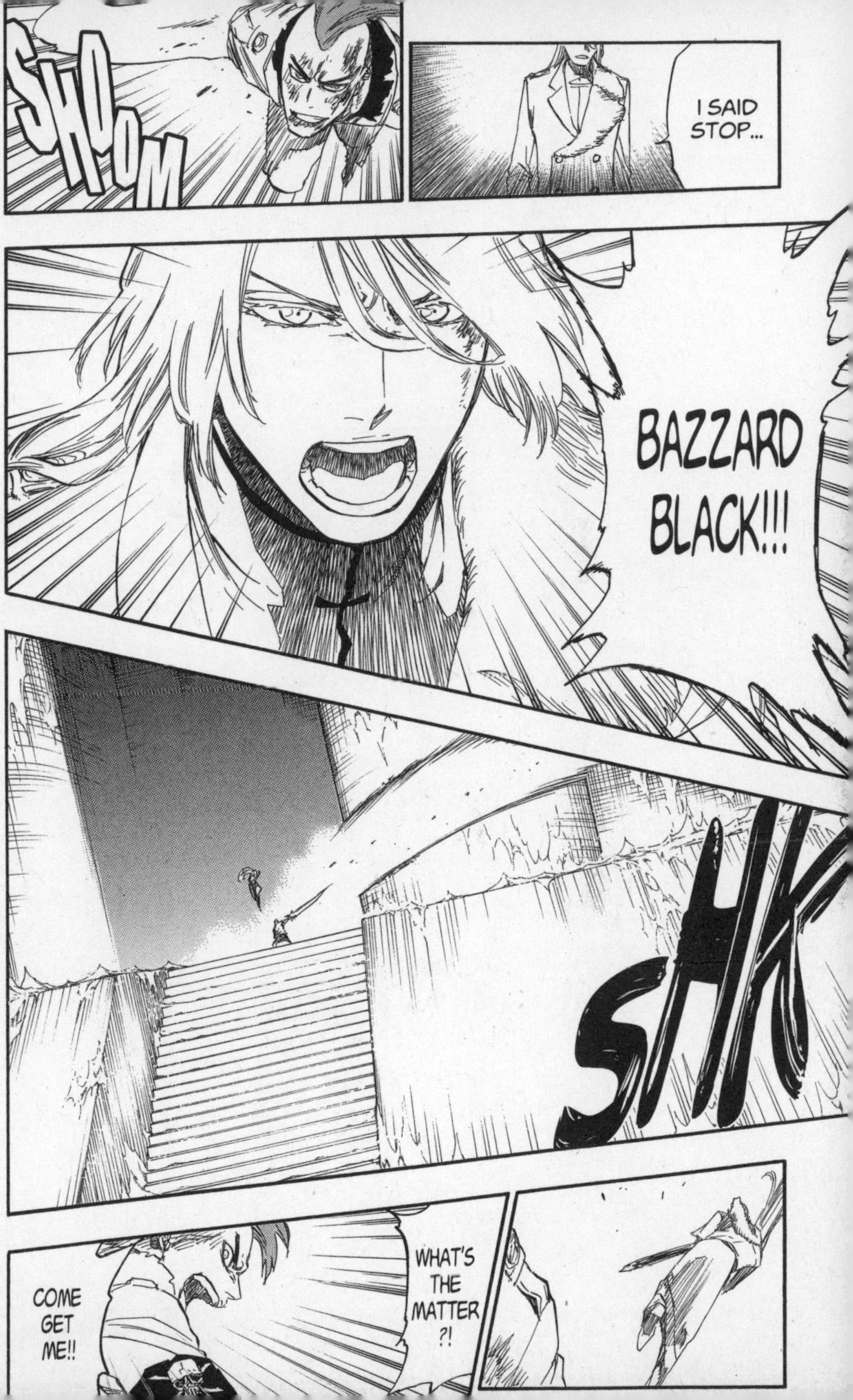
I SAID STOP...
SHOOM
BAZZARD BLACK!!!
SHK
WHAT'S THE MATTER ?!
COME GET ME!!

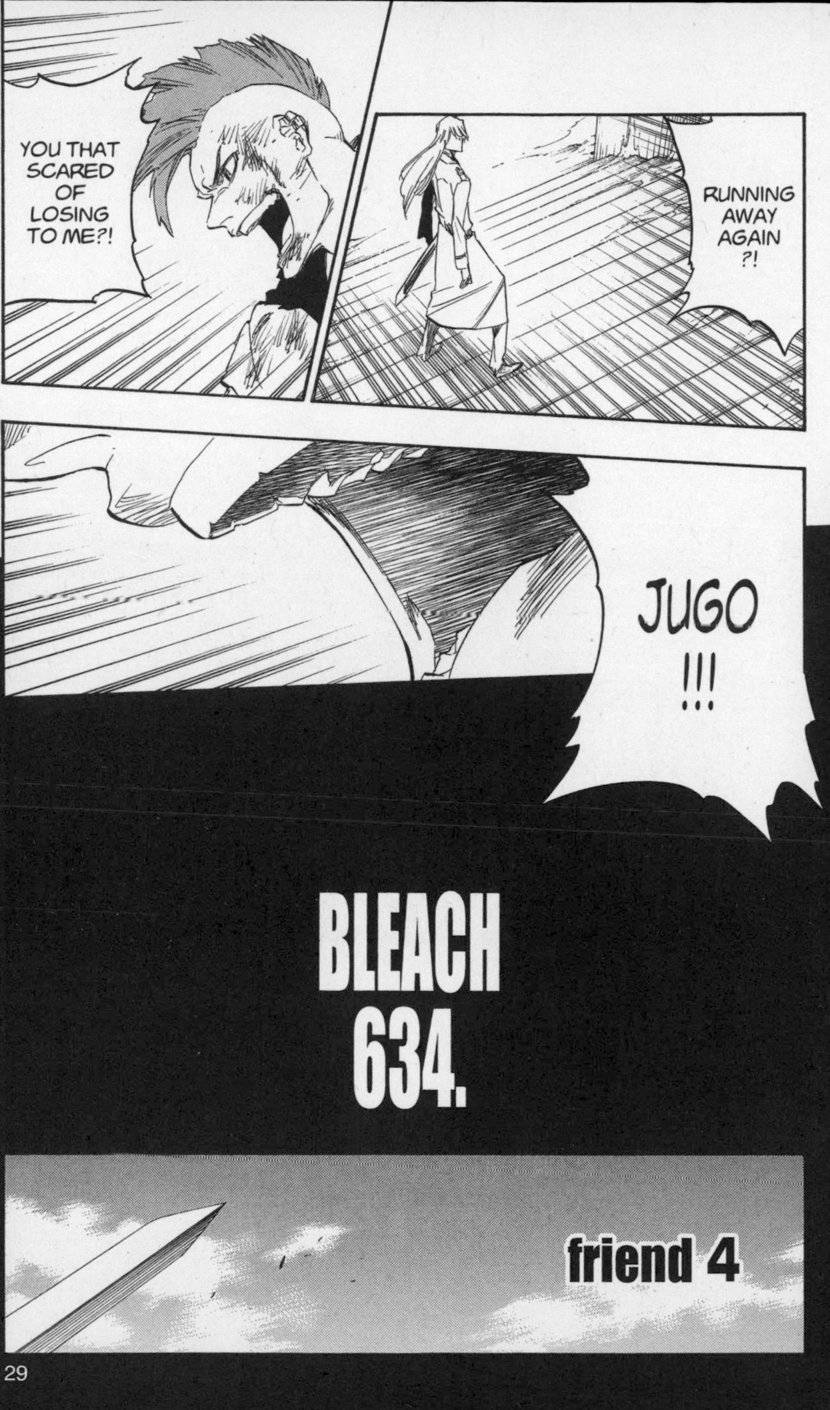
RUNNING AWAY AGAIN ?!
YOU THAT SCARED OF LOSING TO ME?!
JUGO !!!
BLEACH 634.
friend 4

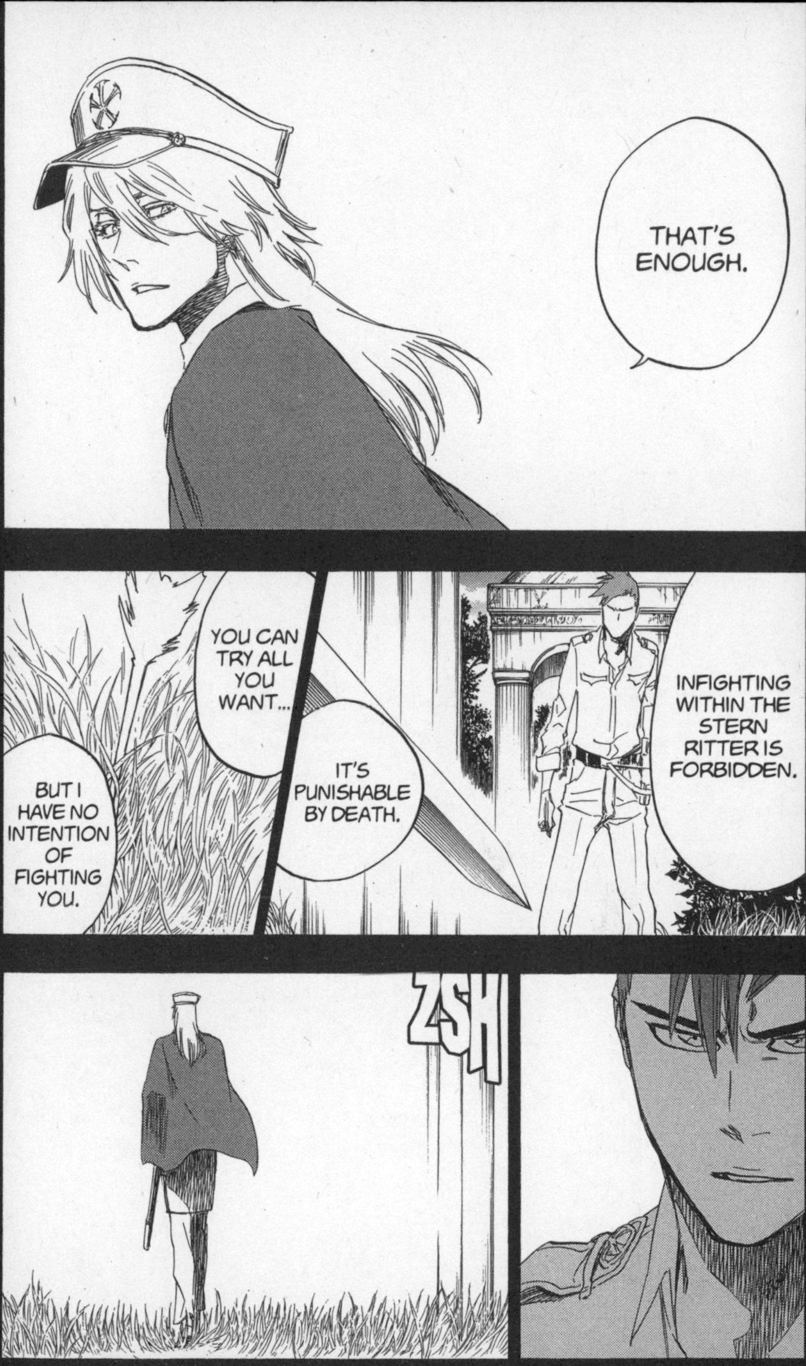
THAT'S ENOUGH.
INFIGHTING WITHIN THE STERN RITTER IS FORBIDDEN.
IT'S PUNISHABLE BY DEATH.
YOU CAN TRY ALL YOU WANT...
BUT I HAVE NO INTENTION OF FIGHTING YOU.
ZSH

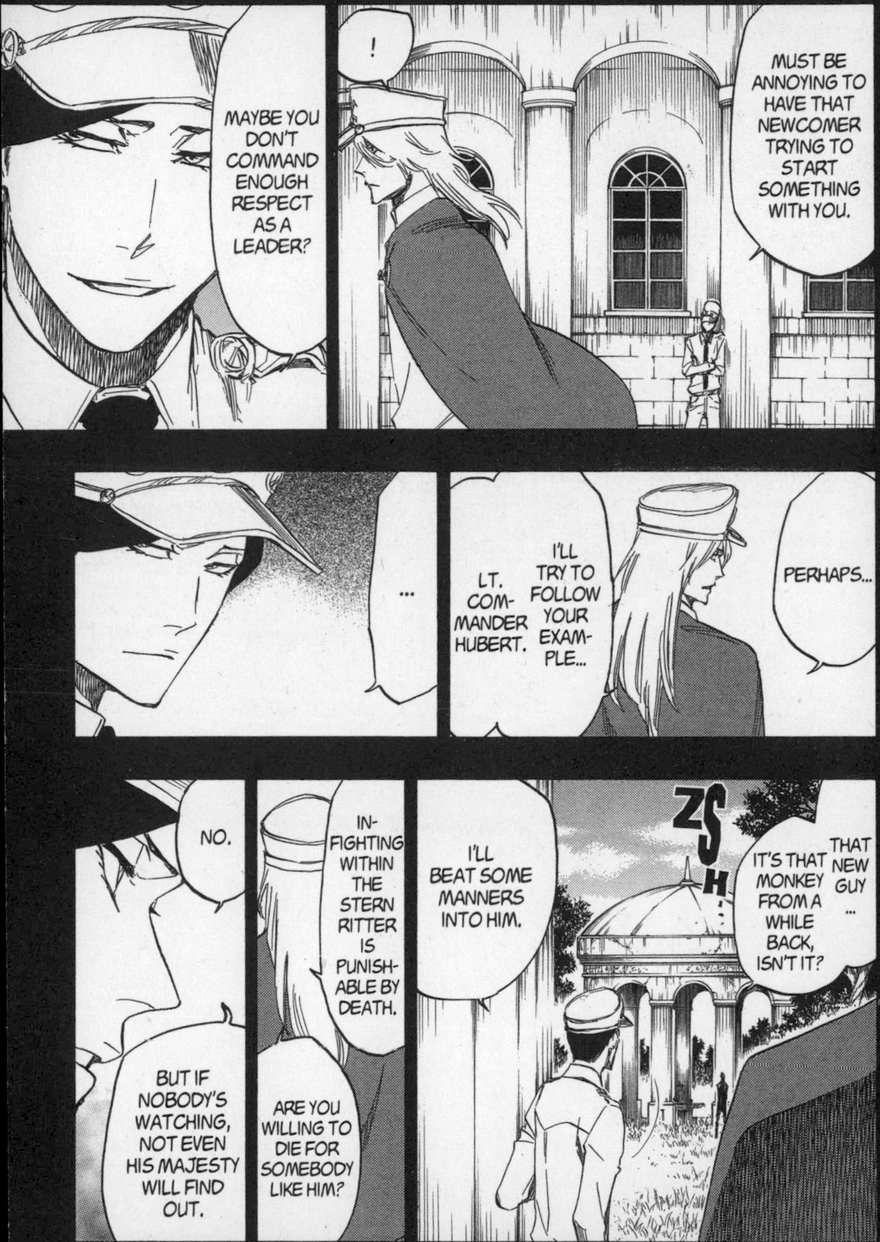
MUST BE ANNOYING TO HAVE THAT NEWCOMER TRYING TO START SOMETHING WITH YOU.
!
MAYBE YOU DON'T COMMAND ENOUGH RESPECT AS A LEADER?
PERHAPS...
I'LL TRY TO FOLLOW YOUR EXAMPLE...
LT. COMMANDER HUBERT.
...
THAT NEW GUY...
IT'S THAT MONKEY FROM A WHILE BACK, ISN'T IT?
ZSH
I'LL BEAT SOME MANNERS INTO HIM.
IN-FIGHTING WITHIN THE STERN RITTER IS PUNISHABLE BY DEATH.
ARE YOU WILLING TO DIE FOR SOMEBODY LIKE HIM?
NO.
BUT IF NOBODY'S WATCHING, NOT EVEN HIS MAJESTY WILL FIND OUT.

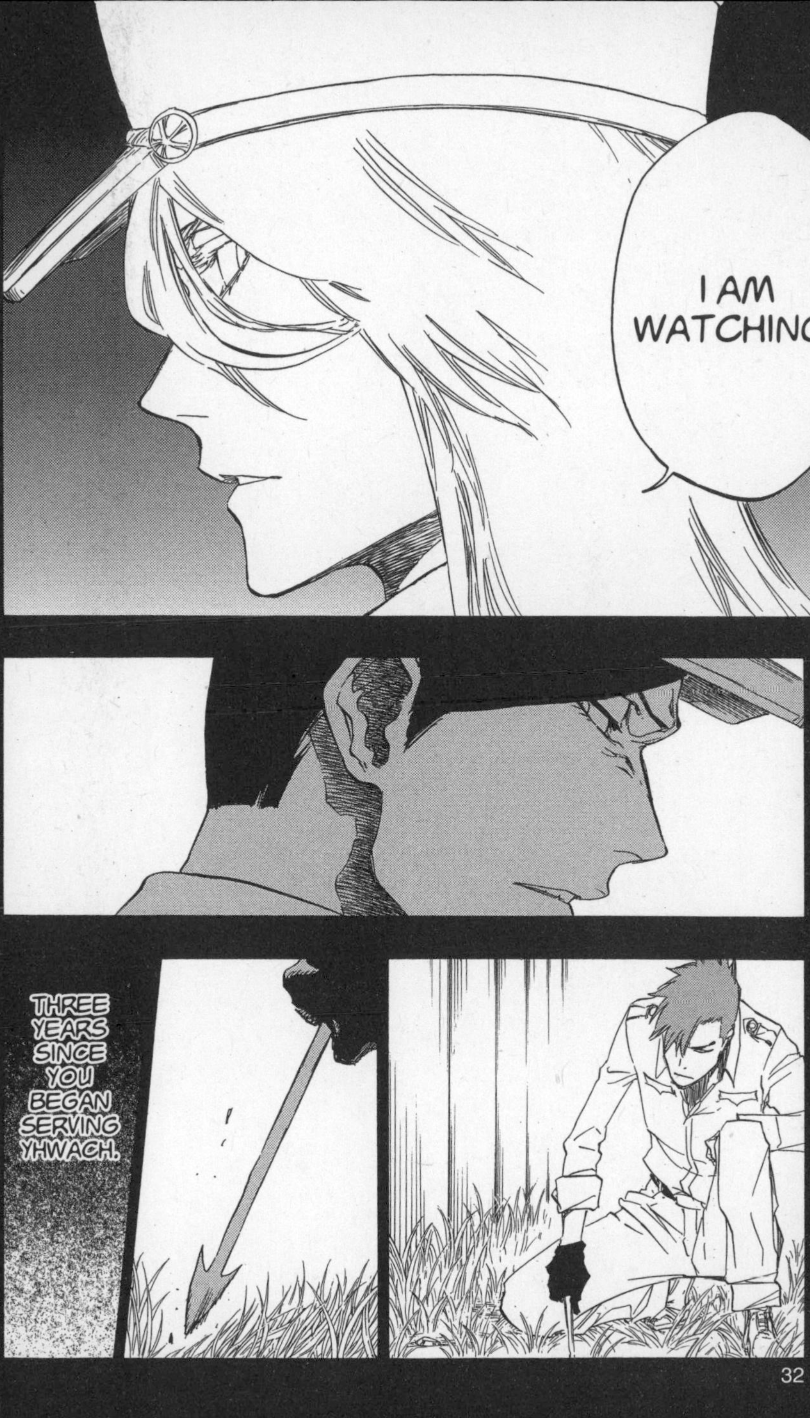
I AM WATCHING.
THREE YEARS SINCE YOU BEGAN SERVING YHWACH.

READ THIS WAY

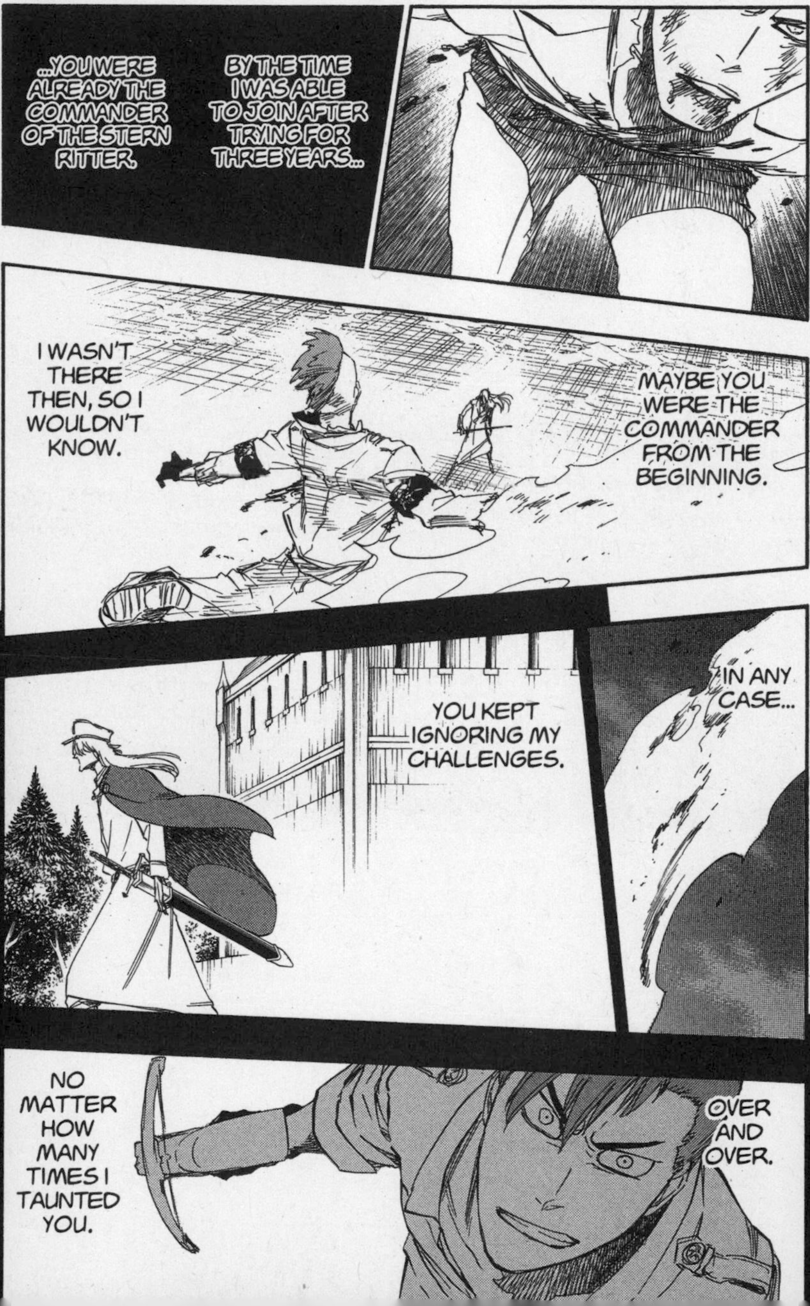
BY THE TIME I WAS ABLE TO JOIN AFTER TRYING FOR THREE YEARS...
...YOU WERE ALREADY THE COMMANDER OF THE STERN RITTER.
MAYBE YOU WERE THE COMMANDER FROM THE BEGINNING.
I WASN'T THERE THEN, SO I WOULDN'T KNOW.
IN ANY CASE...
YOU KEPT IGNORING MY CHALLENGES.
OVER AND OVER.
NO MATTER HOW MANY TIMES I TAUNTED YOU.

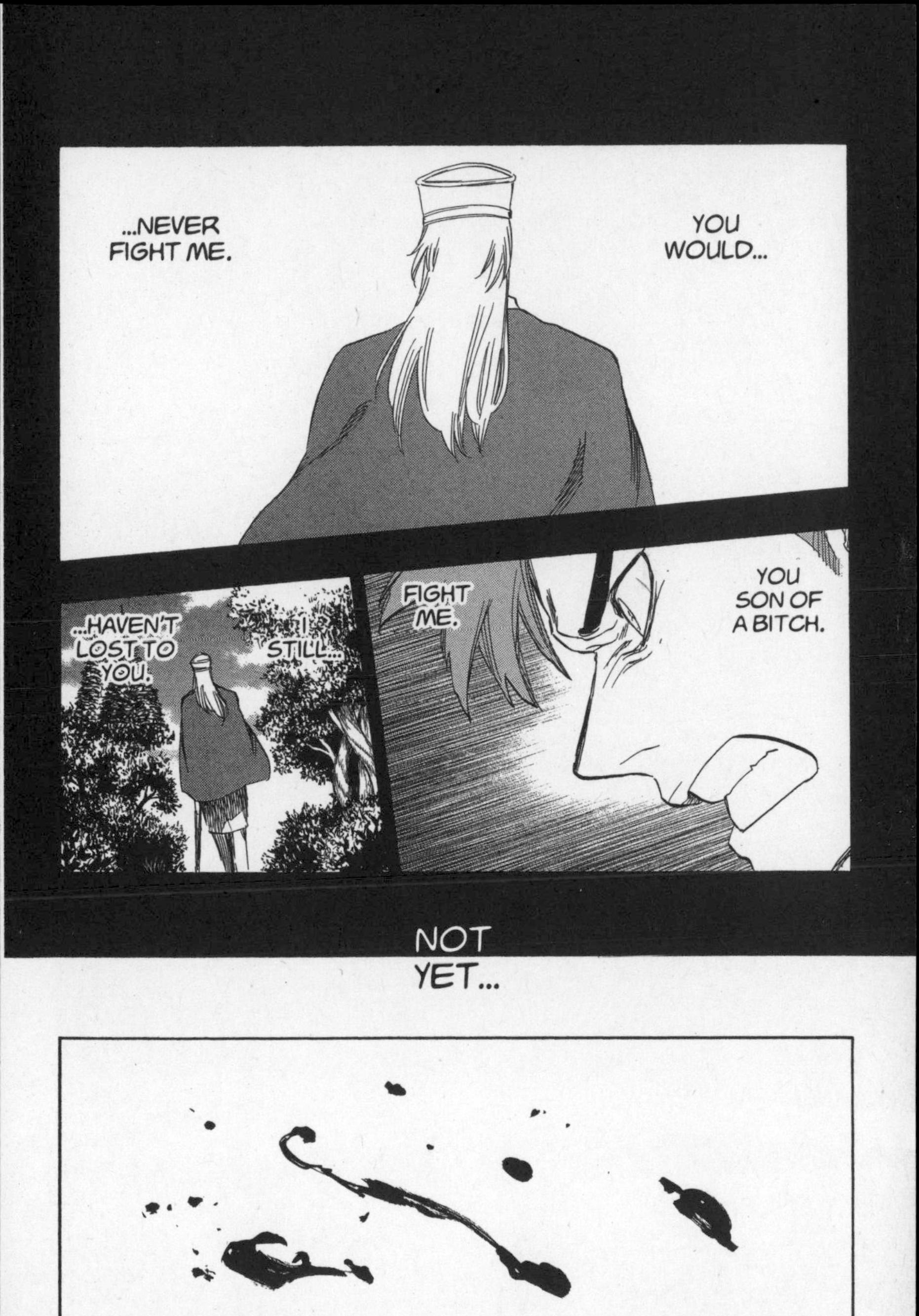
YOU WOULD...
...NEVER FIGHT ME.
YOU SON OF A BITCH.
FIGHT ME.
I STILL...
...HAVEN'T LOST TO YOU.
NOT YET...

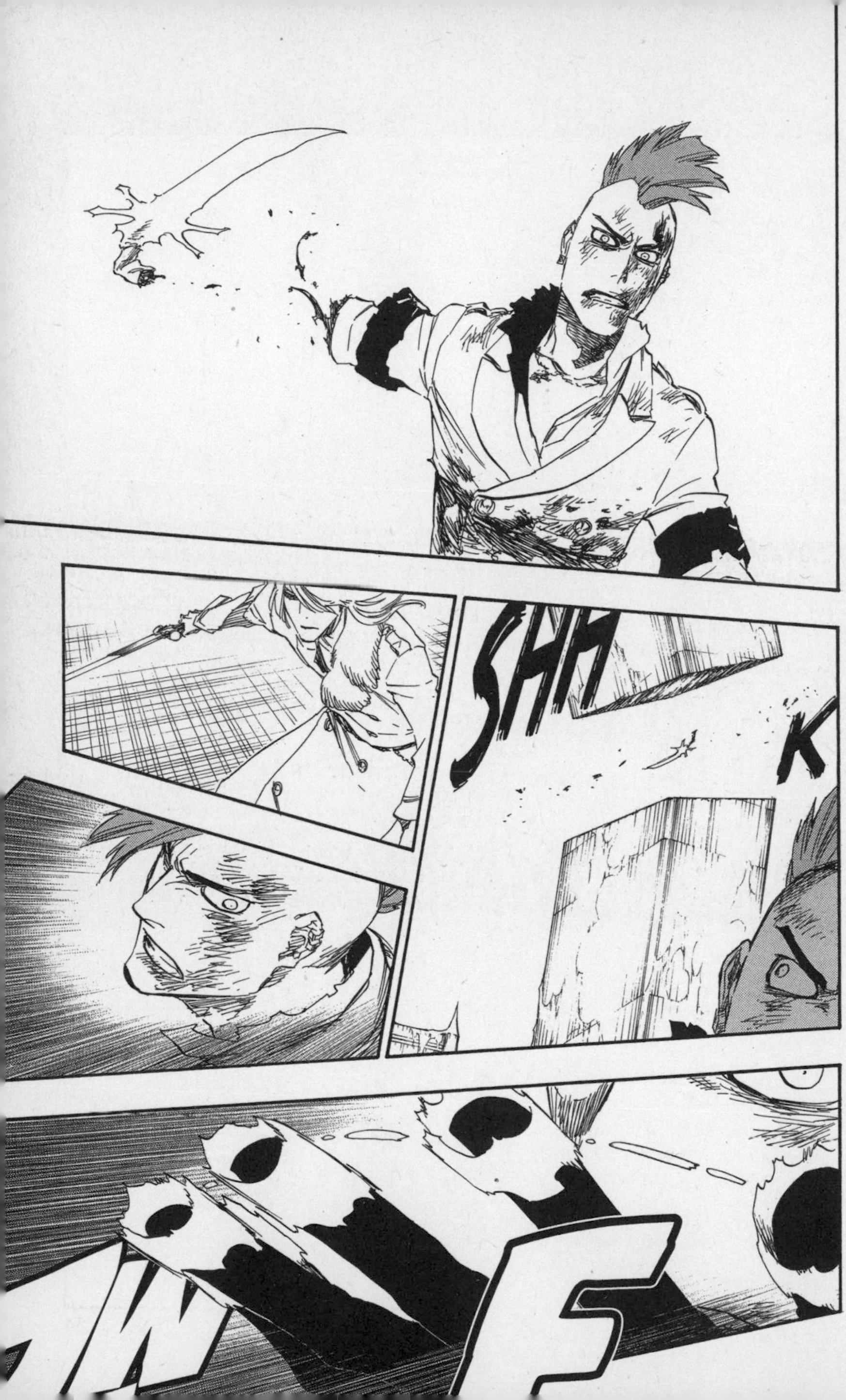
SHH
K

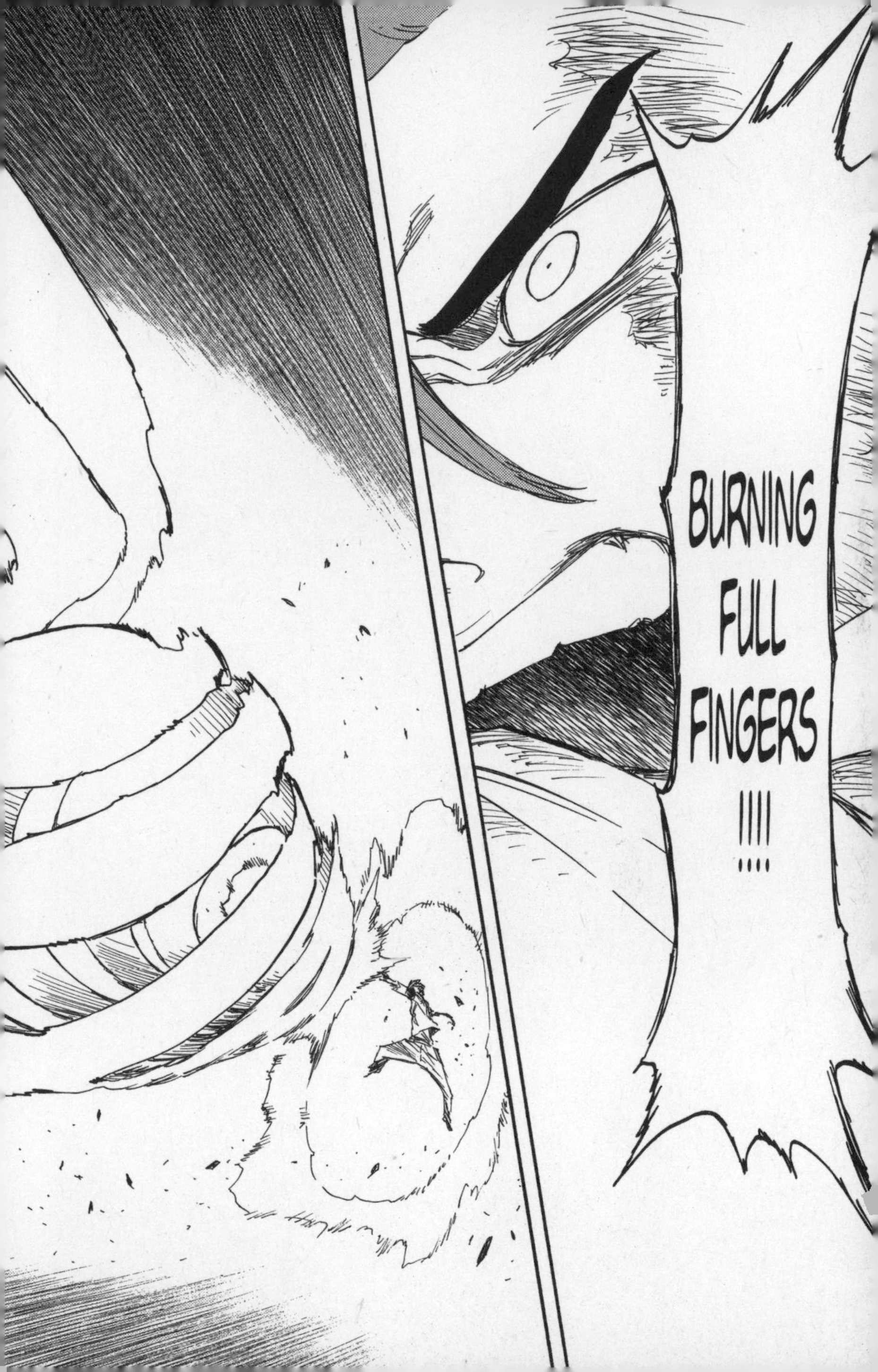
BURNING FULL FINGERS !!!!

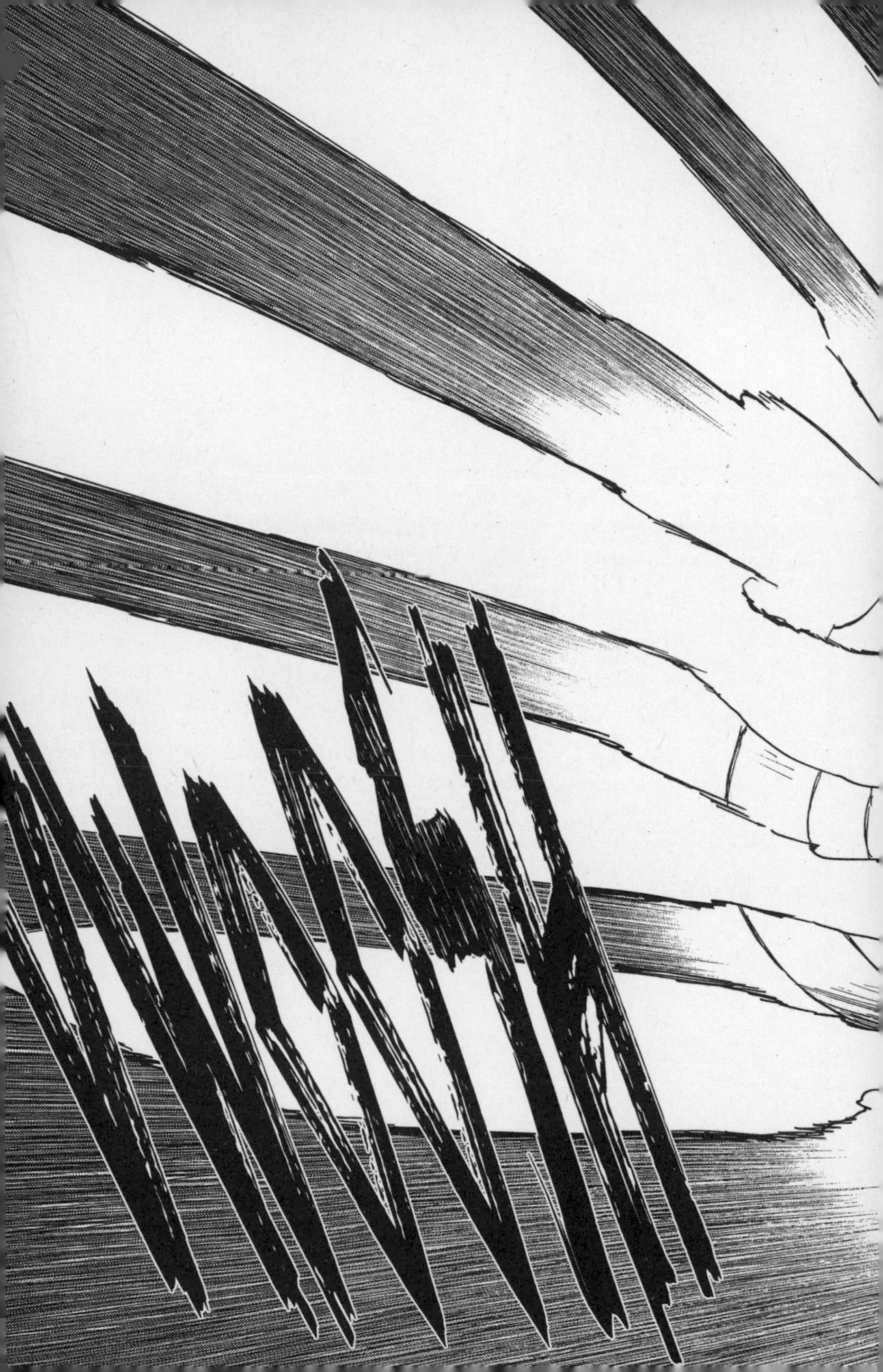

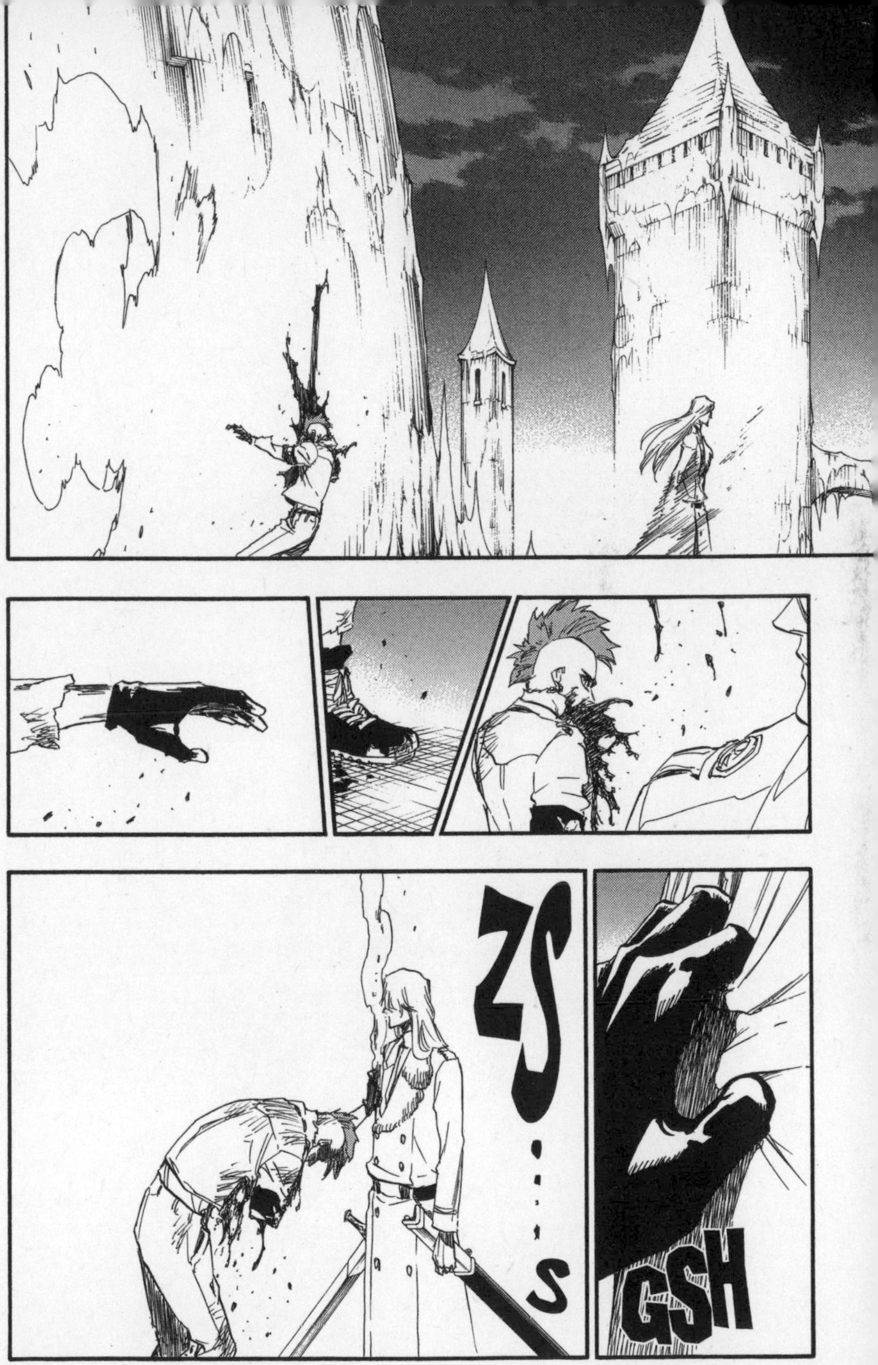
GSH
ZS...S

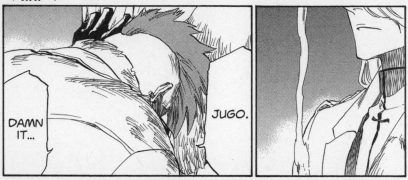

DAMN IT...

JUGO.

YOU WIN...

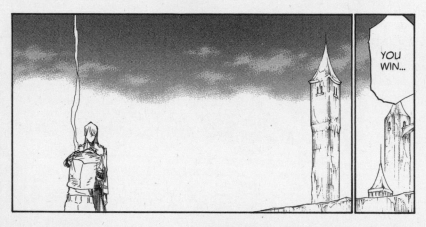

THINGS DON'T ALWAYS GO THE WAY YOU WANT THEM TO, DO THEY...?

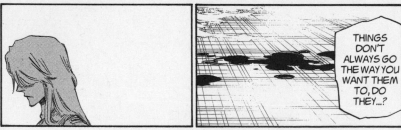

I THOUGHT LOSING TO YOU...

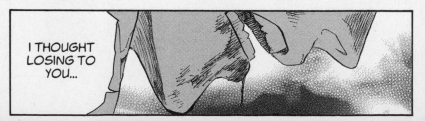

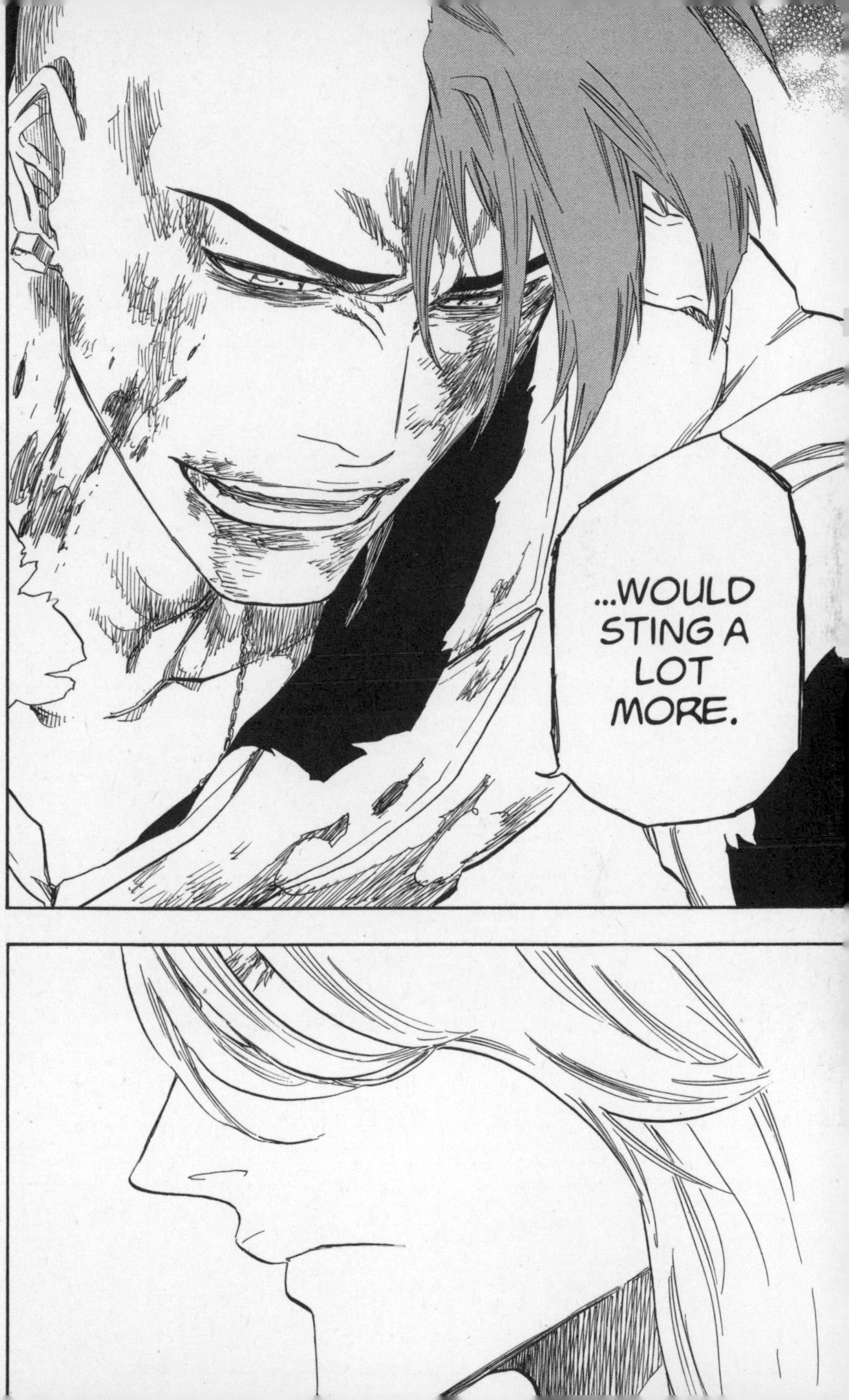
...WOULD STING A LOT MORE.

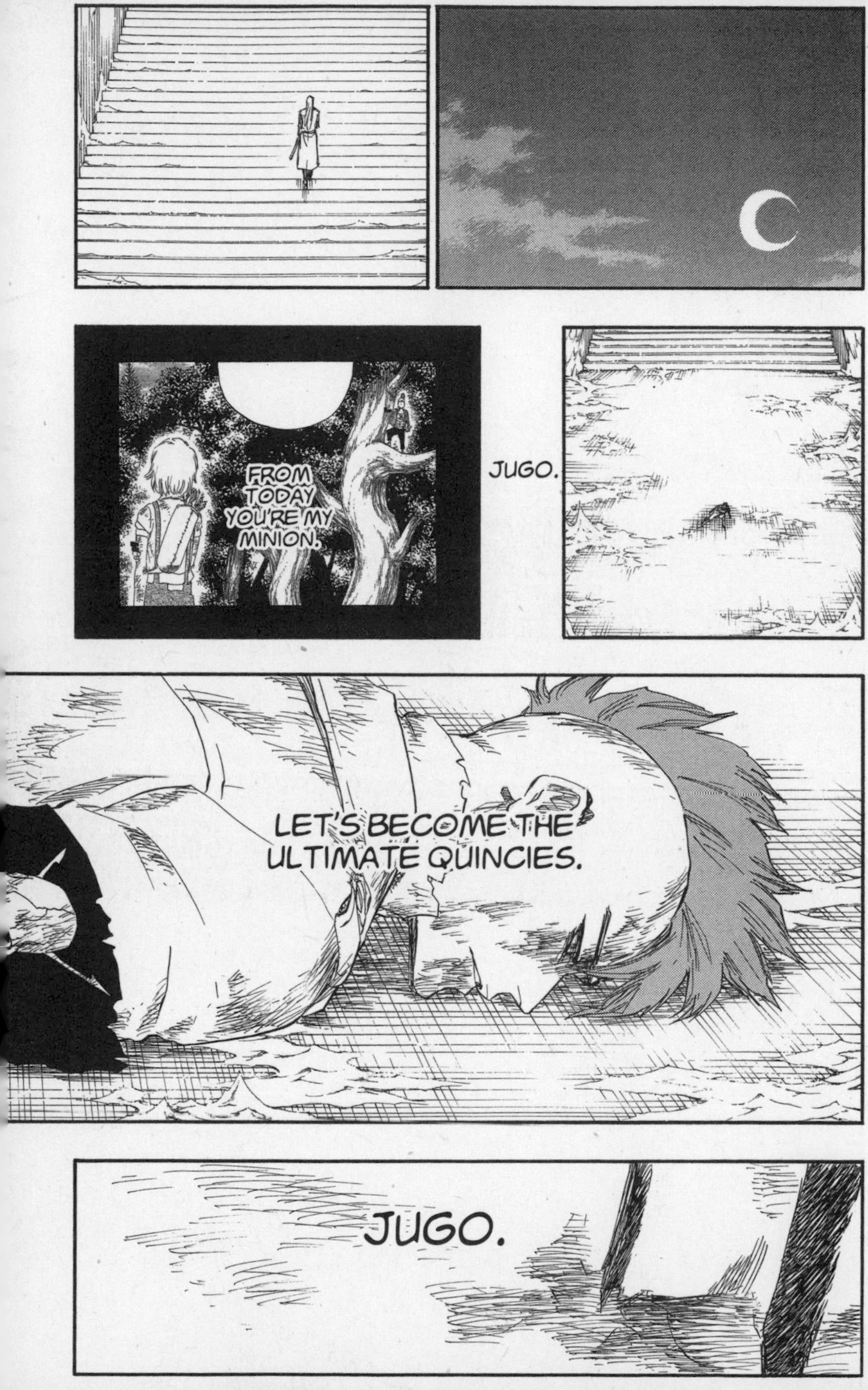
JUGO.
FROM TODAY YOU'RE MY MINION.
LET'S BECOME THE ULTIMATE QUINCIES.
JUGO.

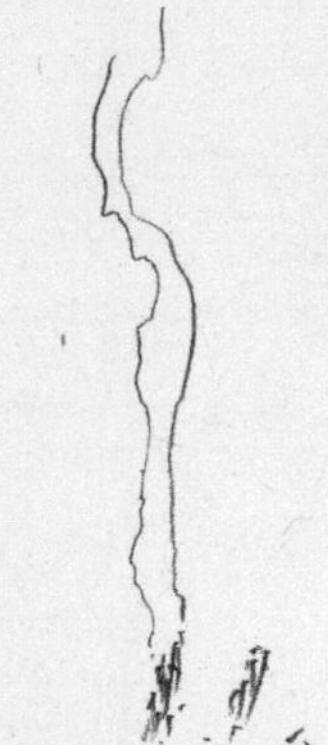

635.HOODED ENIGMA

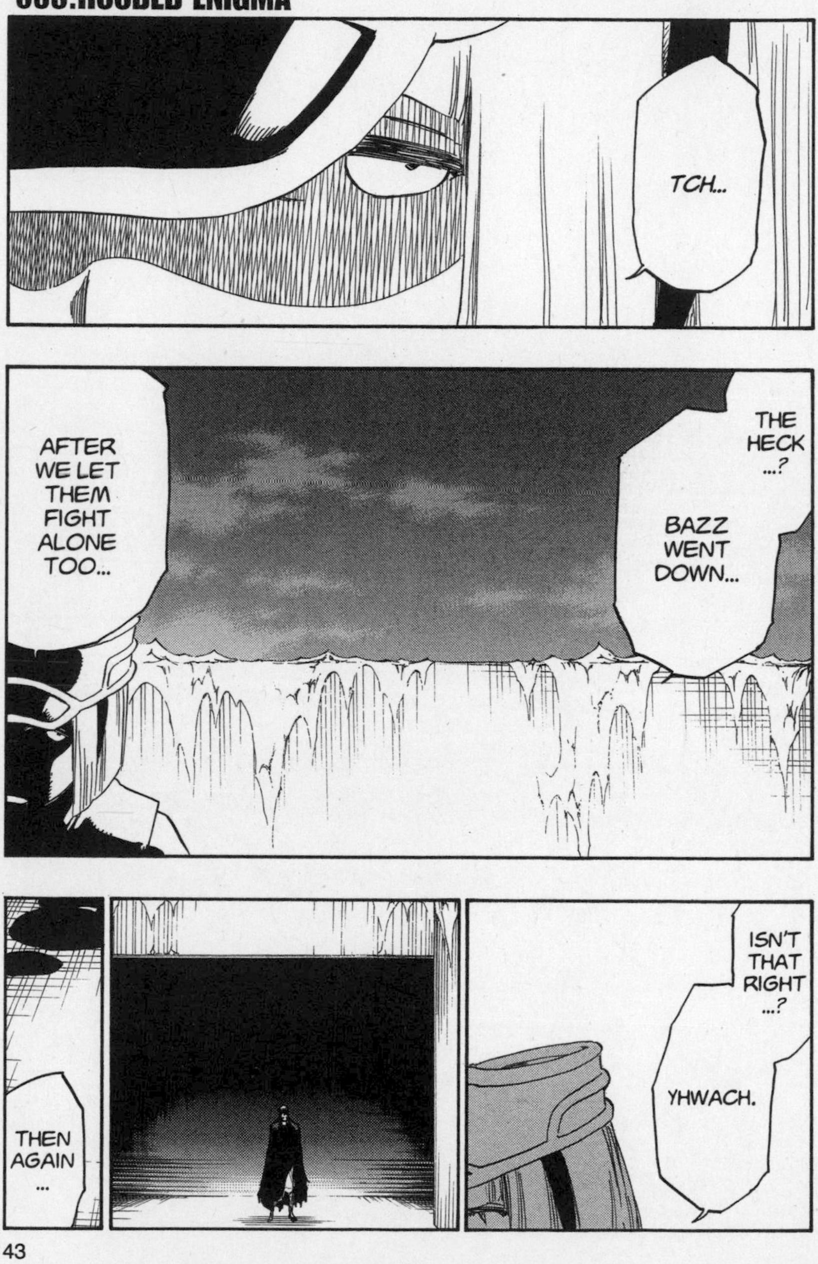
TCH...
THE HECK ...?
BAZZ WENT DOWN...
AFTER WE LET THEM FIGHT ALONE TOO...
ISN'T THAT RIGHT ...?
YHWACH.
THEN AGAIN ...

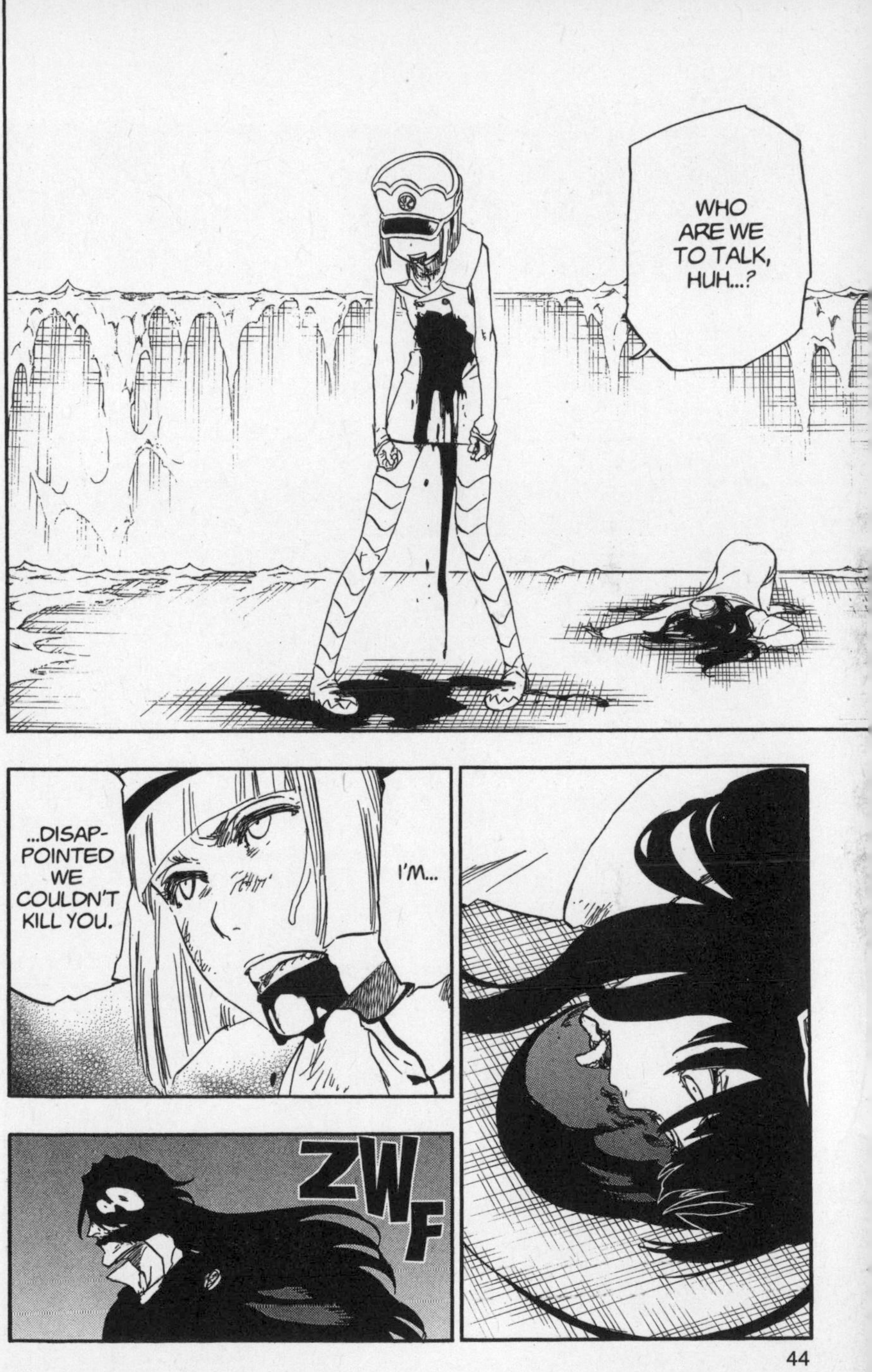
WHO ARE WE TO TALK, HUH...?
I'M...
...DISAP-POINTED WE COULDN'T KILL YOU.
ZWF

READ THIS WAY

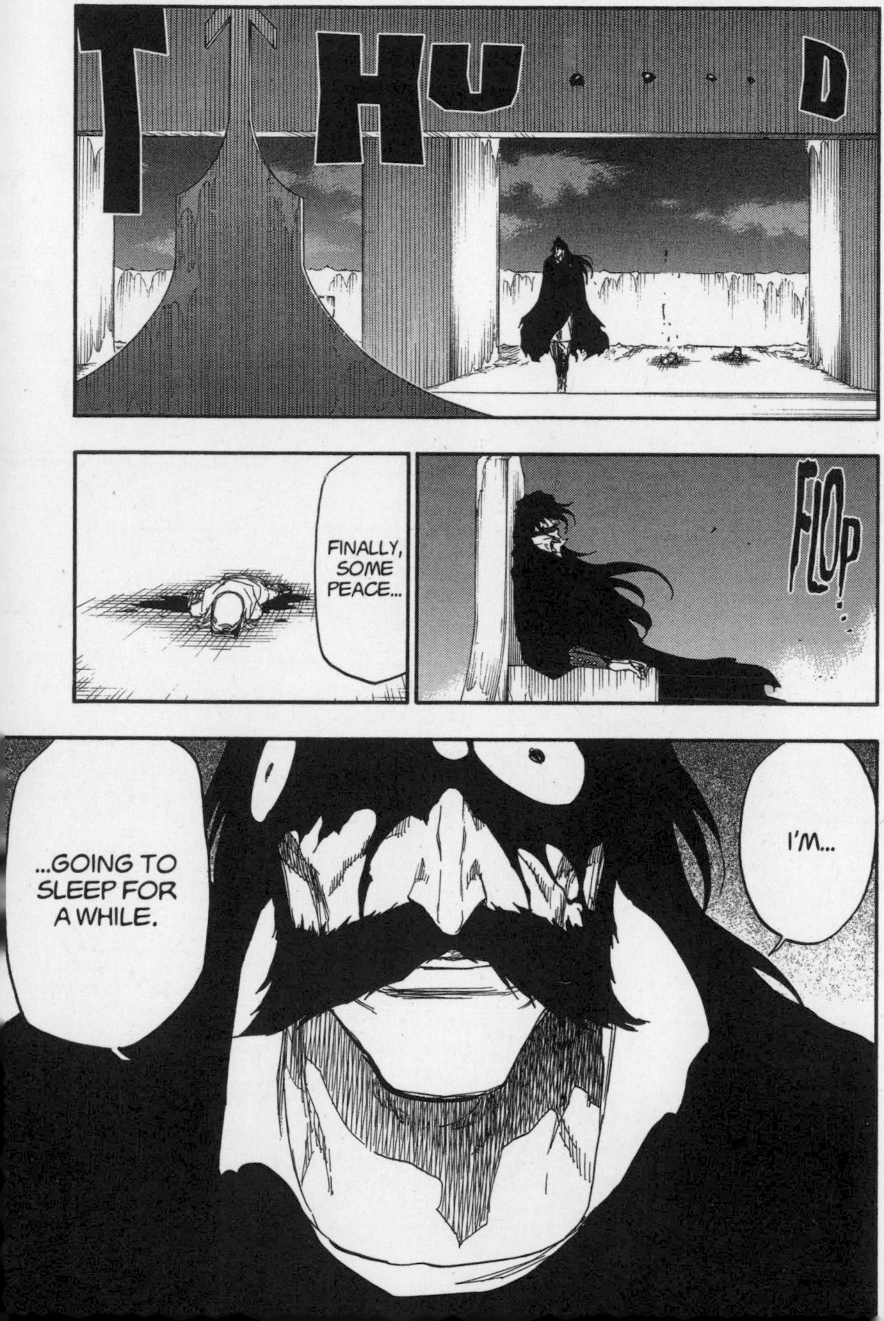
THUD
FLOP!
FINALLY, SOME PEACE...
I'M...
...GOING TO SLEEP FOR A WHILE.

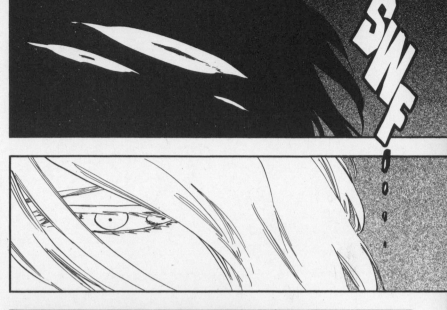

BLEACH

635.

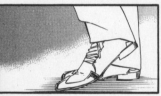

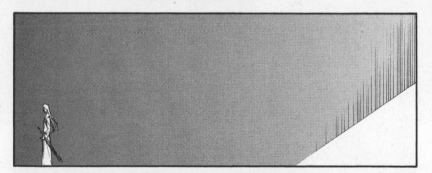

...YOUR MAJ-ESTY?

SUCH A CRUEL POWER, ISN'T IT...

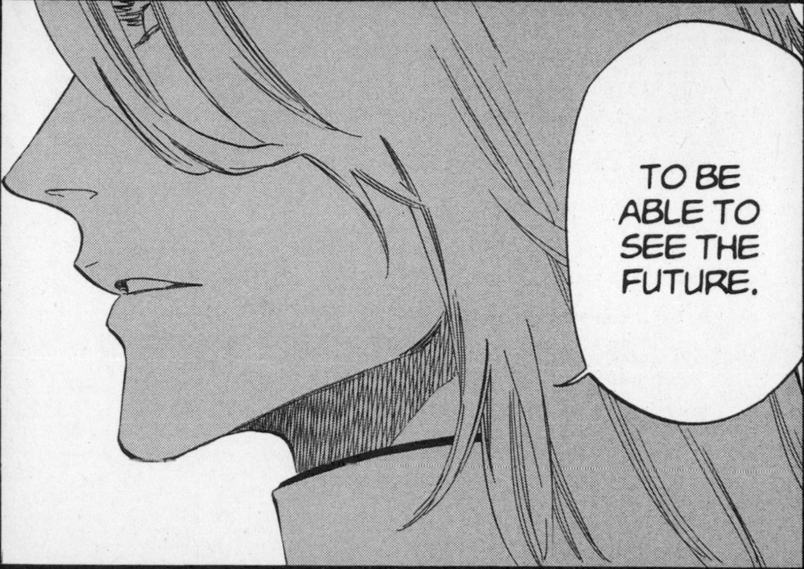
TO BE ABLE TO SEE THE FUTURE.

Hooded Enigma

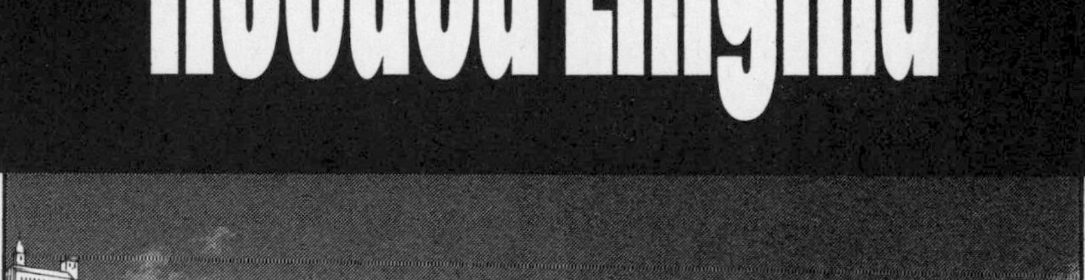

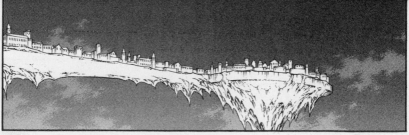

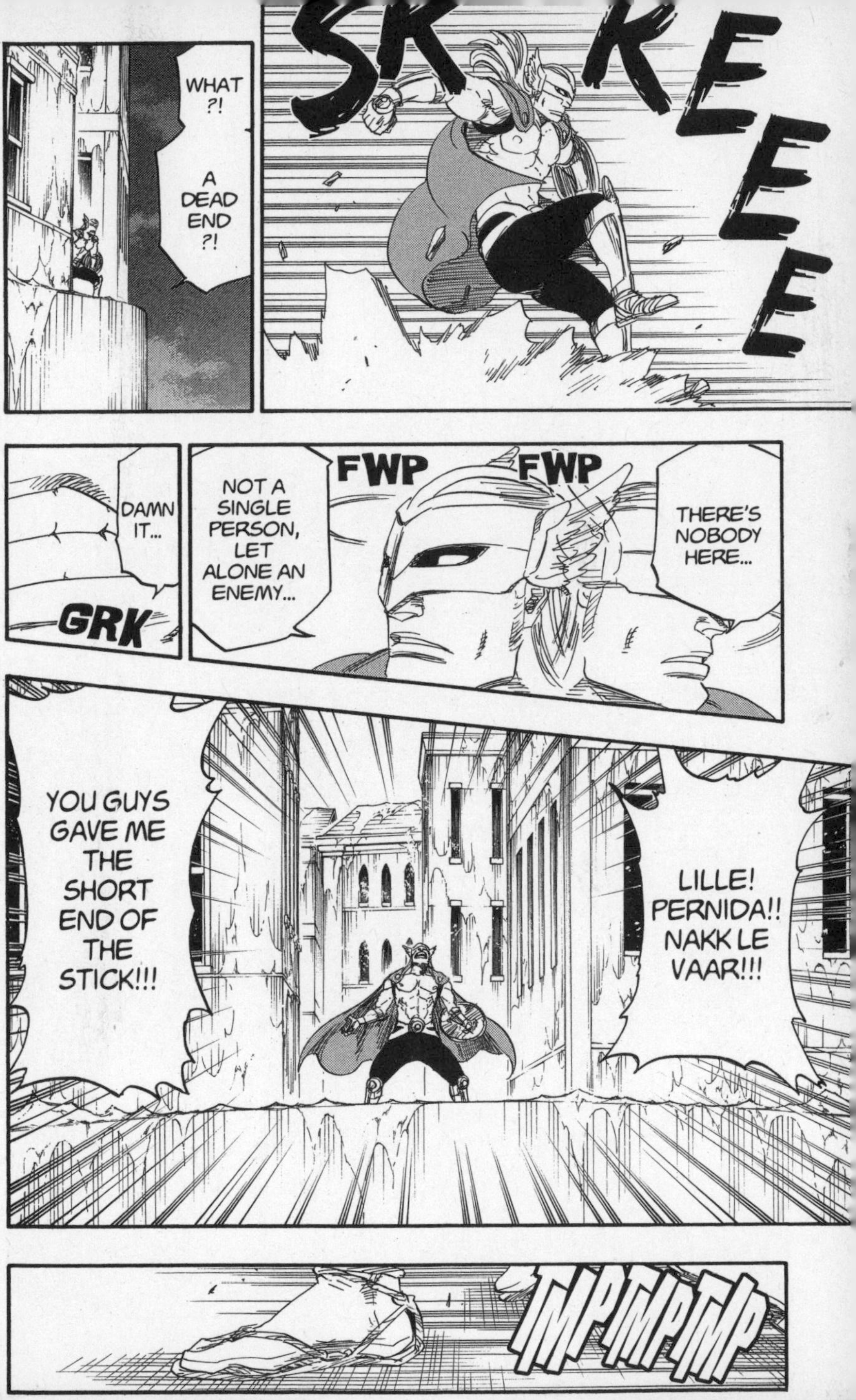
SKREEEE
WHAT?!
A DEAD END?!
FWP FWP
THERE'S NOBODY HERE...
NOT A SINGLE PERSON, LET ALONE AN ENEMY...
DAMN IT...
GRK
LILLE! PERNIDA!! NAKK LE VAAR!!!
YOU GUYS GAVE ME THE SHORT END OF THE STICK!!!
TMPTMPTMP

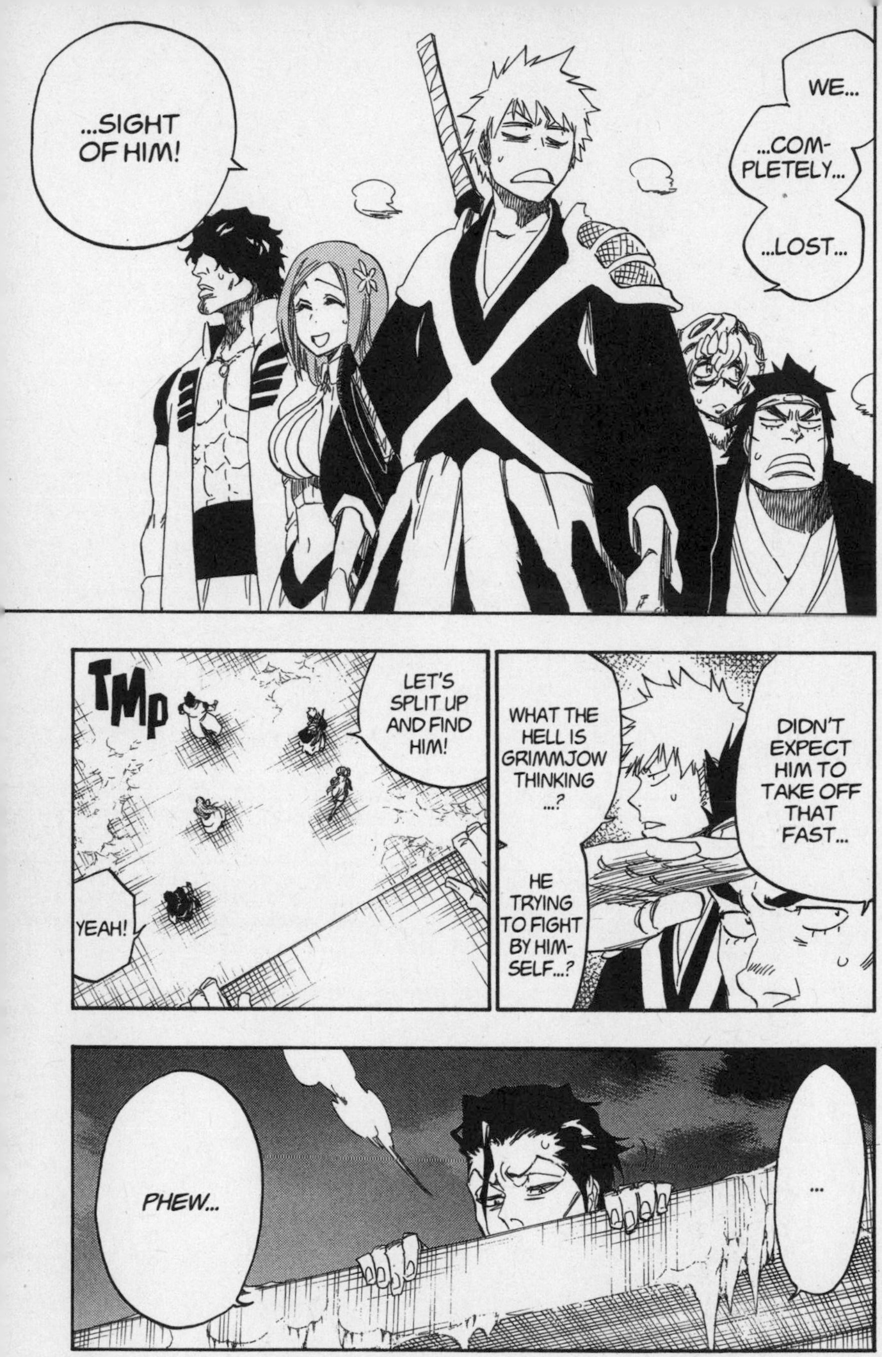
WE... ...COM-PLETELY... ...LOST...
...SIGHT OF HIM!
DIDN'T EXPECT HIM TO TAKE OFF THAT FAST...
WHAT THE HELL IS GRIMMJOW THINKING ...?
HE TRYING TO FIGHT BY HIM-SELF...?
LET'S SPLIT UP AND FIND HIM!
TMP
YEAH!
...
PHEW...

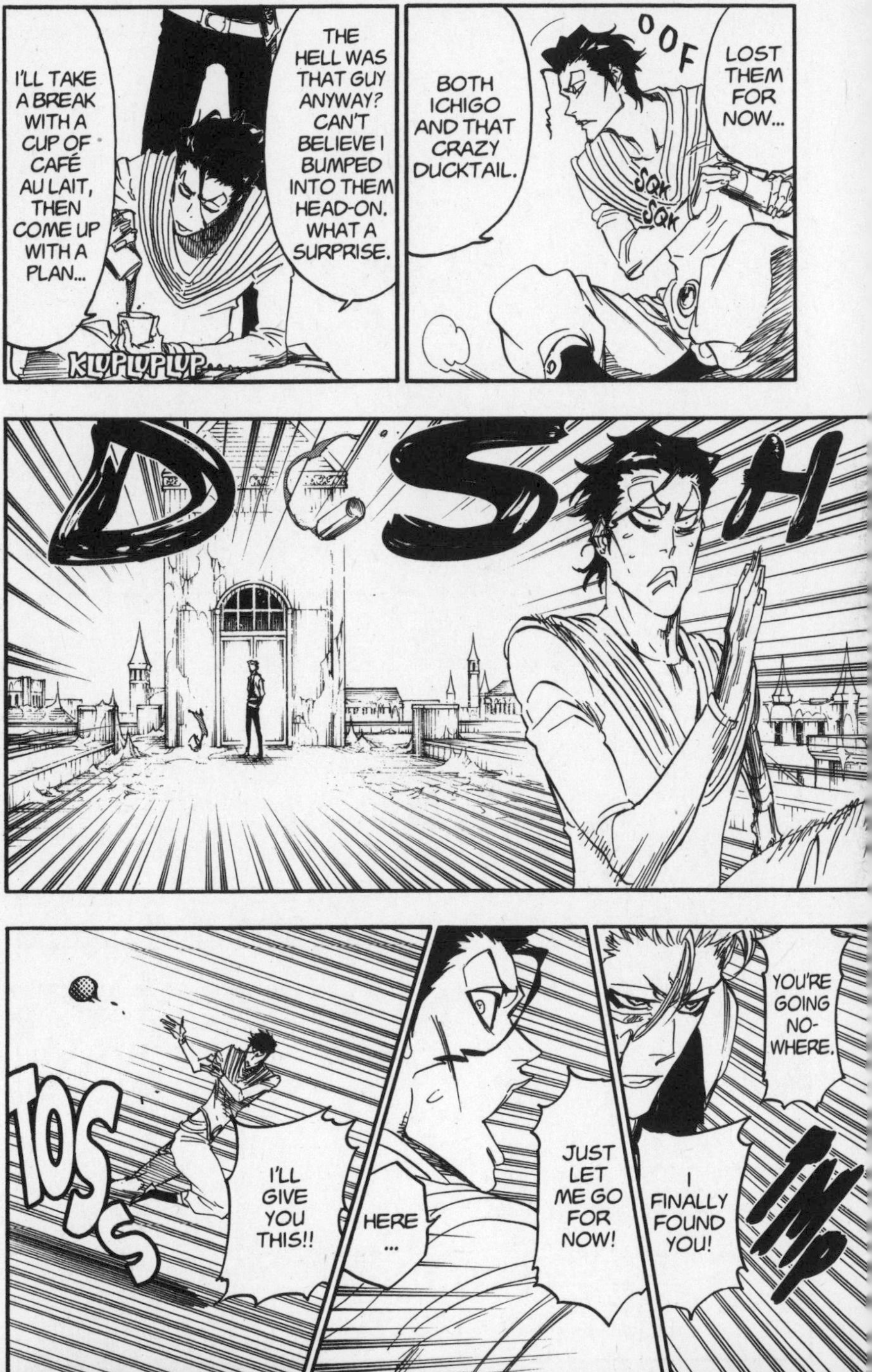
LOST THEM FOR NOW...
OOF
SQK SQK
BOTH ICHIGO AND THAT CRAZY DUCKTAIL.
THE HELL WAS THAT GUY ANYWAY? CAN'T BELIEVE I BUMPED INTO THEM HEAD-ON. WHAT A SURPRISE.
I'LL TAKE A BREAK WITH A CUP OF CAFÉ AU LAIT, THEN COME UP WITH A PLAN...
KLUPLUPLUP
D.S.H
YOU'RE GOING NO-WHERE.
TMP
I FINALLY FOUND YOU!
JUST LET ME GO FOR NOW!
HERE ...
I'LL GIVE YOU THIS!!
TOSS

READ THIS WAY

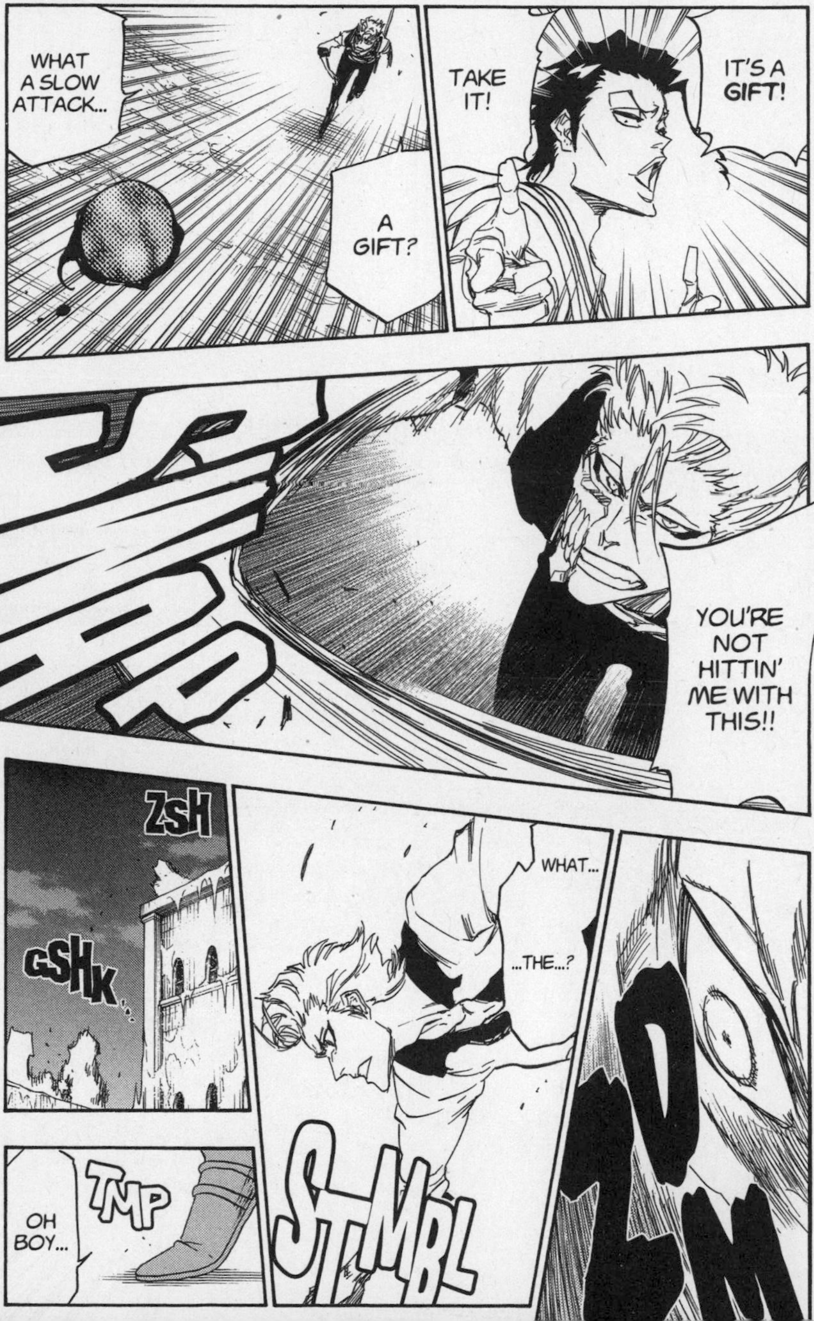
IT'S A GIFT!
TAKE IT!
WHAT A SLOW ATTACK...
A GIFT?
YOU'RE NOT HITTIN' ME WITH THIS!!
WHAT...
...THE...?
STMBL
ZSH
GSHK
TMP
OH BOY...

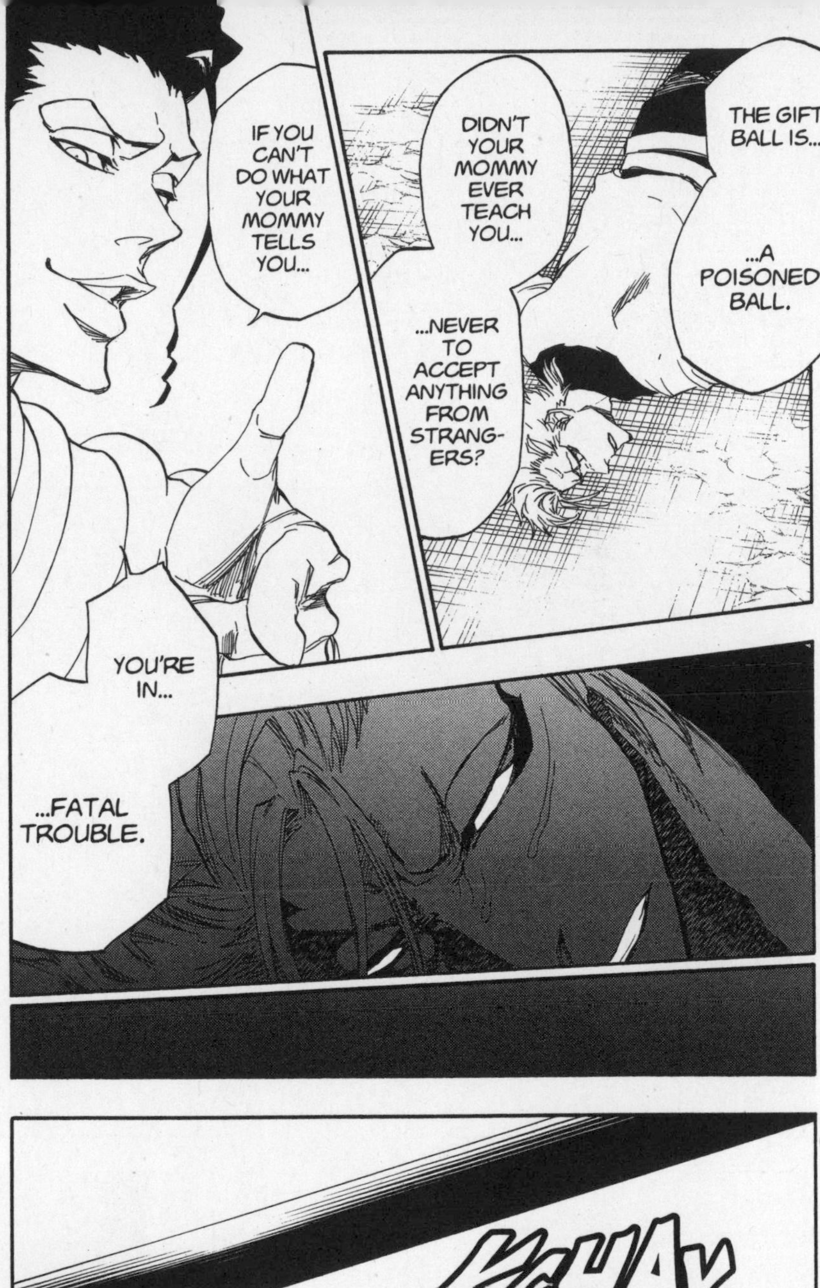
THE GIFT BALL IS...
...A POISONED BALL.
DIDN'T YOUR MOMMY EVER TEACH YOU...
...NEVER TO ACCEPT ANYTHING FROM STRANG-ERS?
IF YOU CAN'T DO WHAT YOUR MOMMY TELLS YOU...
YOU'RE IN...
...FATAL TROUBLE.
KCHAK

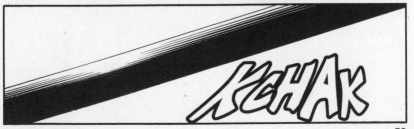

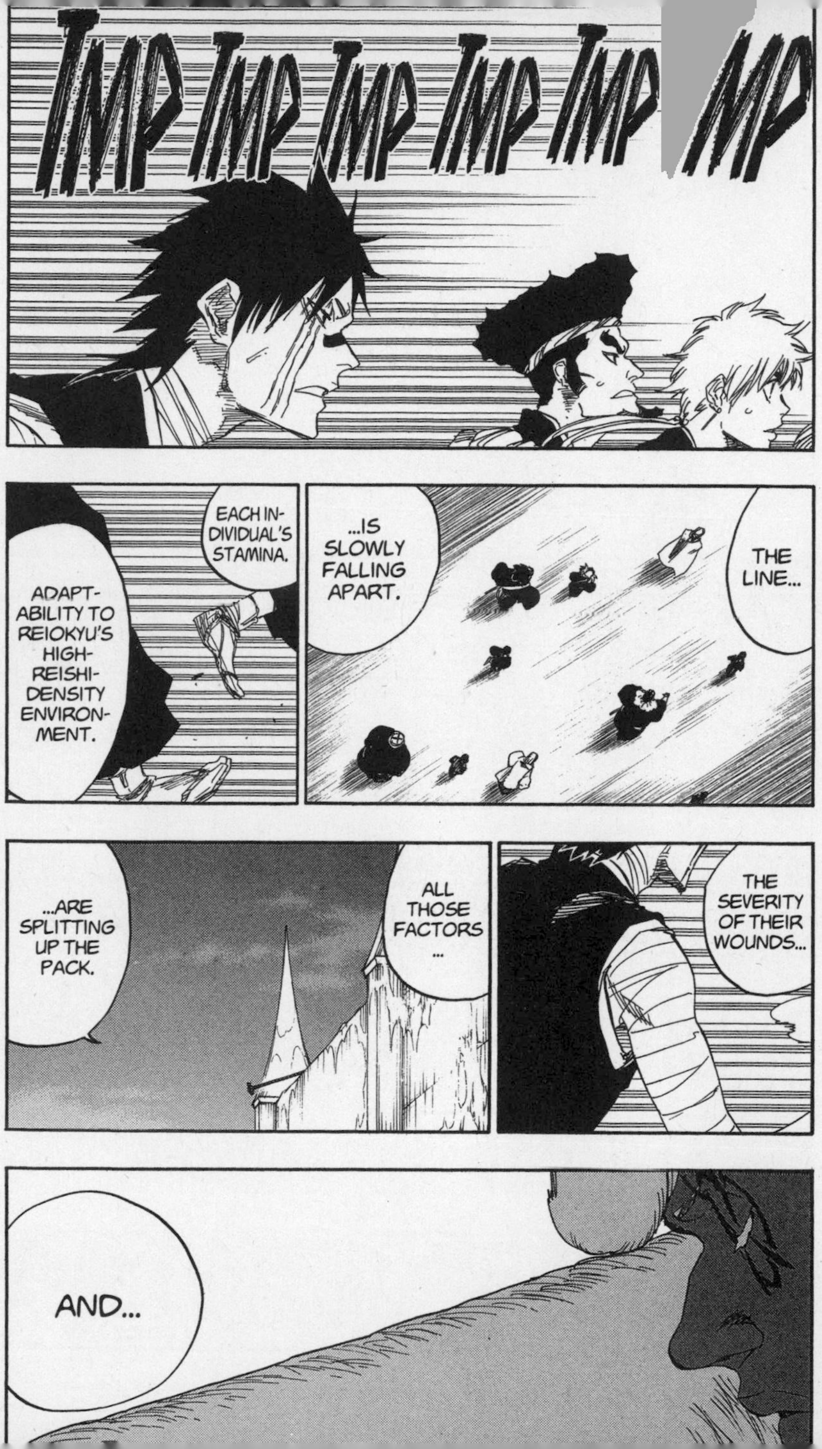
TMP TMP TMP TMP TMP MP
THE LINE...
...IS SLOWLY FALLING APART.
EACH INDIVIDUAL'S STAMINA.
ADAPTABILITY TO REIOKYU'S HIGH-REISHI-DENSITY ENVIRONMENT.
THE SEVERITY OF THEIR WOUNDS...
ALL THOSE FACTORS...
...ARE SPLITTING UP THE PACK.
AND...

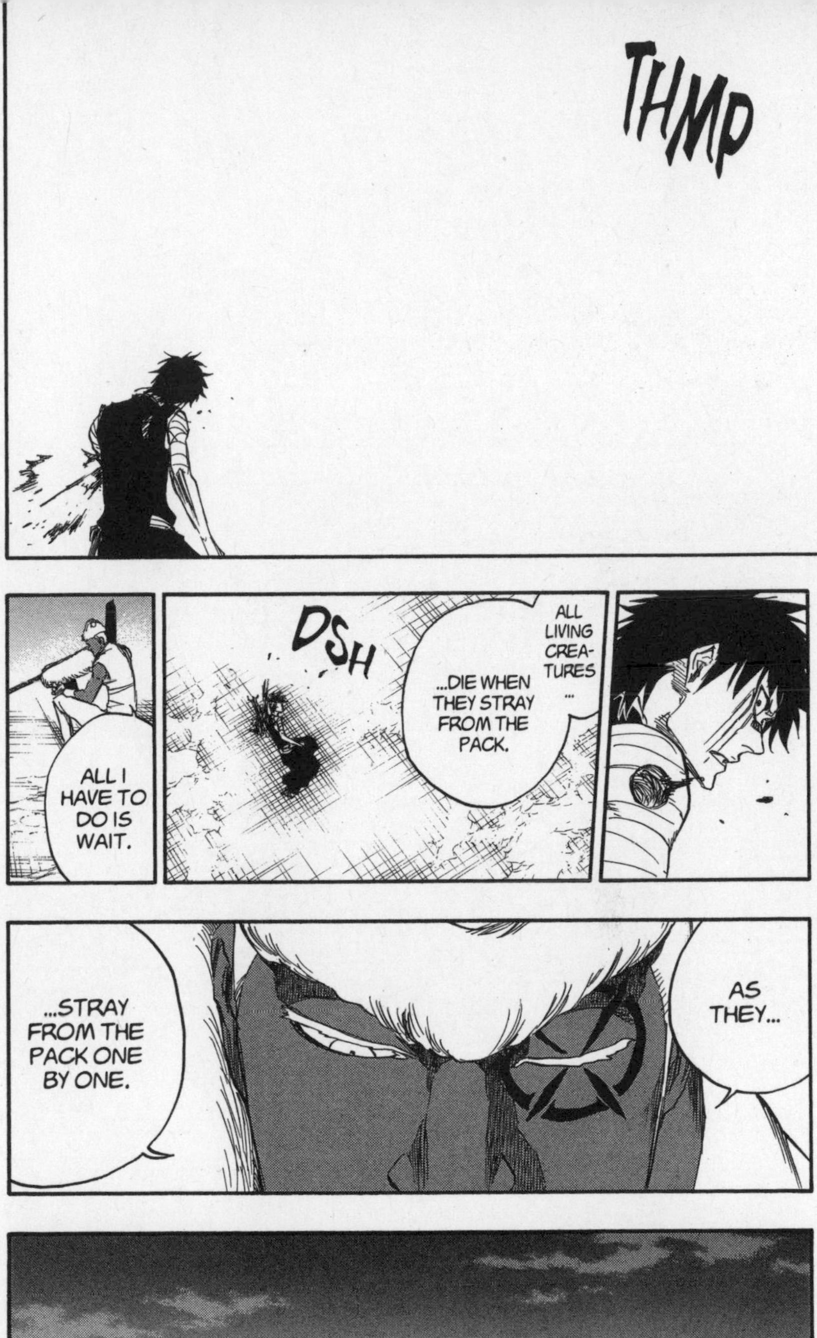
THMP
ALL LIVING CREATURES...
...DIE WHEN THEY STRAY FROM THE PACK.
DSH
ALL I HAVE TO DO IS WAIT.
AS THEY...
...STRAY FROM THE PACK ONE BY ONE.

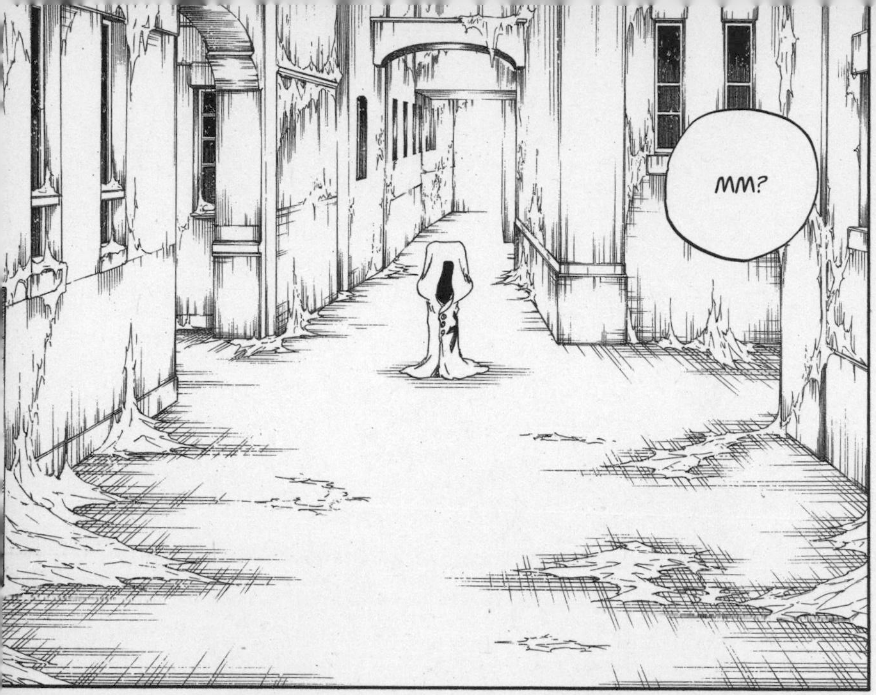
MM?

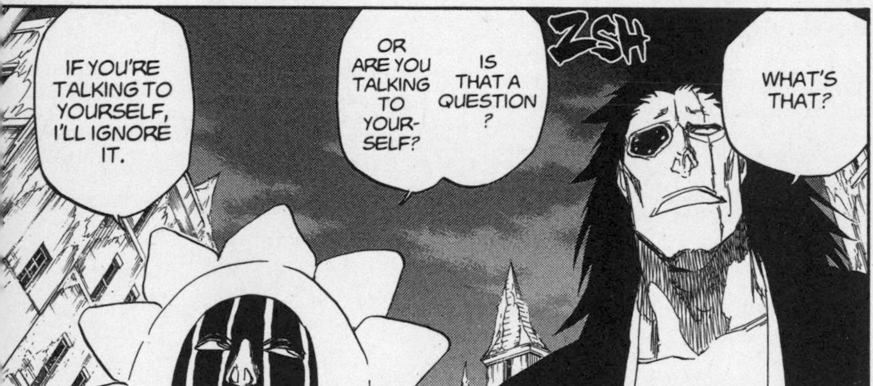
WHAT'S THAT?
ZSH
IS THAT A QUESTION?
OR ARE YOU TALKING TO YOURSELF?
IF YOU'RE TALKING TO YOURSELF, I'LL IGNORE IT.

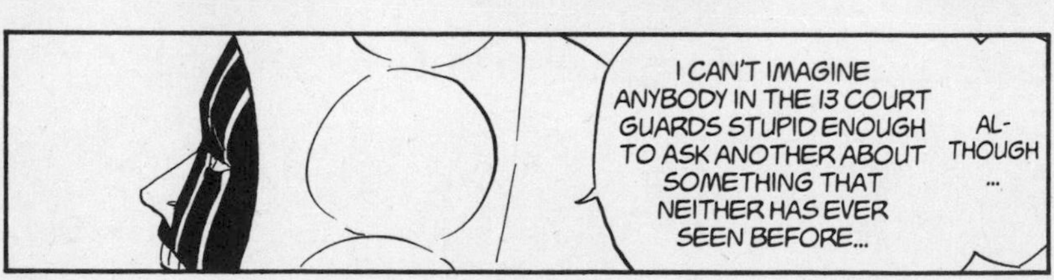
AL-THOUGH...
I CAN'T IMAGINE ANYBODY IN THE 13 COURT GUARDS STUPID ENOUGH TO ASK ANOTHER ABOUT SOMETHING THAT NEITHER HAS EVER SEEN BEFORE...

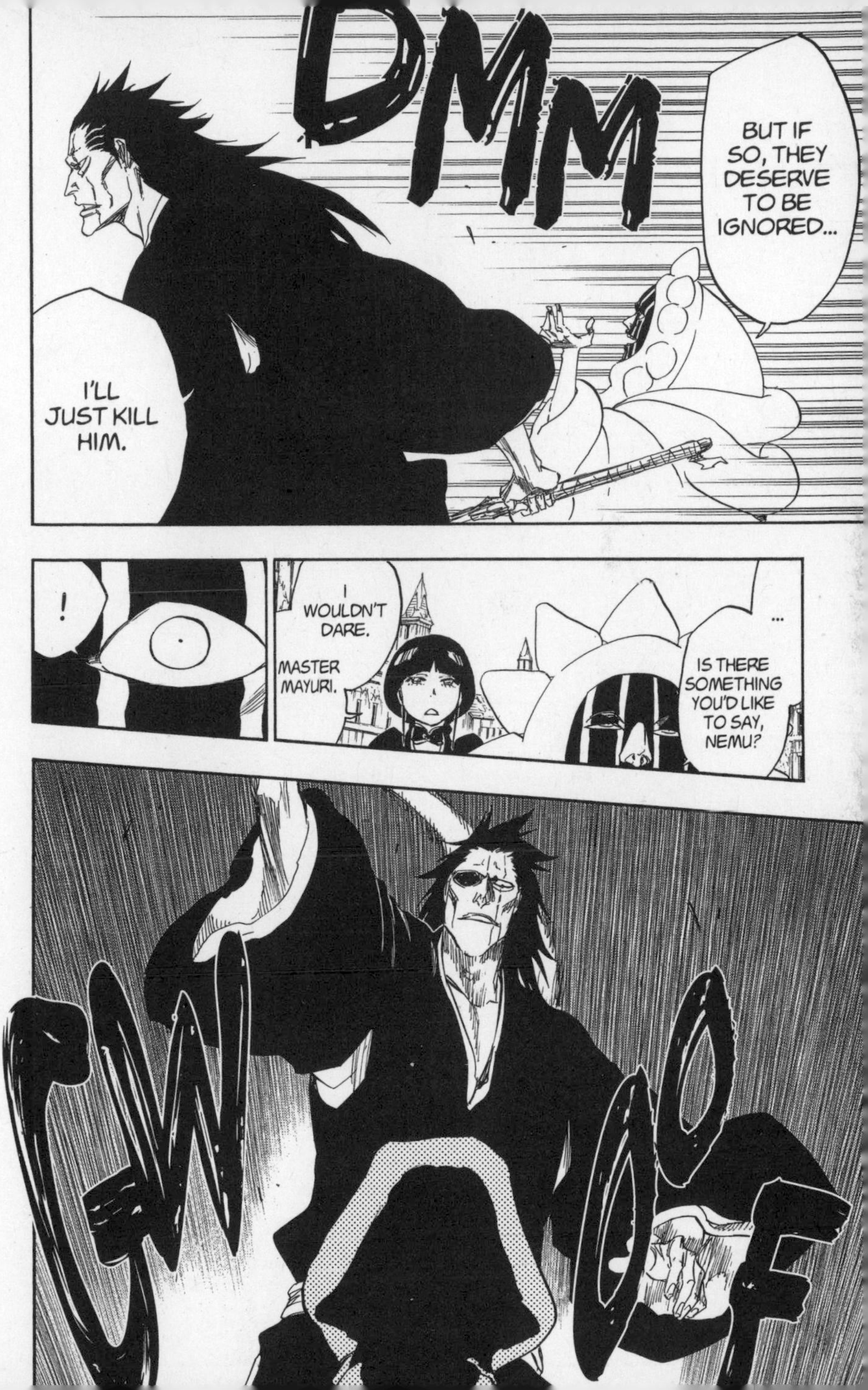
BUT IF SO, THEY DESERVE TO BE IGNORED...
DMM
I'LL JUST KILL HIM.
...
IS THERE SOMETHING YOU'D LIKE TO SAY, NEMU?
I WOULDN'T DARE.
MASTER MAYURI.
!

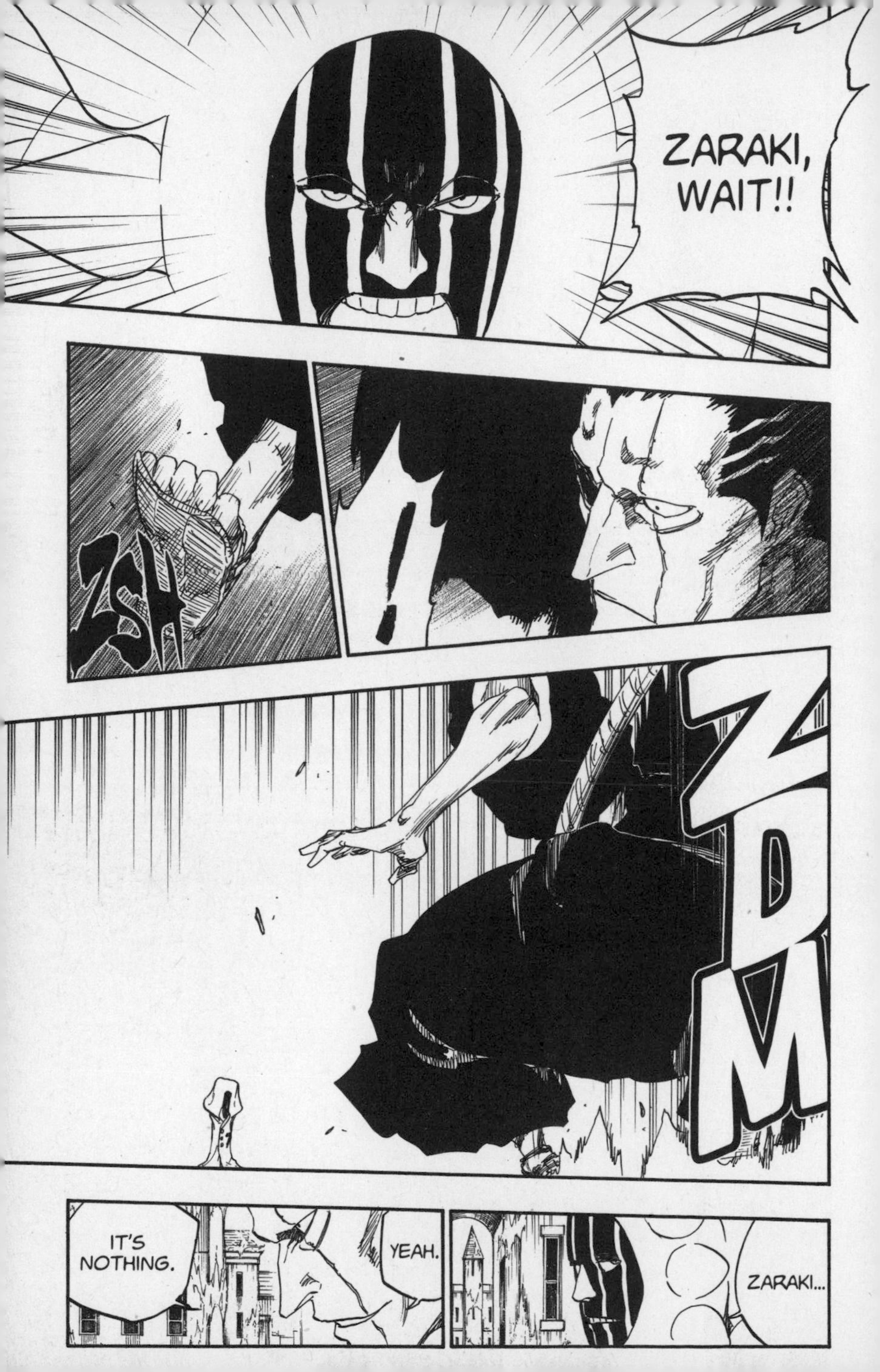
ZARAKI, WAIT!!
!
ZSH
ZDM
YEAH.
IT'S NOTHING.
ZARAKI...

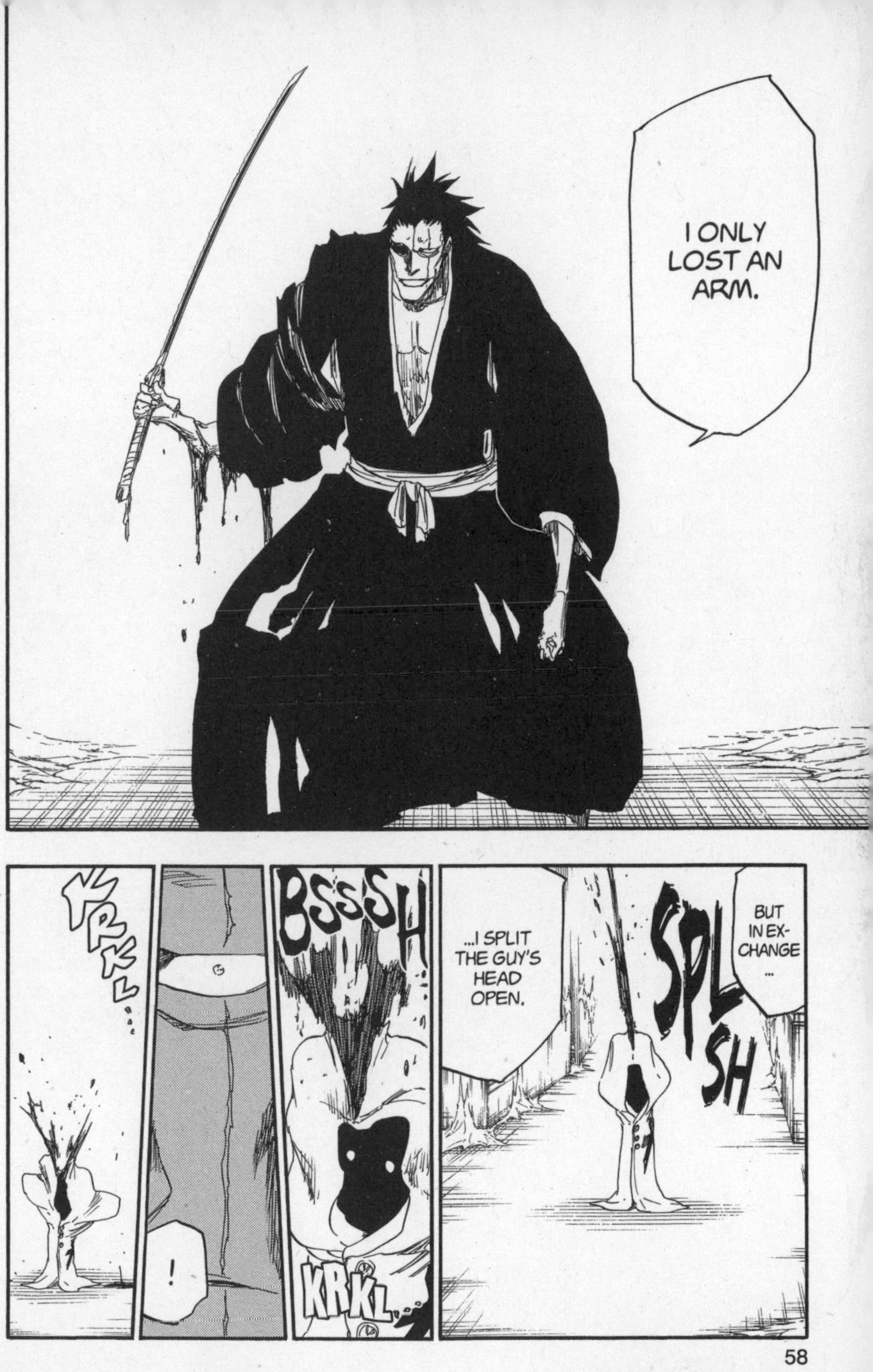
I ONLY LOST AN ARM.
BUT IN EX-CHANGE...
SPLSH
...I SPLIT THE GUY'S HEAD OPEN.
BSSSH
KRKL
!
KRKL

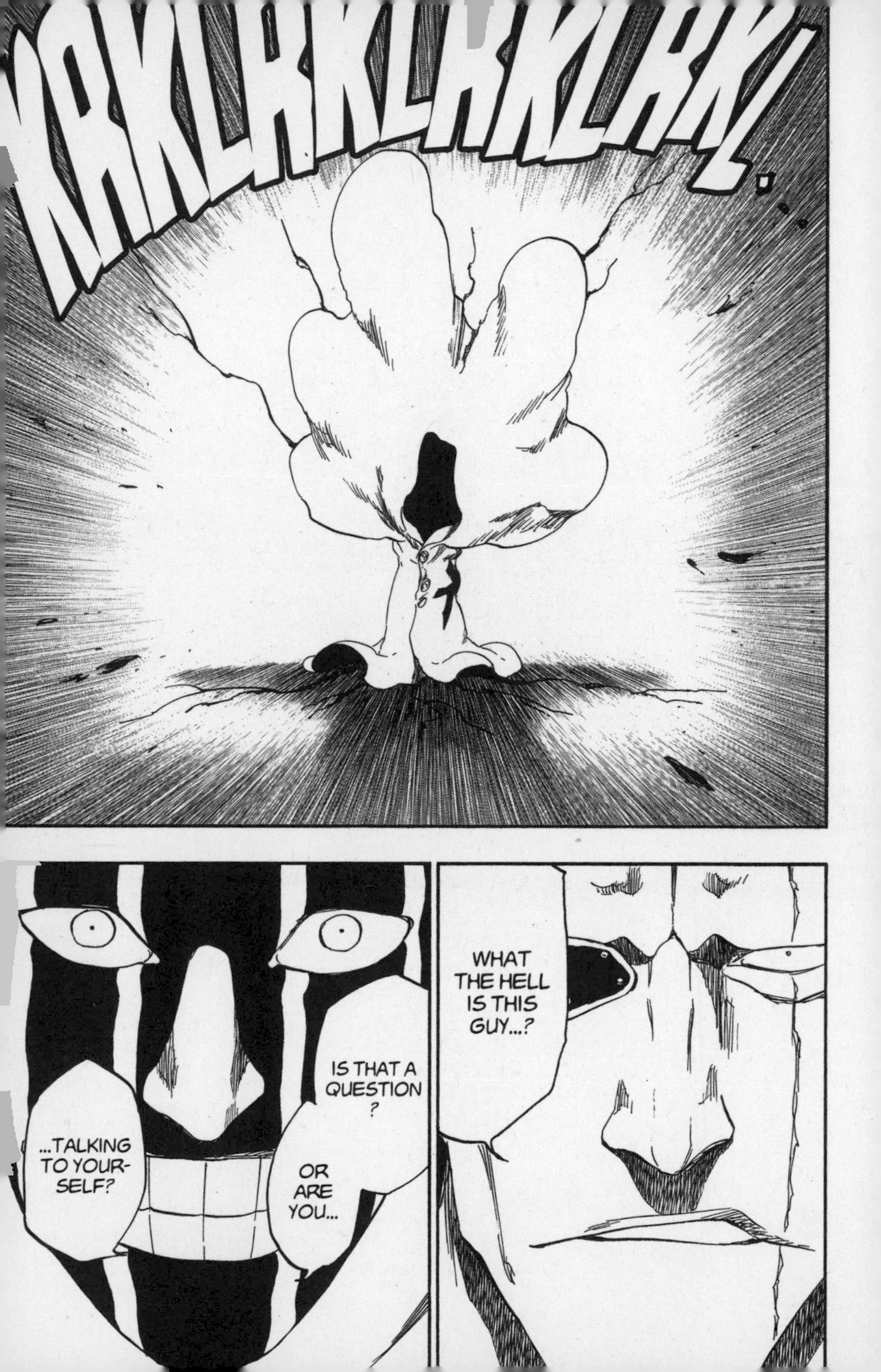
KRAKLAKKLAKKLAKK!
WHAT THE HELL IS THIS GUY...?
IS THAT A QUESTION?
OR ARE YOU...
...TALKING TO YOURSELF?

NAKK LE VAAR
LIKES SWEET
CAFE AU LAIT.

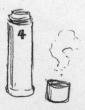

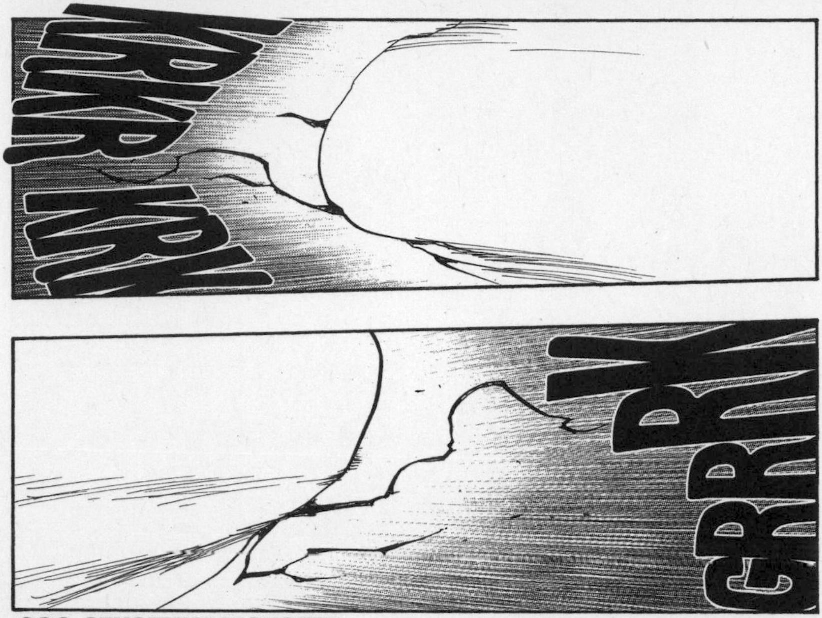
KRAK KRAK
CRRNK

636. SENSITIVE MONSTER

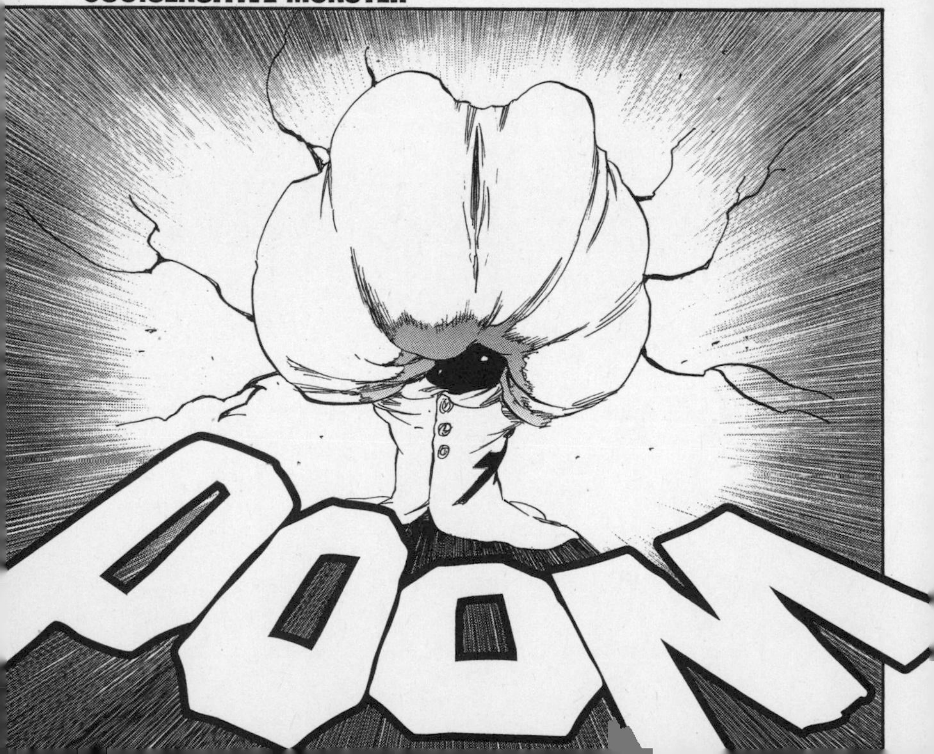
DOOM

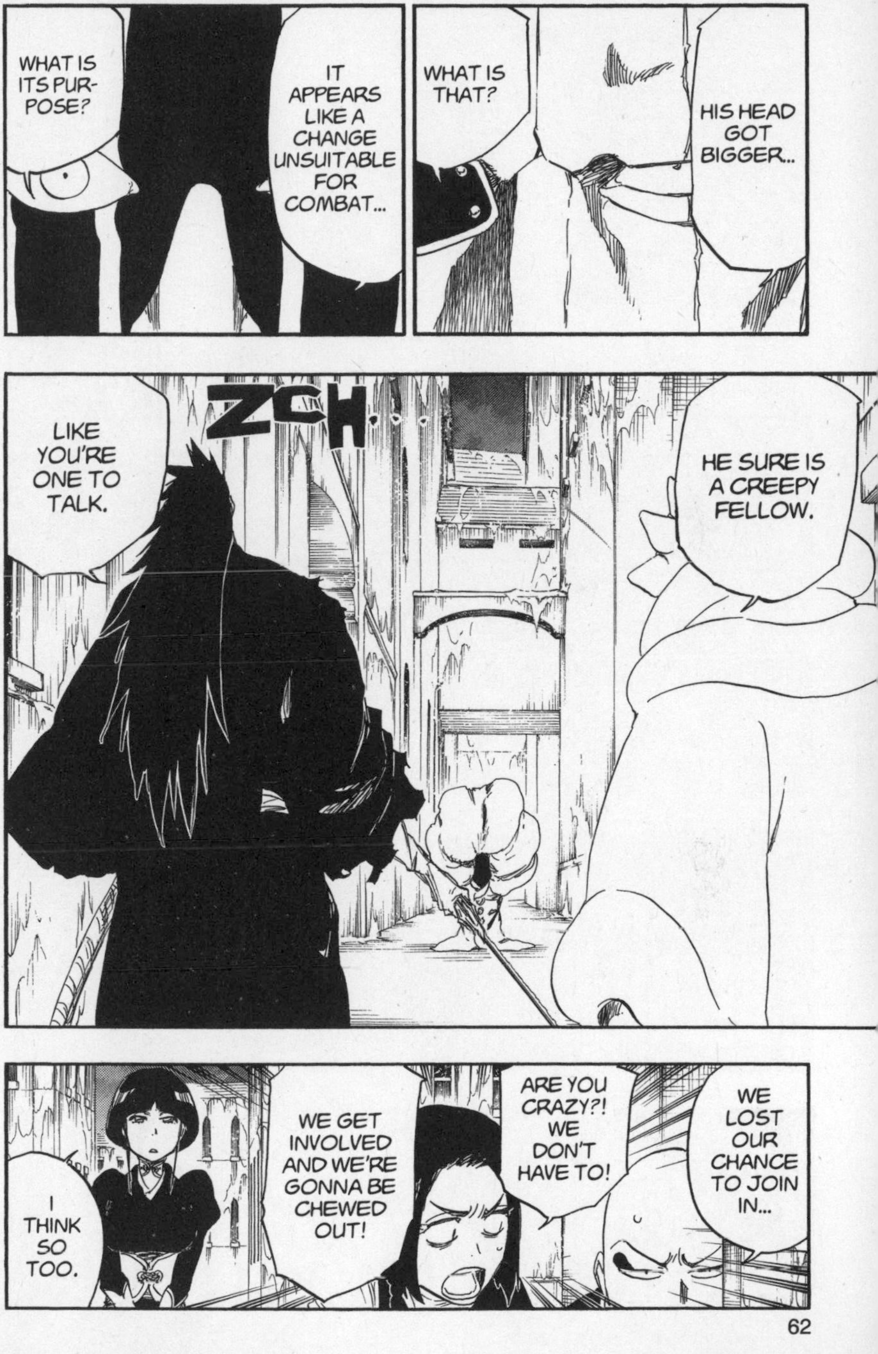
HIS HEAD GOT BIGGER...
WHAT IS THAT?
IT APPEARS LIKE A CHANGE UNSUITABLE FOR COMBAT...
WHAT IS ITS PURPOSE?
HE SURE IS A CREEPY FELLOW.
ZCH...
LIKE YOU'RE ONE TO TALK.
WE LOST OUR CHANCE TO JOIN IN...
ARE YOU CRAZY?! WE DON'T HAVE TO!
WE GET INVOLVED AND WE'RE GONNA BE CHEWED OUT!
I THINK SO TOO.

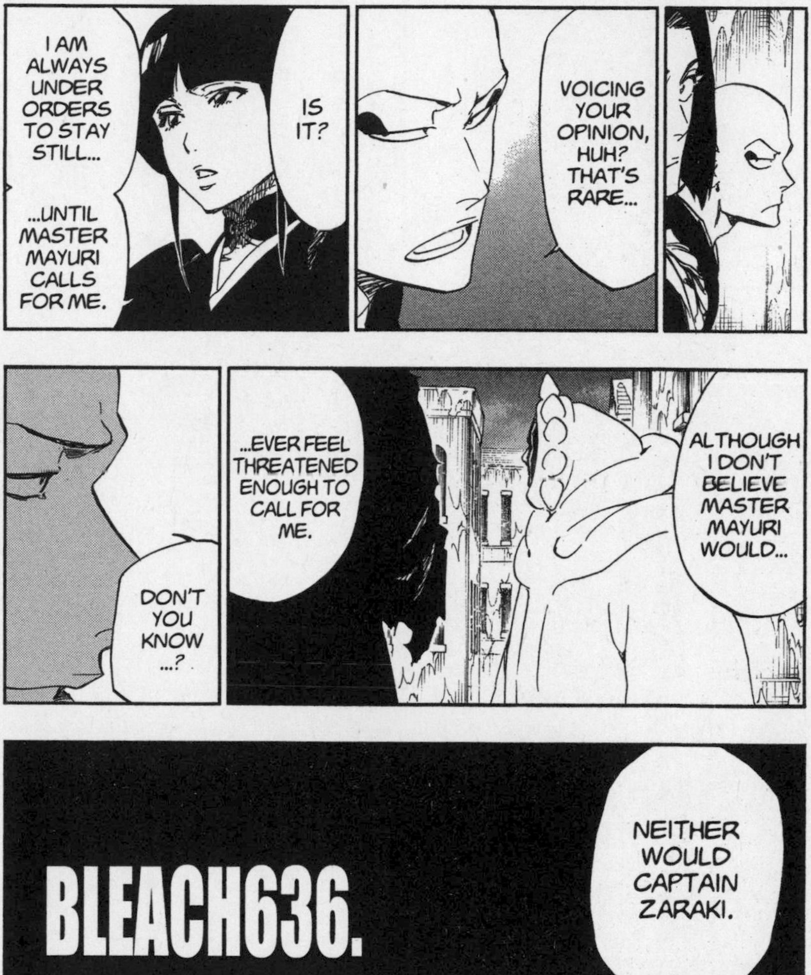
VOICING YOUR OPINION, HUH? THAT'S RARE...
IS IT?
I AM ALWAYS UNDER ORDERS TO STAY STILL...
...UNTIL MASTER MAYURI CALLS FOR ME.
ALTHOUGH I DON'T BELIEVE MASTER MAYURI WOULD...
...EVER FEEL THREATENED ENOUGH TO CALL FOR ME.
DON'T YOU KNOW ...?
NEITHER WOULD CAPTAIN ZARAKI.
BLEACH636.
Sensitive Monster

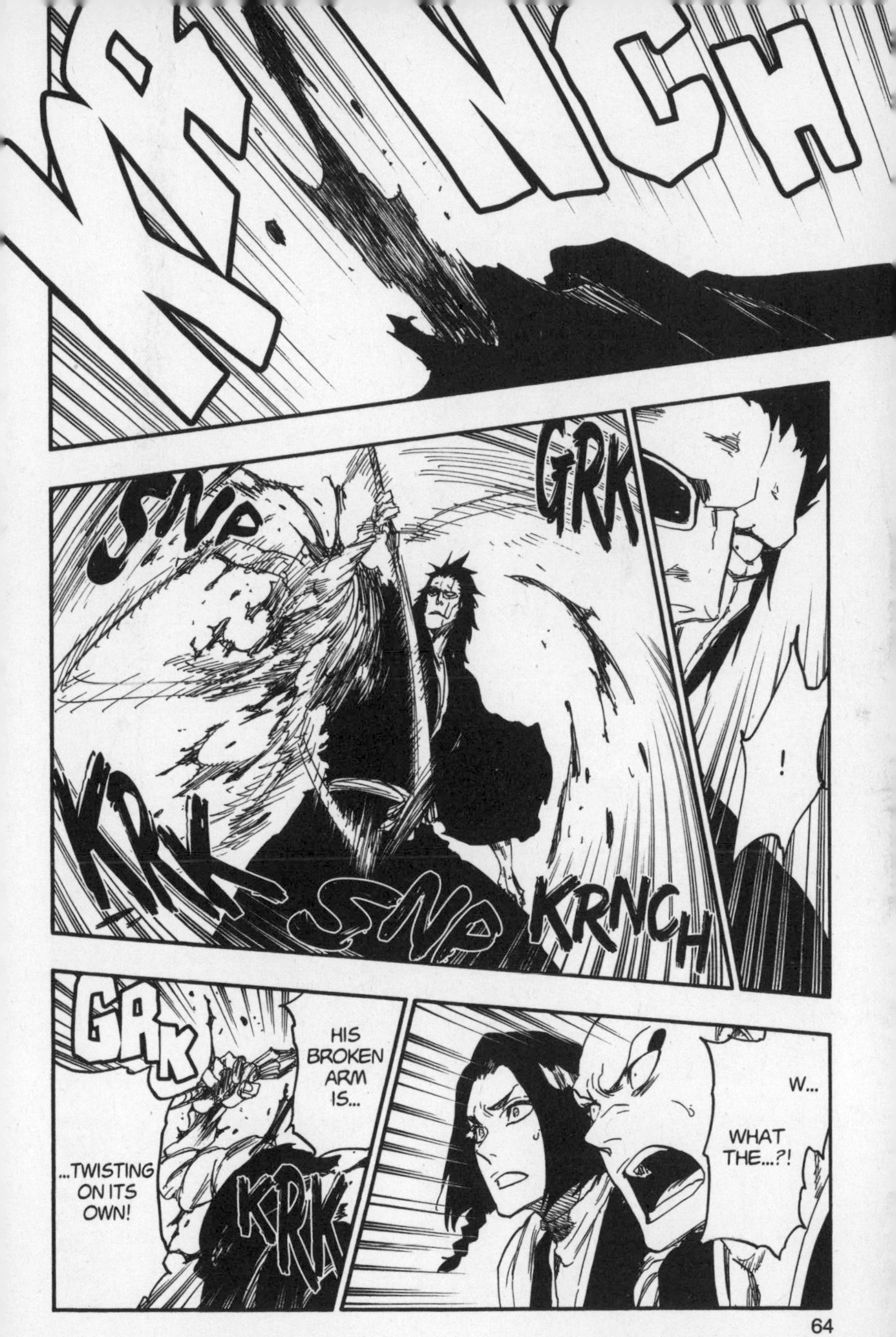
KRUNCH
!
GRK
SNP
KRK
SNP
KRNCH
W...
WHAT THE...?!
GRK
HIS BROKEN ARM IS...
...TWISTING ON ITS OWN!
KRK

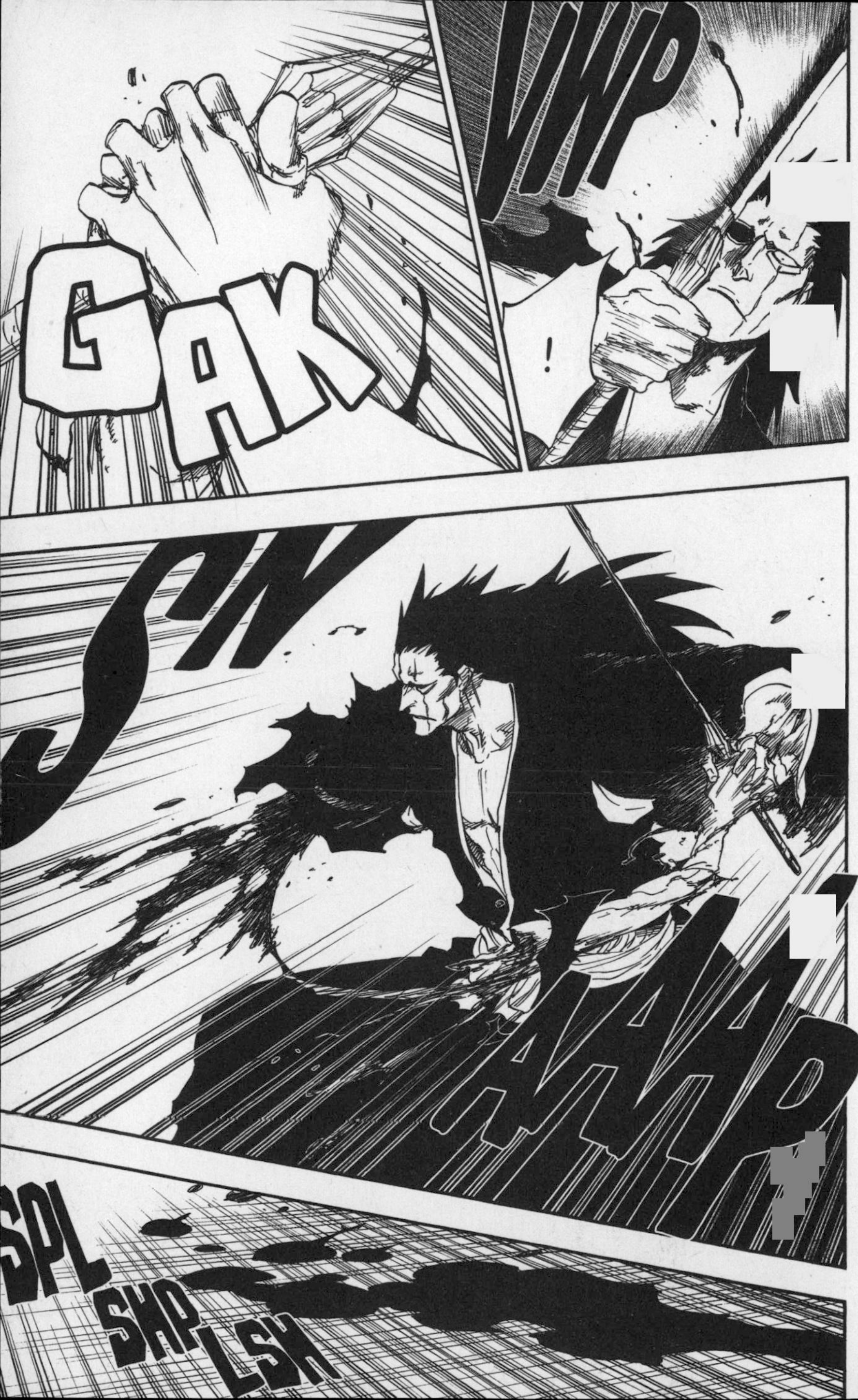
VWP
!
GAK
SPL
SHP
LSH

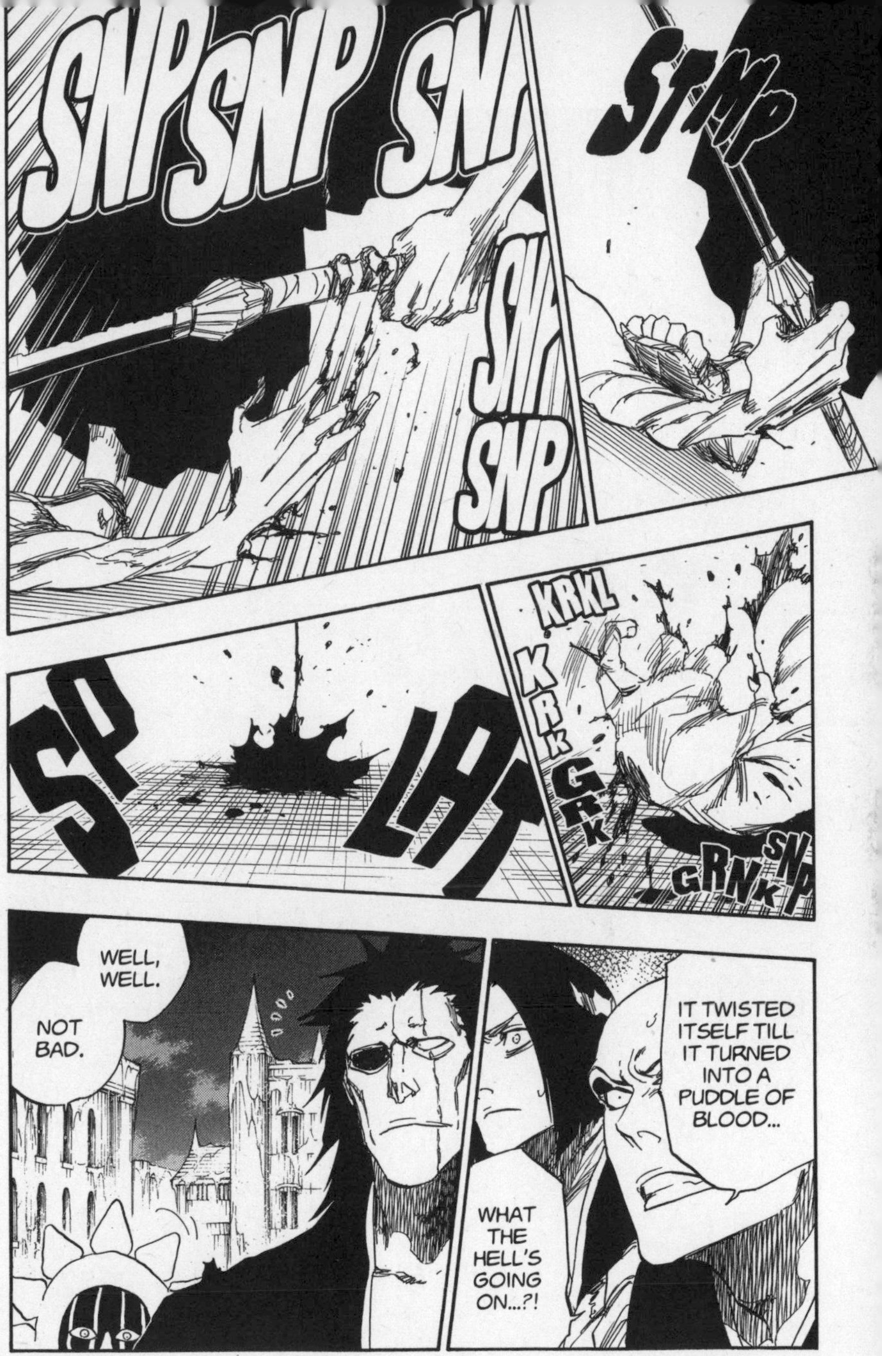
STMP
SNPSNP
SNP
KRKL
KRK
GRK
GRNK
SNP
SPLAT
IT TWISTED ITSELF TILL IT TURNED INTO A PUDDLE OF BLOOD...
WHAT THE HELL'S GOING ON...?!
WELL, WELL.
NOT BAD.

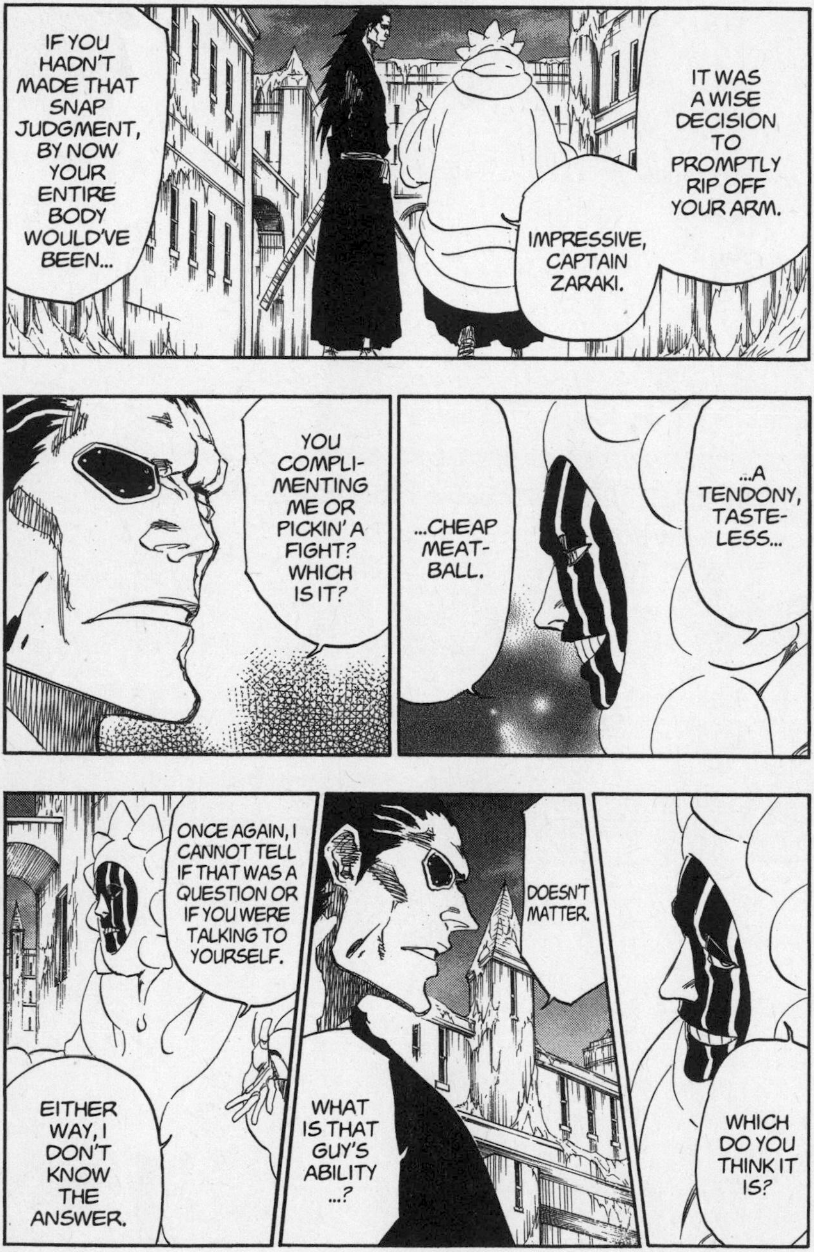
IT WAS A WISE DECISION TO PROMPTLY RIP OFF YOUR ARM.
IMPRESSIVE, CAPTAIN ZARAKI.
IF YOU HADN'T MADE THAT SNAP JUDGMENT, BY NOW YOUR ENTIRE BODY WOULD'VE BEEN...
...A TENDONY, TASTELESS...
...CHEAP MEATBALL.
YOU COMPLIMENTING ME OR PICKIN' A FIGHT? WHICH IS IT?
WHICH DO YOU THINK IT IS?
DOESN'T MATTER.
WHAT IS THAT GUY'S ABILITY ...?
ONCE AGAIN, I CANNOT TELL IF THAT WAS A QUESTION OR IF YOU WERE TALKING TO YOURSELF.
EITHER WAY, I DON'T KNOW THE ANSWER.

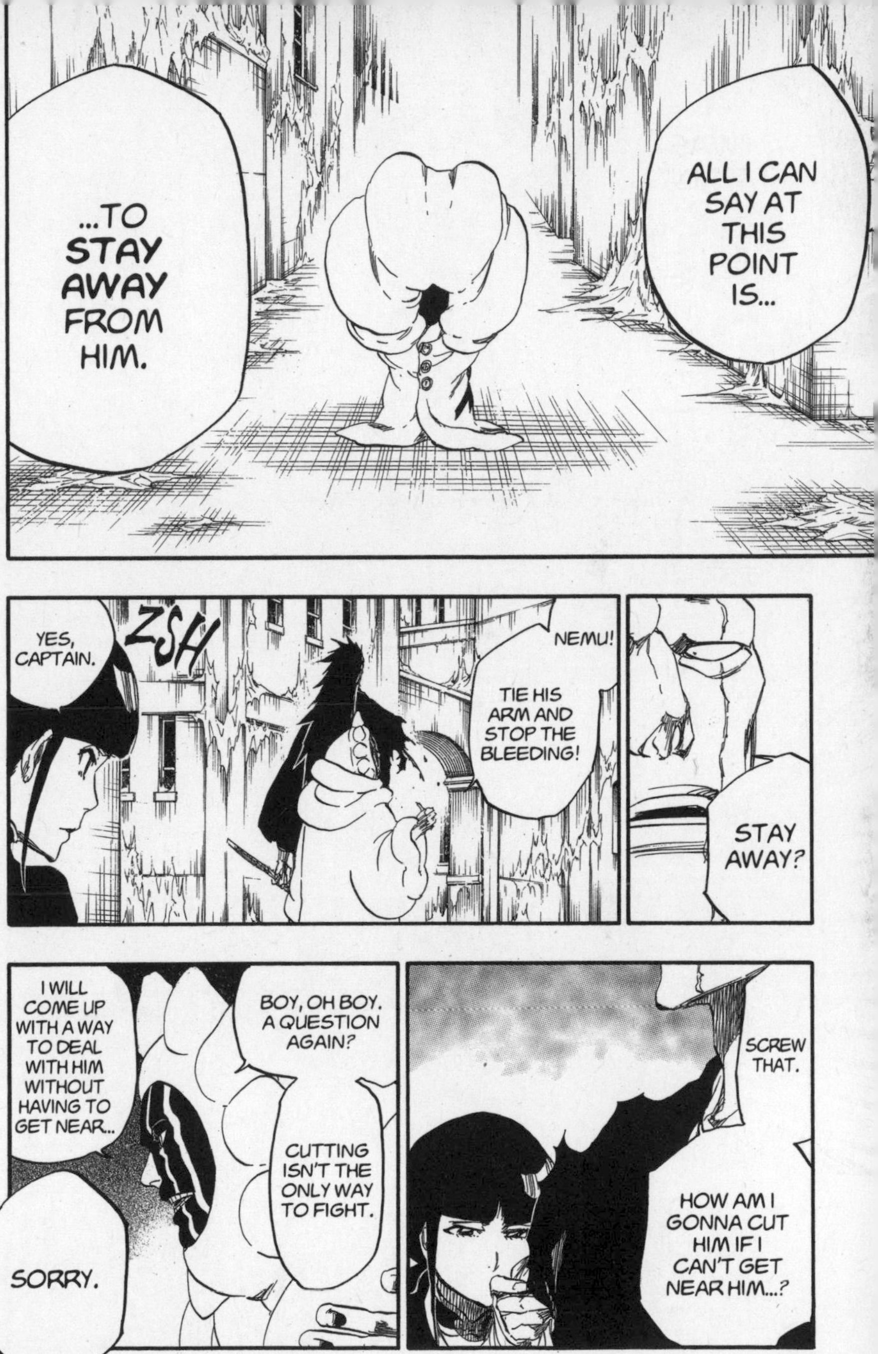
ALL I CAN SAY AT THIS POINT IS...
...TO STAY AWAY FROM HIM.
STAY AWAY?
NEMU!
TIE HIS ARM AND STOP THE BLEEDING!
ZSH
YES, CAPTAIN.
SCREW THAT.
HOW AM I GONNA CUT HIM IF I CAN'T GET NEAR HIM...?
BOY, OH BOY. A QUESTION AGAIN?
CUTTING ISN'T THE ONLY WAY TO FIGHT.
I WILL COME UP WITH A WAY TO DEAL WITH HIM WITHOUT HAVING TO GET NEAR...
SORRY.

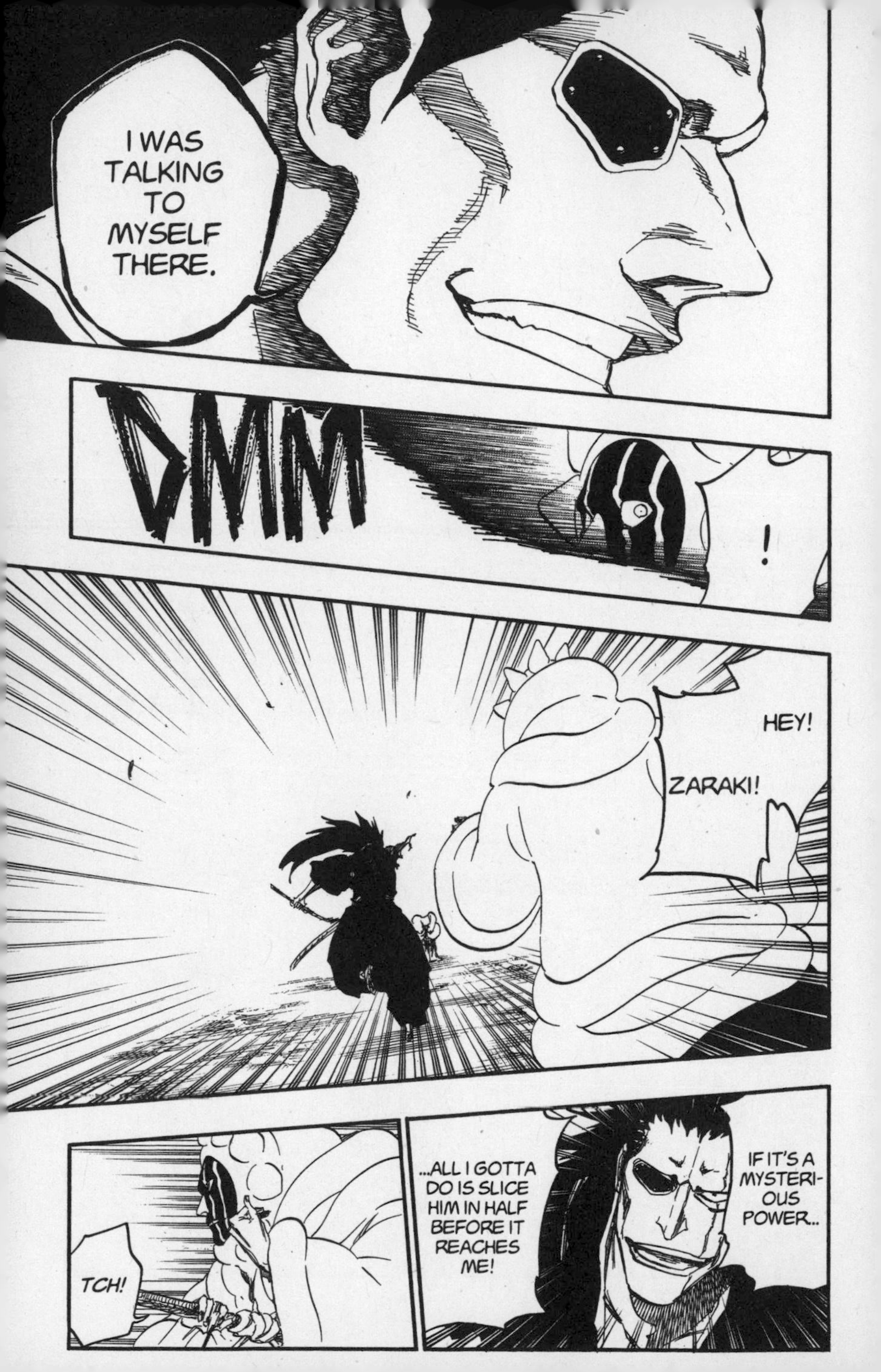
I WAS TALKING TO MYSELF THERE.
DMM
!
HEY!
ZARAKI!
IF IT'S A MYSTERI-OUS POWER...
...ALL I GOTTA DO IS SLICE HIM IN HALF BEFORE IT REACHES ME!
TCH!

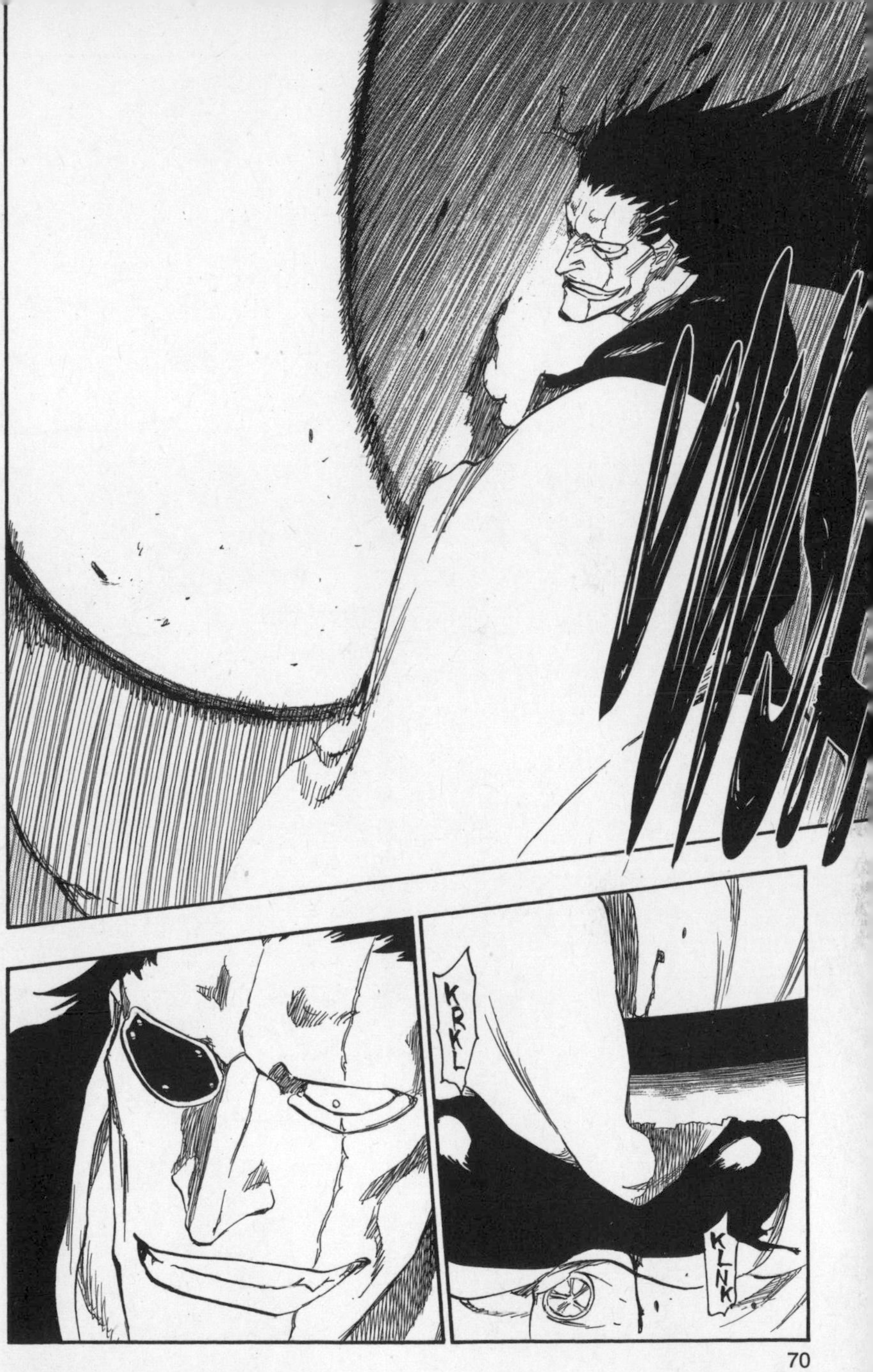
KRKL
KLNK

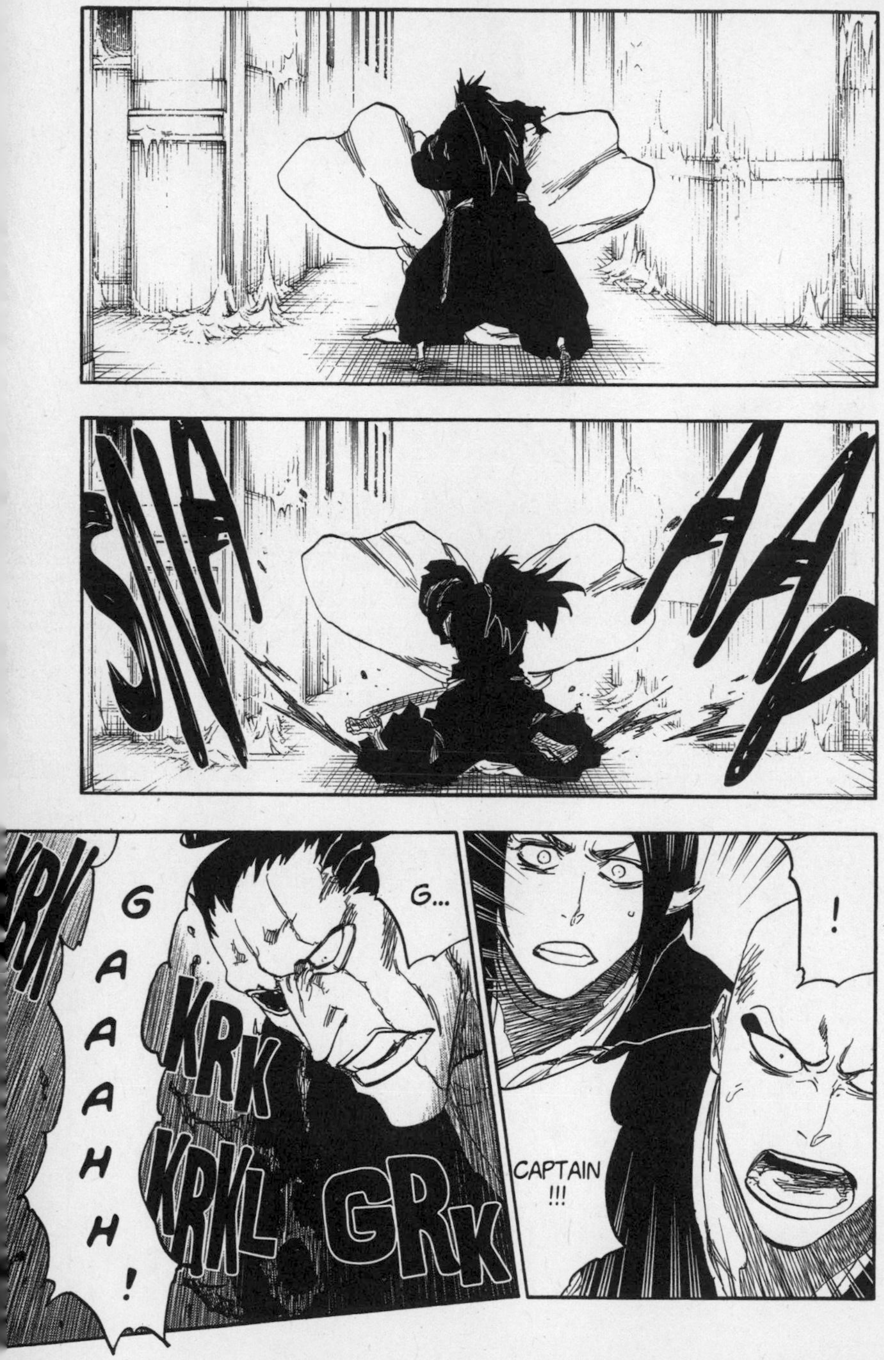
SHA
AAP
!
CAPTAIN !!!
G...
GAAAHH!
KRK
KRK
KRKL
GRK

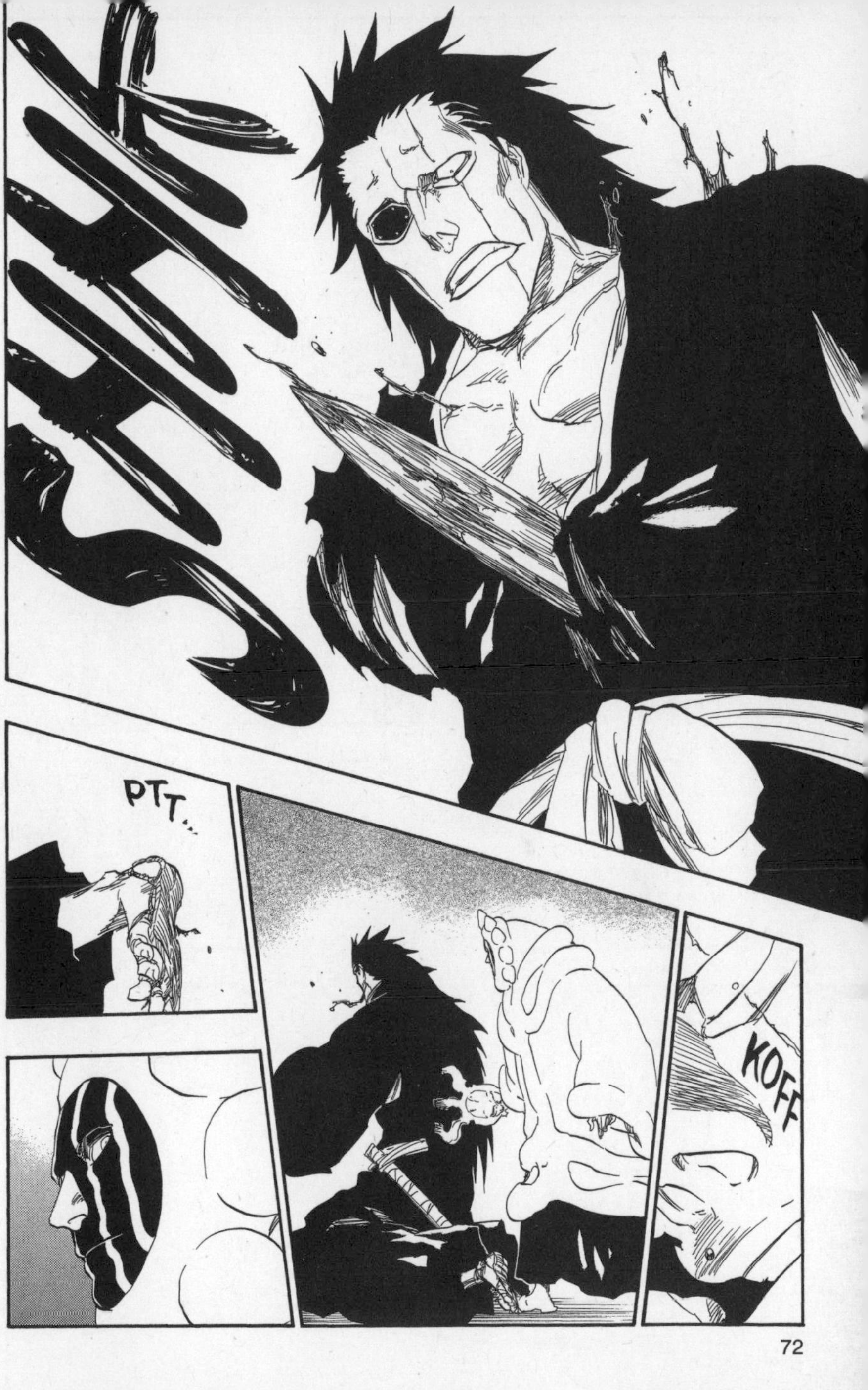
KOFF
PTT...

SNP
K...
KURO-TSUCHI ...
KRK
KRKL
YOU ...!
HMM...
I GUESS STOPPING THE LIMBS ONLY LEADS TO OTHER PARTS BREAK-ING...
ASHISOGI JIZO.
ZRCH
FEAR LEVEL 4.
WAAAAAA

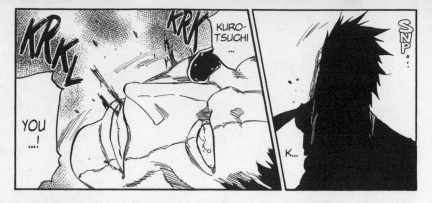

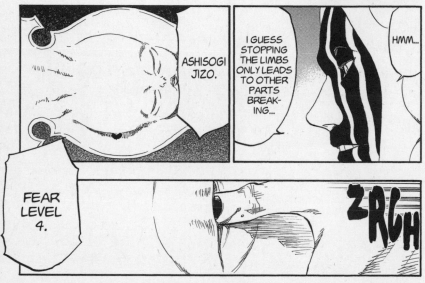

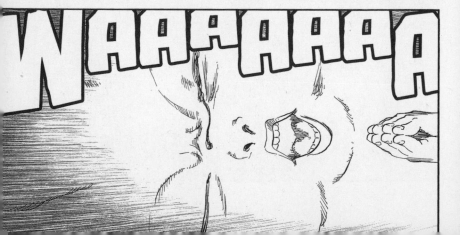

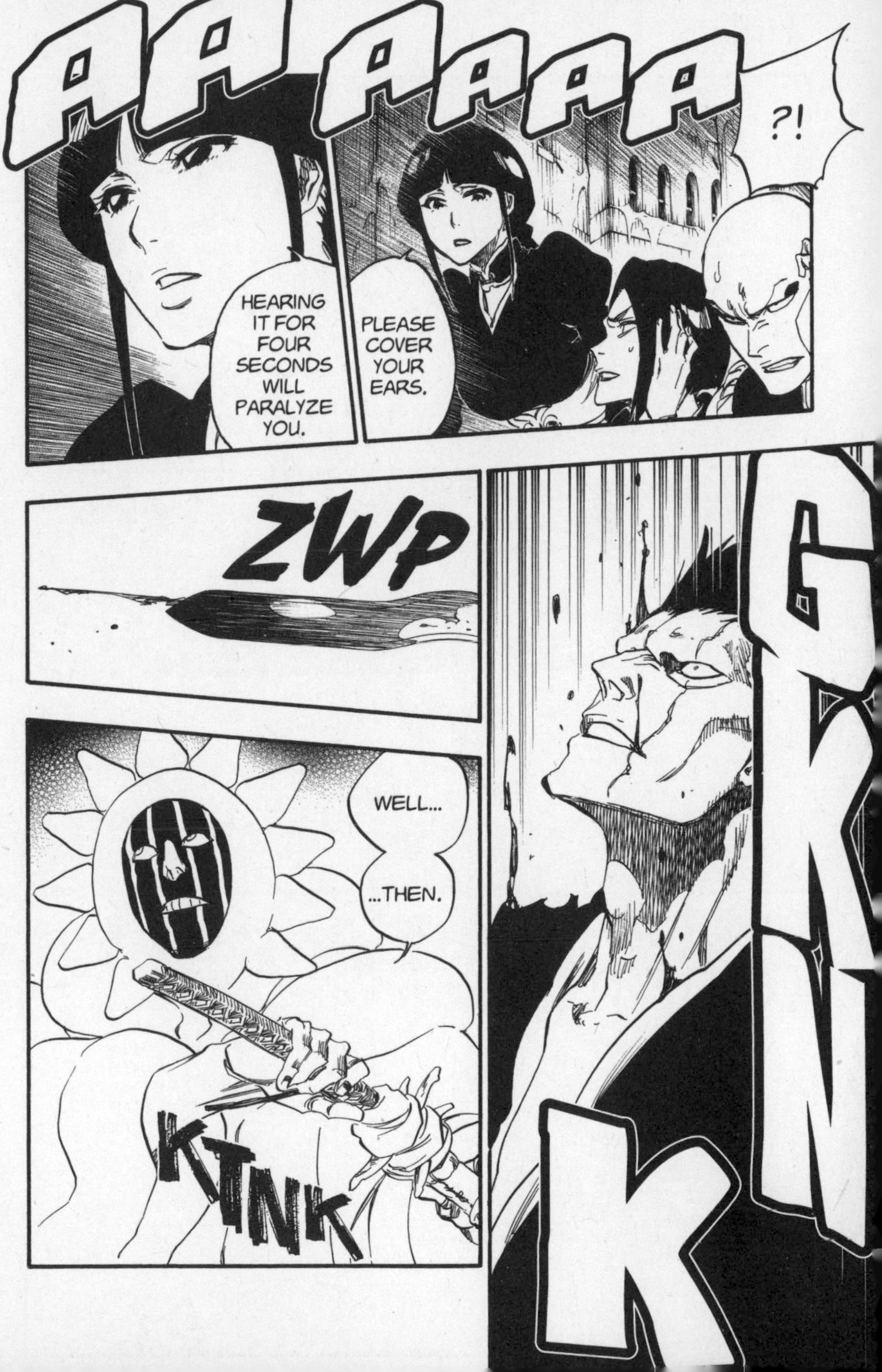
AAAAAAA
?!
PLEASE COVER YOUR EARS.
HEARING IT FOR FOUR SECONDS WILL PARALYZE YOU.
GRNK
ZWP
WELL...
...THEN.
KTNK

READ THIS WAY

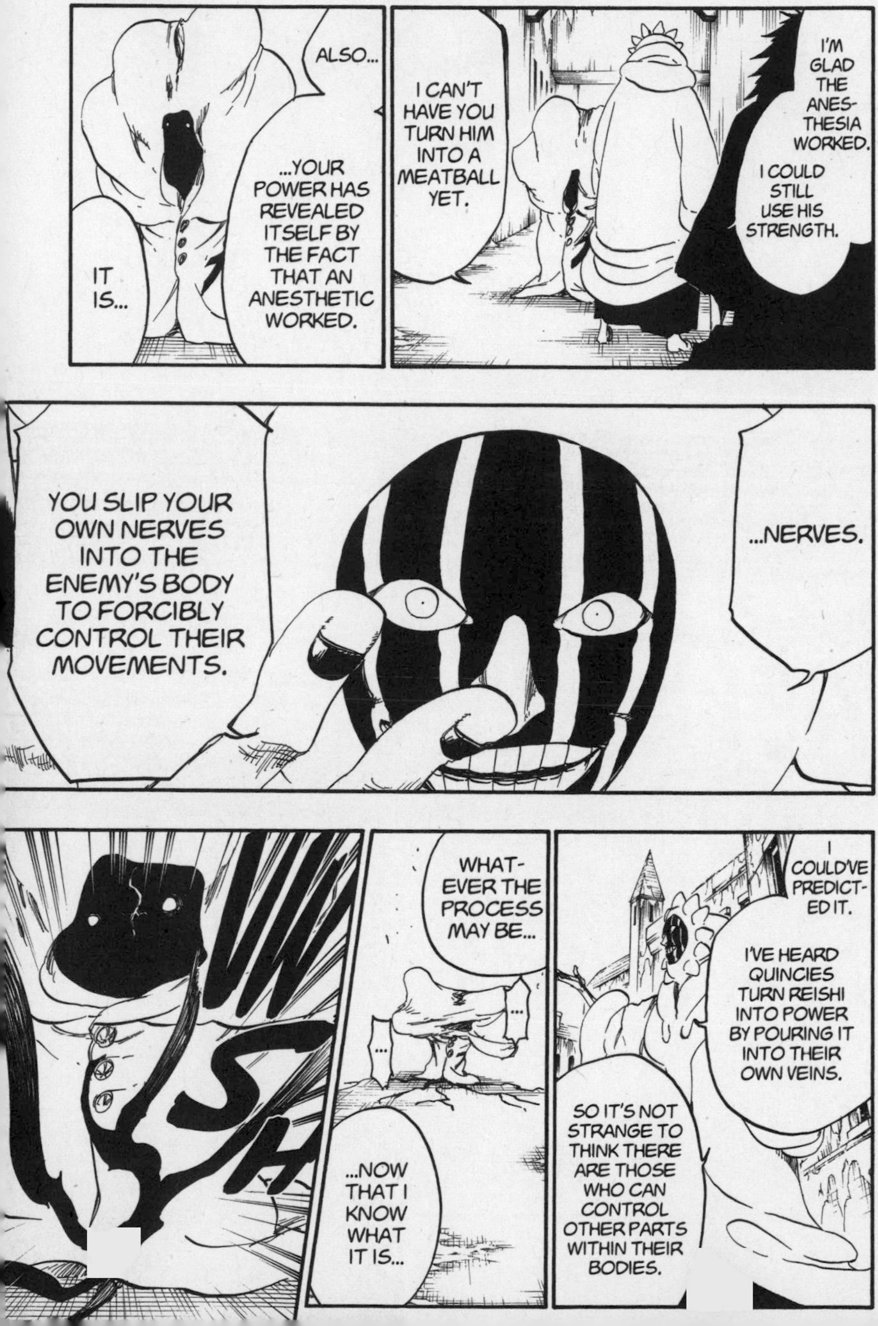
I'M GLAD THE ANESTHESIA WORKED.
I COULD STILL USE HIS STRENGTH.
I CAN'T HAVE YOU TURN HIM INTO A MEATBALL YET.
ALSO...
...YOUR POWER HAS REVEALED ITSELF BY THE FACT THAT AN ANESTHETIC WORKED.
IT IS...
...NERVES.
YOU SLIP YOUR OWN NERVES INTO THE ENEMY'S BODY TO FORCIBLY CONTROL THEIR MOVEMENTS.
I COULD'VE PREDICTED IT.
I'VE HEARD QUINCIES TURN REISHI INTO POWER BY POURING IT INTO THEIR OWN VEINS.
SO IT'S NOT STRANGE TO THINK THERE ARE THOSE WHO CAN CONTROL OTHER PARTS WITHIN THEIR BODIES.
WHATEVER THE PROCESS MAY BE...
...
...
...NOW THAT I KNOW WHAT IT IS...
SH

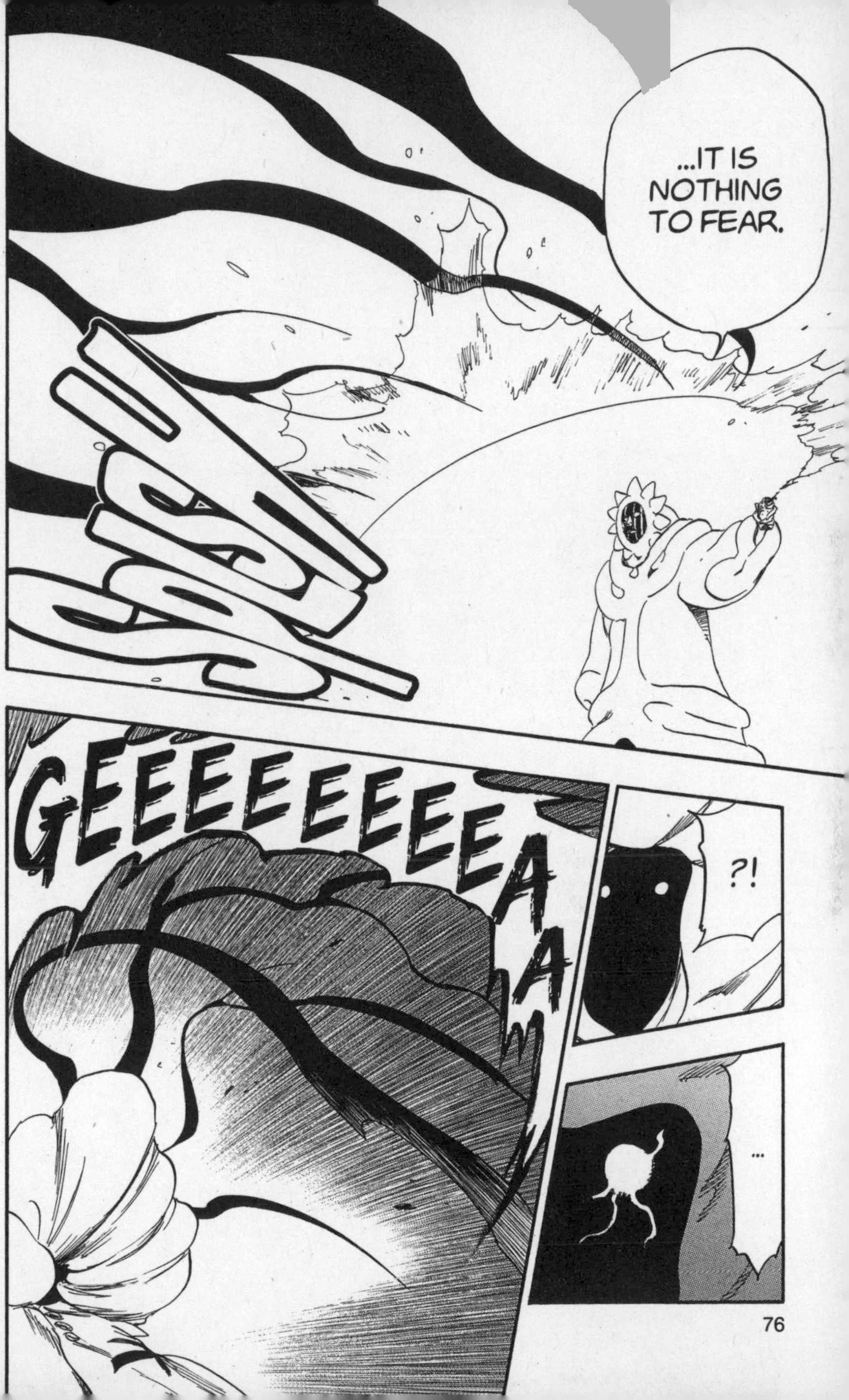
...IT IS NOTHING TO FEAR.
GEEEEEEEEAAA
?!
...

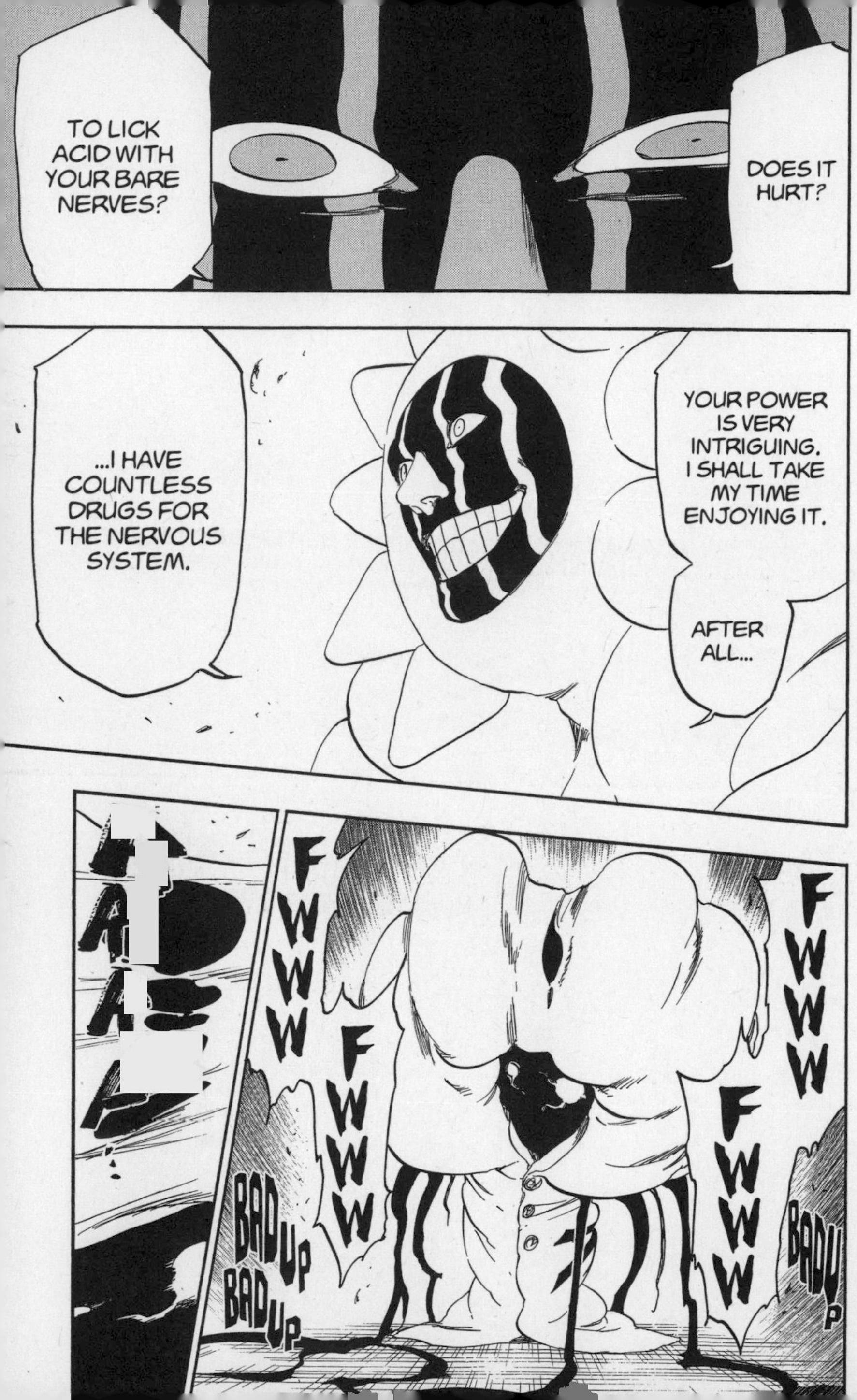
DOES IT HURT?
TO LICK ACID WITH YOUR BARE NERVES?
YOUR POWER IS VERY INTRIGUING. I SHALL TAKE MY TIME ENJOYING IT.
AFTER ALL...
...I HAVE COUNTLESS DRUGS FOR THE NERVOUS SYSTEM.
FWWW
FWWW
BADUP
FWWW
FWWW
BADUP BADUP

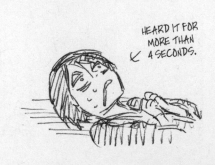
HEARD IT FOR
MORE THAN
4 SECONDS.

637.BABY,HOLD YOUR HAND

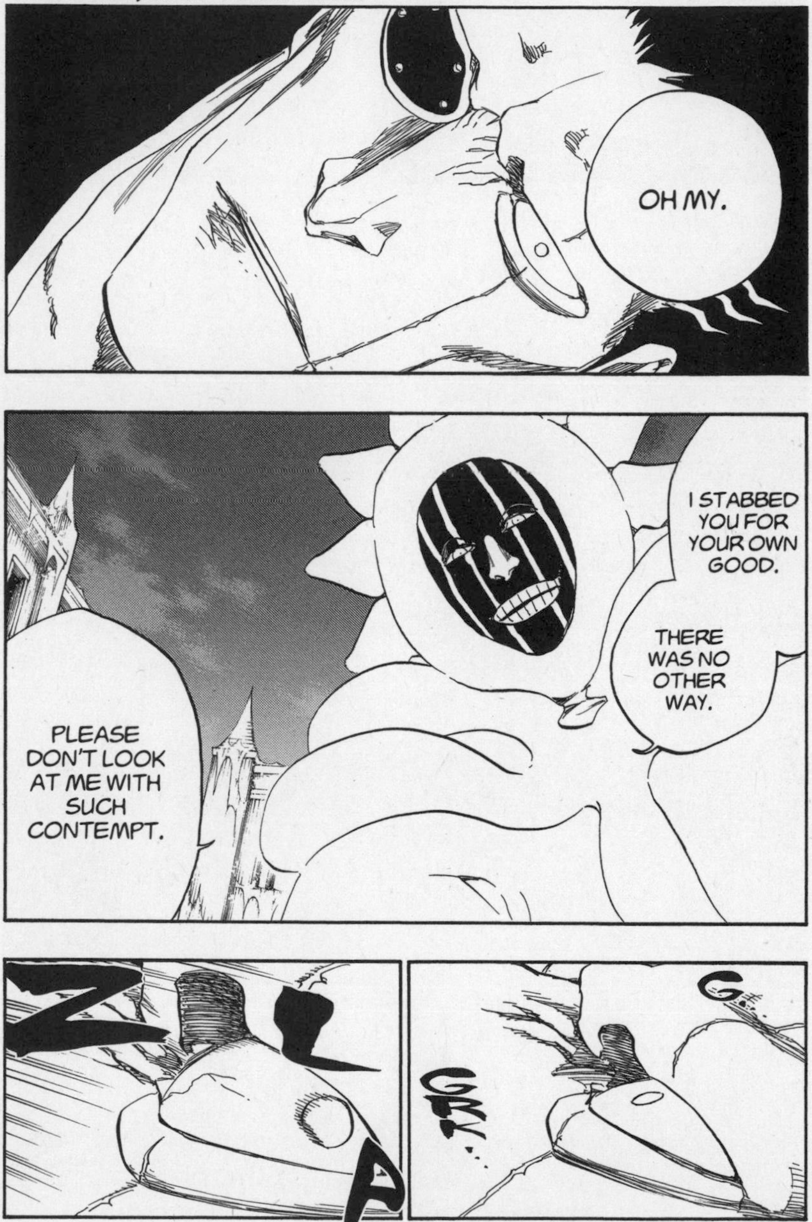
OH MY.
I STABBED YOU FOR YOUR OWN GOOD.
THERE WAS NO OTHER WAY.
PLEASE DON'T LOOK AT ME WITH SUCH CONTEMPT.
G...
GRK...

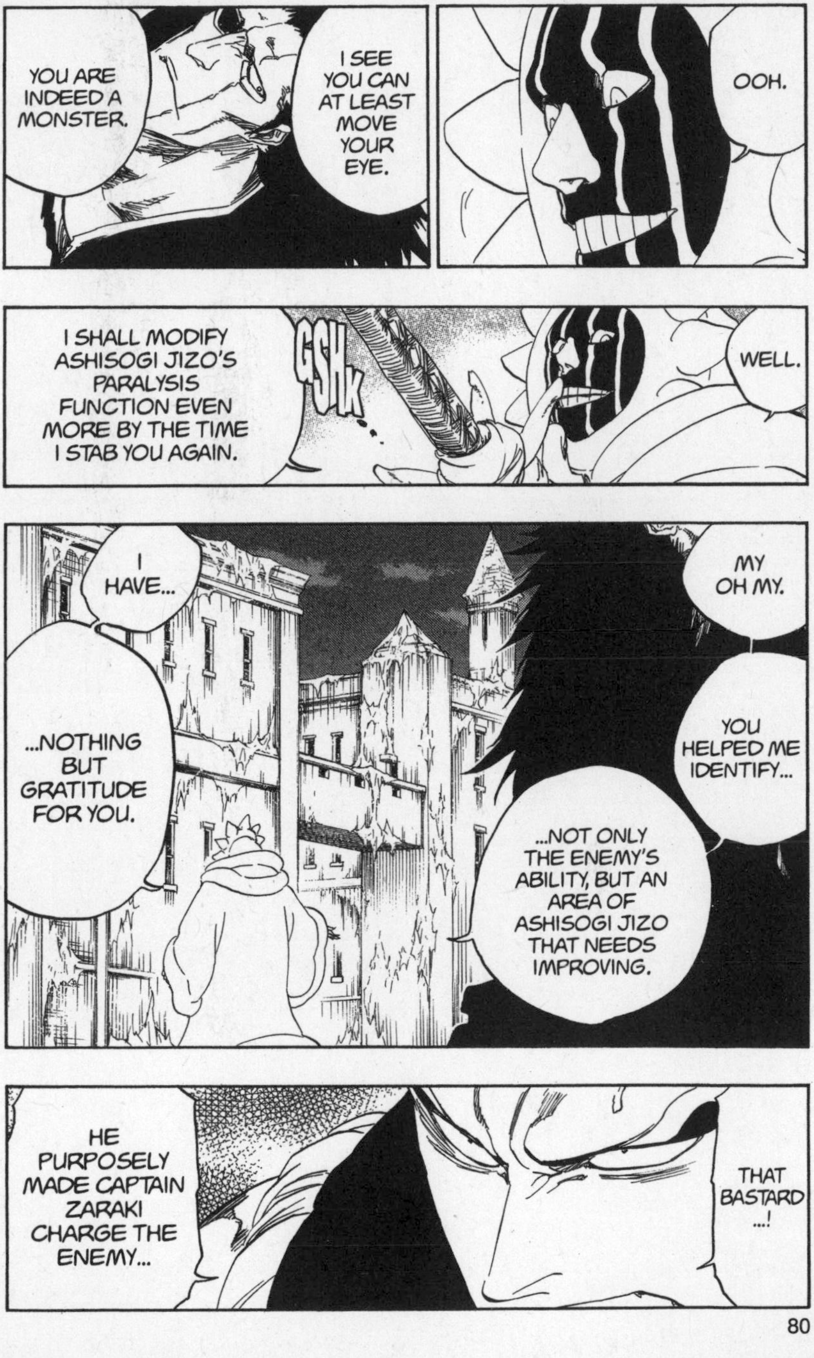
OOH.
I SEE YOU CAN AT LEAST MOVE YOUR EYE.
YOU ARE INDEED A MONSTER.
WELL.
GSHK
I SHALL MODIFY ASHISOGI JIZO'S PARALYSIS FUNCTION EVEN MORE BY THE TIME I STAB YOU AGAIN.
MY OH MY.
YOU HELPED ME IDENTIFY...
...NOT ONLY THE ENEMY'S ABILITY, BUT AN AREA OF ASHISOGI JIZO THAT NEEDS IMPROVING.
I HAVE...
...NOTHING BUT GRATITUDE FOR YOU.
THAT BASTARD ...!
HE PURPOSELY MADE CAPTAIN ZARAKI CHARGE THE ENEMY...

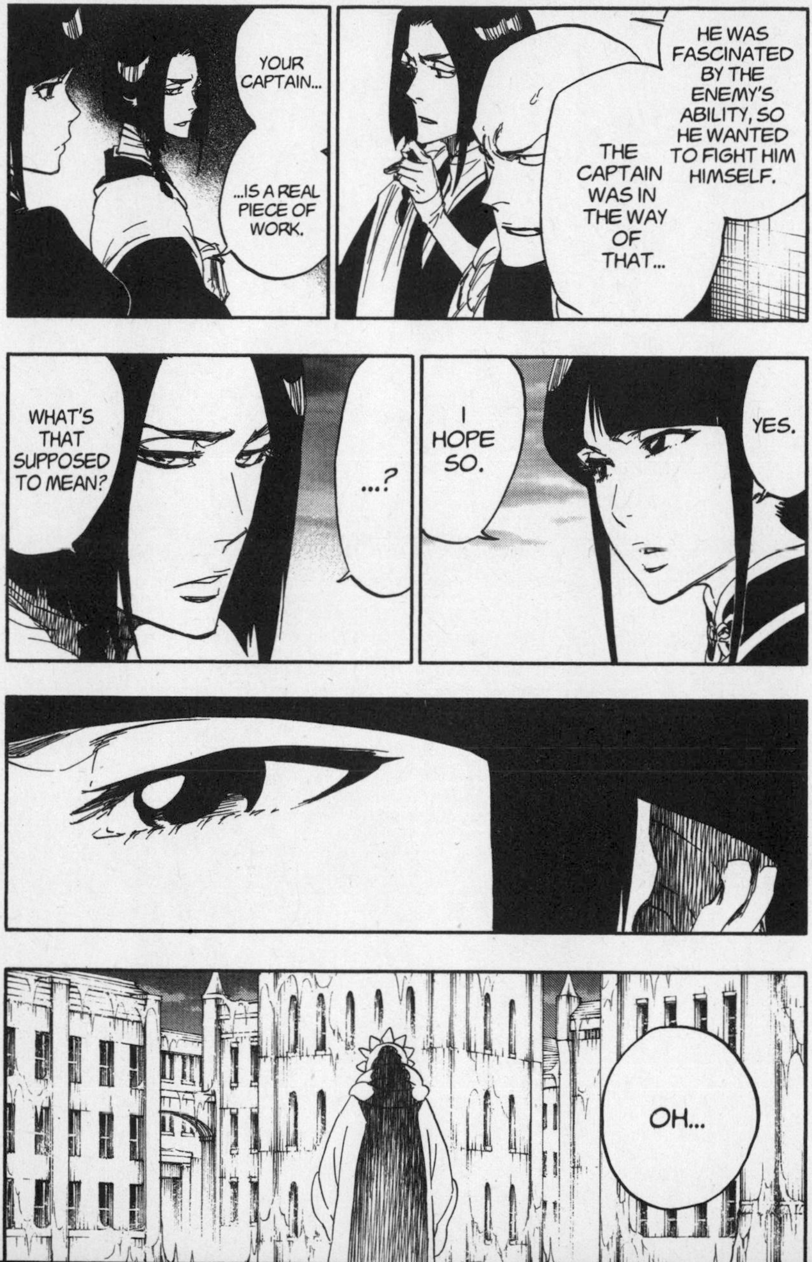
HE WAS FASCINATED BY THE ENEMY'S ABILITY, SO HE WANTED TO FIGHT HIM HIMSELF.
THE CAPTAIN WAS IN THE WAY OF THAT...
YOUR CAPTAIN...
...IS A REAL PIECE OF WORK.
YES.
I HOPE SO.
...?
WHAT'S THAT SUPPOSED TO MEAN?
OH...

BLEACH 637.

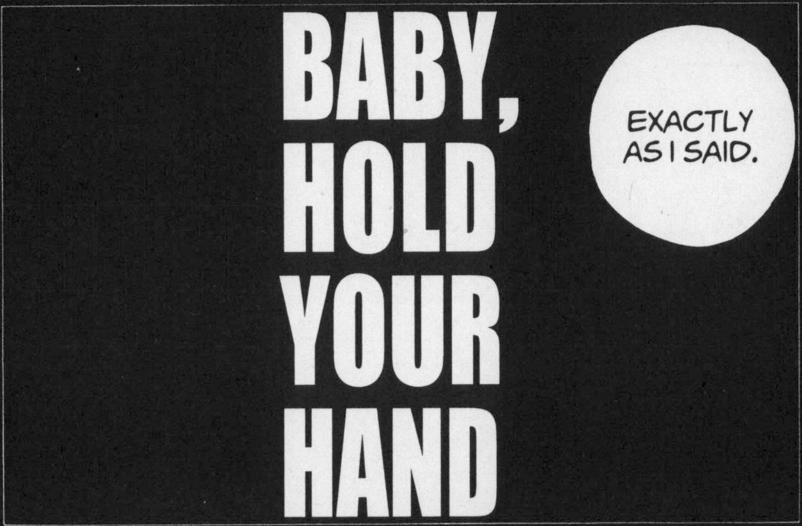
EXACTLY AS I SAID.
BABY, HOLD YOUR HAND
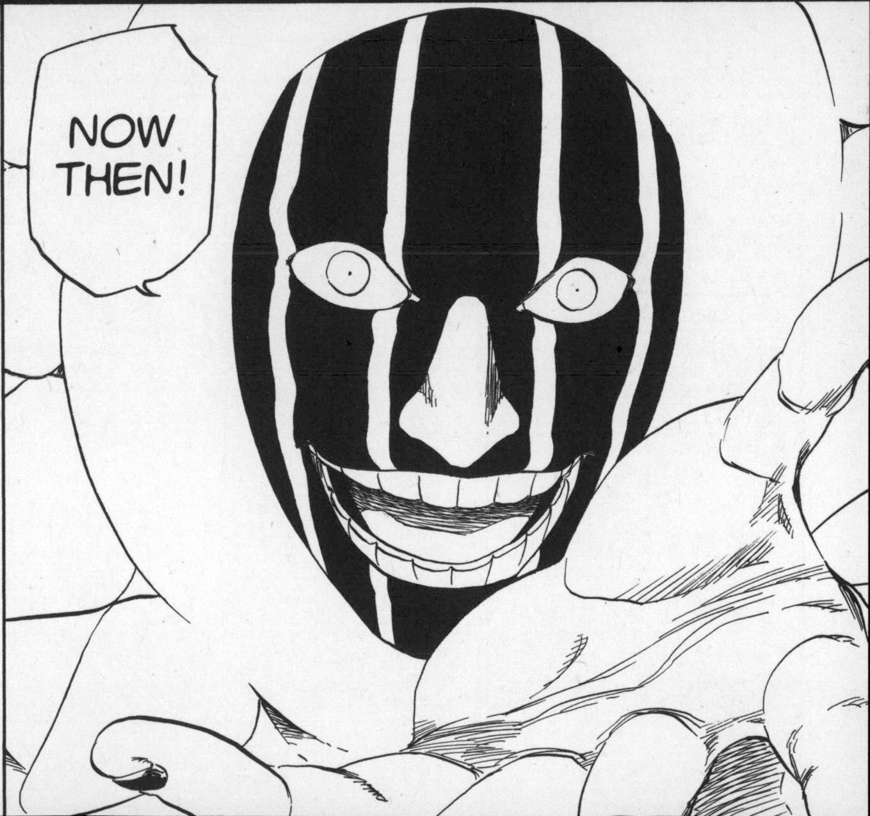
NOW THEN!

READ THIS WAY

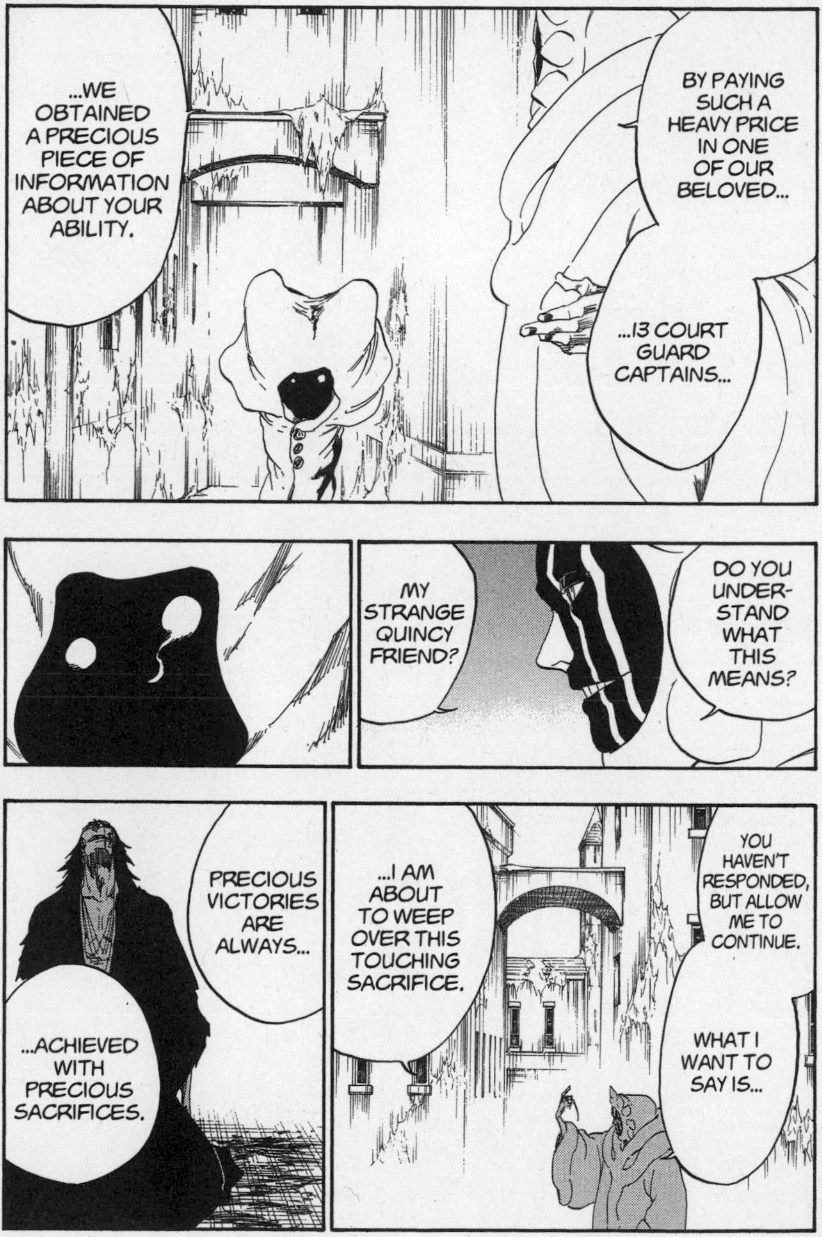
BY PAYING SUCH A HEAVY PRICE IN ONE OF OUR BELOVED...
...13 COURT GUARD CAPTAINS...
...WE OBTAINED A PRECIOUS PIECE OF INFORMATION ABOUT YOUR ABILITY.
DO YOU UNDER-STAND WHAT THIS MEANS?
MY STRANGE QUINCY FRIEND?
YOU HAVEN'T RESPONDED, BUT ALLOW ME TO CONTINUE.
WHAT I WANT TO SAY IS...
...I AM ABOUT TO WEEP OVER THIS TOUCHING SACRIFICE.
PRECIOUS VICTORIES ARE ALWAYS...
...ACHIEVED WITH PRECIOUS SACRIFICES.

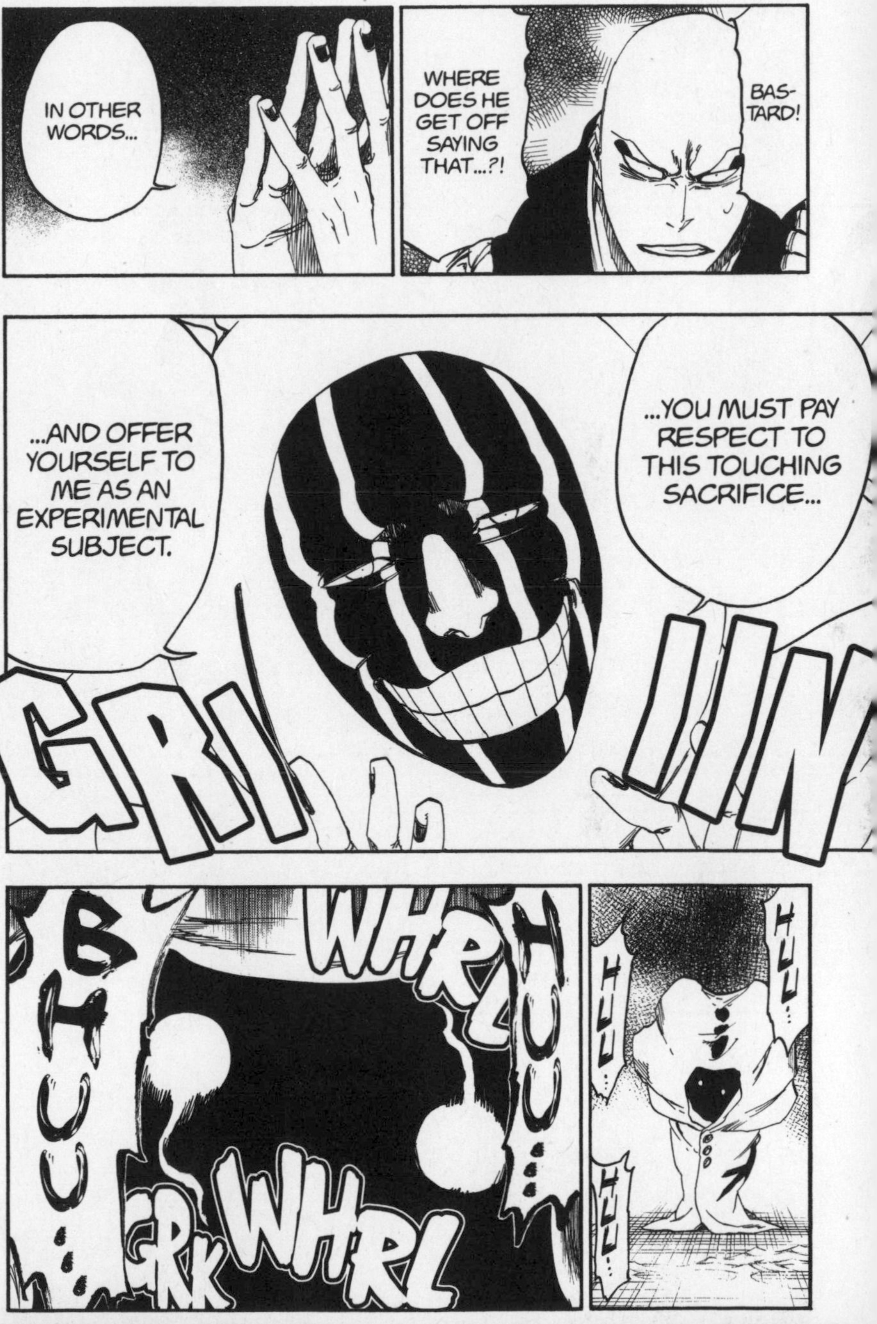
BAS-TARD!
WHERE DOES HE GET OFF SAYING THAT...?!
IN OTHER WORDS...
...YOU MUST PAY RESPECT TO THIS TOUCHING SACRIFICE...
...AND OFFER YOURSELF TO ME AS AN EXPERIMENTAL SUBJECT.
GRI
IIN
HULL...
HULL...
HULL...
WHRL
HUUU...
BHUU...
WHRL
GRK

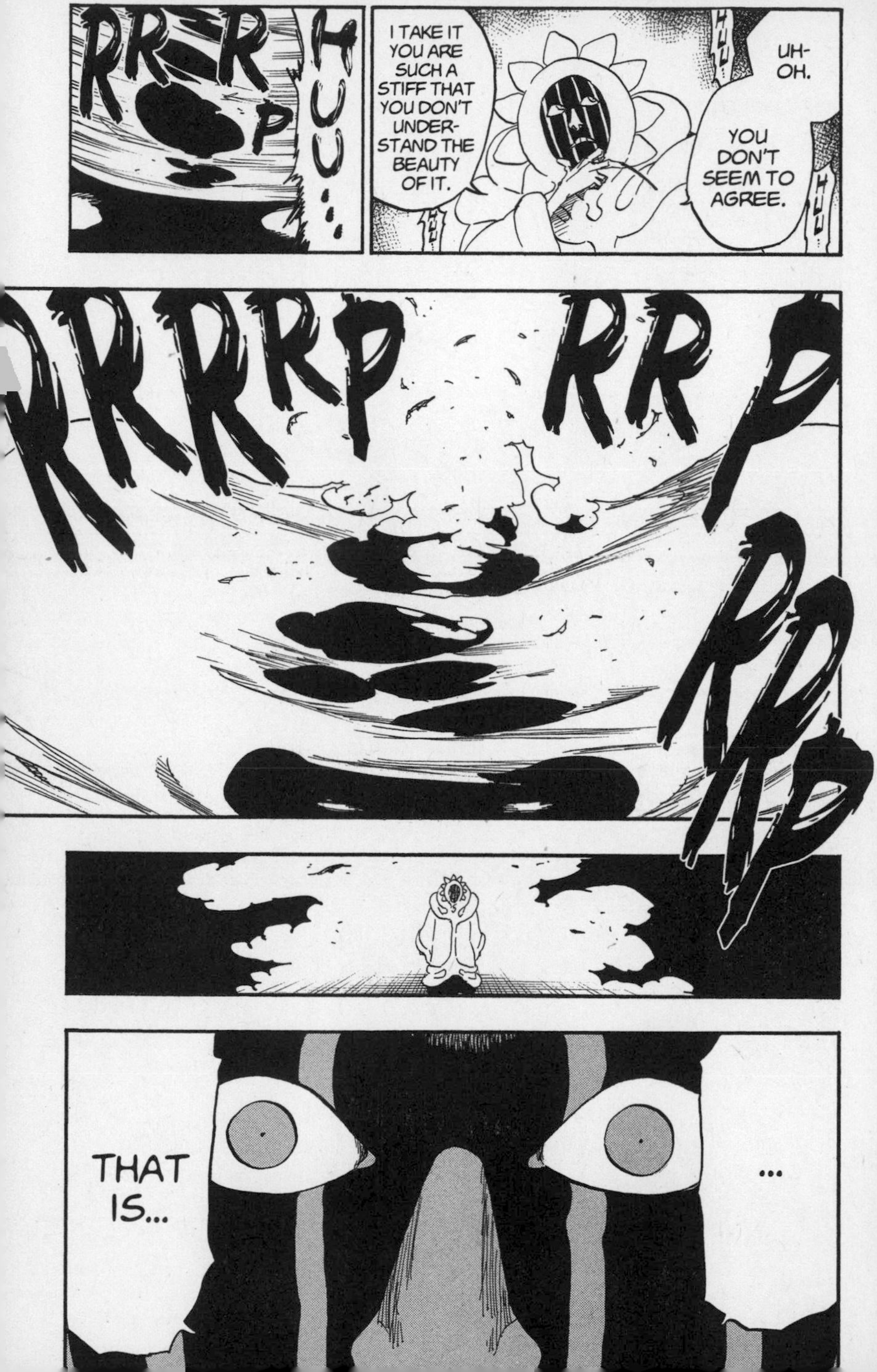

UH-OH.
YOU DON'T SEEM TO AGREE.
I TAKE IT YOU ARE SUCH A STIFF THAT YOU DON'T UNDER-STAND THE BEAUTY OF IT.
HUUU
RRRP
RRRRP RRP
RRRP
...
THAT IS...

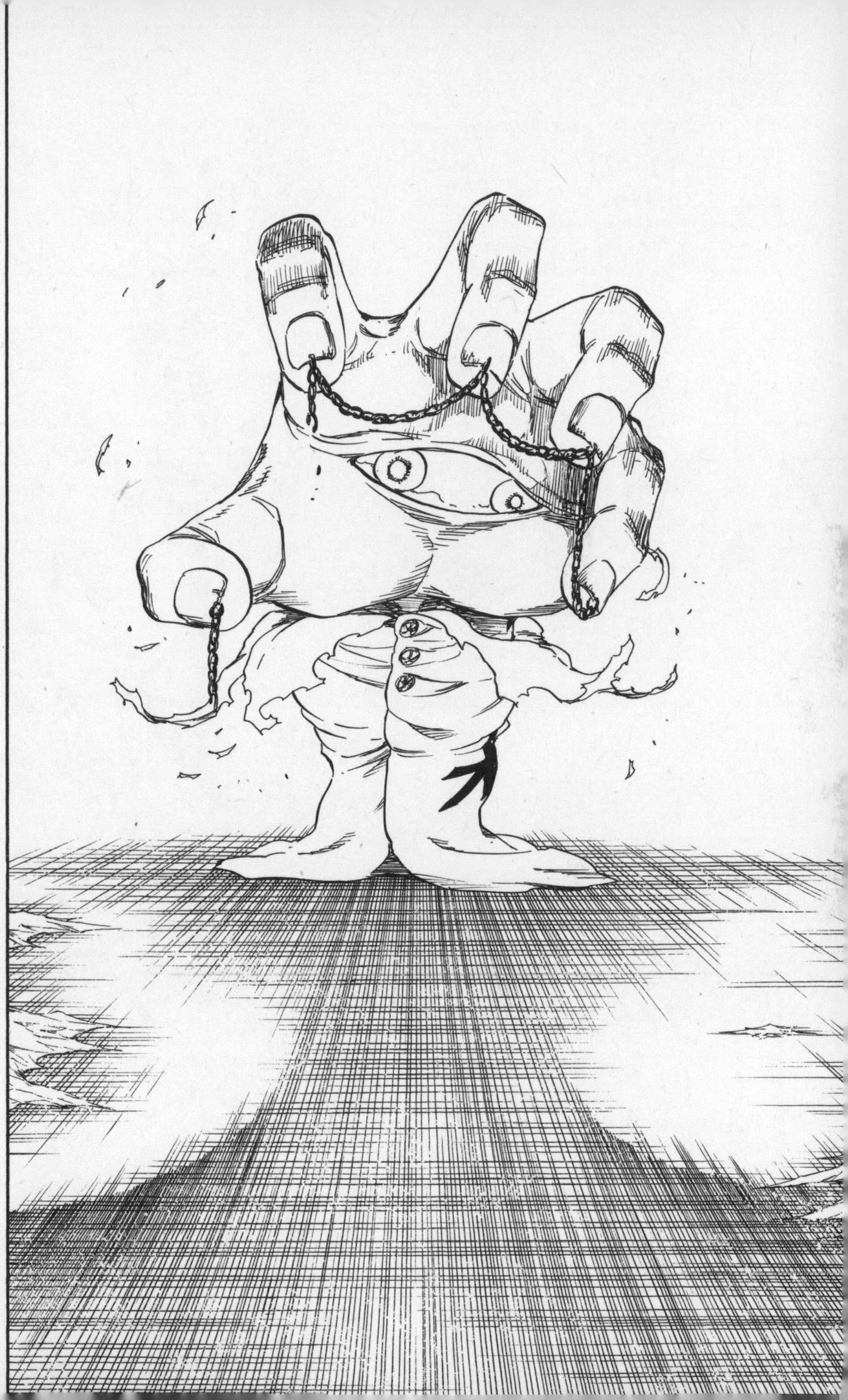

READ THIS WAY

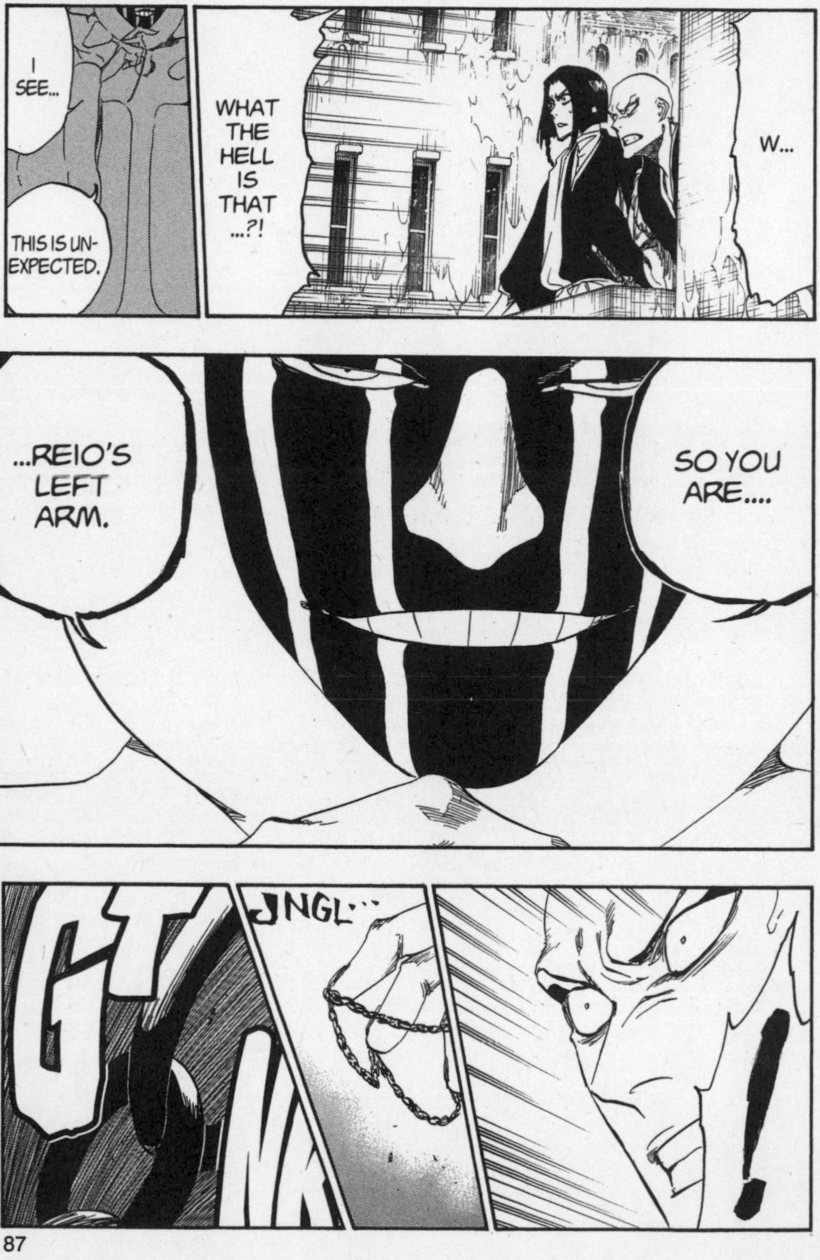

W...
WHAT THE HELL IS THAT...?!
I SEE...
THIS IS UN-EXPECTED.
SO YOU ARE....
...REIO'S LEFT ARM.
!
JNGL...

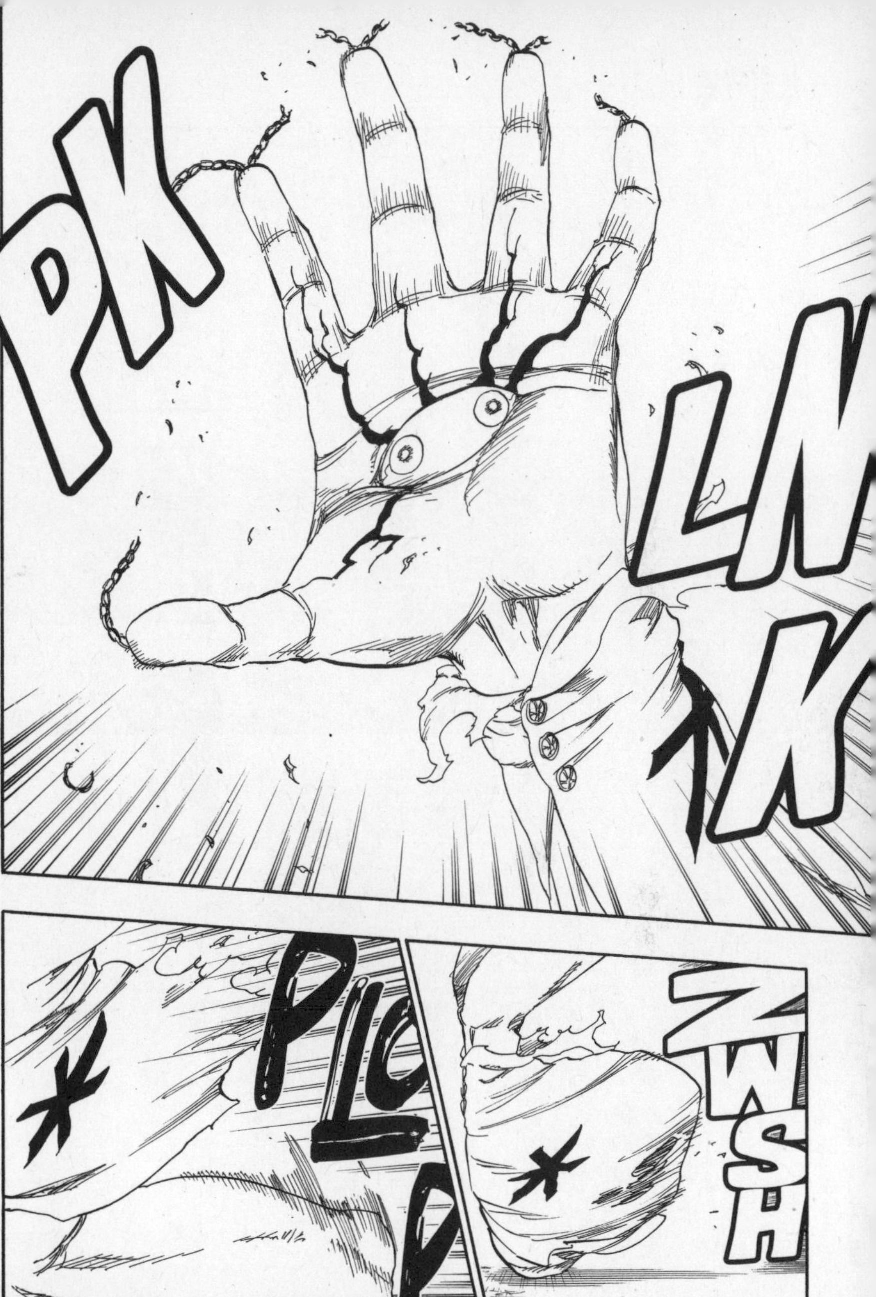
PK
PLOP

READ THIS WAY

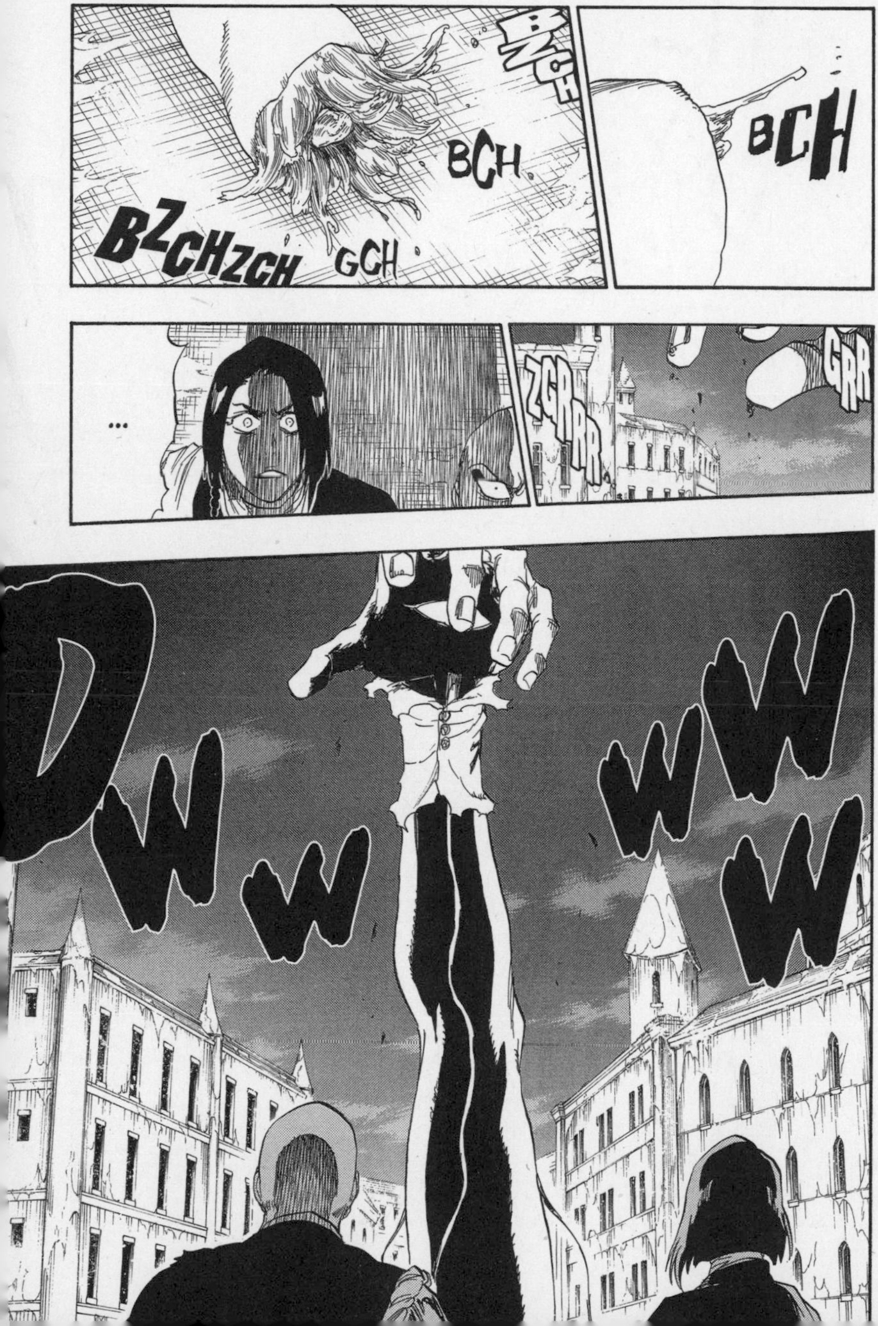
BCH
BZNCH
BCH
BZCHZCH
GCH
ZGRRR
GRR
...
DWWWWWWW

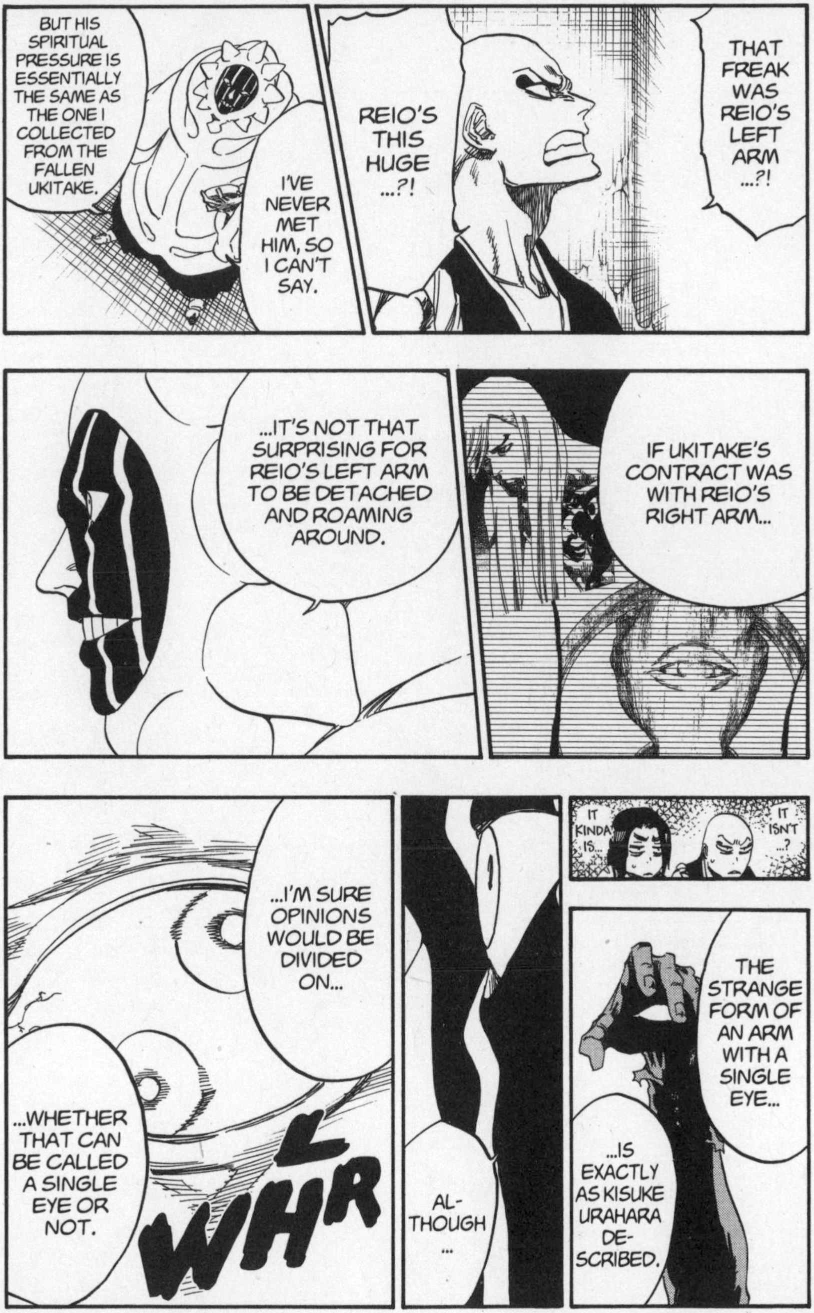
THAT FREAK WAS REIO'S LEFT ARM ...?!
REIO'S THIS HUGE ...?!
I'VE NEVER MET HIM, SO I CAN'T SAY.
BUT HIS SPIRITUAL PRESSURE IS ESSENTIALLY THE SAME AS THE ONE I COLLECTED FROM THE FALLEN UKITAKE.
IF UKITAKE'S CONTRACT WAS WITH REIO'S RIGHT ARM...
...IT'S NOT THAT SURPRISING FOR REIO'S LEFT ARM TO BE DETACHED AND ROAMING AROUND.
IT ISN'T ...?
IT KINDA IS...
THE STRANGE FORM OF AN ARM WITH A SINGLE EYE...
...IS EXACTLY AS KISUKE URAHARA DE-SCRIBED.
AL-THOUGH ...
...I'M SURE OPINIONS WOULD BE DIVIDED ON...
...WHETHER THAT CAN BE CALLED A SINGLE EYE OR NOT.
WHRL

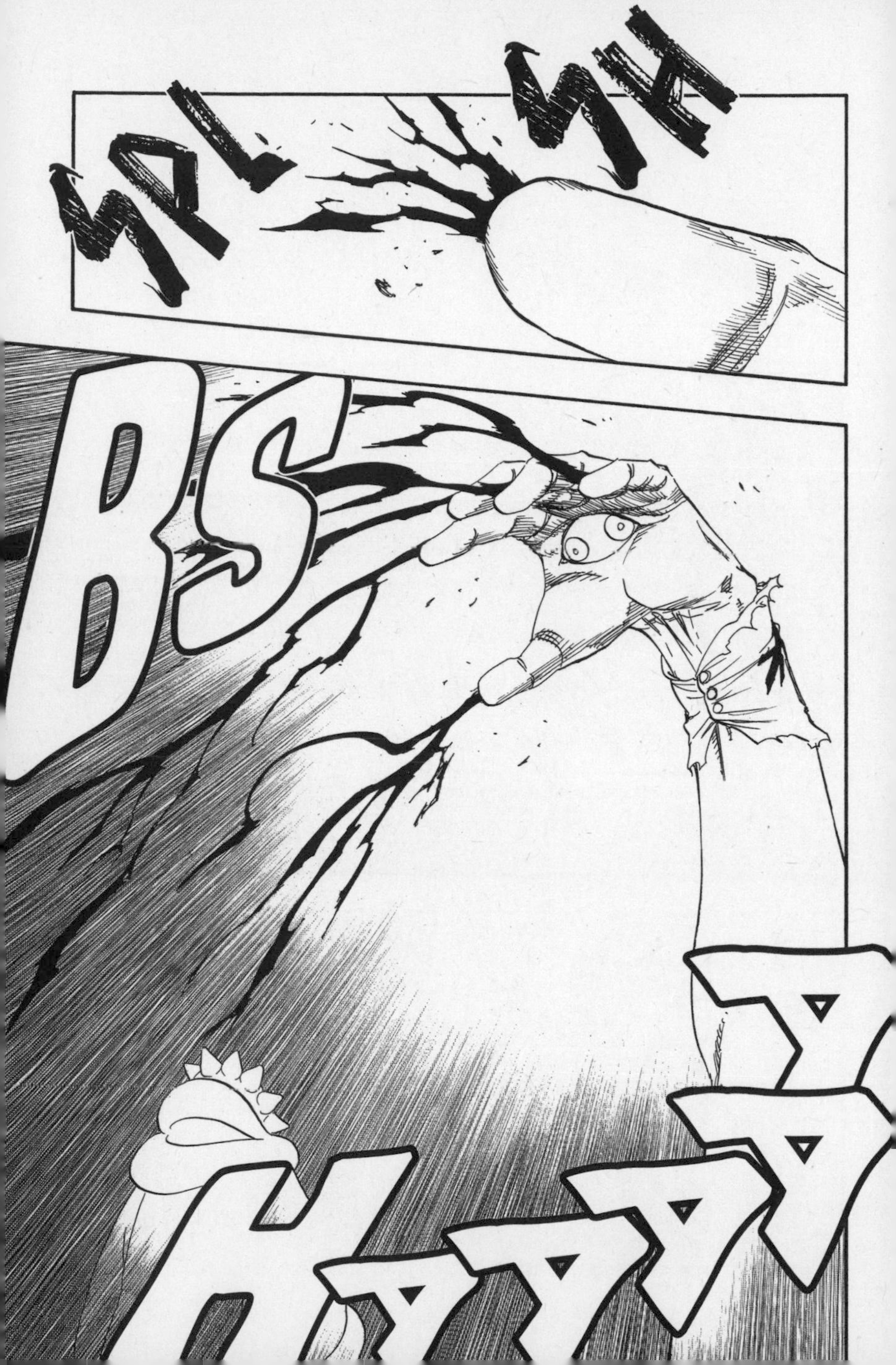
SPLSHA
BS
HAAAAA

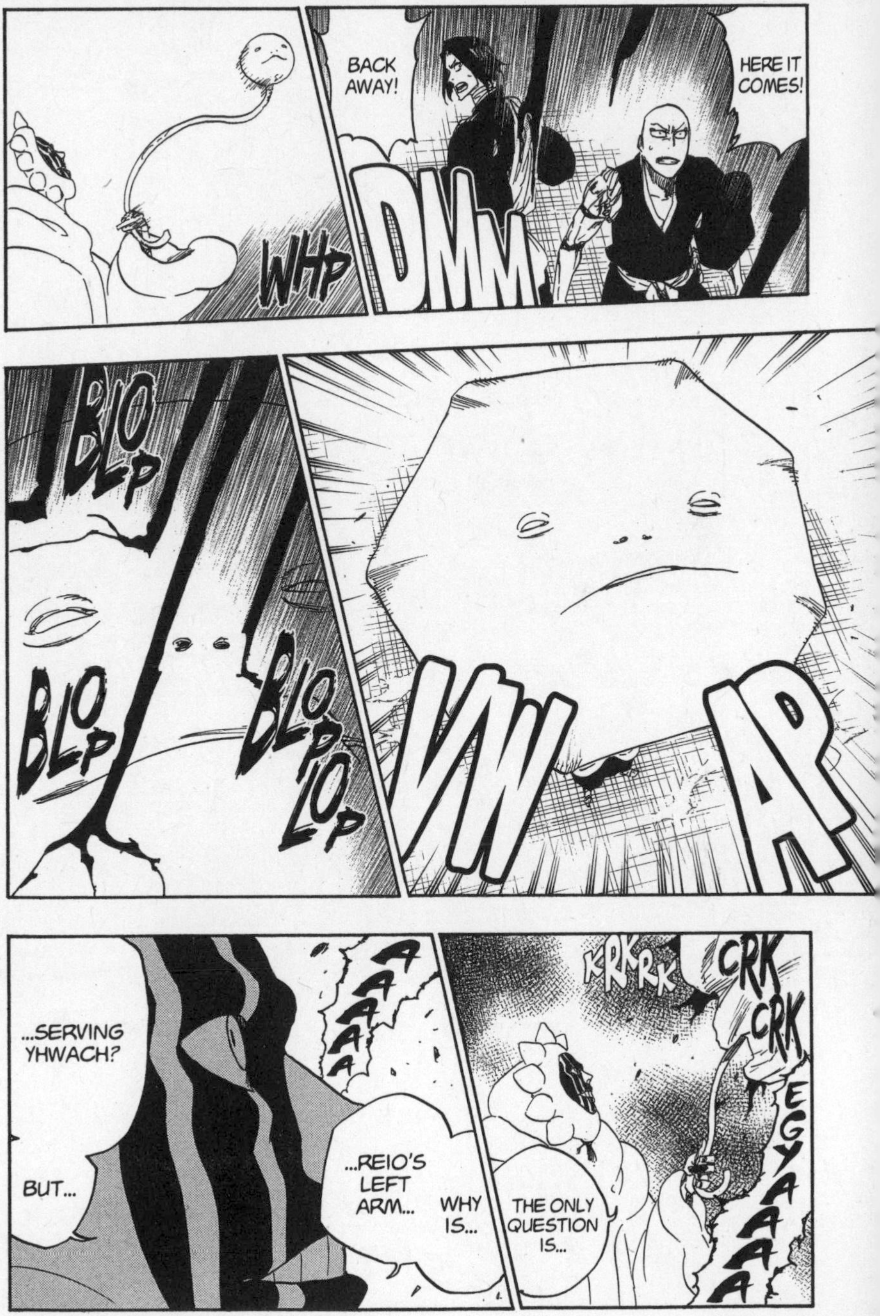
HERE IT COMES!
BACK AWAY!
DMM
WHP
VWAR
BLOP
BLOPLOP
BLOP
KRKRK
CRK CRK
EGYAAAAAA
THE ONLY QUESTION IS...
WHY IS...
...REIO'S LEFT ARM...
AAAAAA
...SERVING YHWACH?
BUT...

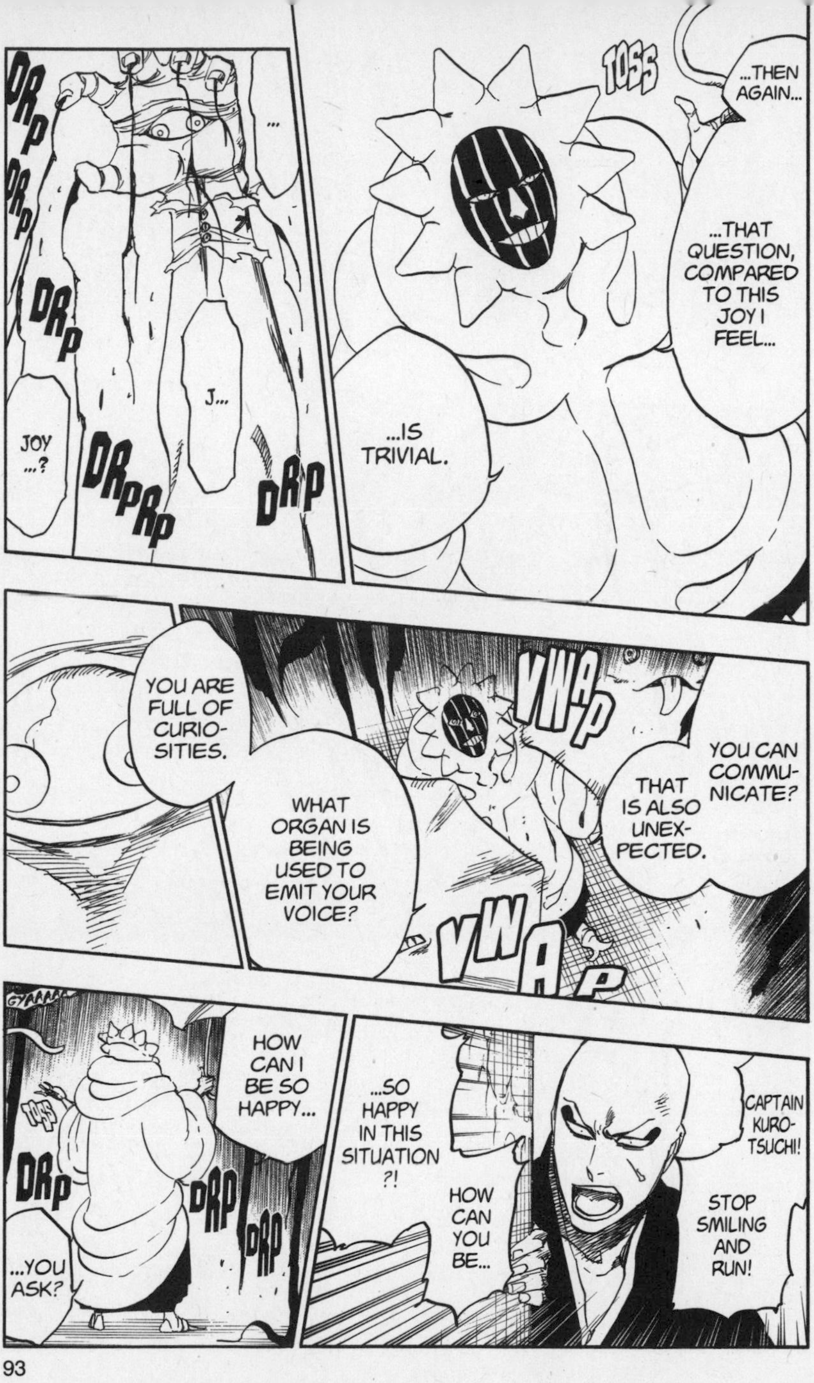
TOSS
...THEN AGAIN...
...THAT QUESTION, COMPARED TO THIS JOY I FEEL...
...IS TRIVIAL.
...
J...
JOY ...?
DRP DRP DRP DRP DRPRP DRP
VWAP
YOU CAN COMMUNICATE?
THAT IS ALSO UNEXPECTED.
WHAT ORGAN IS BEING USED TO EMIT YOUR VOICE?
YOU ARE FULL OF CURIOSITIES.
VWAP
CAPTAIN KUROTSUCHI!
STOP SMILING AND RUN!
HOW CAN YOU BE...
...SO HAPPY IN THIS SITUATION?!
HOW CAN I BE SO HAPPY...
GYAAAAA
TOSS
DRP DRP DRP
...YOU ASK?

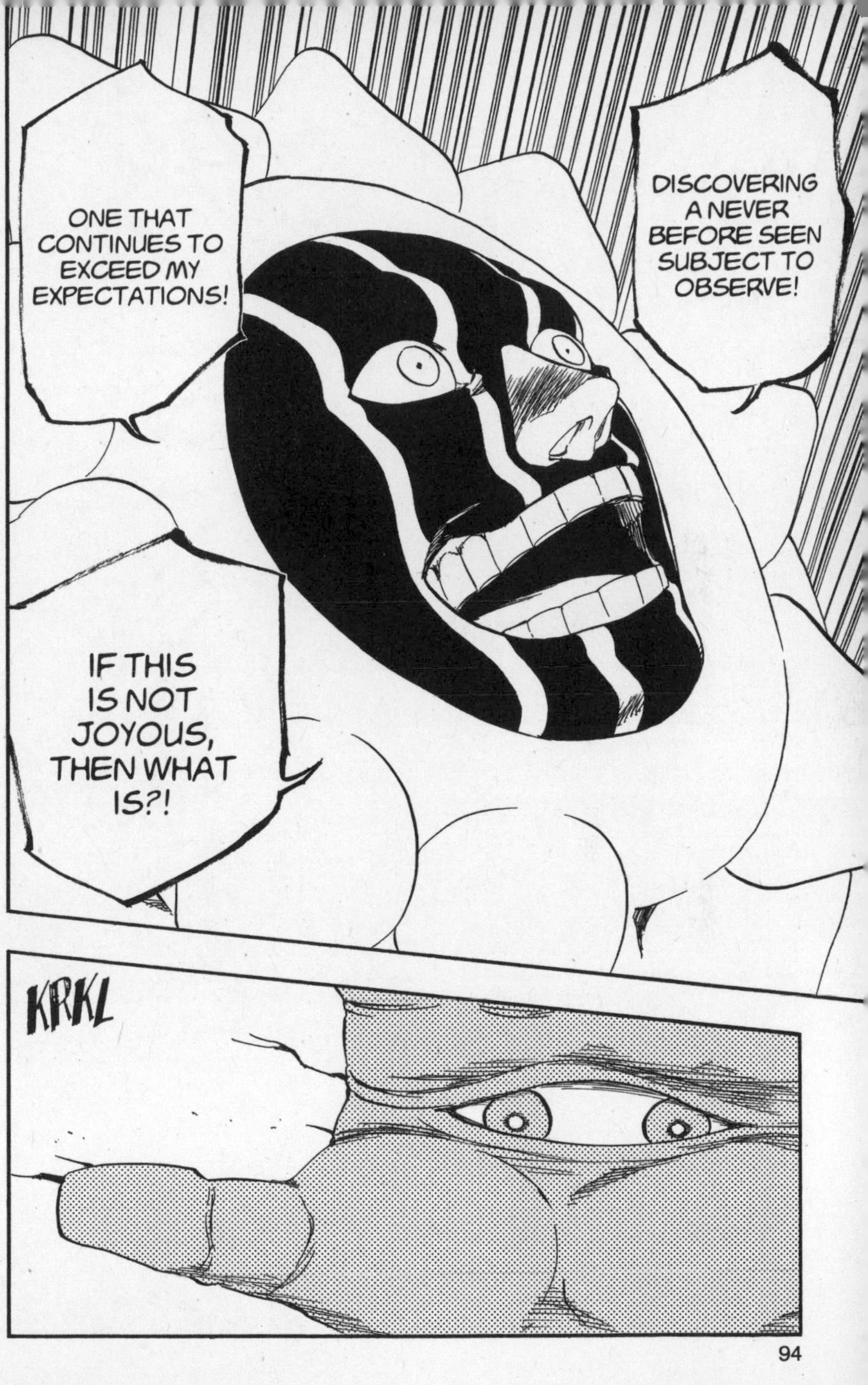
DISCOVERING A NEVER BEFORE SEEN SUBJECT TO OBSERVE!
ONE THAT CONTINUES TO EXCEED MY EXPECTATIONS!
IF THIS IS NOT JOYOUS, THEN WHAT IS?!
KRKL

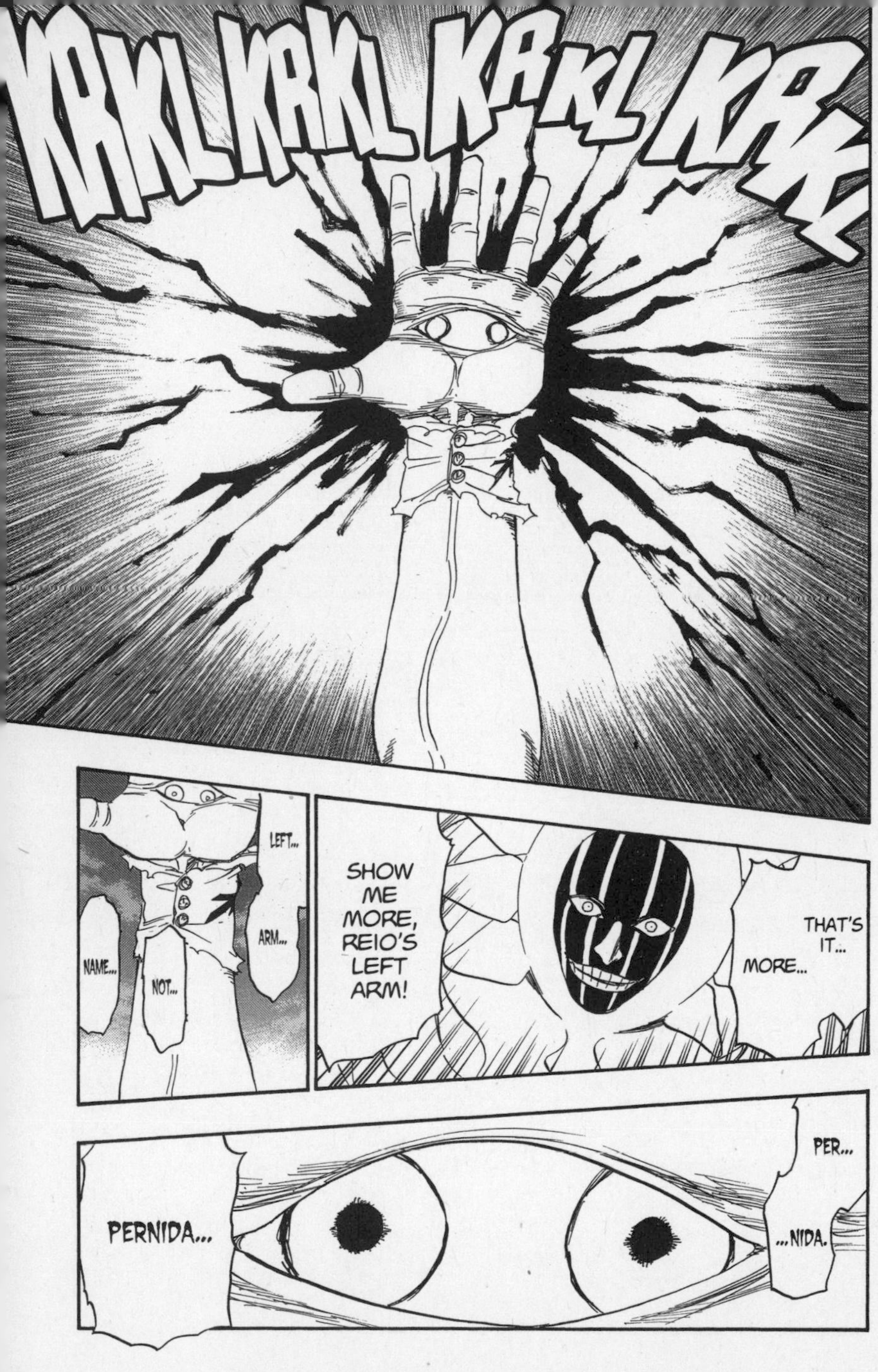
KRAKI KRAKI KRAKI KRAKI
THAT'S IT...
MORE...
SHOW ME MORE, REIO'S LEFT ARM!
LEFT...
ARM...
NOT...
NAME...
PER...
...NIDA.
PERNIDA...

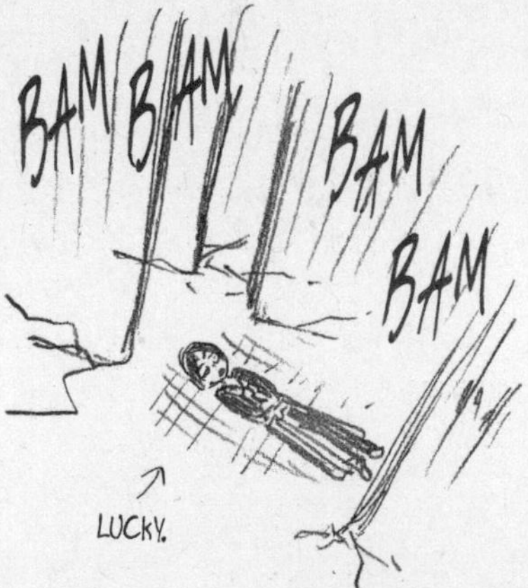
BAM BAM
BAM
BAM
LUCKY.

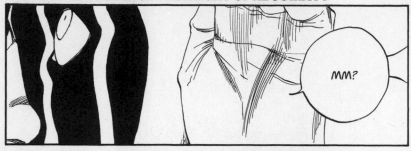

638. SEETHING MALICE THE HEIGHT OF ABSURDITY

MM?
COME AGAIN?
PLEASE SPEAK A LITTLE LOUDER.
LEFT... ARM...
NAME...
NOT...
NAME...
PER-NIDA...
PERNIDA...
PARNKGNJAS...

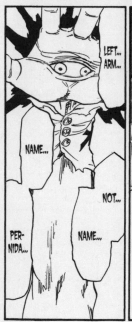

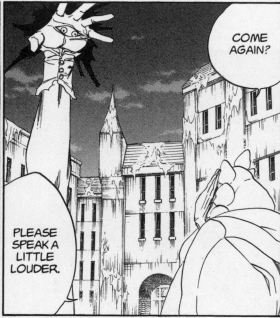

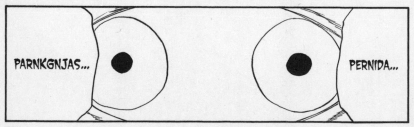

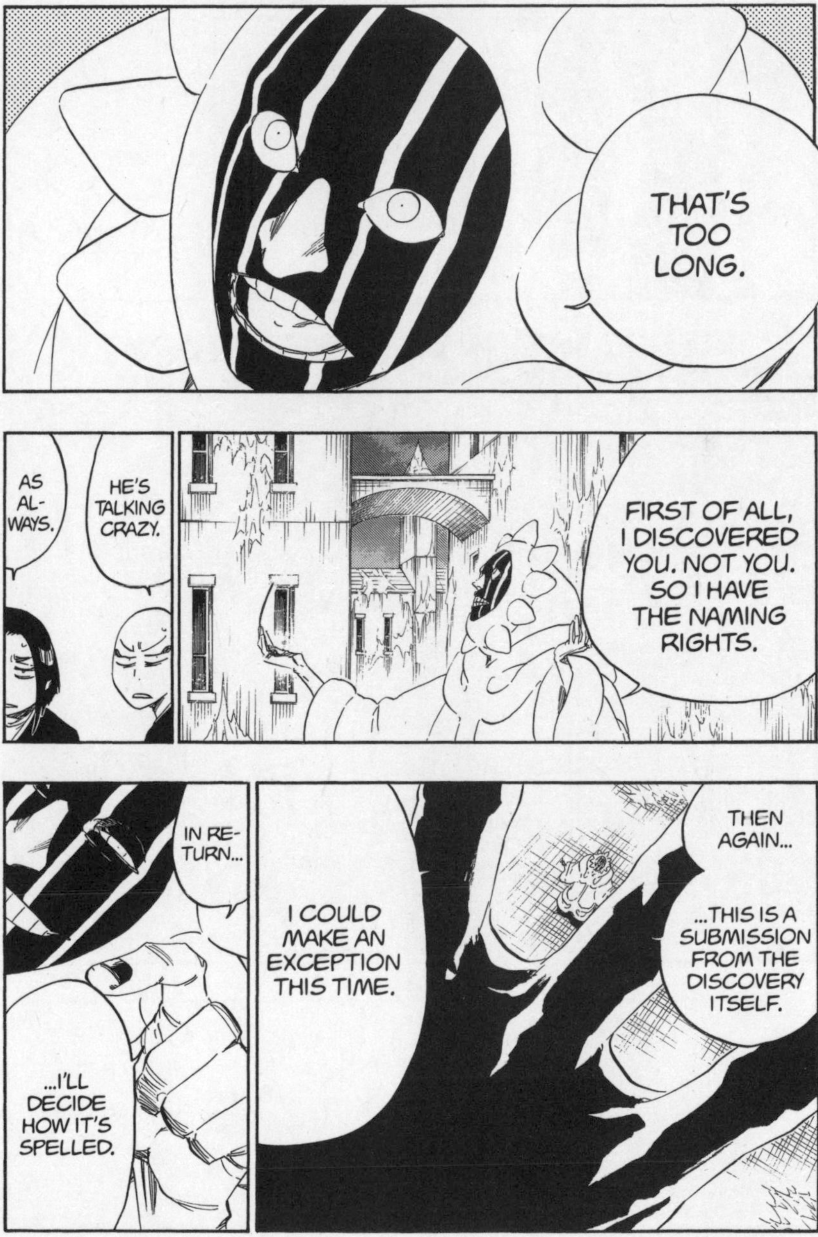
THAT'S TOO LONG.
FIRST OF ALL, I DISCOVERED YOU. NOT YOU. SO I HAVE THE NAMING RIGHTS.
HE'S TALKING CRAZY.
AS ALWAYS.
THEN AGAIN...
...THIS IS A SUBMISSION FROM THE DISCOVERY ITSELF.
I COULD MAKE AN EXCEPTION THIS TIME.
IN RETURN...
...I'LL DECIDE HOW IT'S SPELLED.

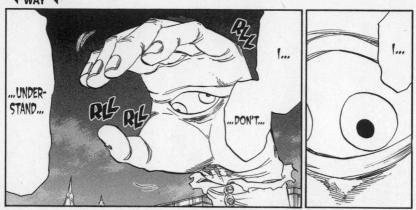

...UNDER- STAND...

RLL

RLL RLL

I....

...DON'T...

I...

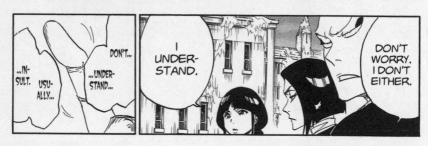

...IN- SULT.

DON'T...

USU- ALLY...

...UNDER- STAND...

I UNDER- STAND.

DON'T WORRY. I DON'T EITHER.

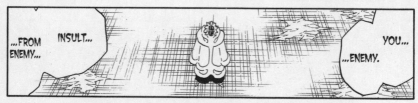

...FROM ENEMY...

INSULT...

YOU...

...ENEMY.

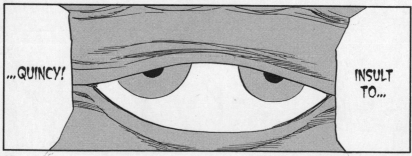

...QUINCY!

INSULT TO...

99

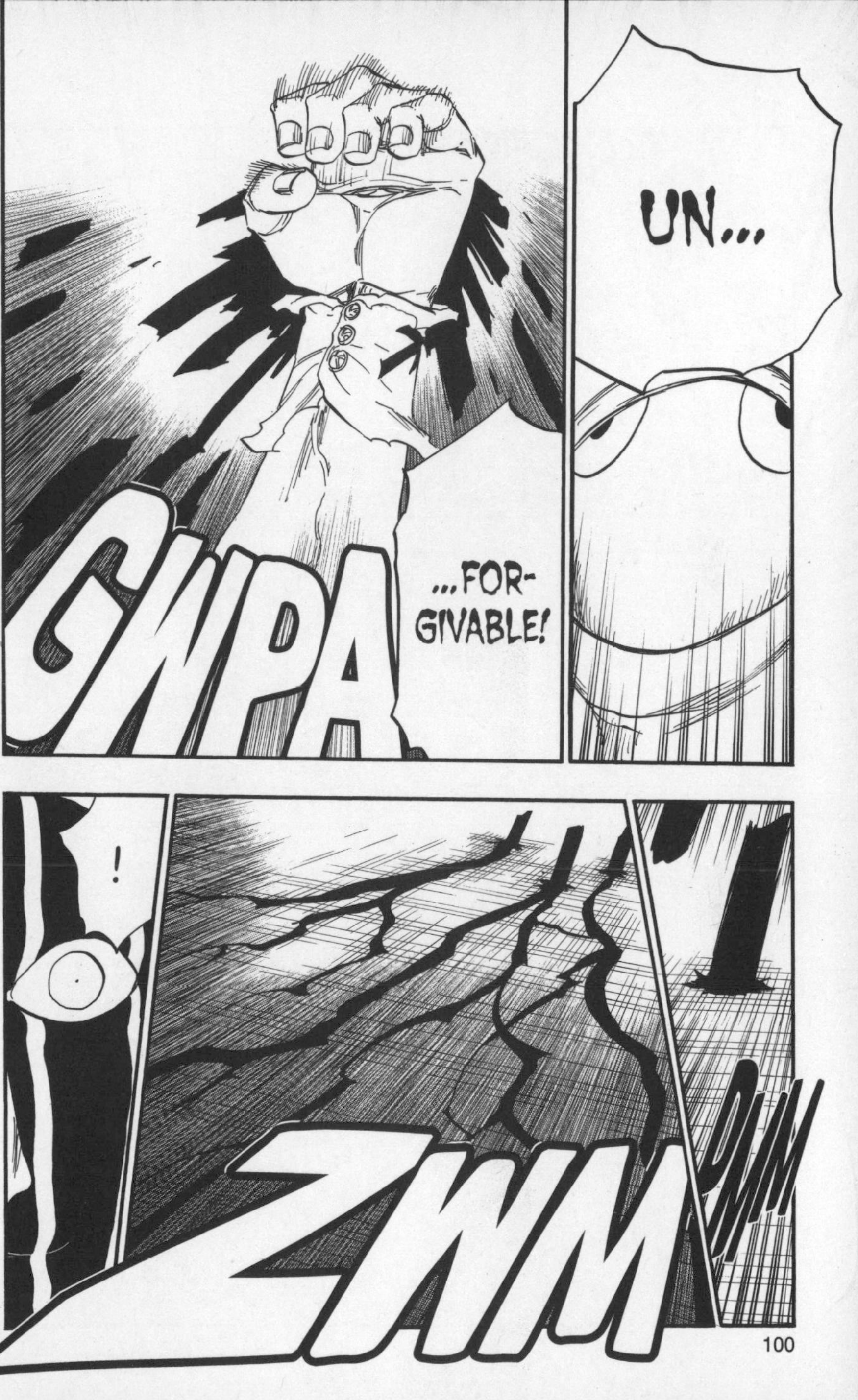
UN...
GWPA
...FOR-
GIVABLE!
ZWM
!

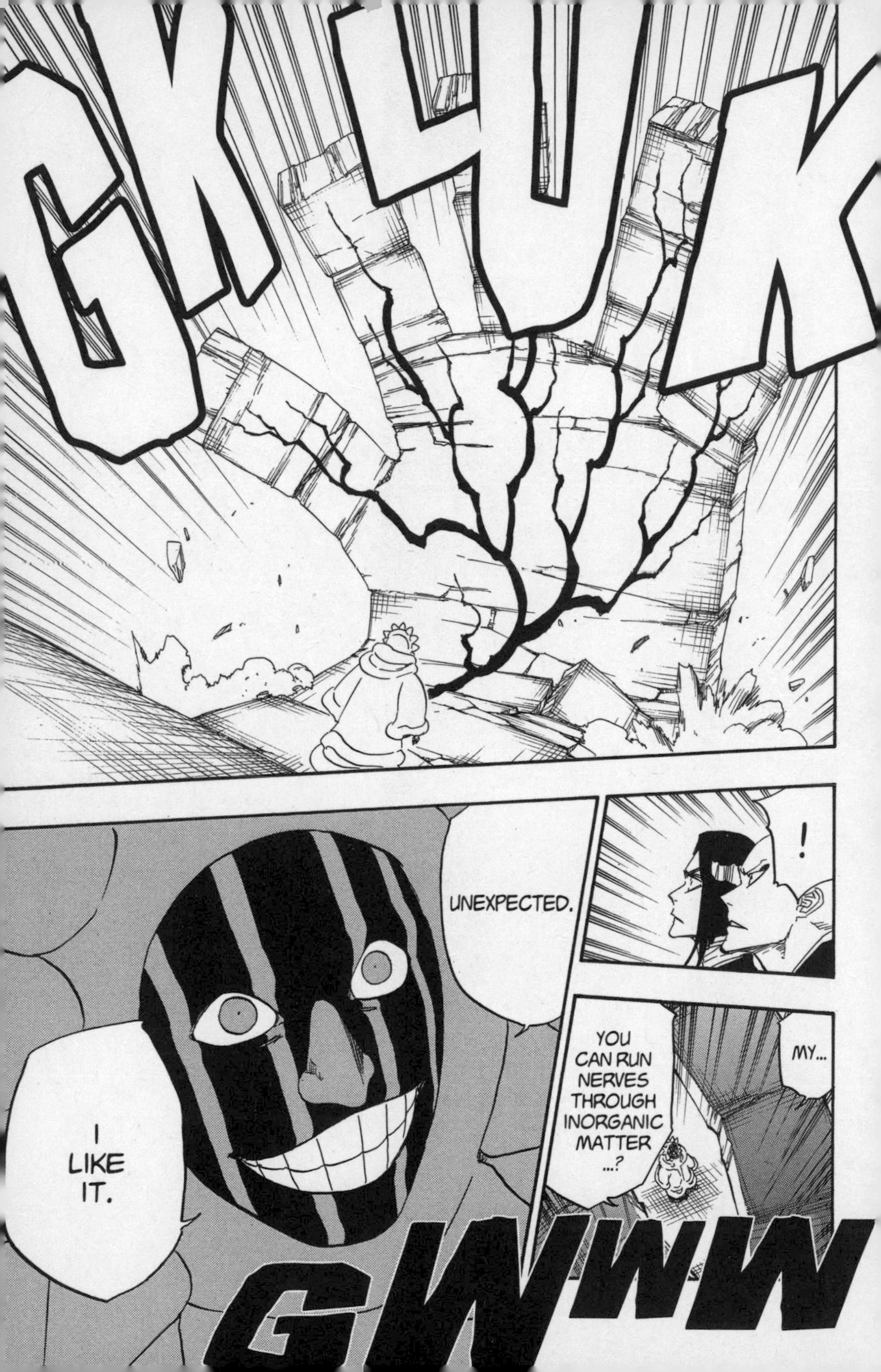
GKLUK
!
MY...
YOU CAN RUN NERVES THROUGH INORGANIC MATTER ...?
UNEXPECTED.
I LIKE IT.
GWWW

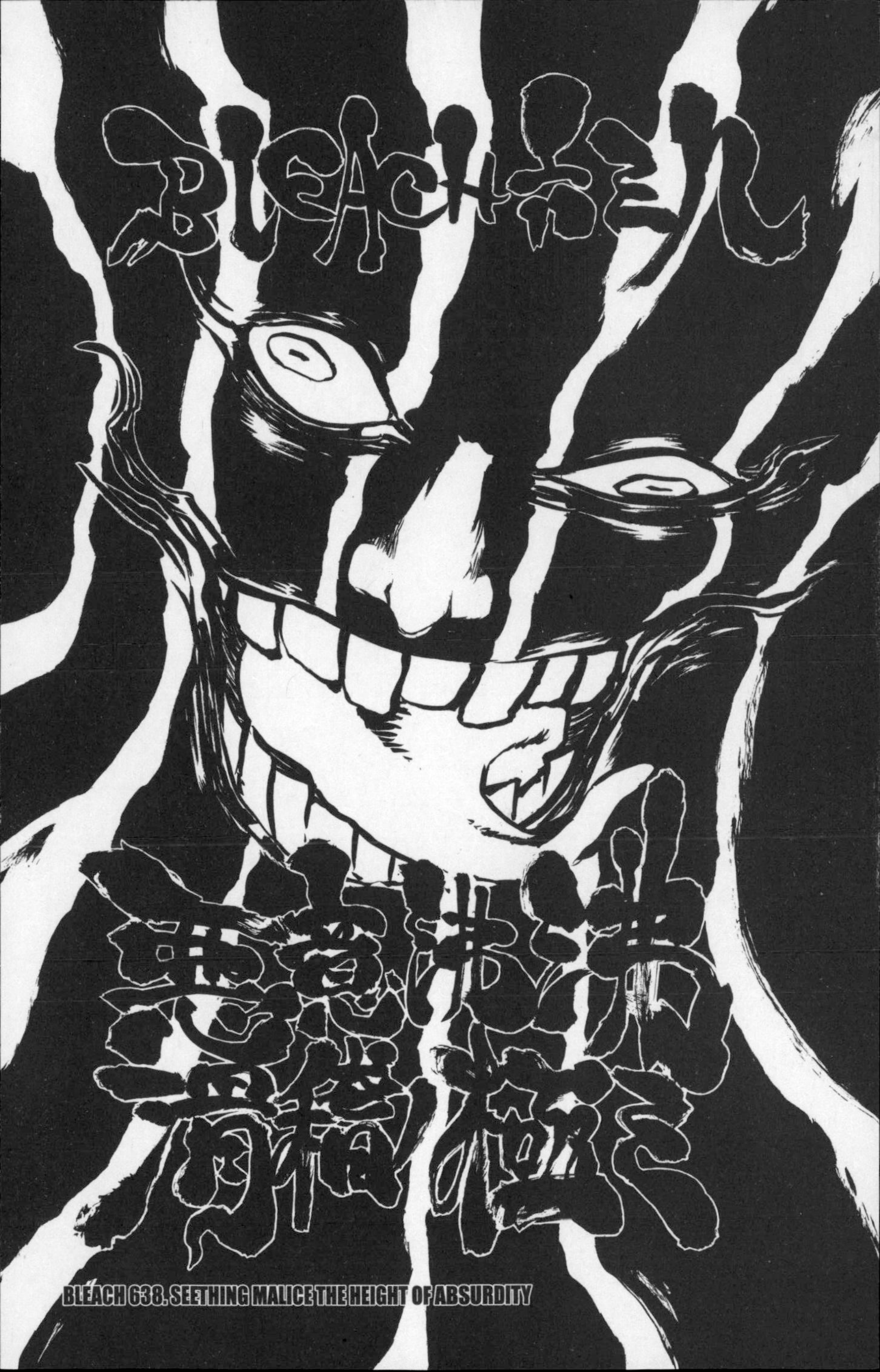
BLEACH
BLEACH 638. SEETHING MALICE THE HEIGHT OF ABSURDITY

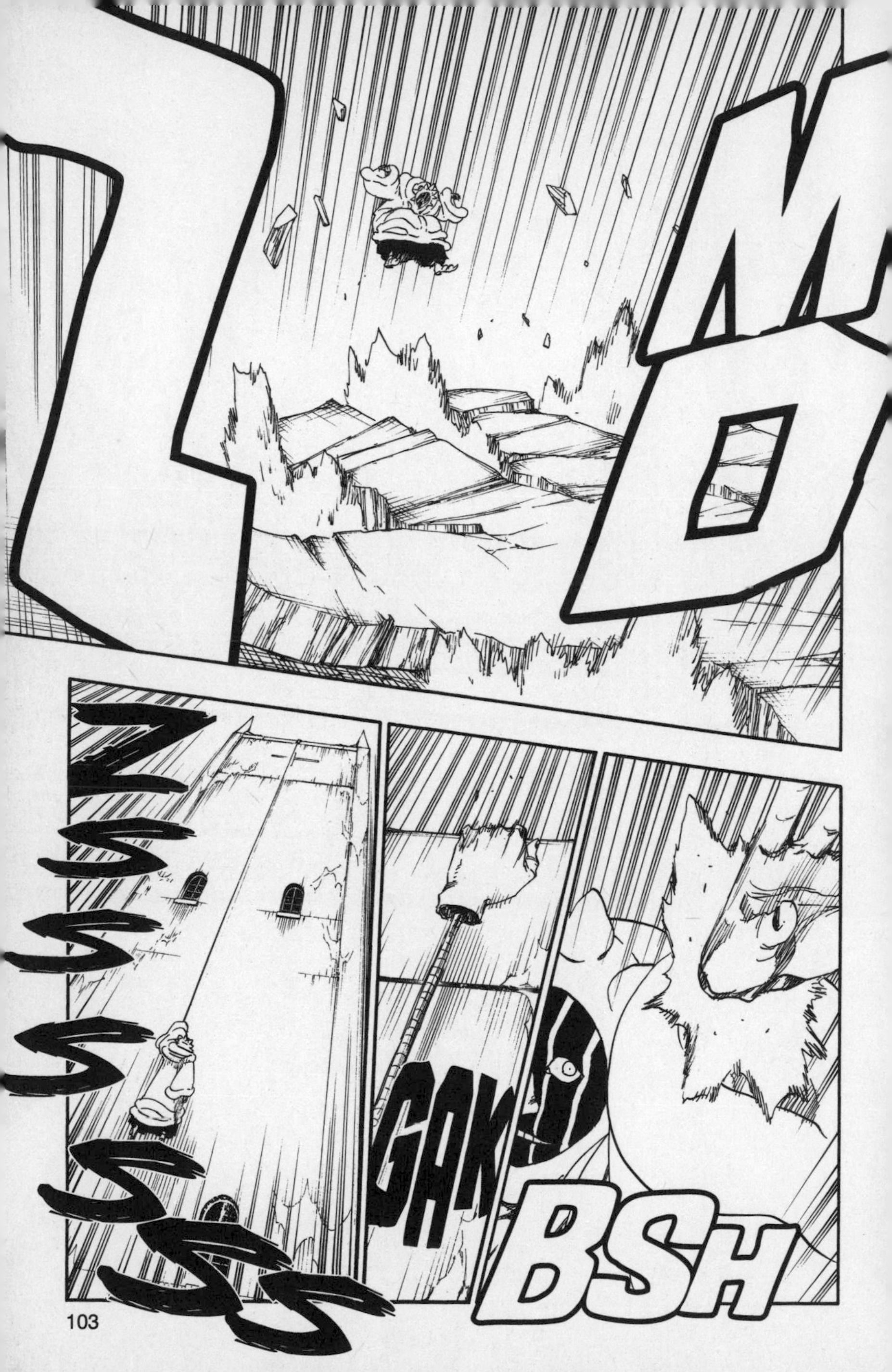
BSH
GAK

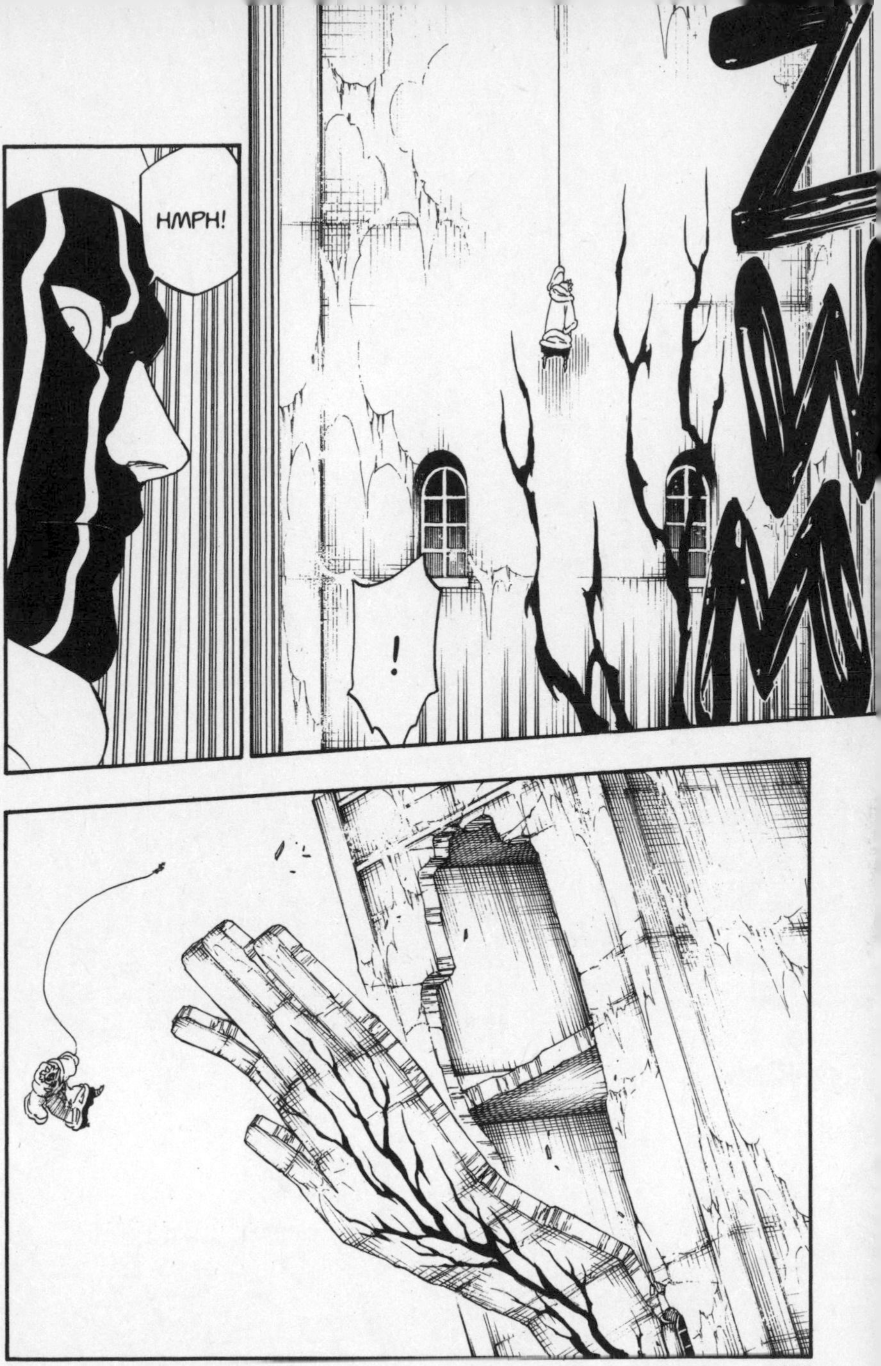
!
HMPH!

READ THIS WAY

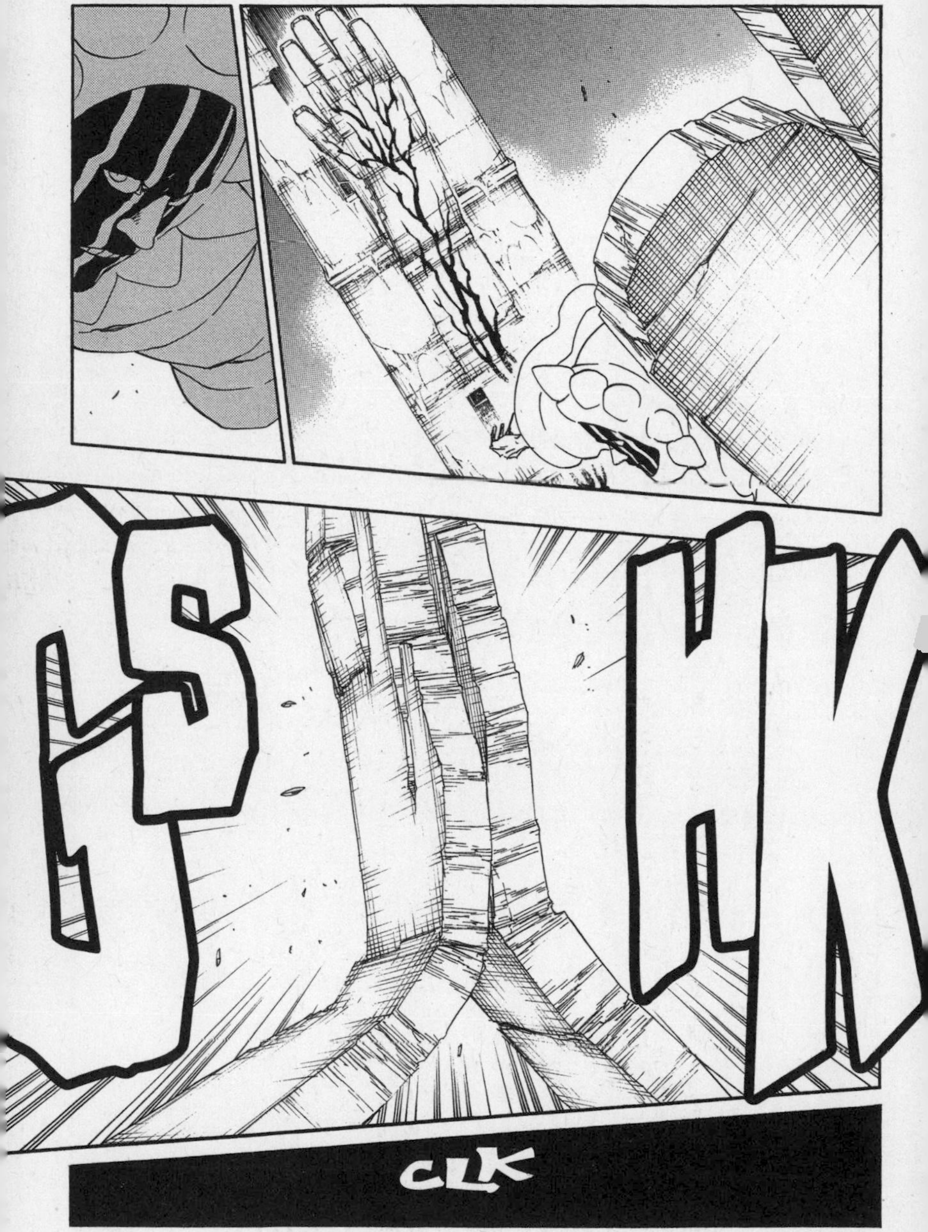
SHK
CLK

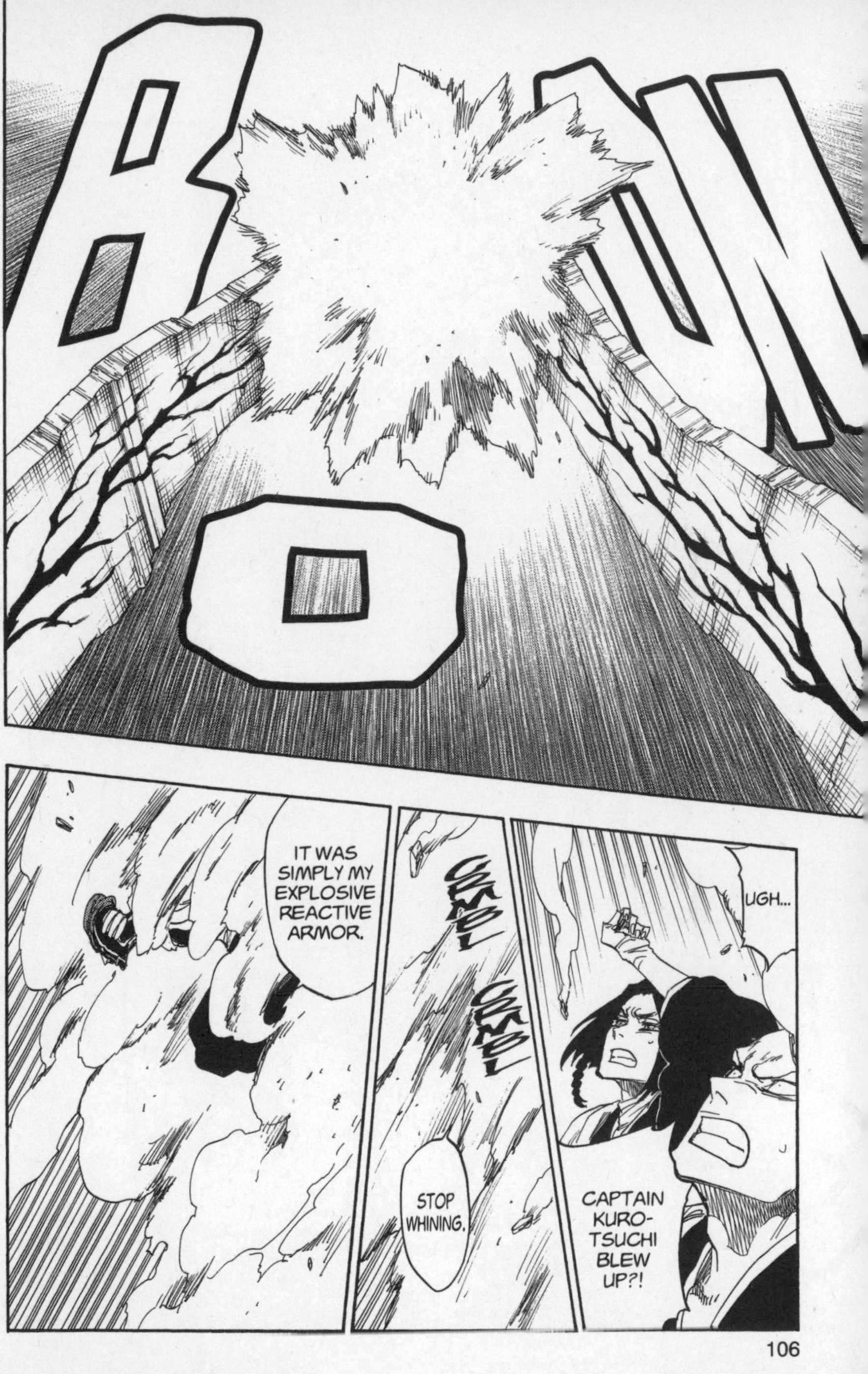
UGH...
CAPTAIN KURO-TSUCHI BLEW UP?!
STOP WHINING.
IT WAS SIMPLY MY EXPLOSIVE REACTIVE ARMOR.

READ THIS WAY

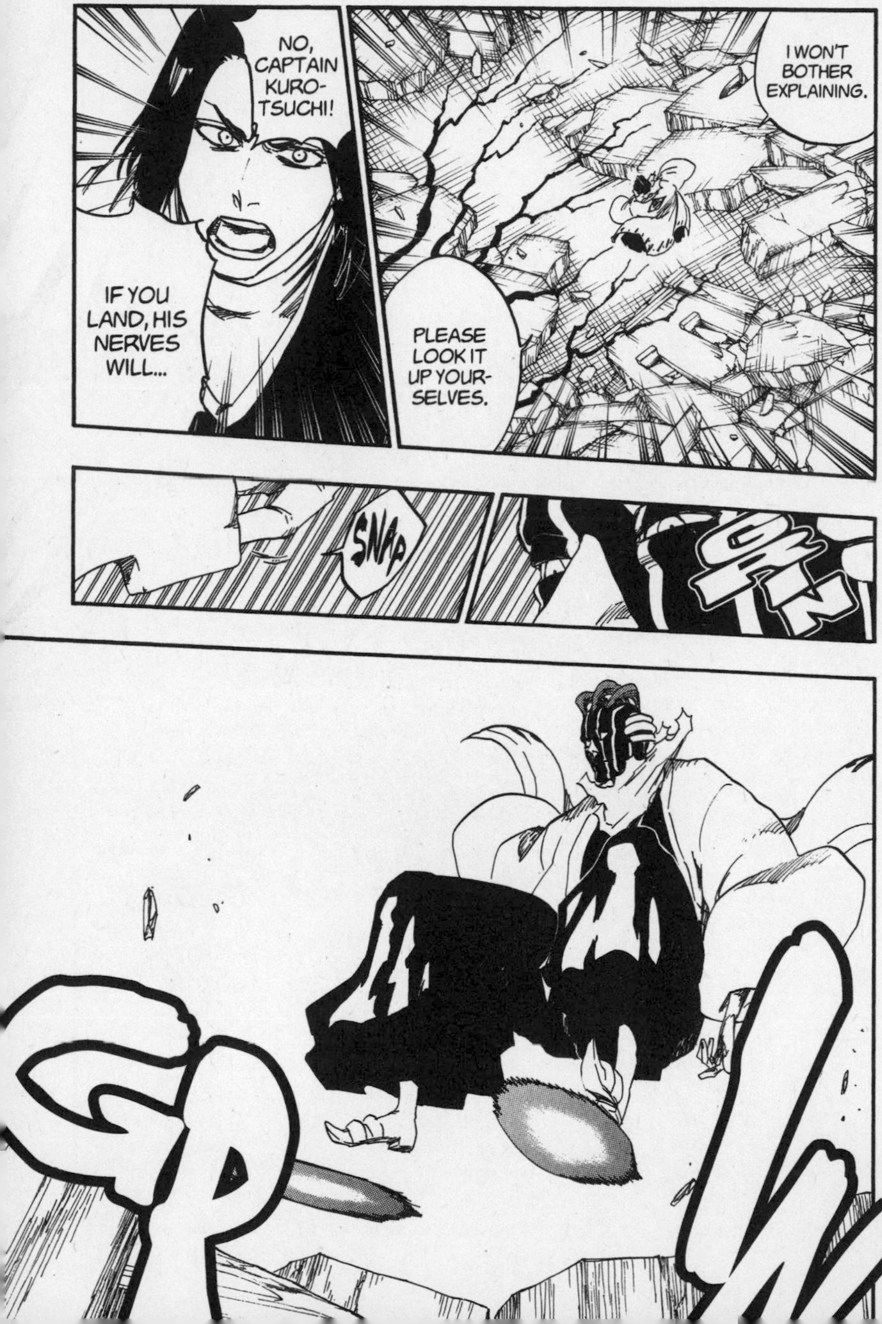
I WON'T BOTHER EXPLAINING.
PLEASE LOOK IT UP YOUR-SELVES.
NO, CAPTAIN KURO-TSUCHI!
IF YOU LAND, HIS NERVES WILL...
SNAP

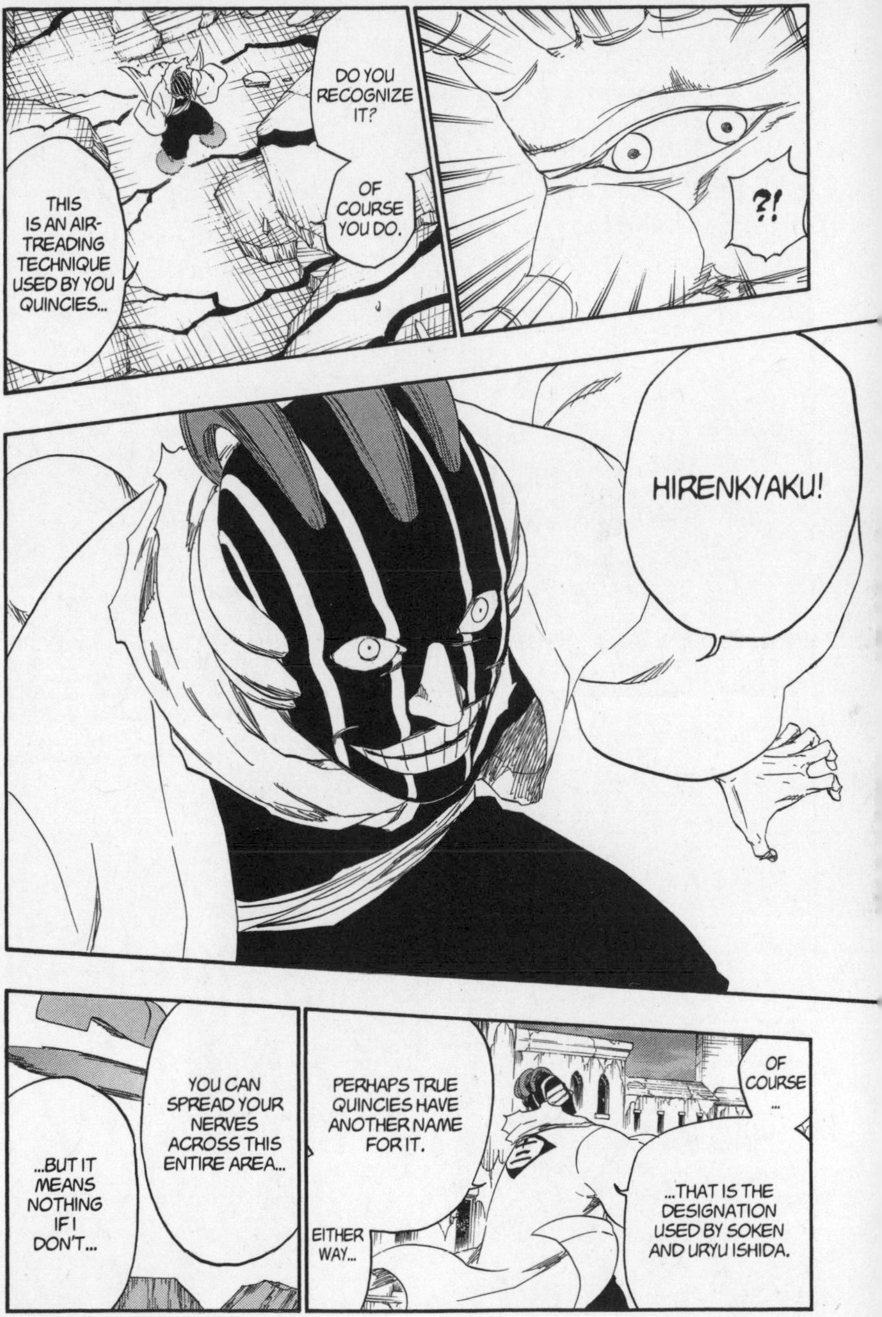
?!
DO YOU RECOGNIZE IT?
OF COURSE YOU DO.
THIS IS AN AIR-TREADING TECHNIQUE USED BY YOU QUINCIES...
HIRENKYAKU!
OF COURSE...
...THAT IS THE DESIGNATION USED BY SOKEN AND URYU ISHIDA.
PERHAPS TRUE QUINCIES HAVE ANOTHER NAME FOR IT.
EITHER WAY...
YOU CAN SPREAD YOUR NERVES ACROSS THIS ENTIRE AREA...
...BUT IT MEANS NOTHING IF I DON'T...

READ THIS WAY

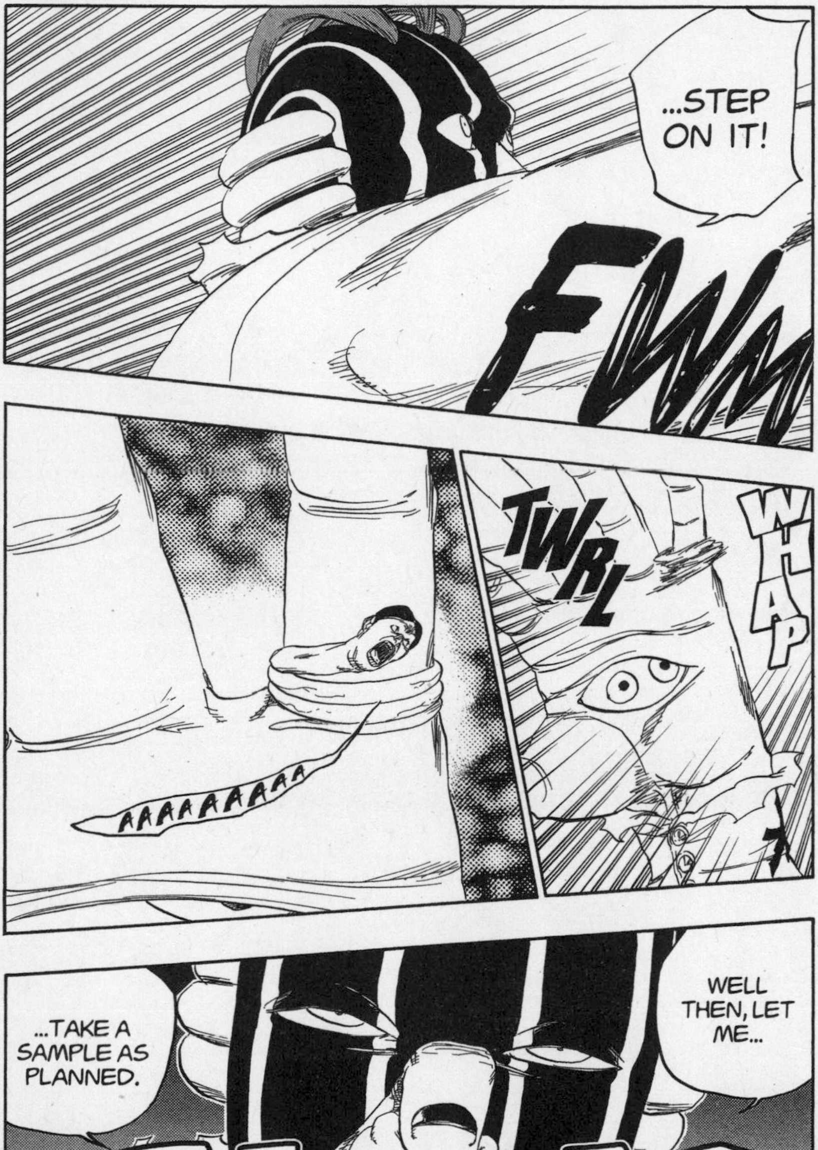

...STEP ON IT!
FWM
TWRL
WHAP
AAAAAAAAA
WELL THEN, LET ME...
...TAKE A SAMPLE AS PLANNED.
CLK

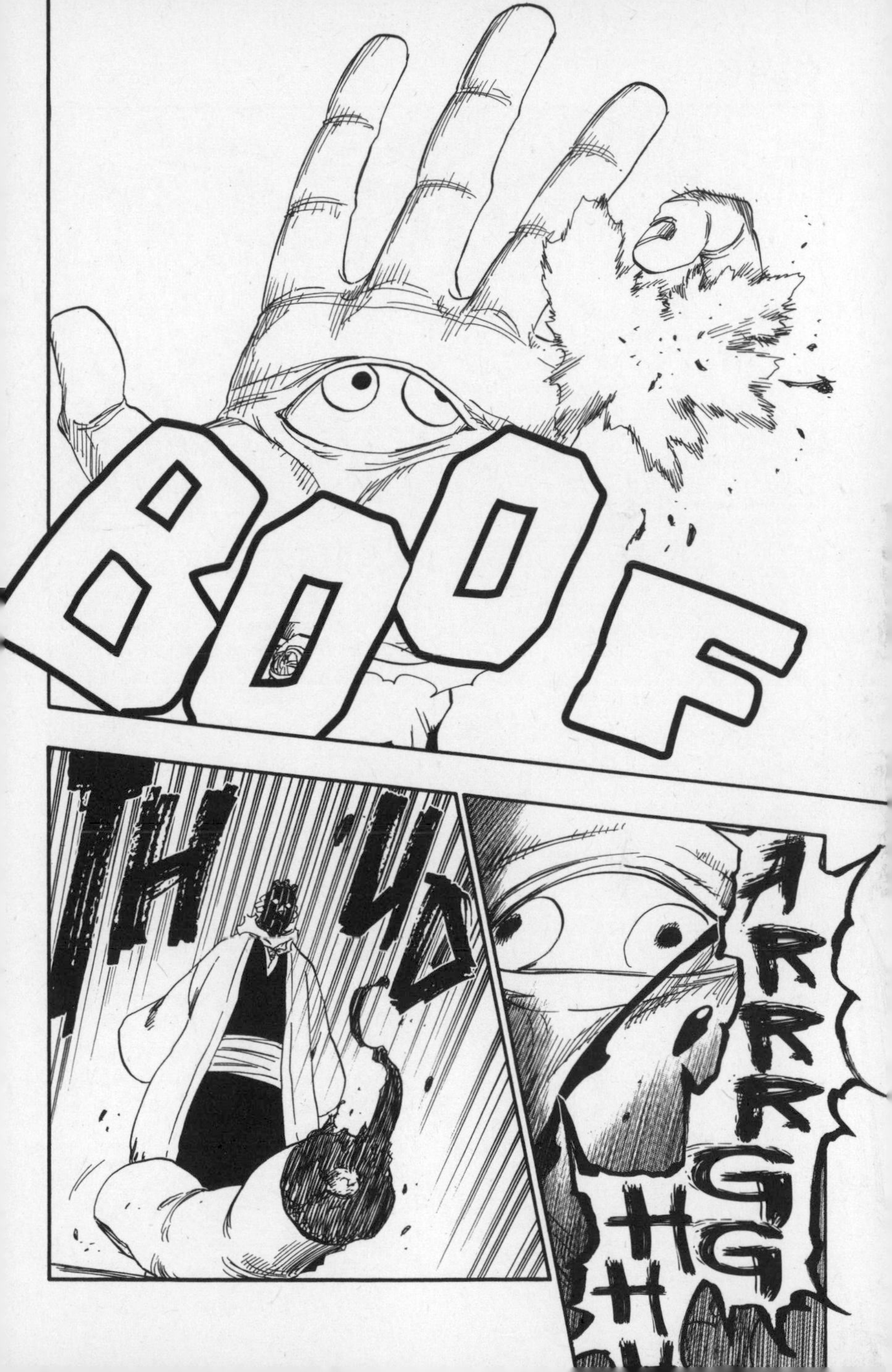
BOOF
ARRRGGHH
THUD

READ THIS WAY

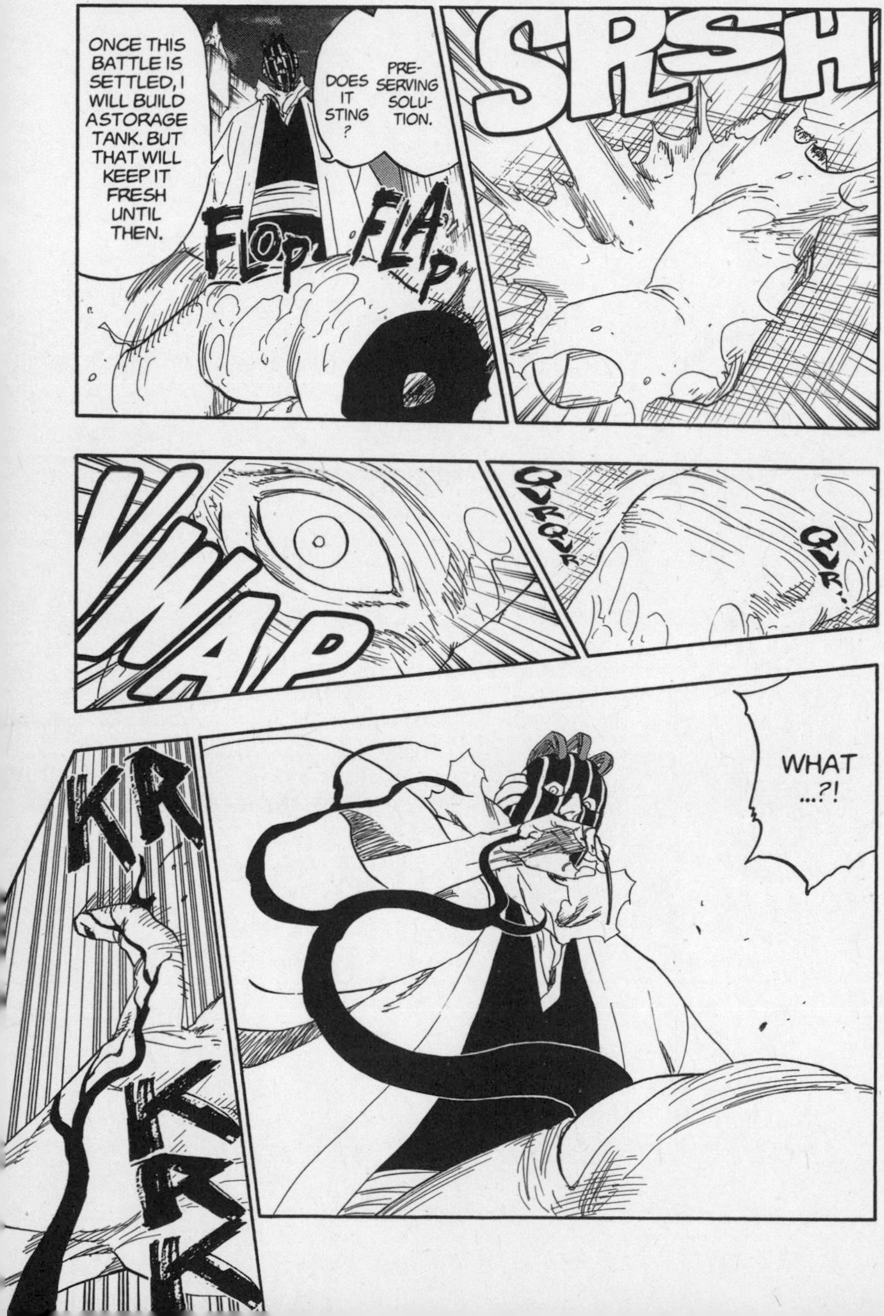
SRSH
PRE-SERVING SOLUTION.
DOES IT STING?
ONCE THIS BATTLE IS SETTLED, I WILL BUILD ASTORAGE TANK. BUT THAT WILL KEEP IT FRESH UNTIL THEN.
FLAP
FLOP
QVR...
QVRQVR
VWAP
WHAT ...?!
KR
KRK

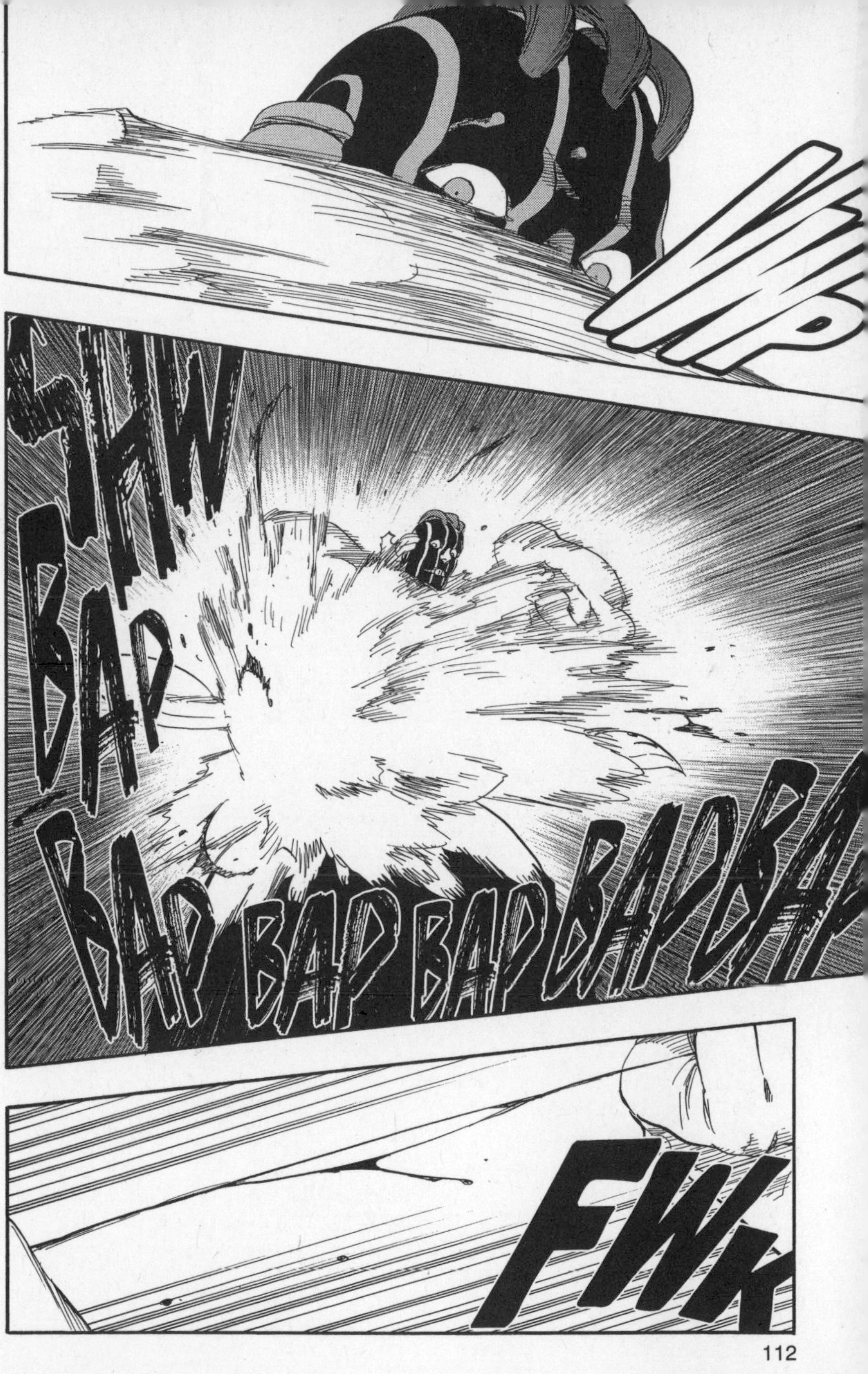
WHIP
SHW
BAP
BAP BAP BAP BAP BAP BAP
FWK

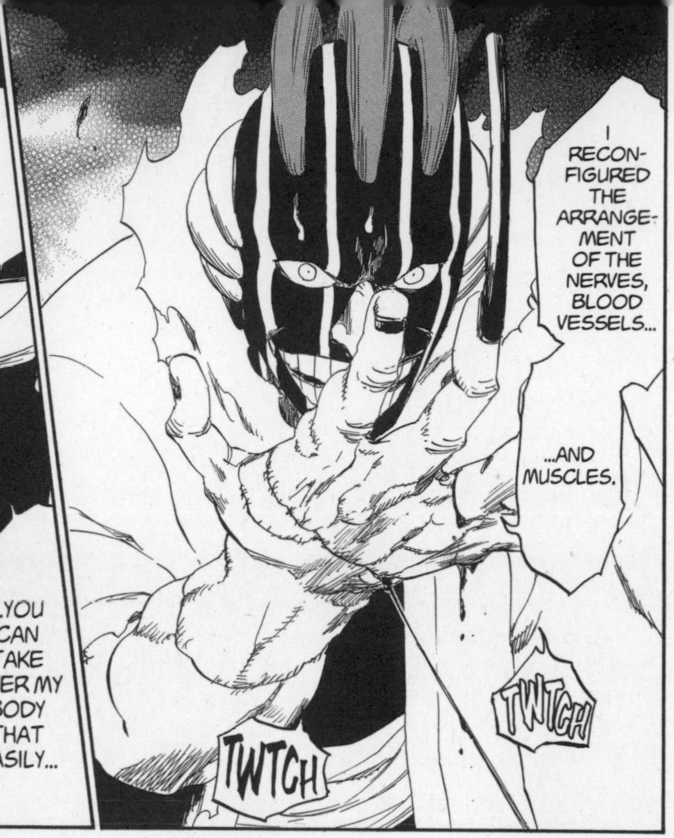
I RECON-FIGURED THE ARRANGE-MENT OF THE NERVES, BLOOD VESSELS...
...AND MUSCLES.
TWTCH
TWTCH

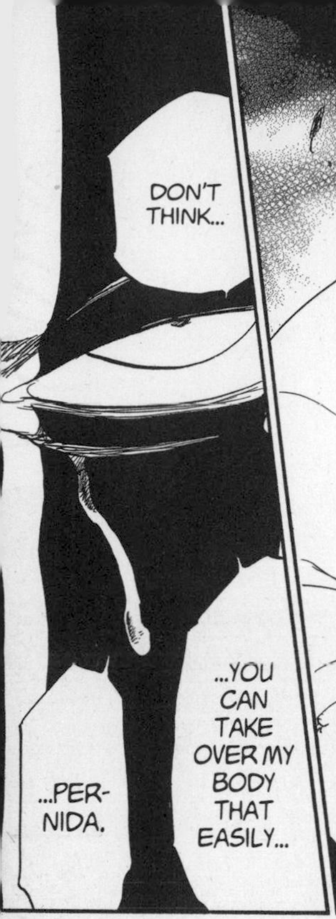
DON'T THINK...
...YOU CAN TAKE OVER MY BODY THAT EASILY...
...PER-NIDA.

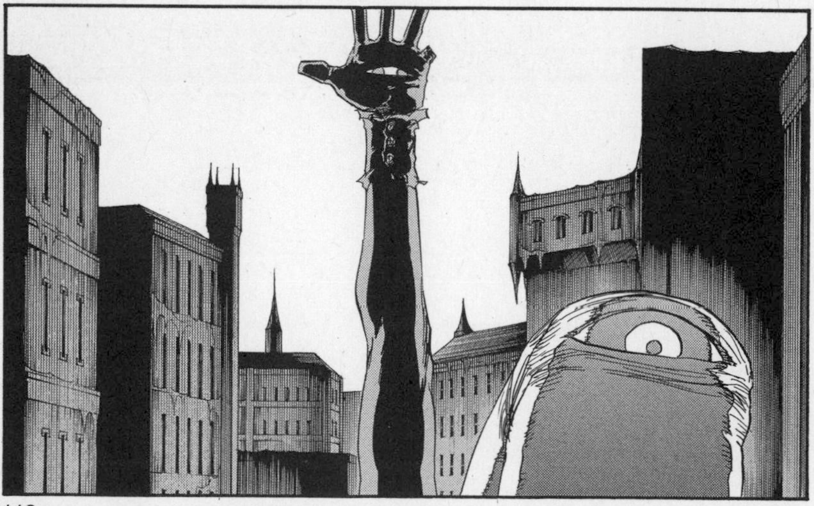

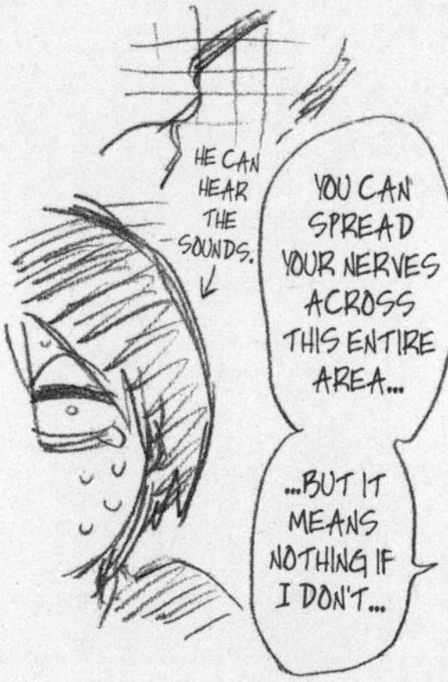
YOU CAN SPREAD YOUR NERVES ACROSS THIS ENTIRE AREA...
...BUT IT MEANS NOTHING IF I DON'T...
HE CAN HEAR THE SOUNDS.

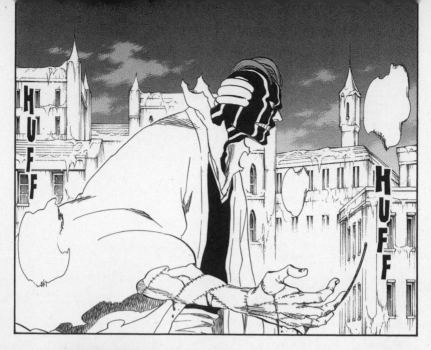

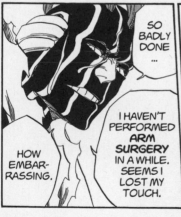

SO BADLY DONE ...

I HAVEN'T PERFORMED **ARM SURGERY** IN A WHILE. SEEMS I LOST MY TOUCH.

HOW EMBAR-RASSING.

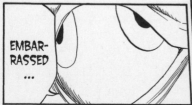

EMBAR-RASSED ...

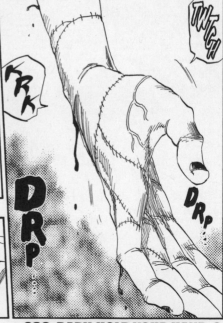

115

639. BABY, HOLD YOUR HAND 2

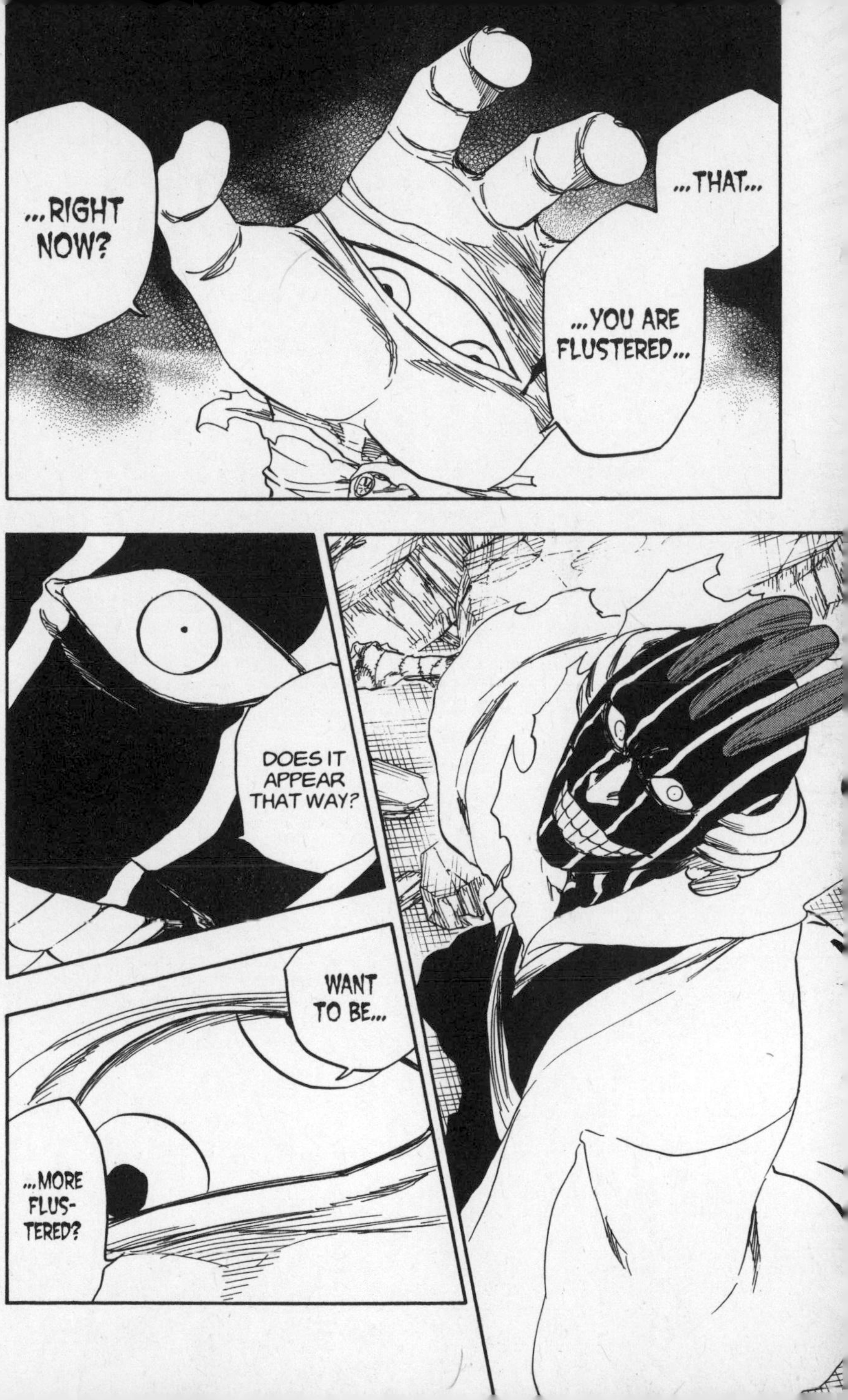
...THAT...
...YOU ARE FLUSTERED...
...RIGHT NOW?
DOES IT APPEAR THAT WAY?
WANT TO BE...
...MORE FLUS-TERED?

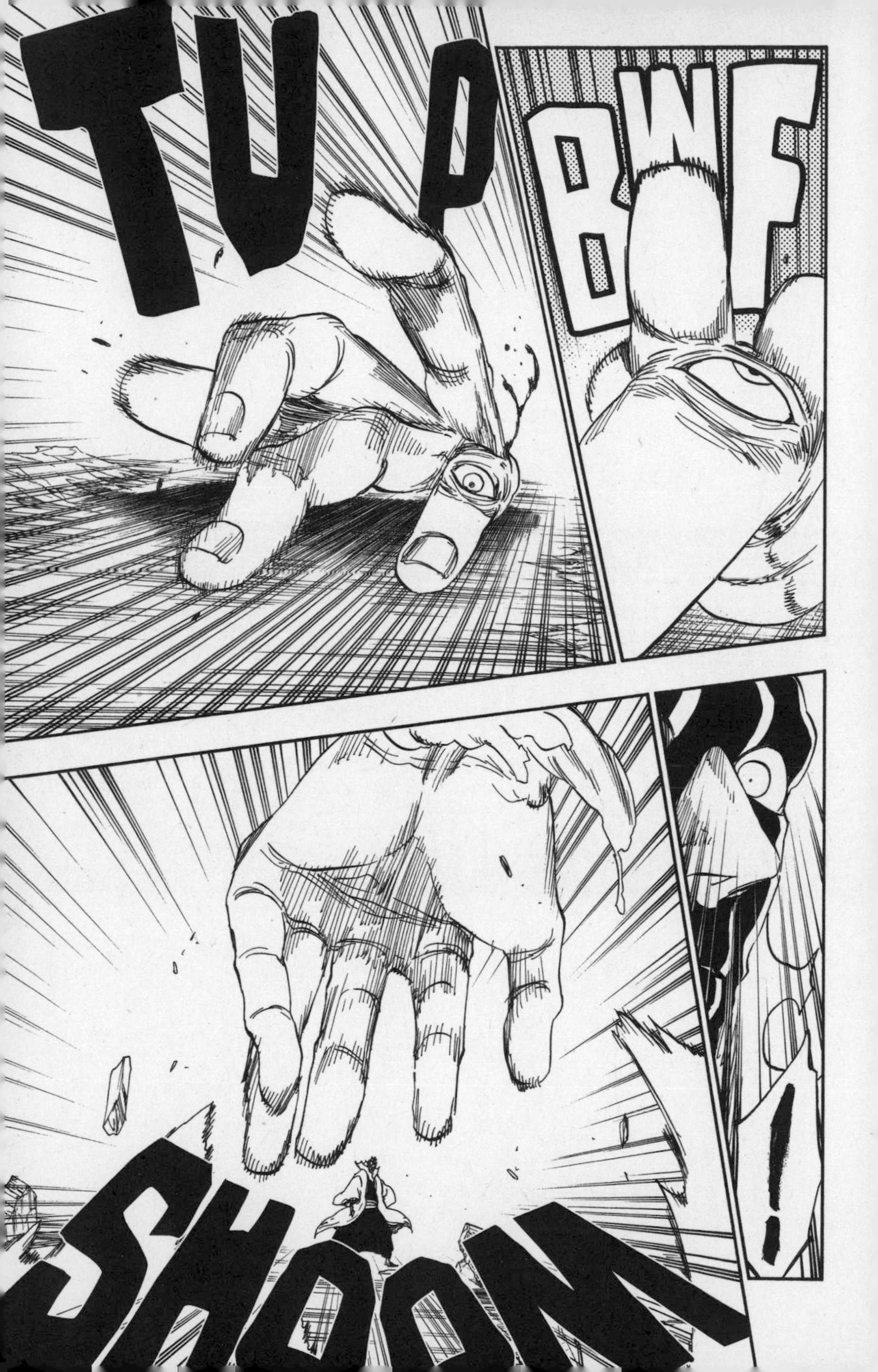
BWF
TUP
!
SHOON

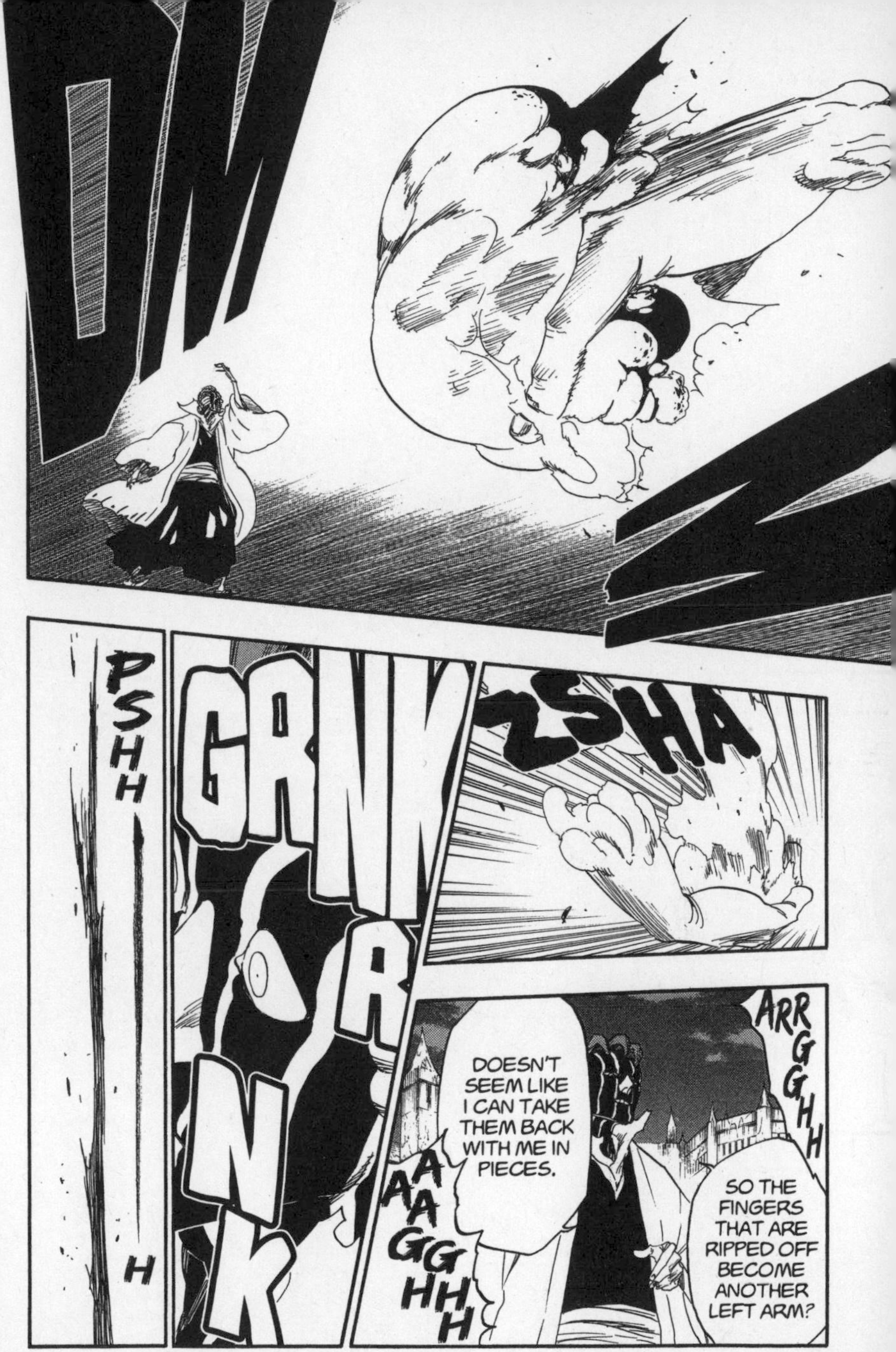
ZSHA
ARRGGHH
SO THE FINGERS THAT ARE RIPPED OFF BECOME ANOTHER LEFT ARM?
DOESN'T SEEM LIKE I CAN TAKE THEM BACK WITH ME IN PIECES.
AAAAGGHHH
GRNK
RNK
PSHHH

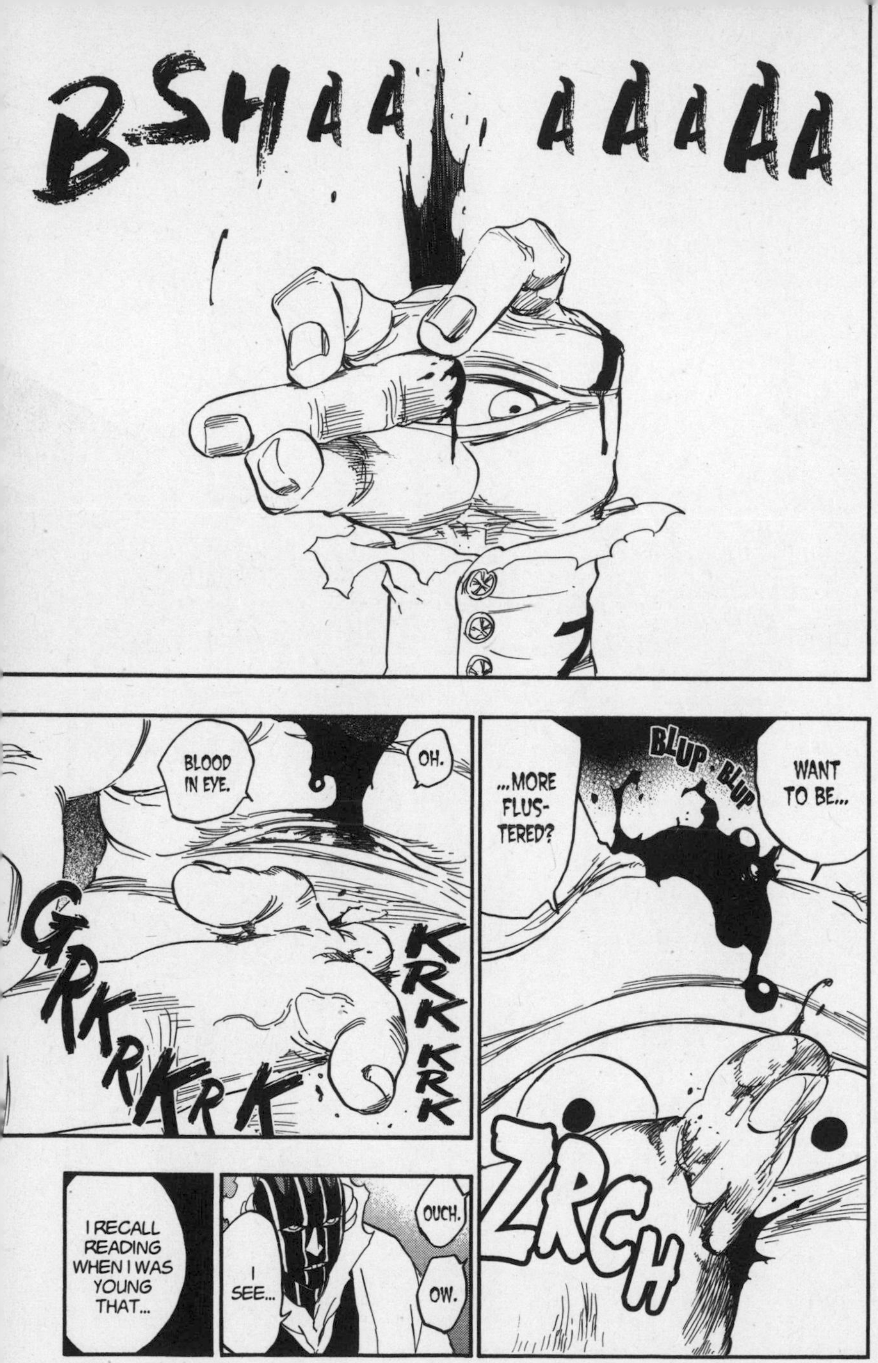
BSHAAAAAAA
WANT TO BE...
BLUP BLUP
...MORE FLUSTERED?
ZRCH
OH.
BLOOD IN EYE.
KRKKRKKRK
GRKRKRKRK
OUCH.
OW.
I SEE...
I RECALL READING WHEN I WAS YOUNG THAT...

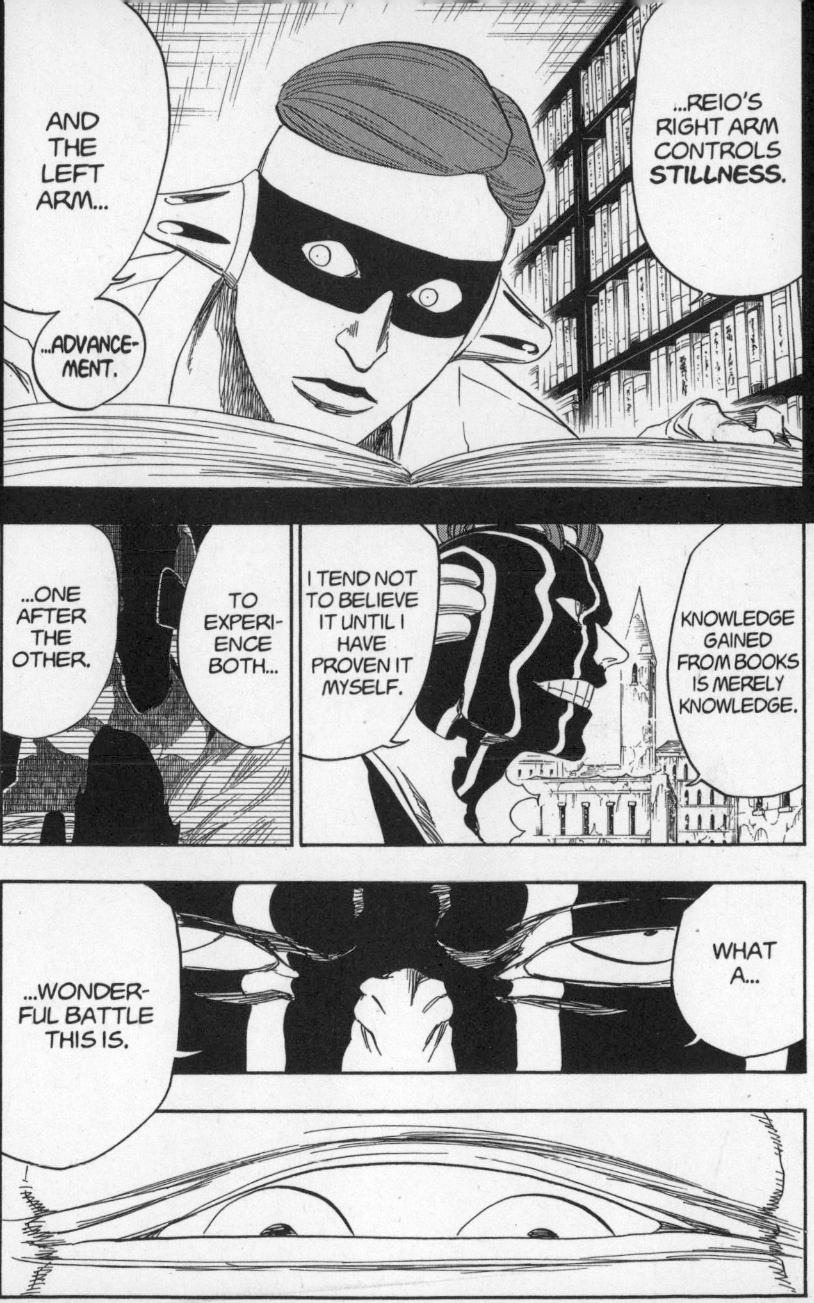
...REIO'S RIGHT ARM CONTROLS **STILLNESS.**
AND THE LEFT ARM...
...ADVANCEMENT.
KNOWLEDGE GAINED FROM BOOKS IS MERELY KNOWLEDGE.
I TEND NOT TO BELIEVE IT UNTIL I HAVE PROVEN IT MYSELF.
TO EXPERIENCE BOTH...
...ONE AFTER THE OTHER.
WHAT A...
...WONDERFUL BATTLE THIS IS.

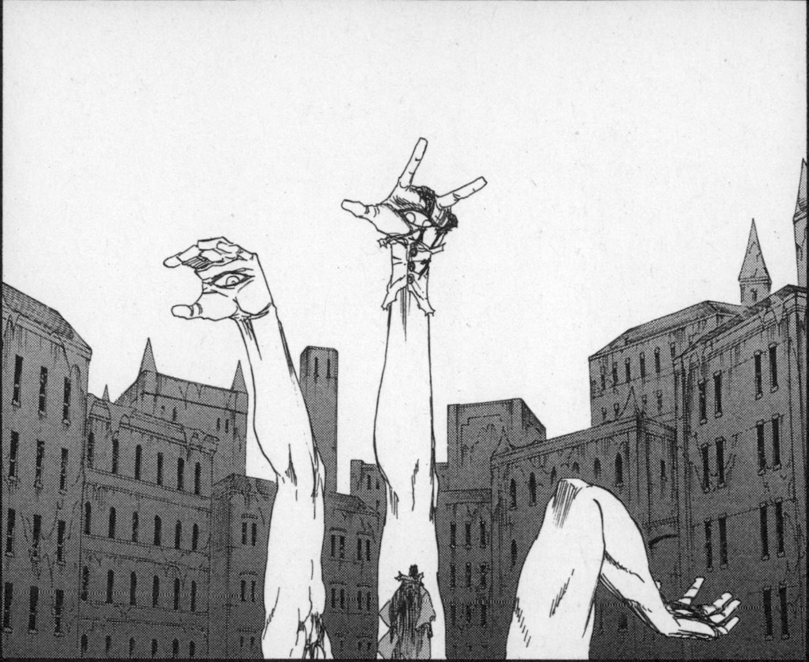

BLEACH 639.

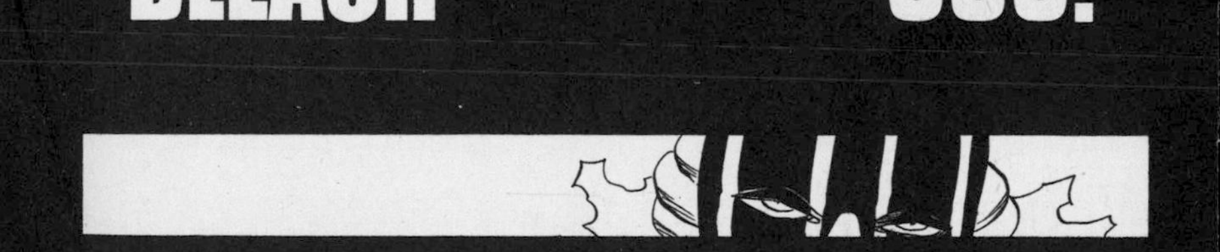

BABY,HOLD YOUR HAND 2

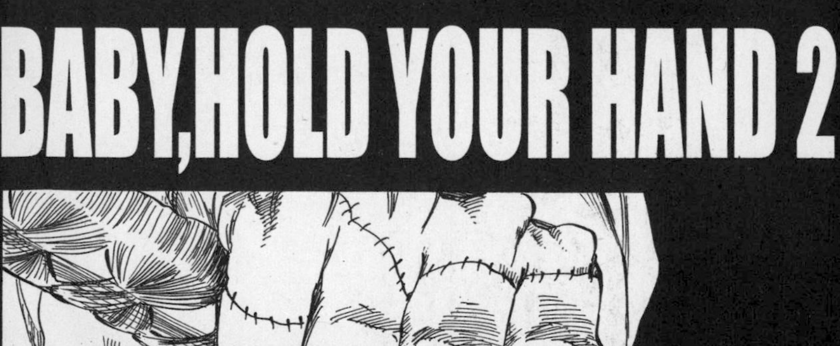

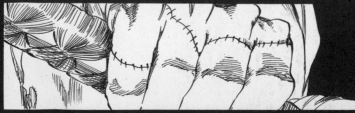

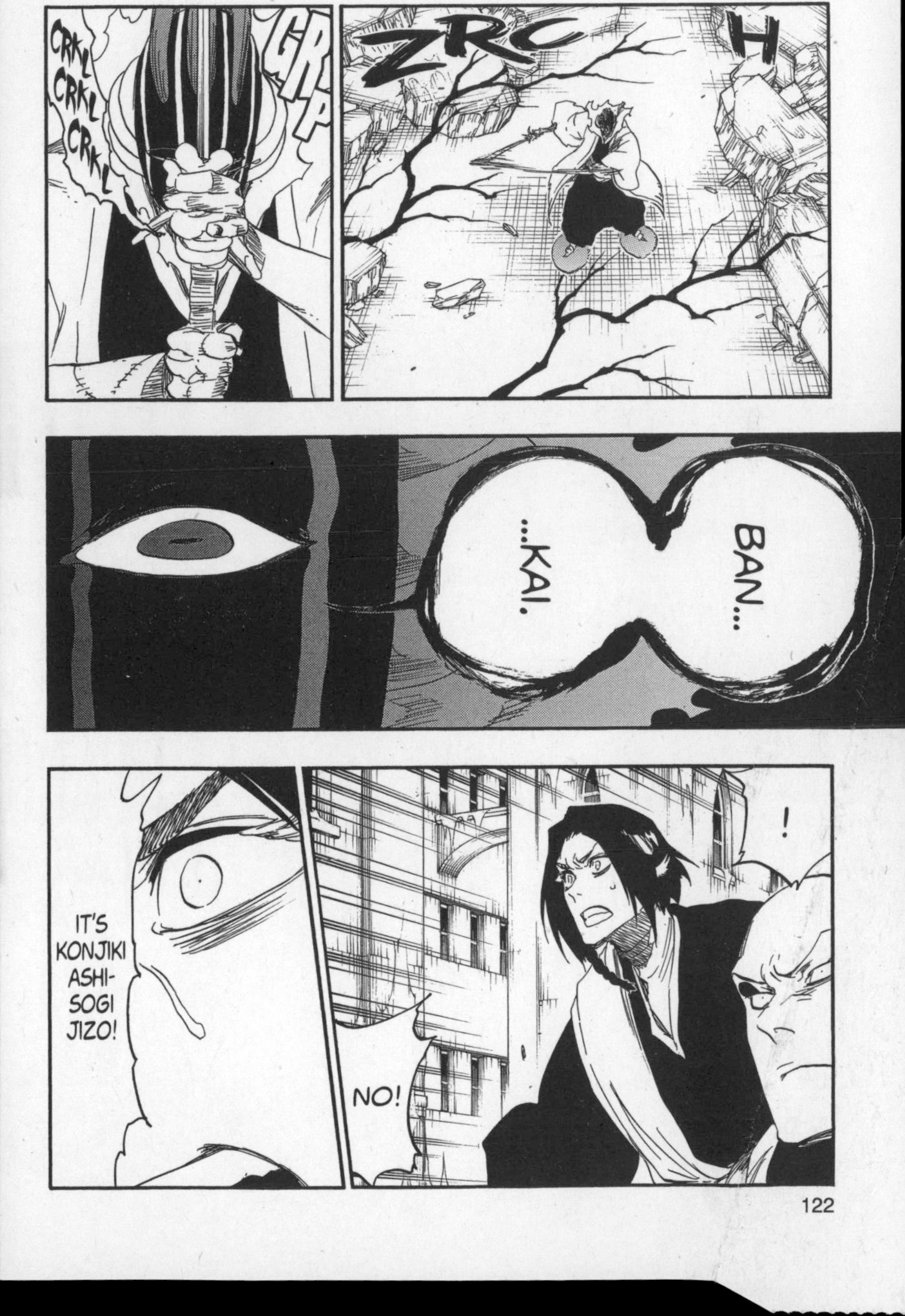
ZRCH
GRP
CRKL CRKL CRKL
BAN...
...KAI.
!
NO!
IT'S KONJIKI ASHI-SOGI JIZO!

READ THIS WAY

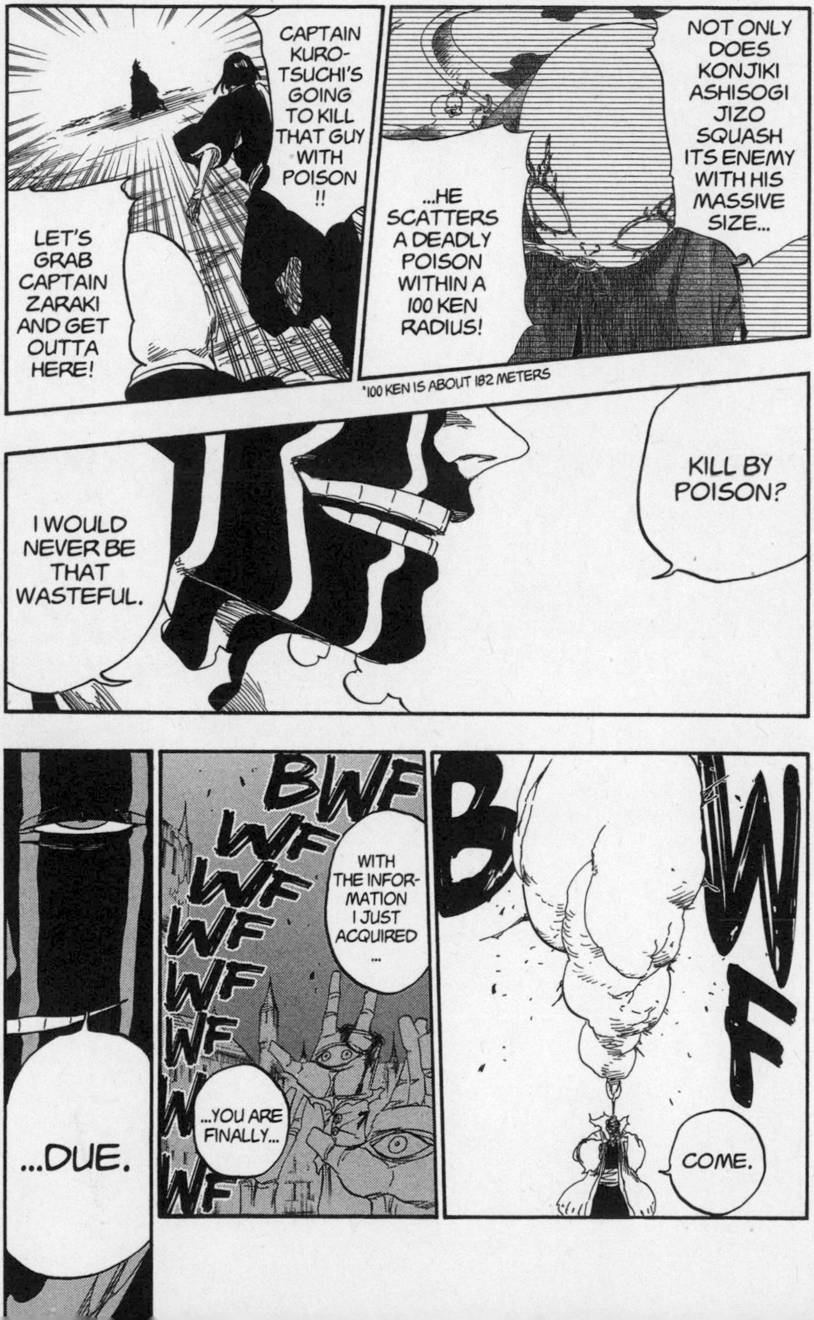
NOT ONLY DOES KONJIKI ASHISOGI JIZO SQUASH ITS ENEMY WITH HIS MASSIVE SIZE...
...HE SCATTERS A DEADLY POISON WITHIN A 100 KEN RADIUS!
CAPTAIN KURO-TSUCHI'S GOING TO KILL THAT GUY WITH POISON !!
LET'S GRAB CAPTAIN ZARAKI AND GET OUTTA HERE!
*100 KEN IS ABOUT 182 METERS
KILL BY POISON?
I WOULD NEVER BE THAT WASTEFUL.
BWF
COME.
BWF WF WF WF WF WF W WF
WITH THE INFORMATION I JUST ACQUIRED ...
...YOU ARE FINALLY...
...DUE.

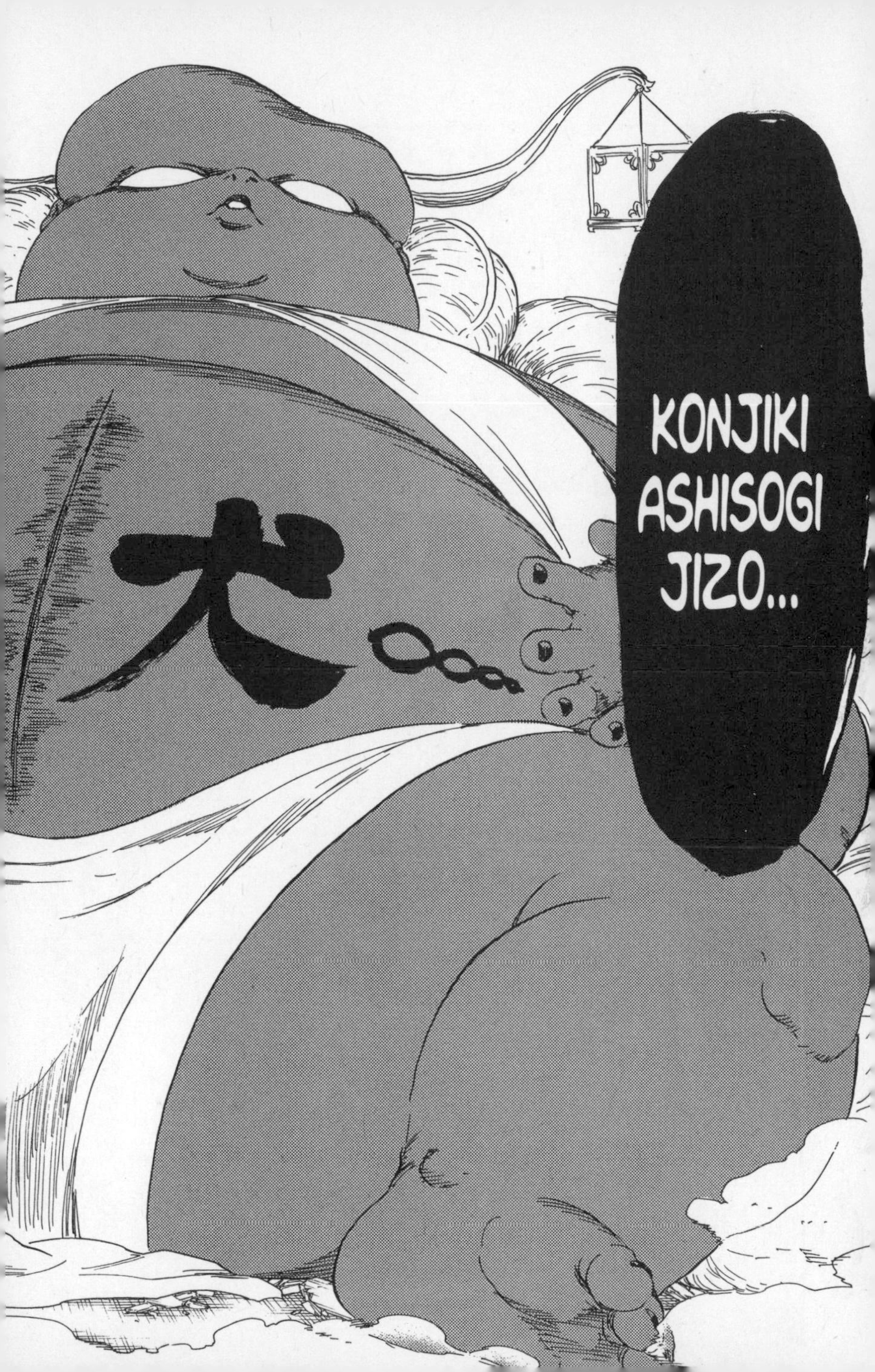
KONJIKI ASHISOGI JIZO...

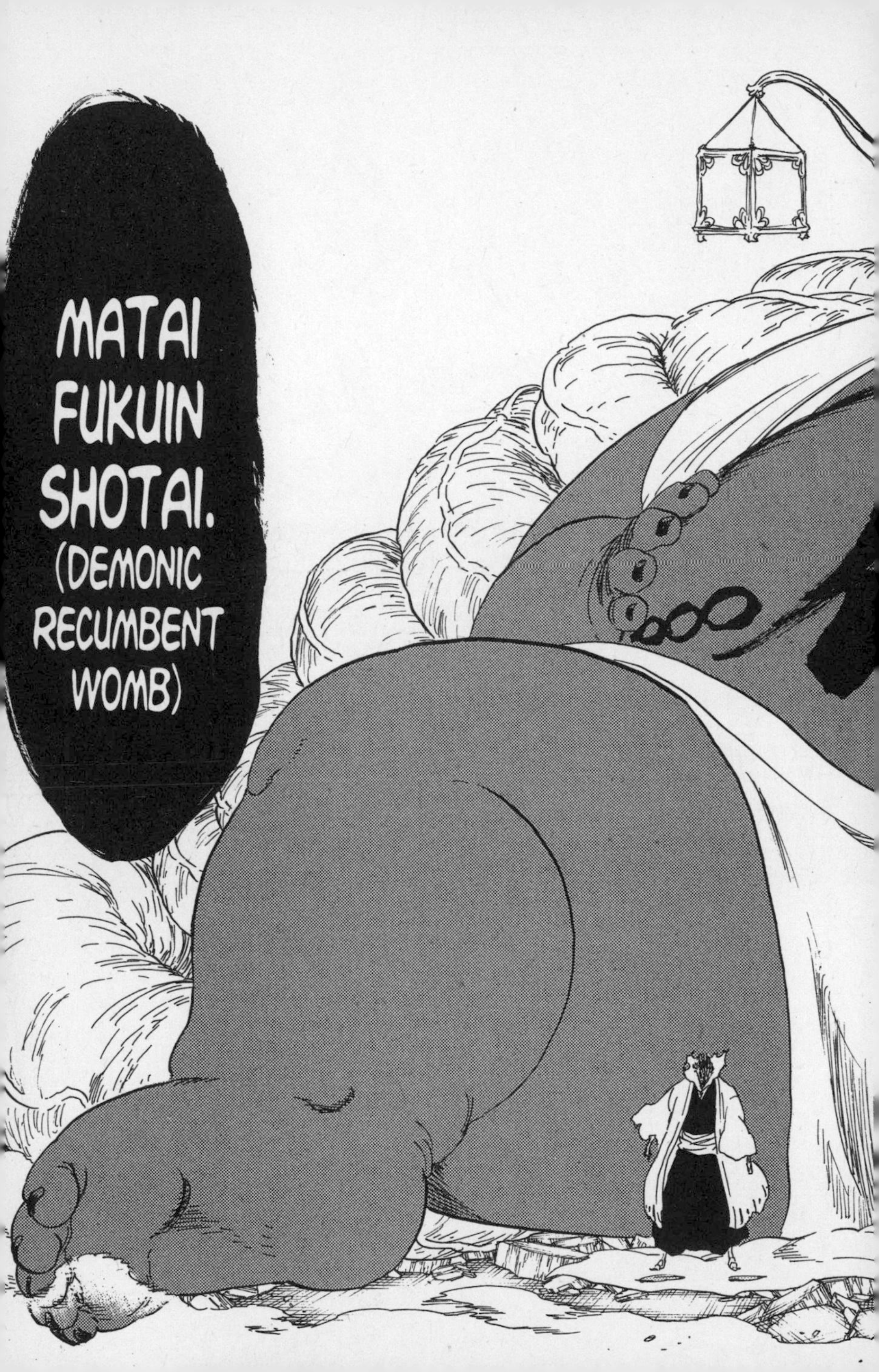
MATAI FUKUIN SHOTAI.
(DEMONIC RECUMBENT WOMB)

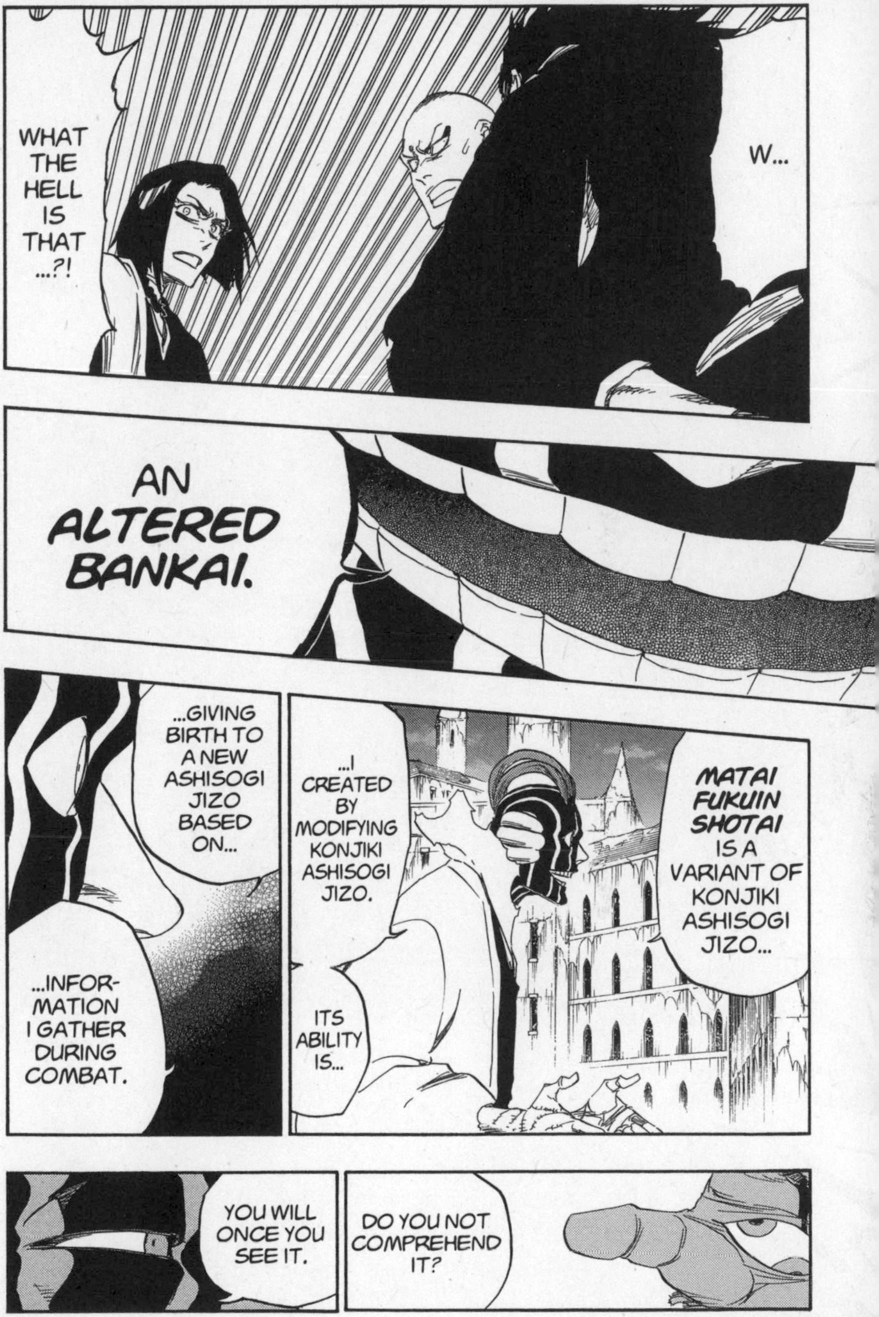
W...
WHAT THE HELL IS THAT ...?!
AN ALTERED BANKAI.
MATAI FUKUIN SHOTAI IS A VARIANT OF KONJIKI ASHISOGI JIZO...
...I CREATED BY MODIFYING KONJIKI ASHISOGI JIZO.
ITS ABILITY IS...
...GIVING BIRTH TO A NEW ASHISOGI JIZO BASED ON...
...INFORMATION I GATHER DURING COMBAT.
DO YOU NOT COMPREHEND IT?
YOU WILL ONCE YOU SEE IT.

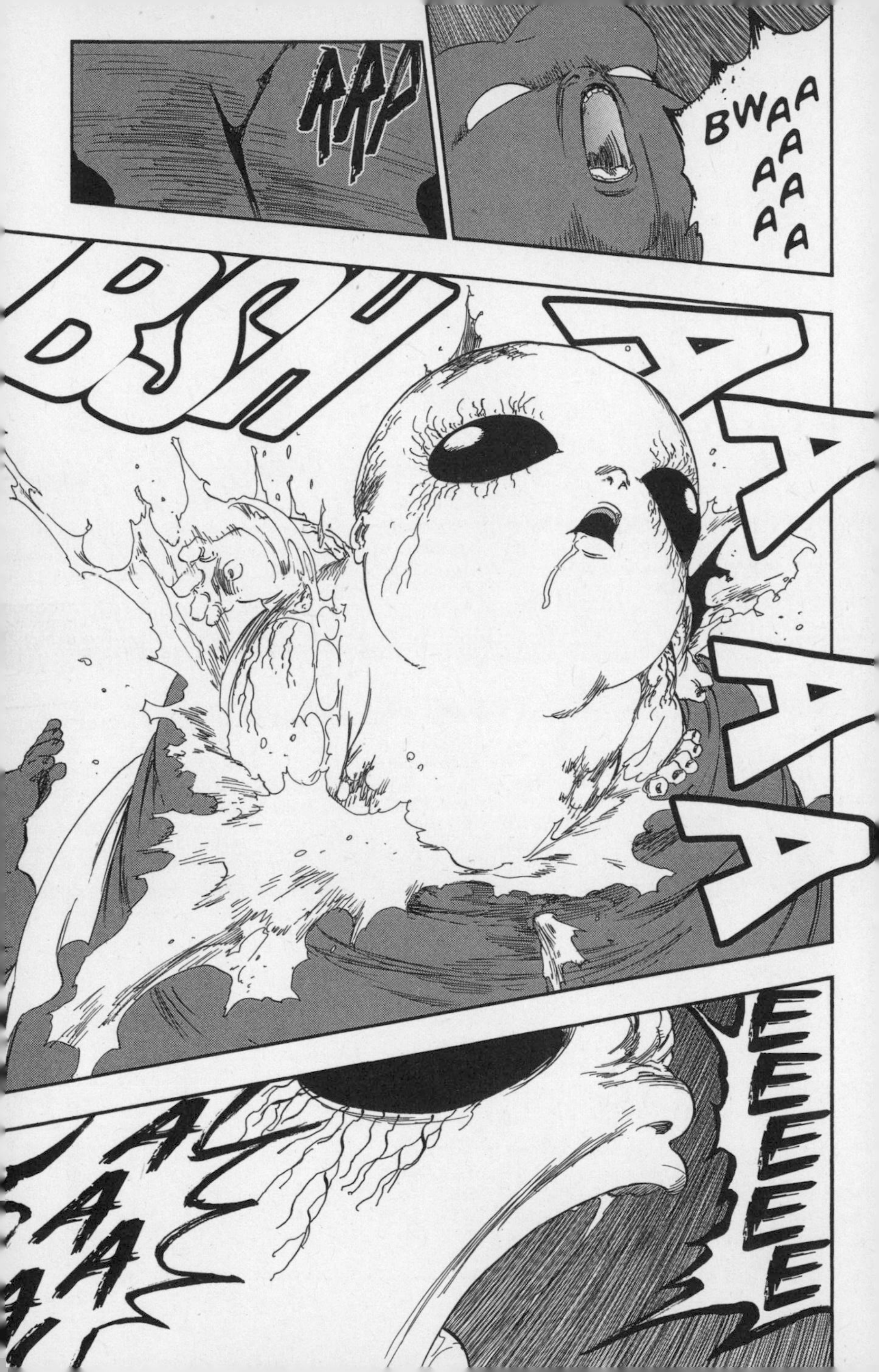
BWAAAAAAA
RRP
BSHAAAA
EEEEEEEEE

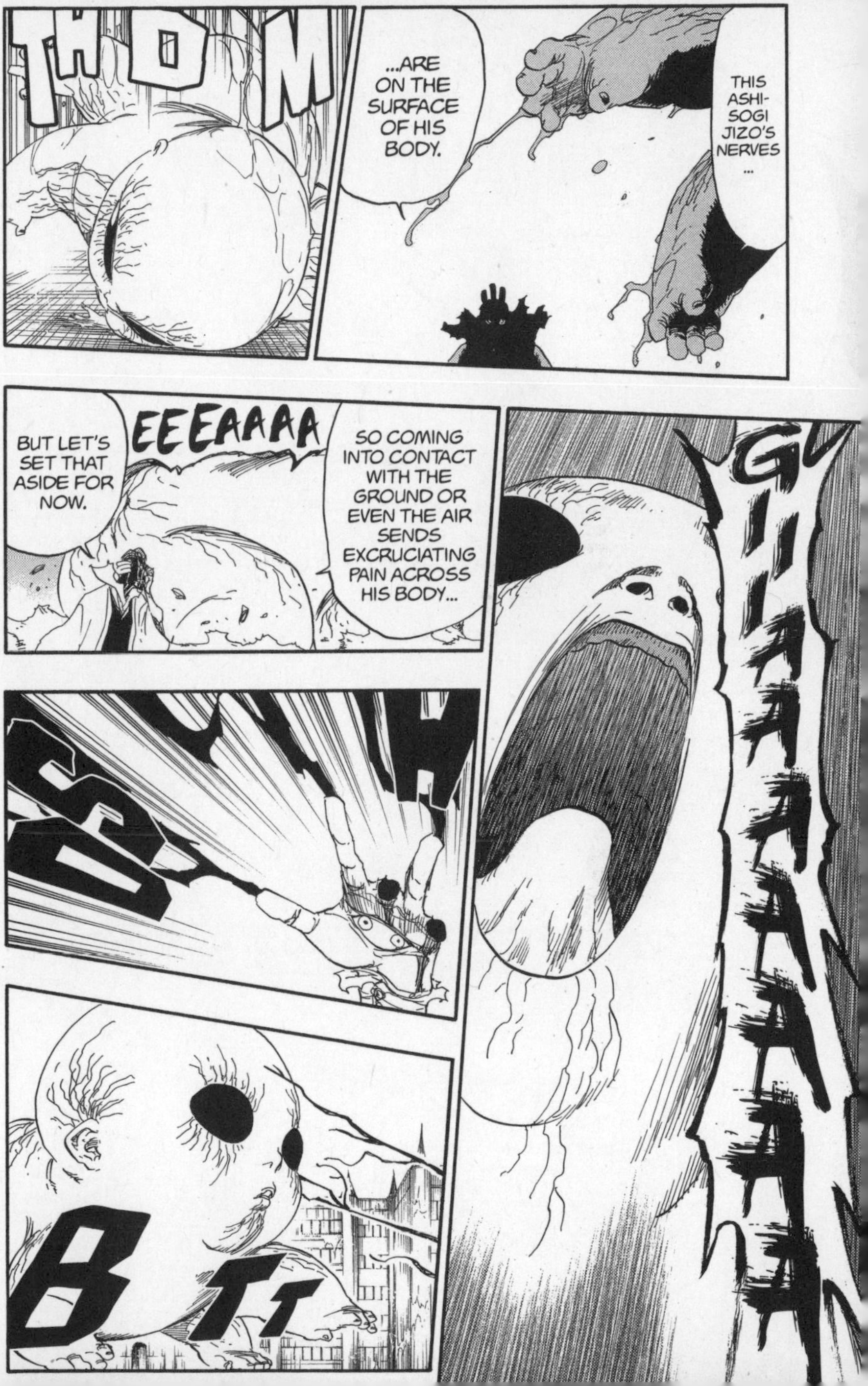

THIS ASHI-SOGI JIZO'S NERVES ...
...ARE ON THE SURFACE OF HIS BODY.
THOOM
SO COMING INTO CONTACT WITH THE GROUND OR EVEN THE AIR SENDS EXCRUCIATING PAIN ACROSS HIS BODY...
EEEAAAA
BUT LET'S SET THAT ASIDE FOR NOW.

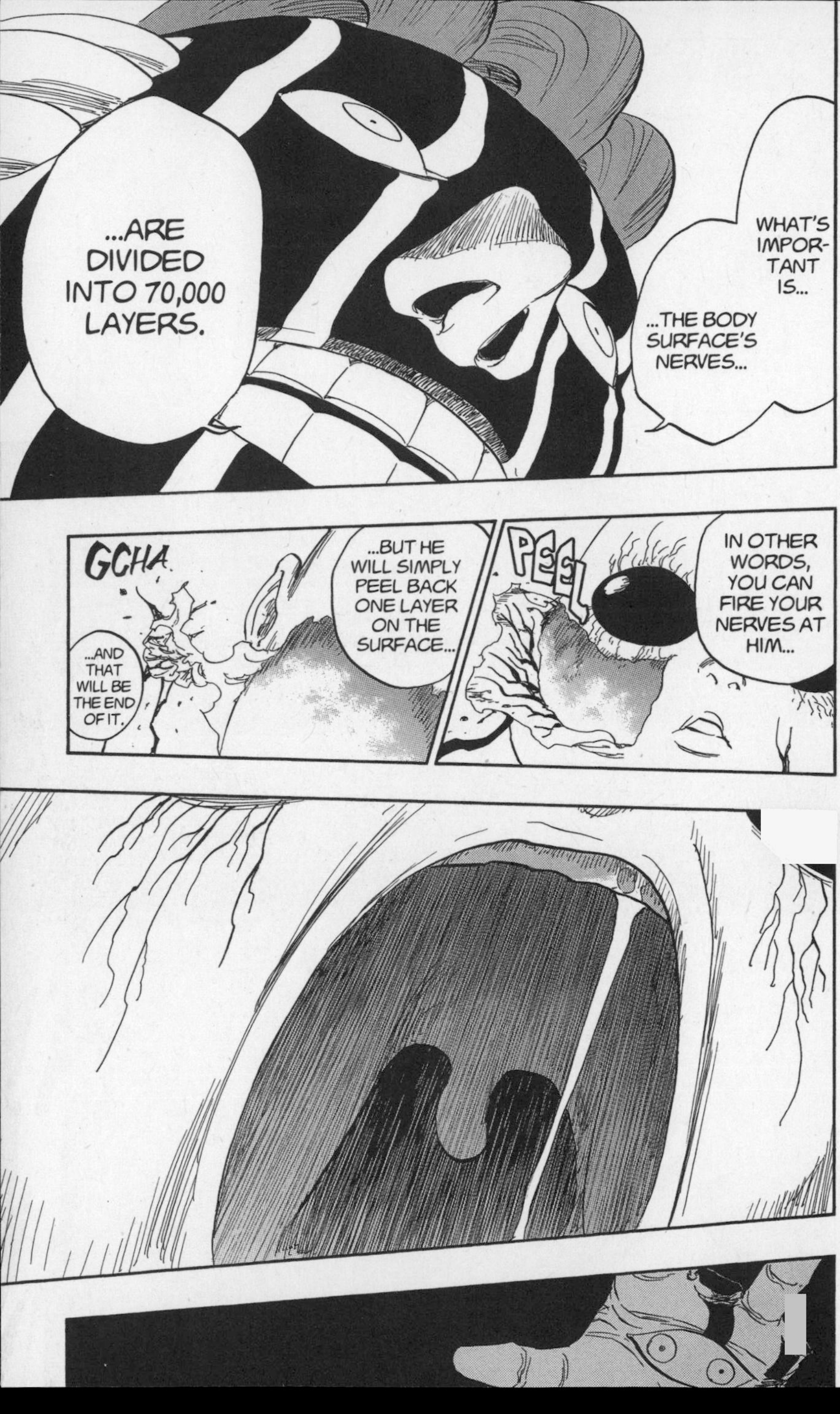
WHAT'S IMPORTANT IS...
...THE BODY SURFACE'S NERVES...
...ARE DIVIDED INTO 70,000 LAYERS.
IN OTHER WORDS, YOU CAN FIRE YOUR NERVES AT HIM...
PEEL
...BUT HE WILL SIMPLY PEEL BACK ONE LAYER ON THE SURFACE...
GCHA
...AND THAT WILL BE THE END OF IT.

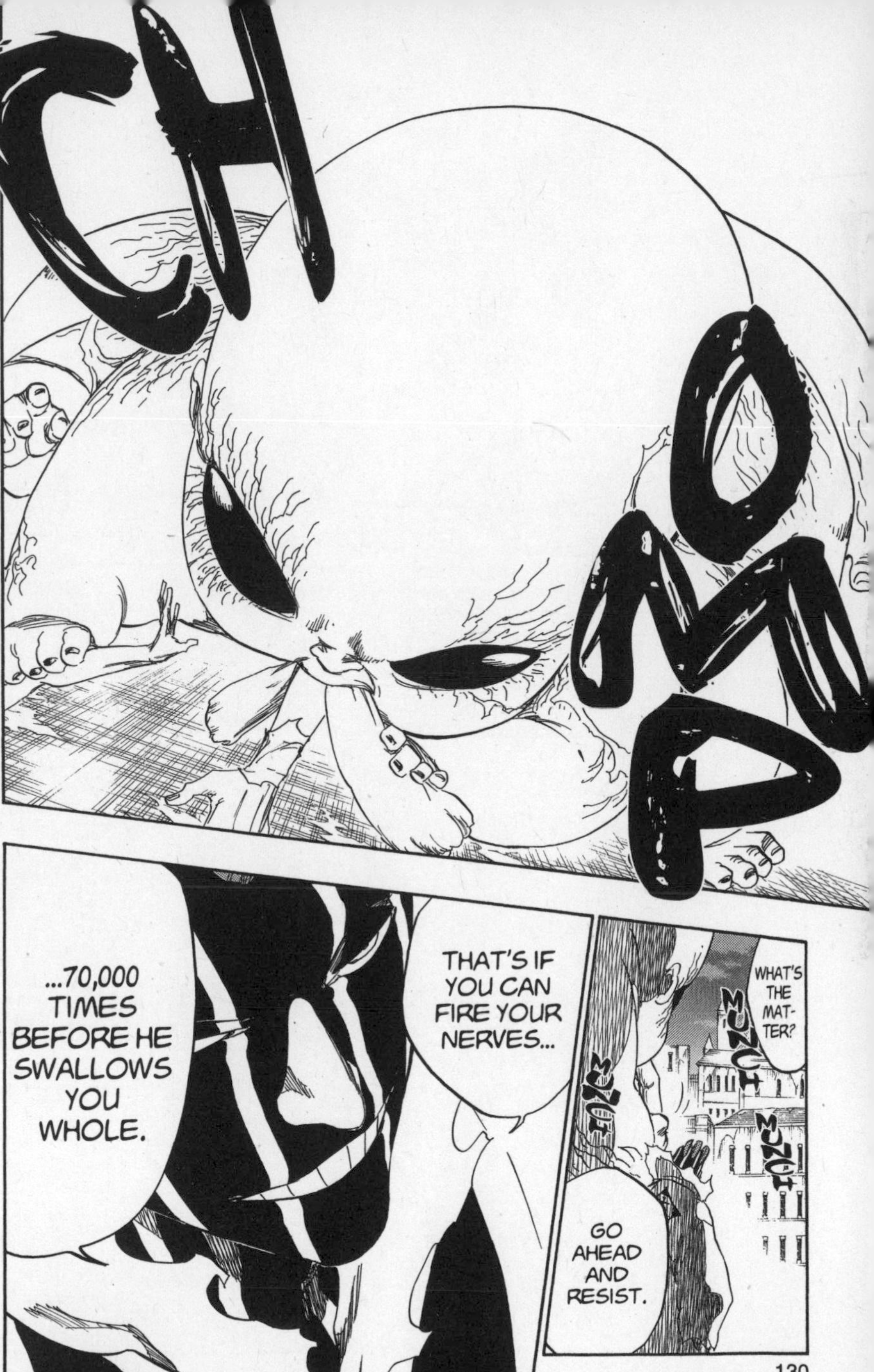
CHOMP
WHAT'S THE MATTER?
MUNCH
MUNCH
MUNCH
GO AHEAD AND RESIST.
THAT'S IF YOU CAN FIRE YOUR NERVES...
...70,000 TIMES BEFORE HE SWALLOWS YOU WHOLE.

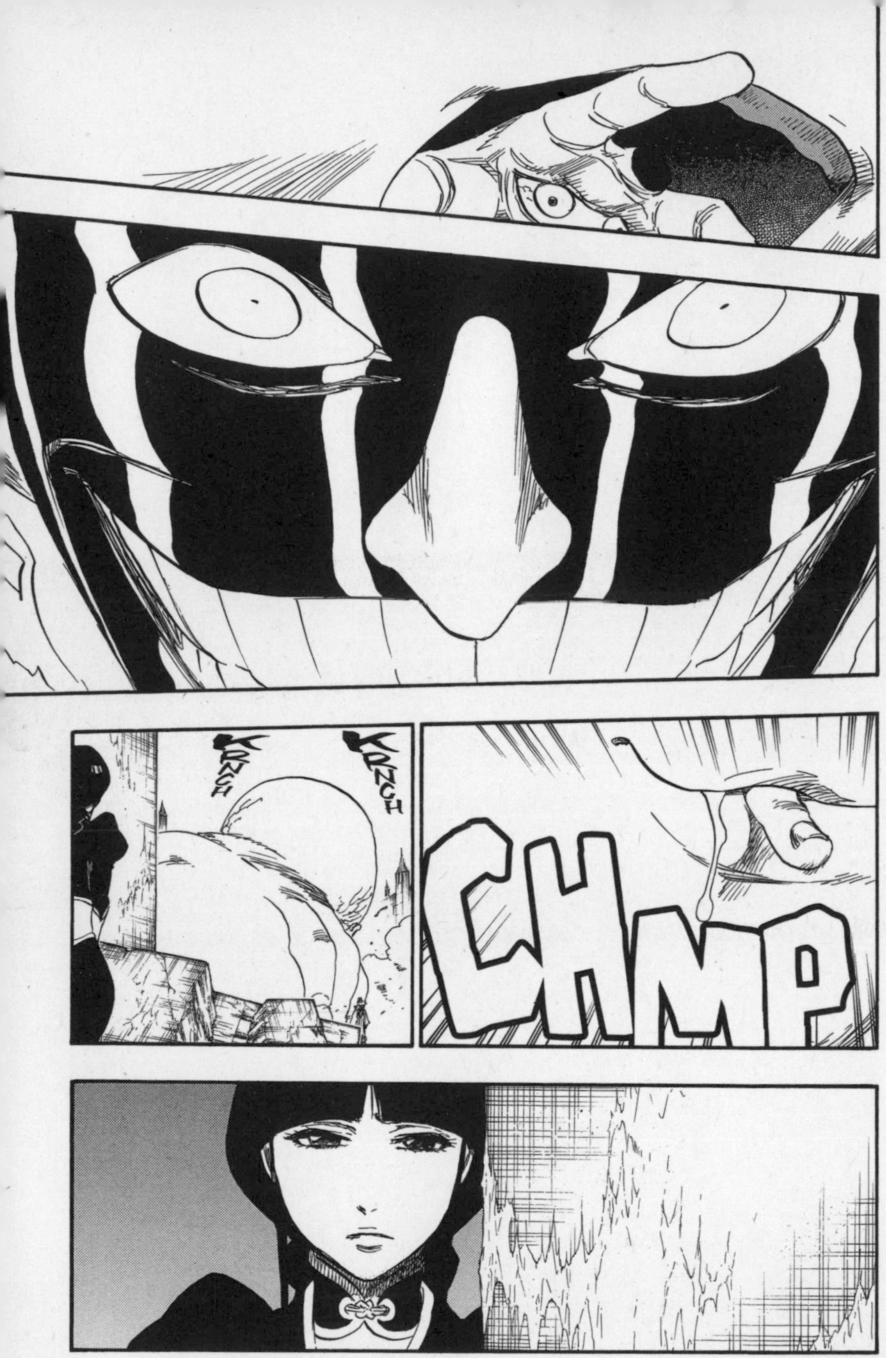
CHMP
KRNCH
KRNCH

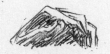

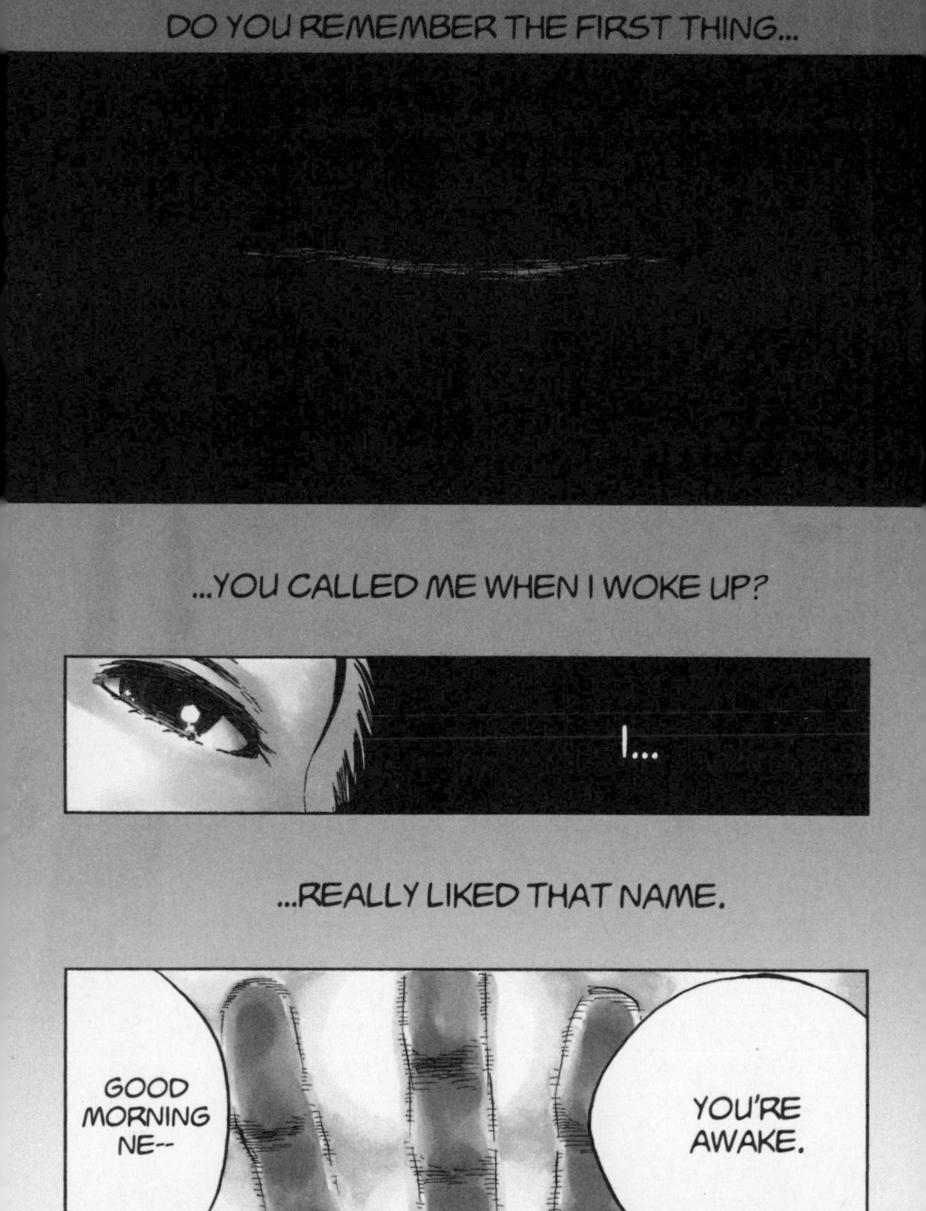

DO YOU REMEMBER THE FIRST THING...

...YOU CALLED ME WHEN I WOKE UP?

I...

...REALLY LIKED THAT NAME.

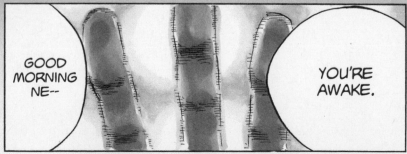

GOOD MORNING NE--

YOU'RE AWAKE.

640. BABY, HOLD YOUR HAND 3 (MAD LULLABY NO.7)

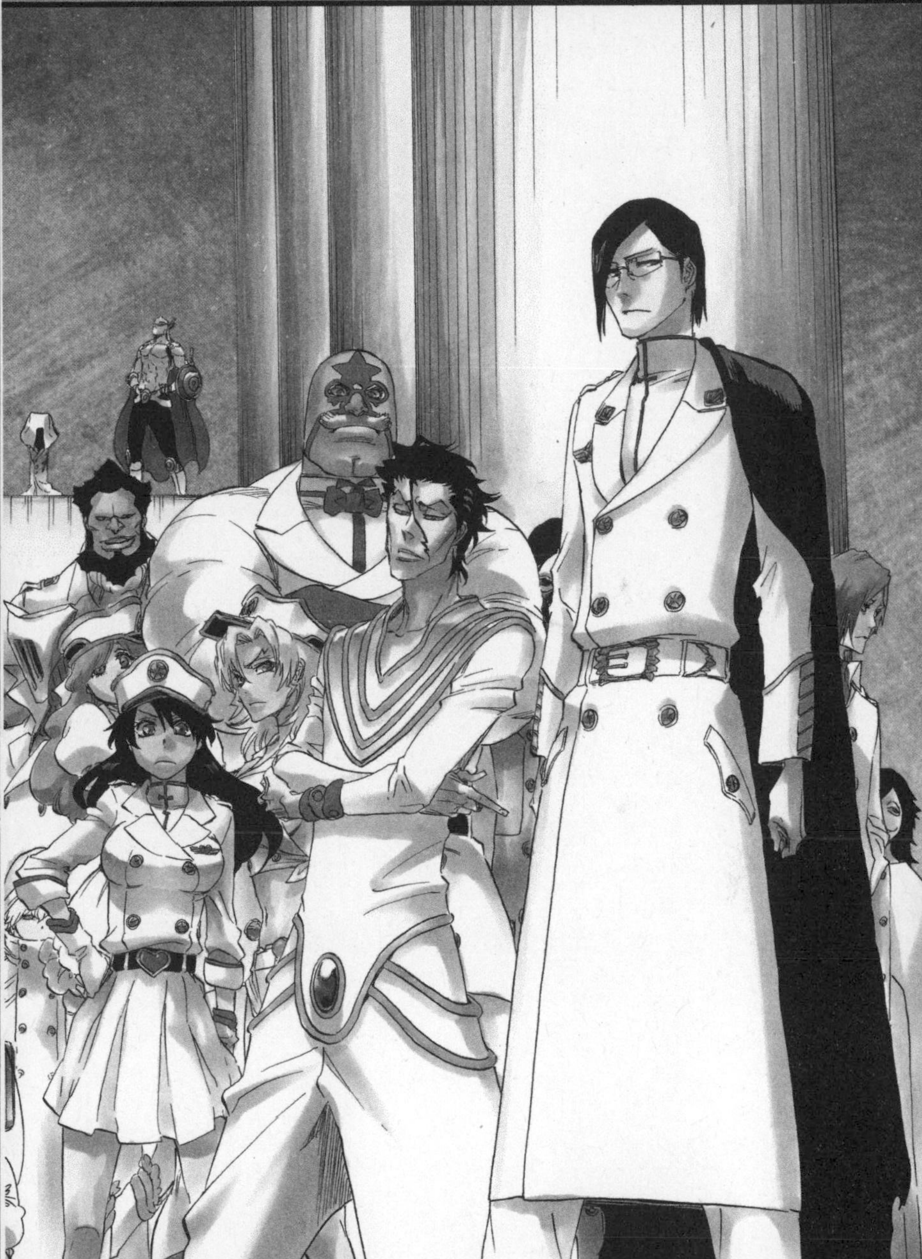

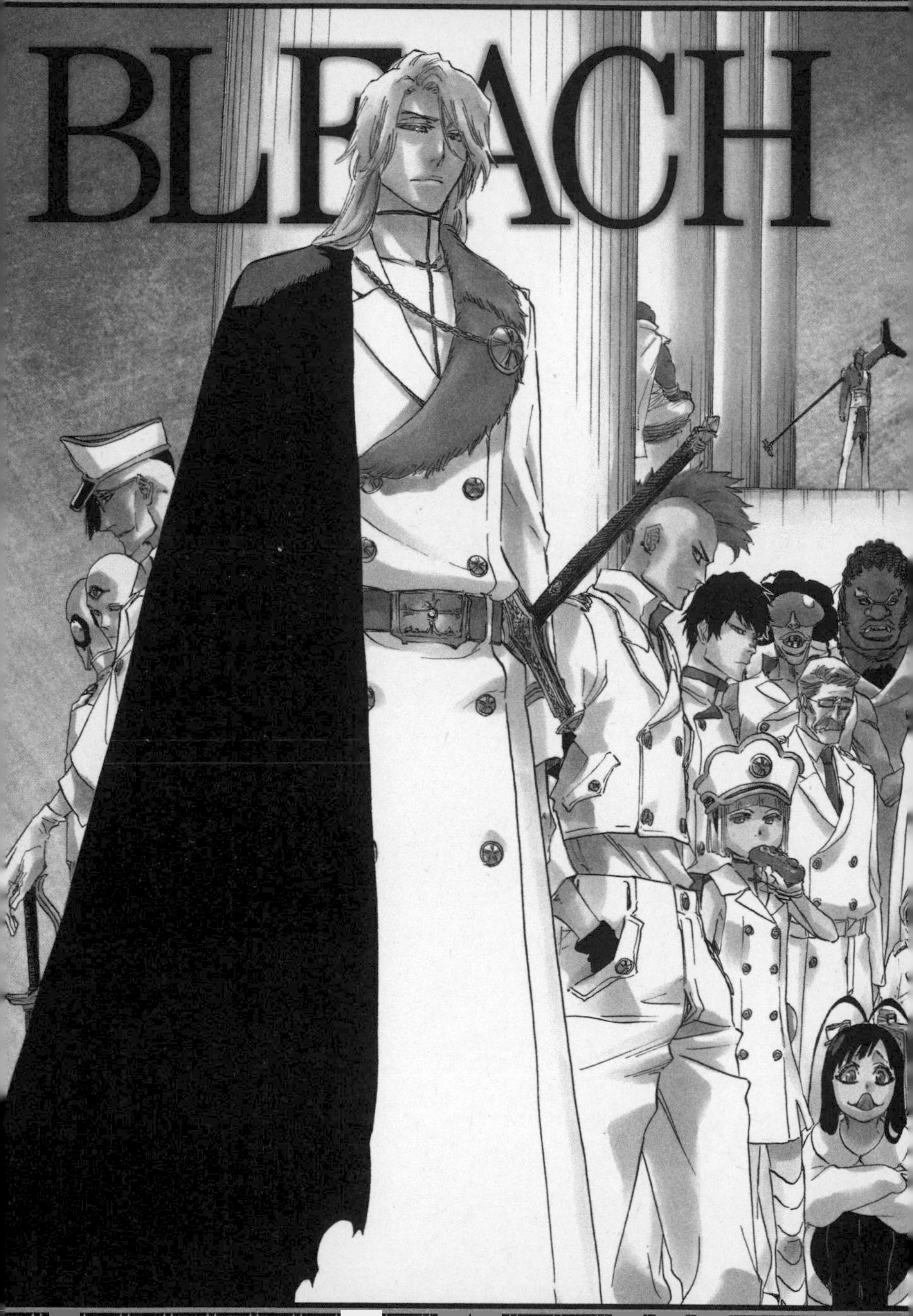
BLEACH

BLEACH
ブリーチ

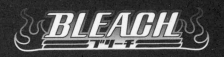

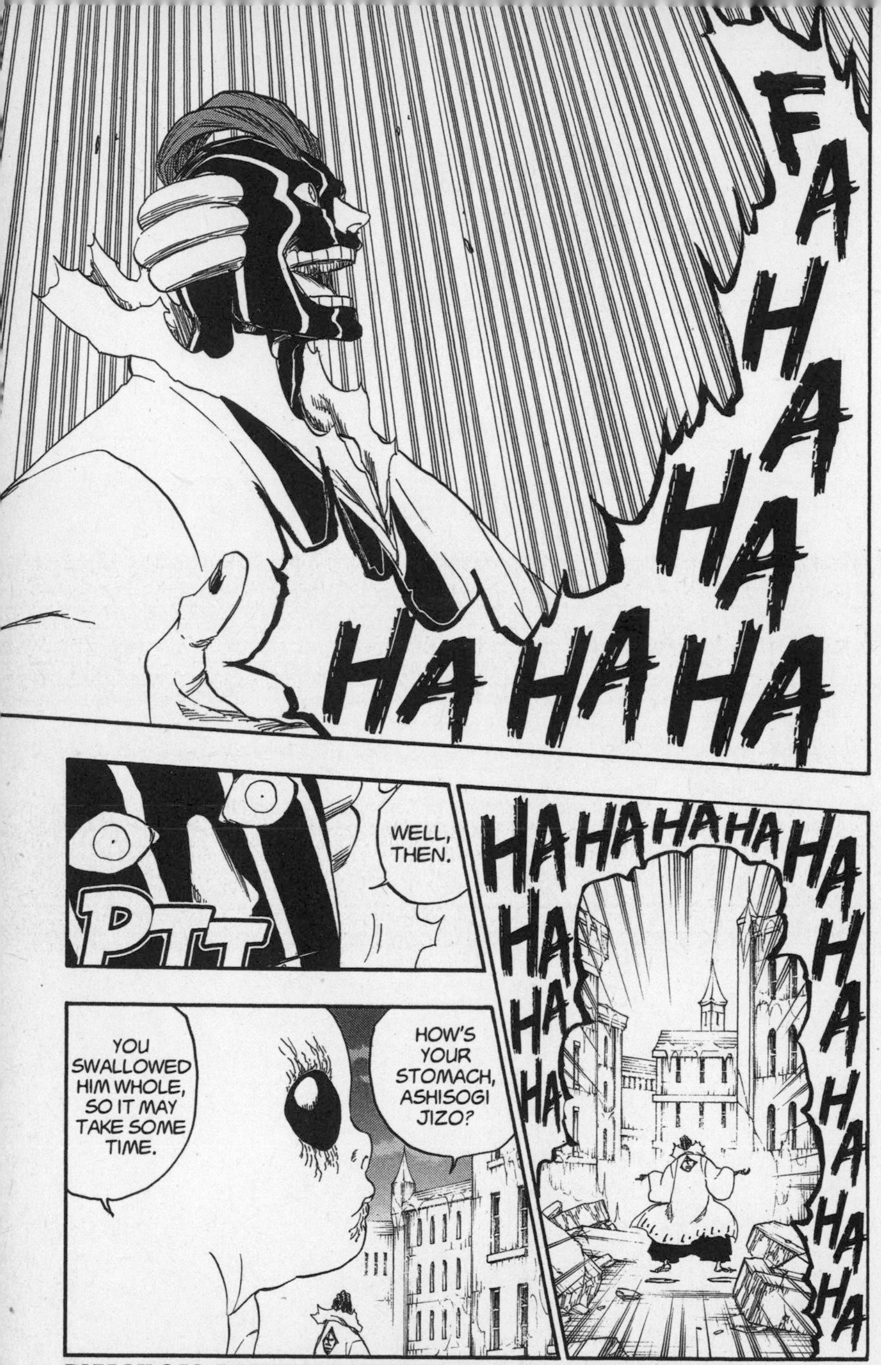
FAHAHAHAHAHA
HA HA HA HA
HAHAHAHAHAHA
HA HA HA HA
HAHAHAHAHAHAHAHAHA
PTT
WELL, THEN.
HOW'S YOUR STOMACH, ASHISOGI JIZO?
YOU SWALLOWED HIM WHOLE, SO IT MAY TAKE SOME TIME.

BLEACH 640. BABY,HOLD YOUR HAND 3 〔Mad Lullaby no.7〕

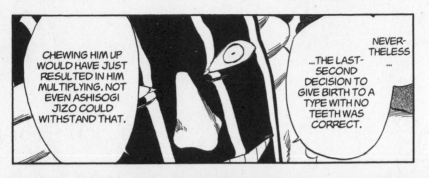

NEVERTHELESS...

...THE LAST-SECOND DECISION TO GIVE BIRTH TO A TYPE WITH NO TEETH WAS CORRECT.

CHEWING HIM UP WOULD HAVE JUST RESULTED IN HIM MULTIPLYING. NOT EVEN ASHISOGI JIZO COULD WITHSTAND THAT.

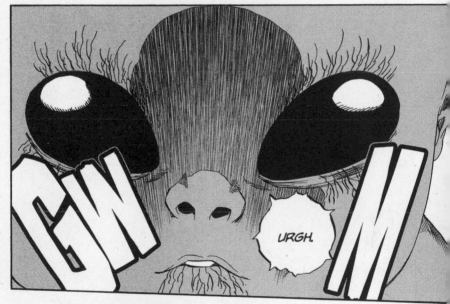

URGH.

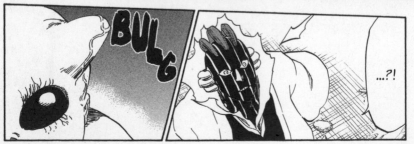

BULG

...?!

138

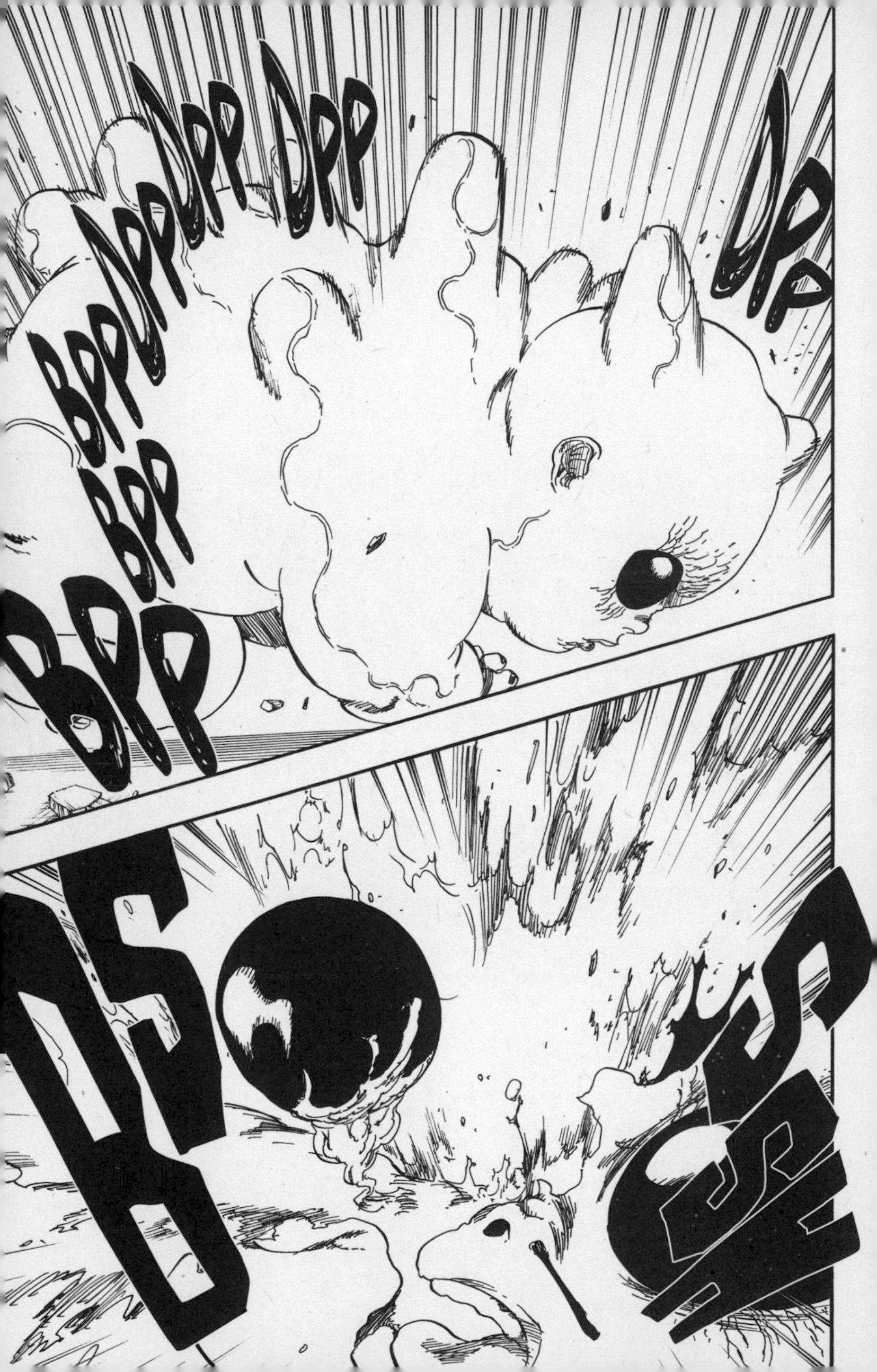
DPP
BPP BPP BPP DPP DPP DPP DPP

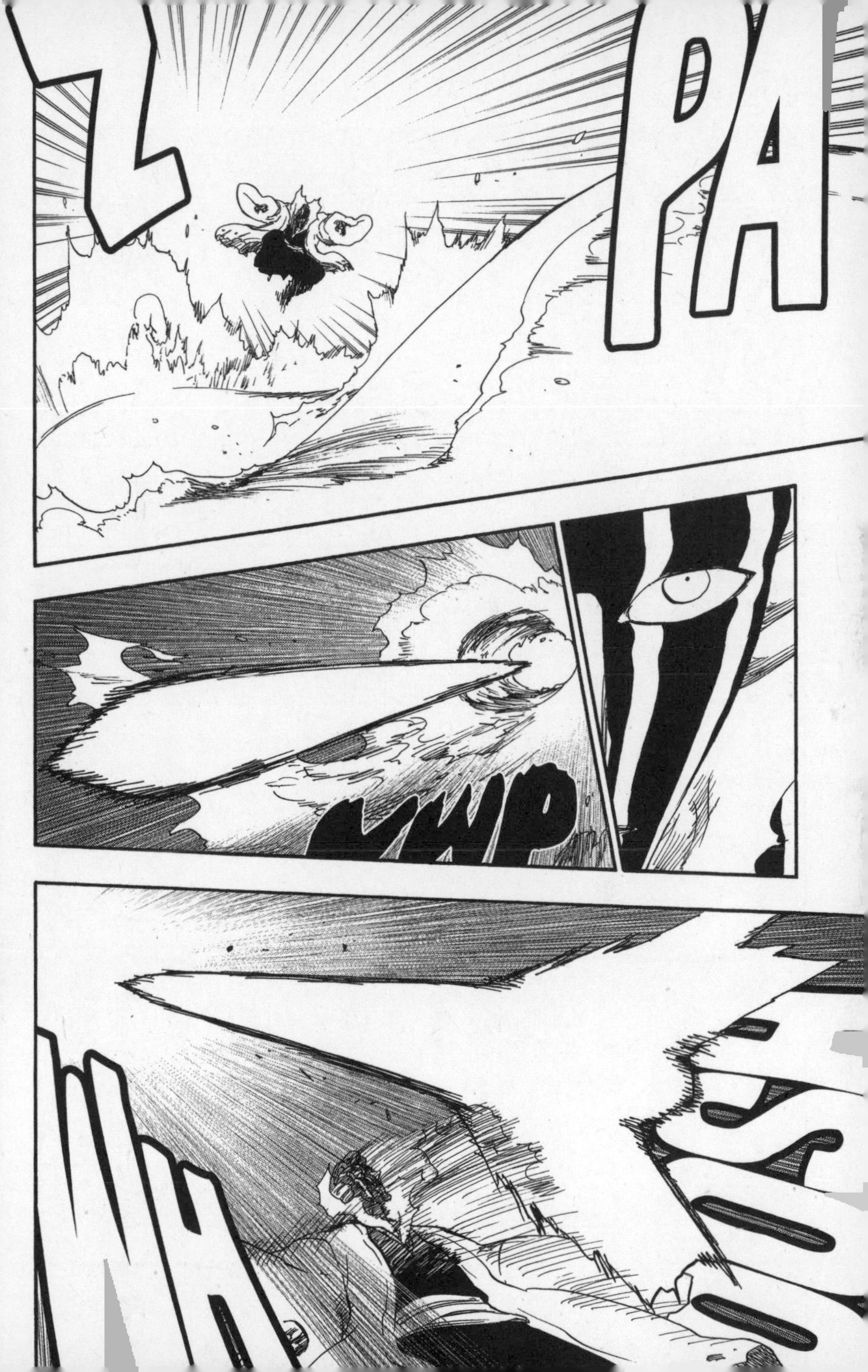
PA
Z
WMP
WH
OOSH

READ THIS WAY

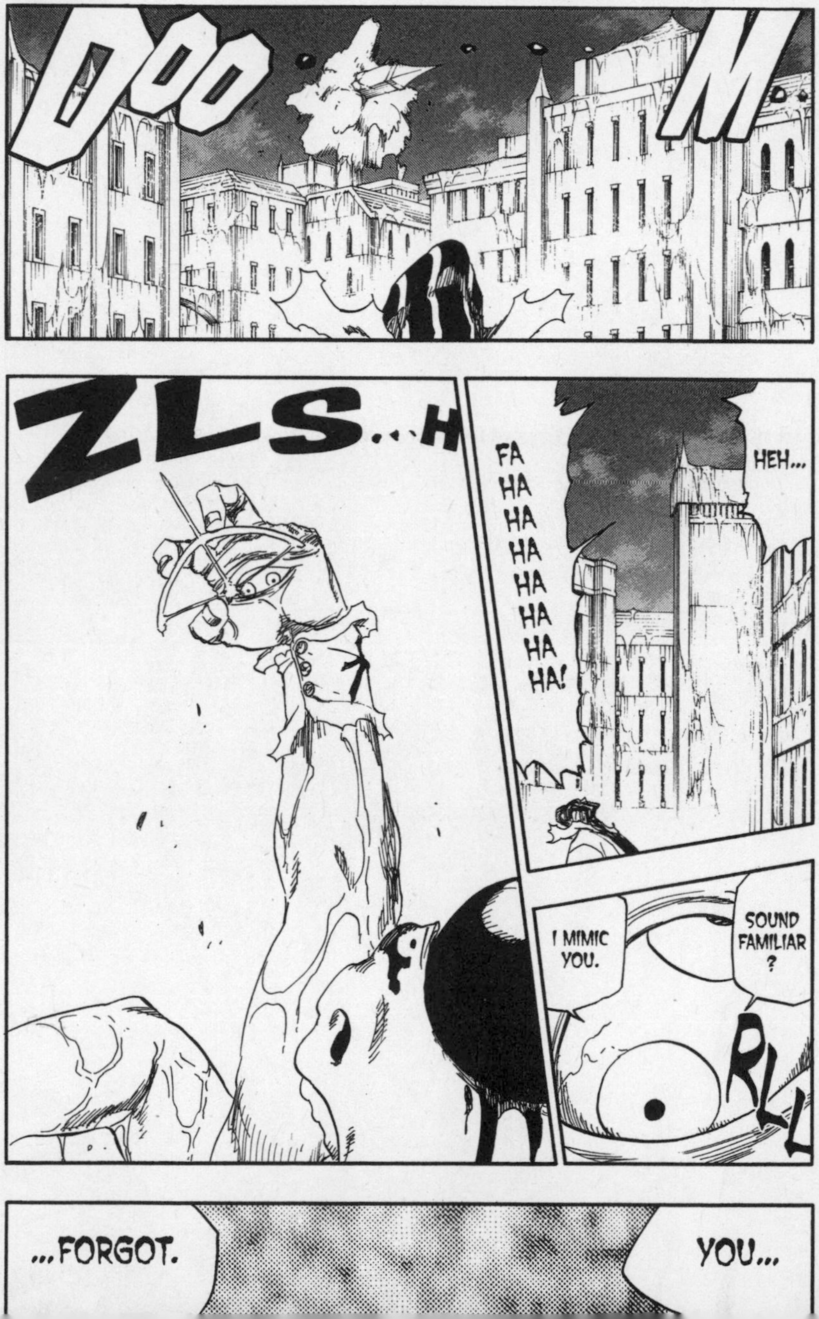

DOO
M
HEH...
FA HA HA HA HA HA HA HA!
SOUND FAMILIAR ?
I MIMIC YOU.
RLL
ZLS...H
YOU...
...FORGOT.

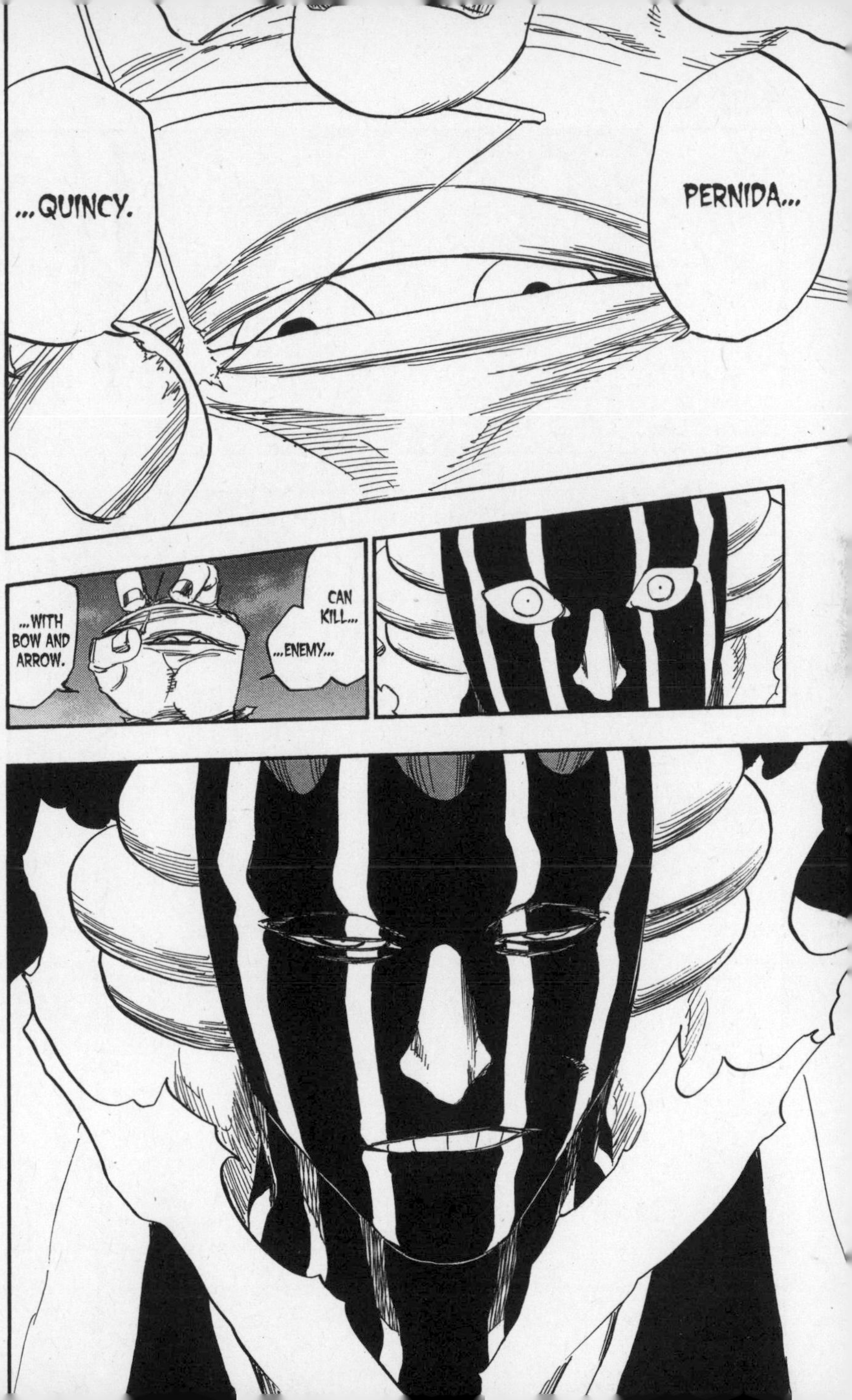
PERNIDA...
...QUINCY.
CAN KILL...
...ENEMY...
...WITH BOW AND ARROW.

READ THIS WAY

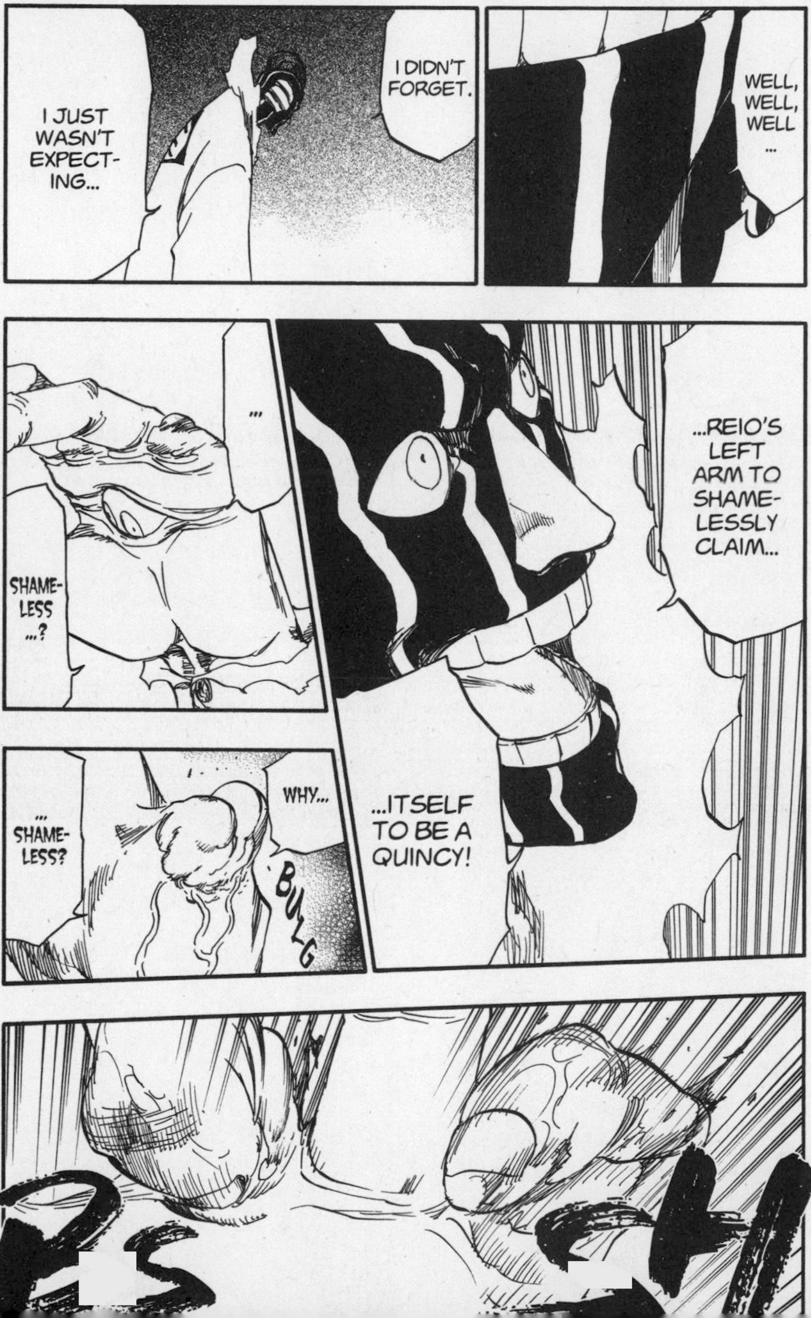
WELL, WELL, WELL ...
I DIDN'T FORGET.
I JUST WASN'T EXPECTING...
...REIO'S LEFT ARM TO SHAMELESSLY CLAIM...
...ITSELF TO BE A QUINCY!
...
SHAMELESS ...?
WHY...
... SHAMELESS?
BULG

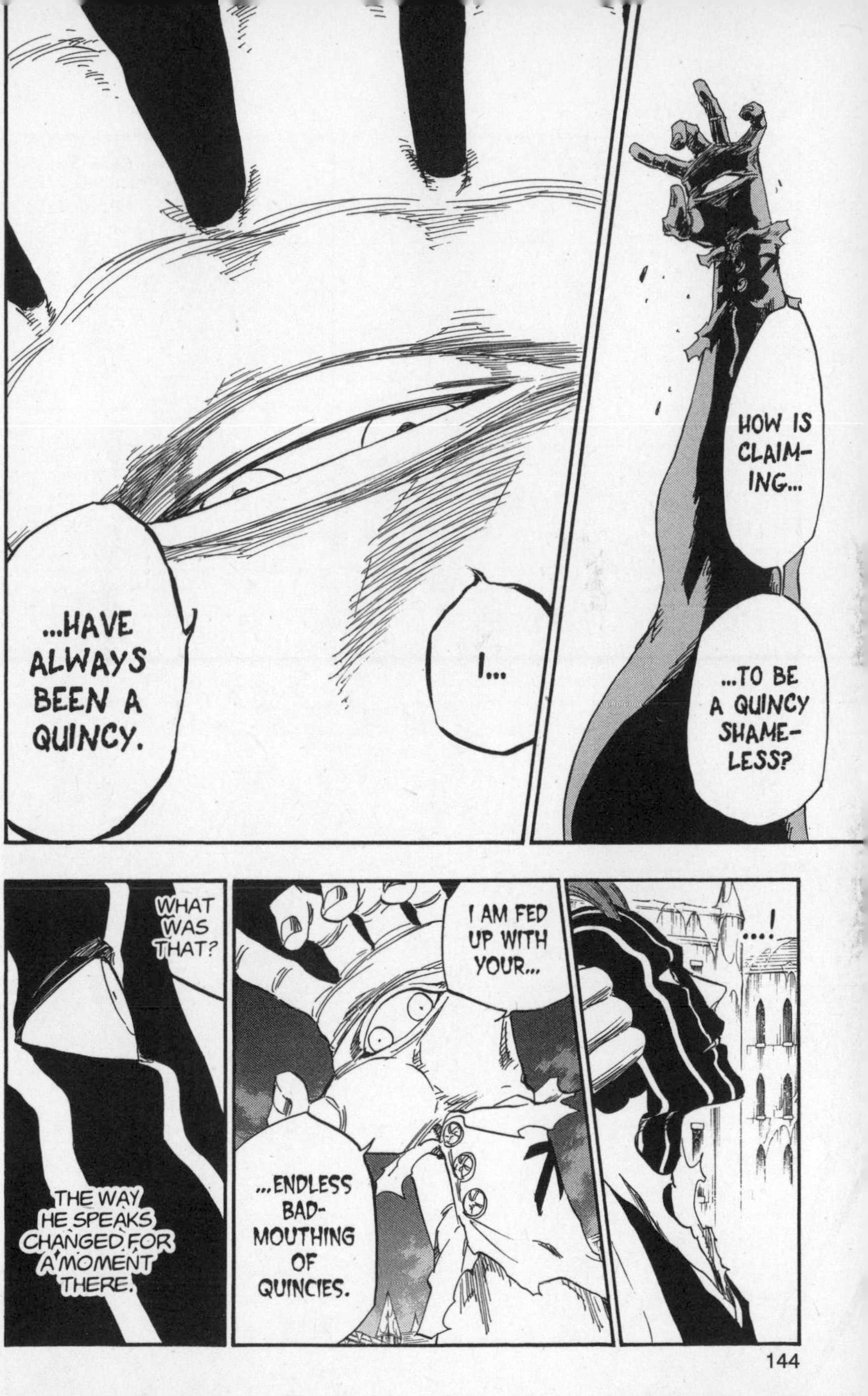
HOW IS CLAIMING...
...TO BE A QUINCY SHAMELESS?
I...
...HAVE ALWAYS BEEN A QUINCY.
...!
I AM FED UP WITH YOUR...
...ENDLESS BAD-MOUTHING OF QUINCIES.
WHAT WAS THAT?
THE WAY HE SPEAKS CHANGED FOR A MOMENT THERE.

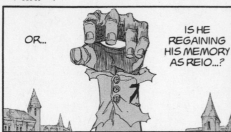

READ THIS WAY

HIS VOCABULARY HAS BEEN INCREASING...
...LITTLE BY LITTLE SINCE THIS BATTLE BEGAN.
IS HE REGAINING HIS MEMORY AS REIO...?
OR...
...IS HE SOME-HOW...
...EVOLVING?
KT...
NK...
WHAP

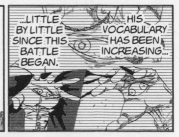

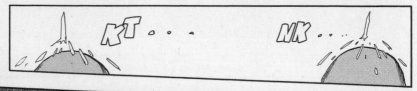

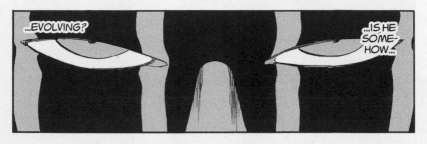

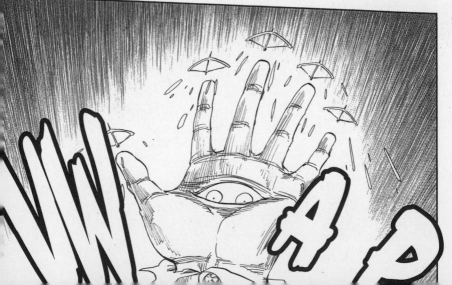

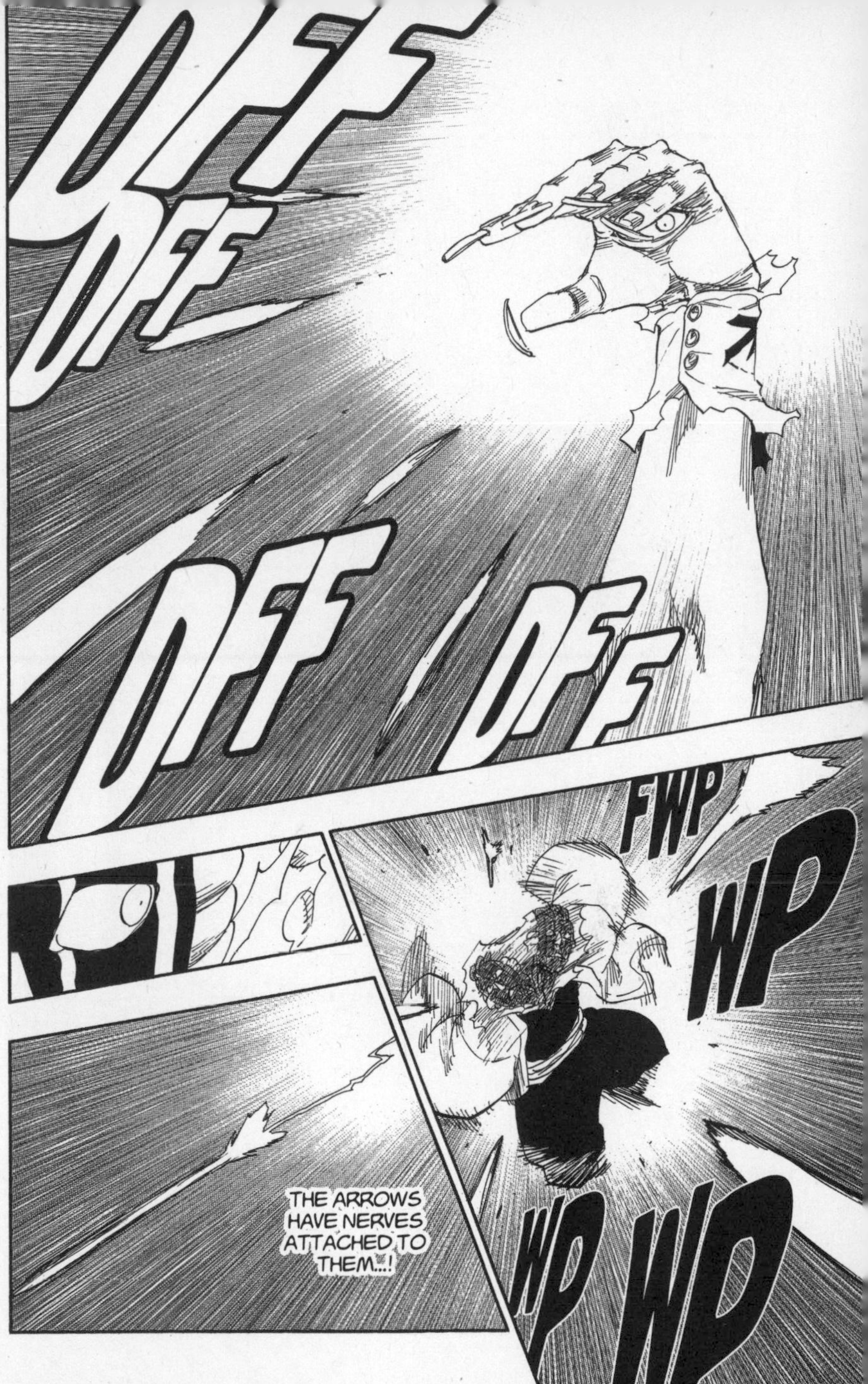
DFF
DFF
DFF
DFF
FWP
WP
WP
WP
THE ARROWS HAVE NERVES ATTACHED TO THEM...!

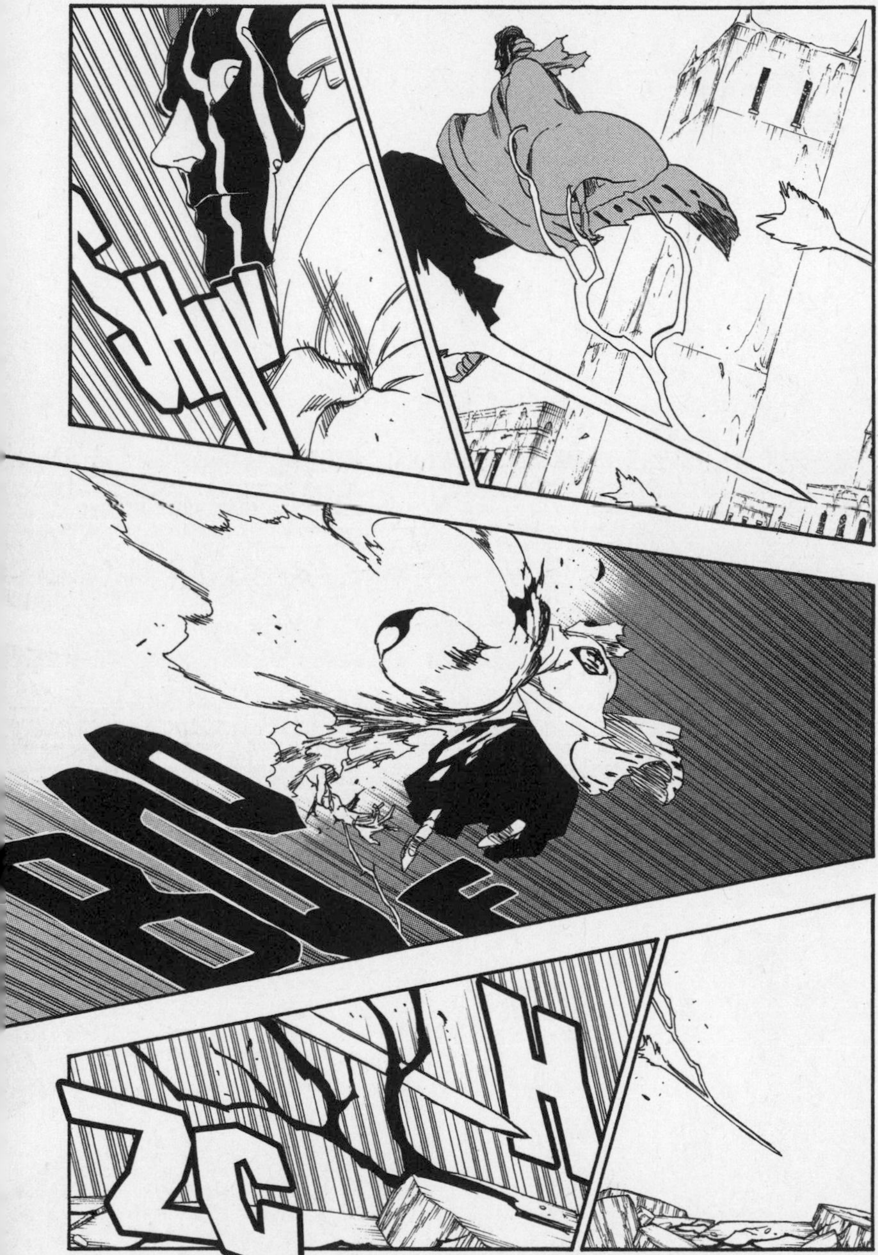
SHIV

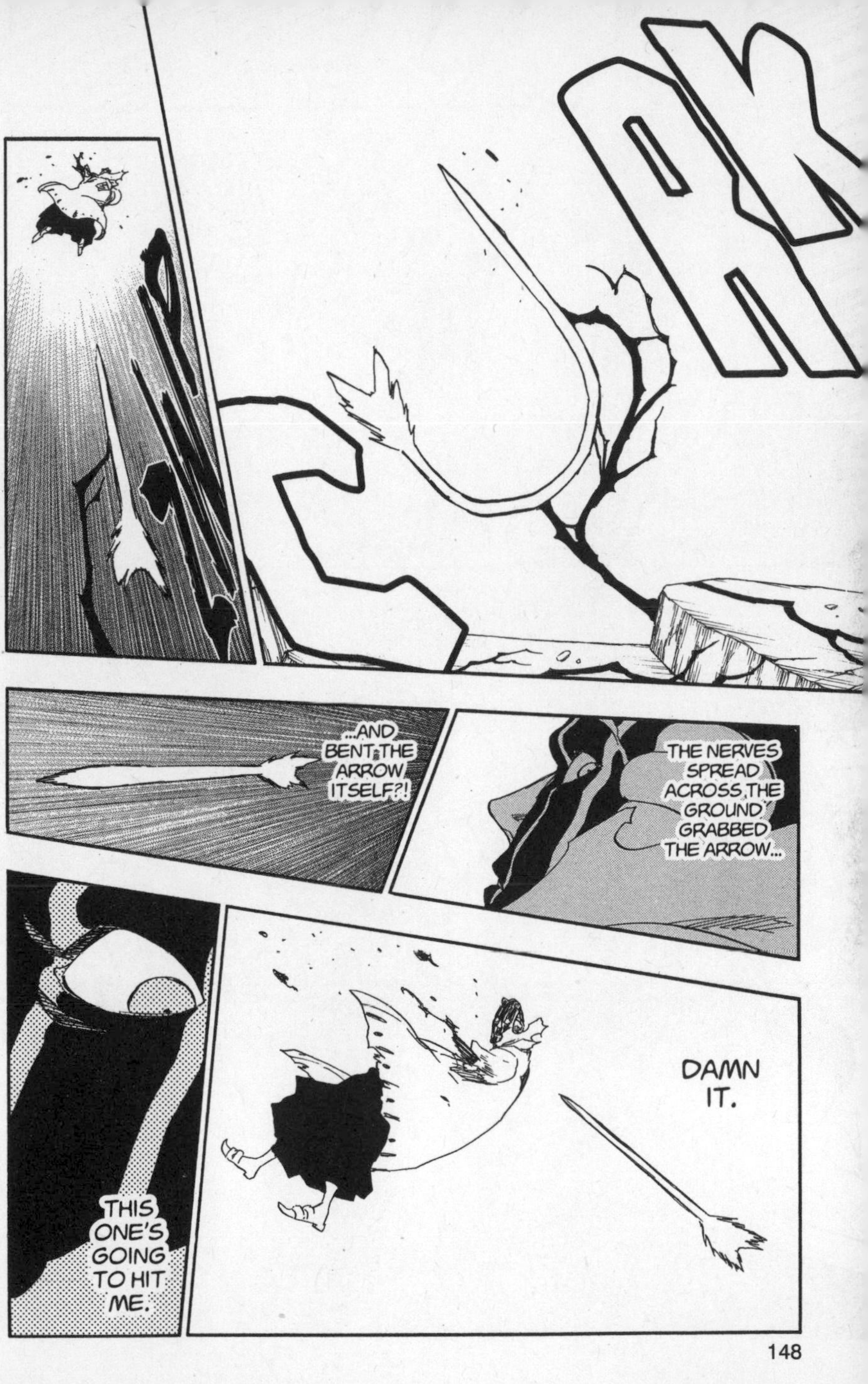
THE NERVES SPREAD ACROSS THE GROUND GRABBED THE ARROW...
...AND BENT THE ARROW ITSELF?!
DAMN IT.
THIS ONE'S GOING TO HIT ME.

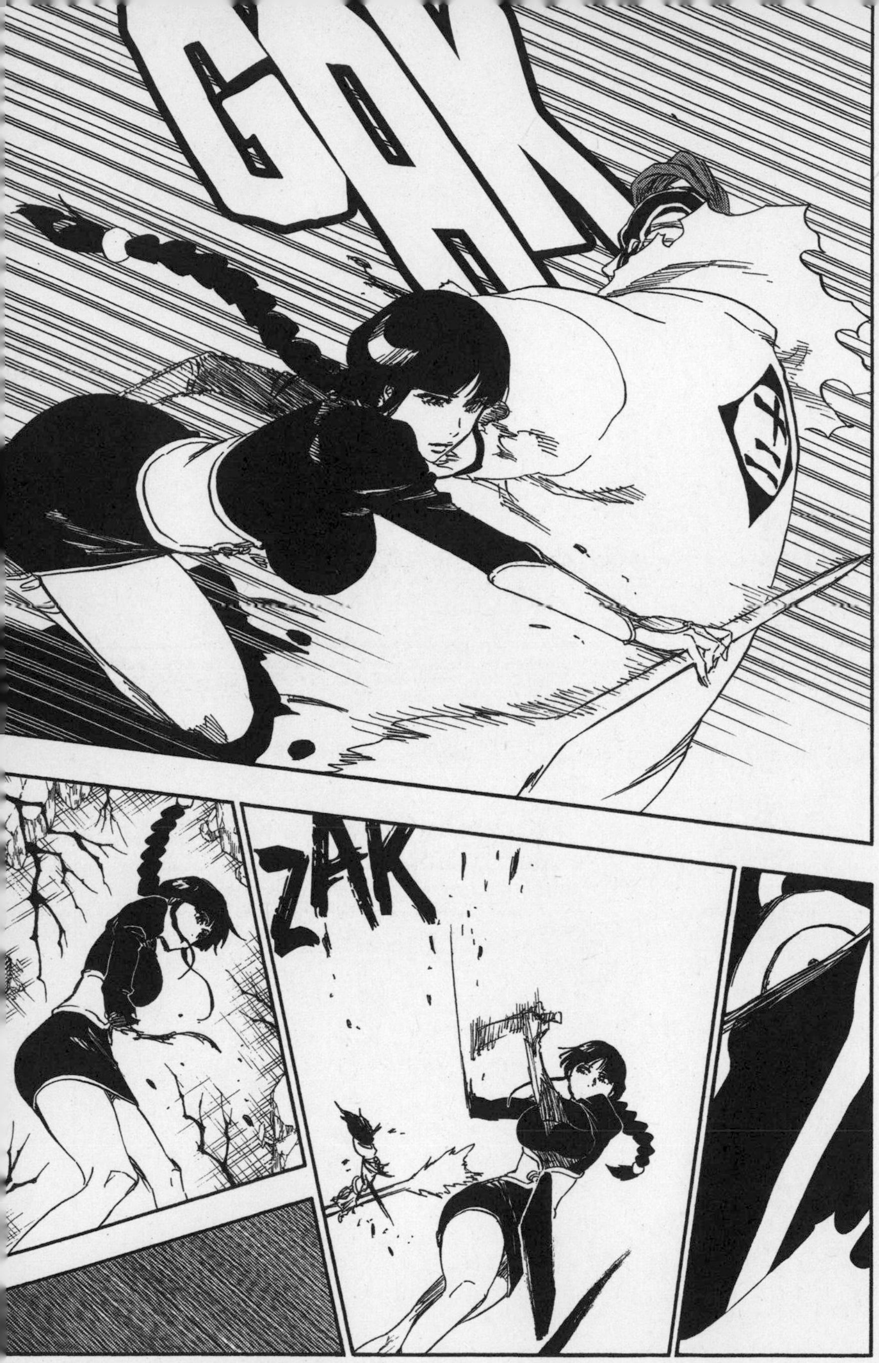
ZAK

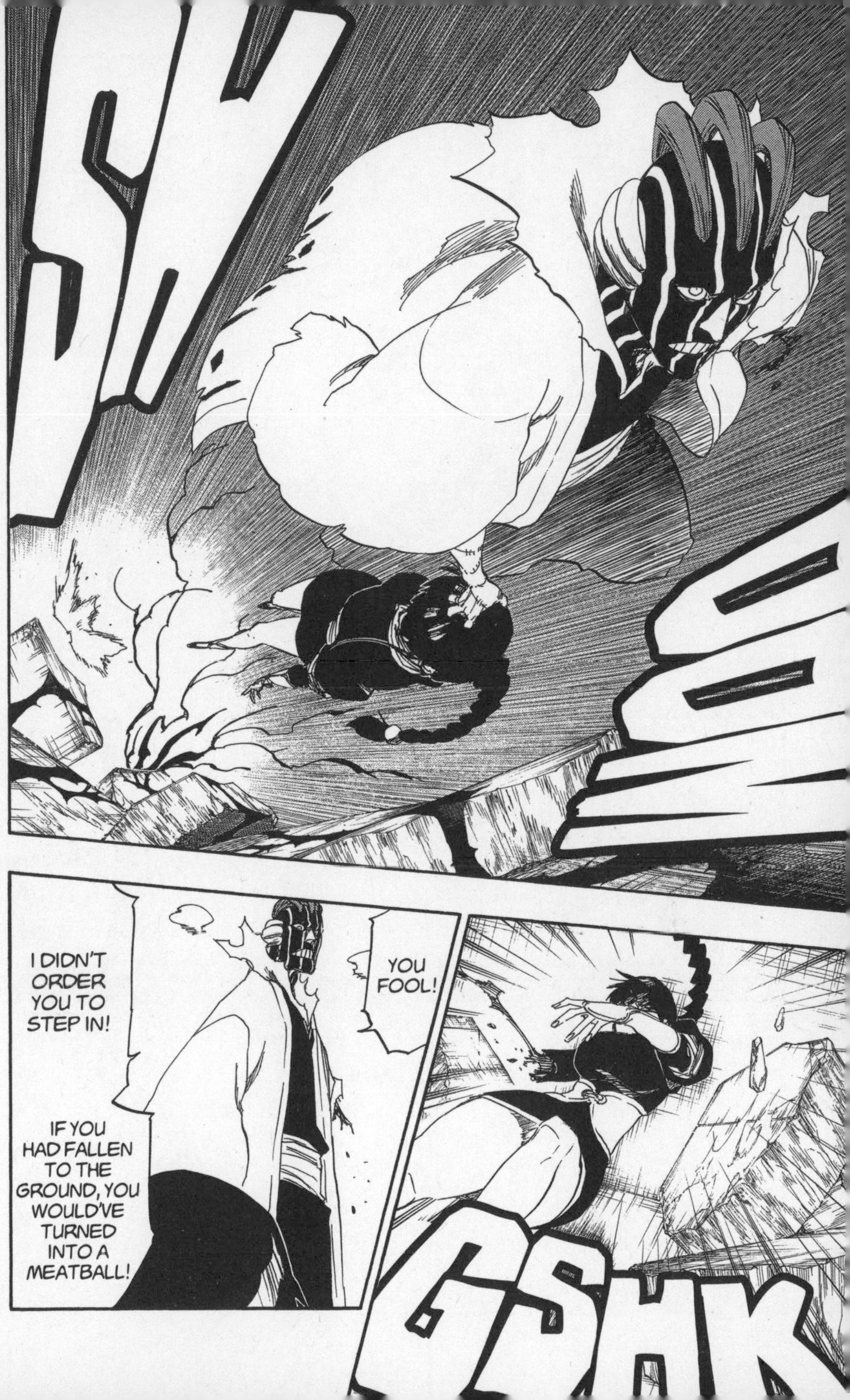
GSHK
YOU FOOL!
I DIDN'T ORDER YOU TO STEP IN!
IF YOU HAD FALLEN TO THE GROUND, YOU WOULD'VE TURNED INTO A MEATBALL!

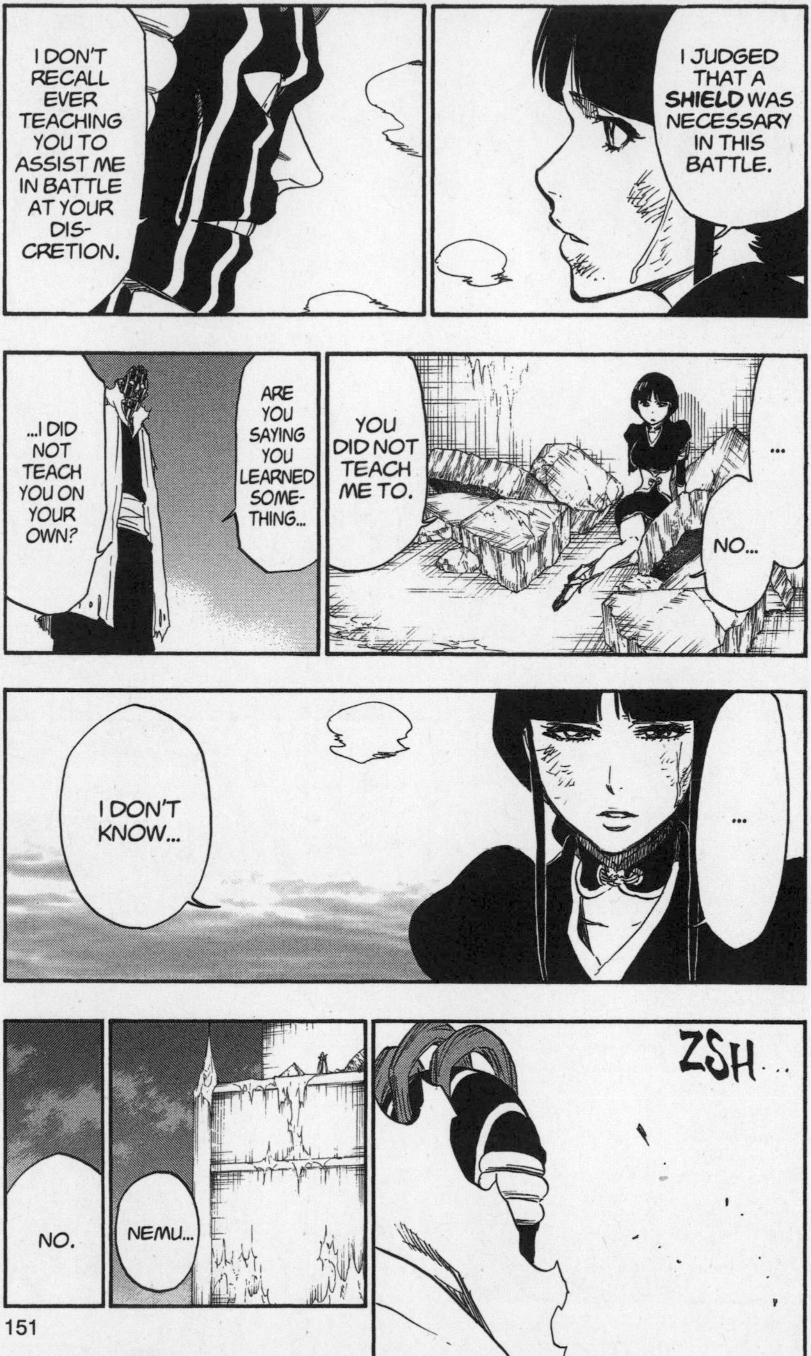
I JUDGED THAT A SHIELD WAS NECESSARY IN THIS BATTLE.
I DON'T RECALL EVER TEACHING YOU TO ASSIST ME IN BATTLE AT YOUR DIS-CRETION.
...
NO...
YOU DID NOT TEACH ME TO.
ARE YOU SAYING YOU LEARNED SOME-THING...
...I DID NOT TEACH YOU ON YOUR OWN?
...
I DON'T KNOW...
ZSH...
NEMU...
NO.

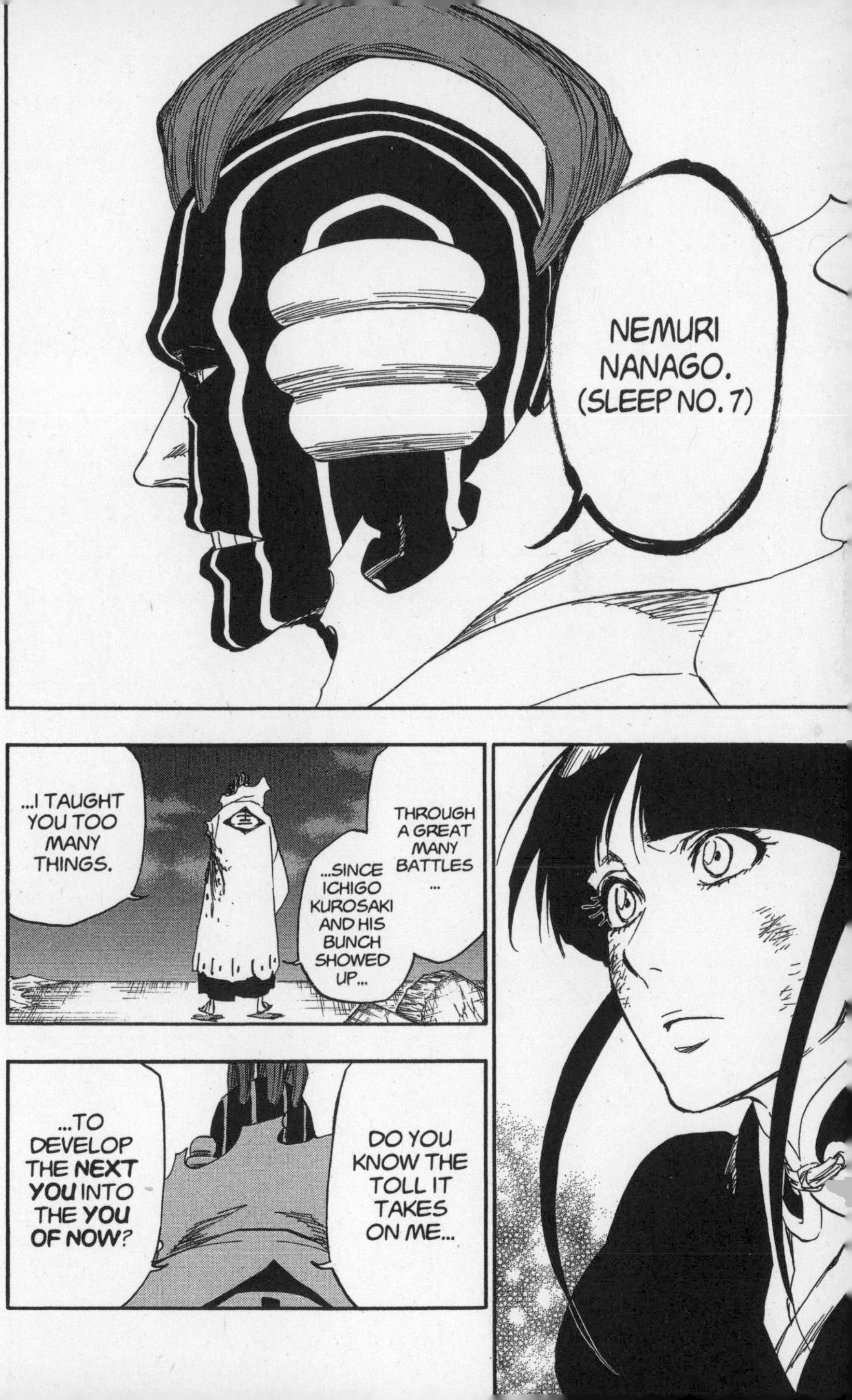
NEMURI NANAGO. (SLEEP NO. 7)
THROUGH A GREAT MANY BATTLES ...
...SINCE ICHIGO KUROSAKI AND HIS BUNCH SHOWED UP...
...I TAUGHT YOU TOO MANY THINGS.
DO YOU KNOW THE TOLL IT TAKES ON ME...
...TO DEVELOP THE NEXT YOU INTO THE YOU OF NOW?

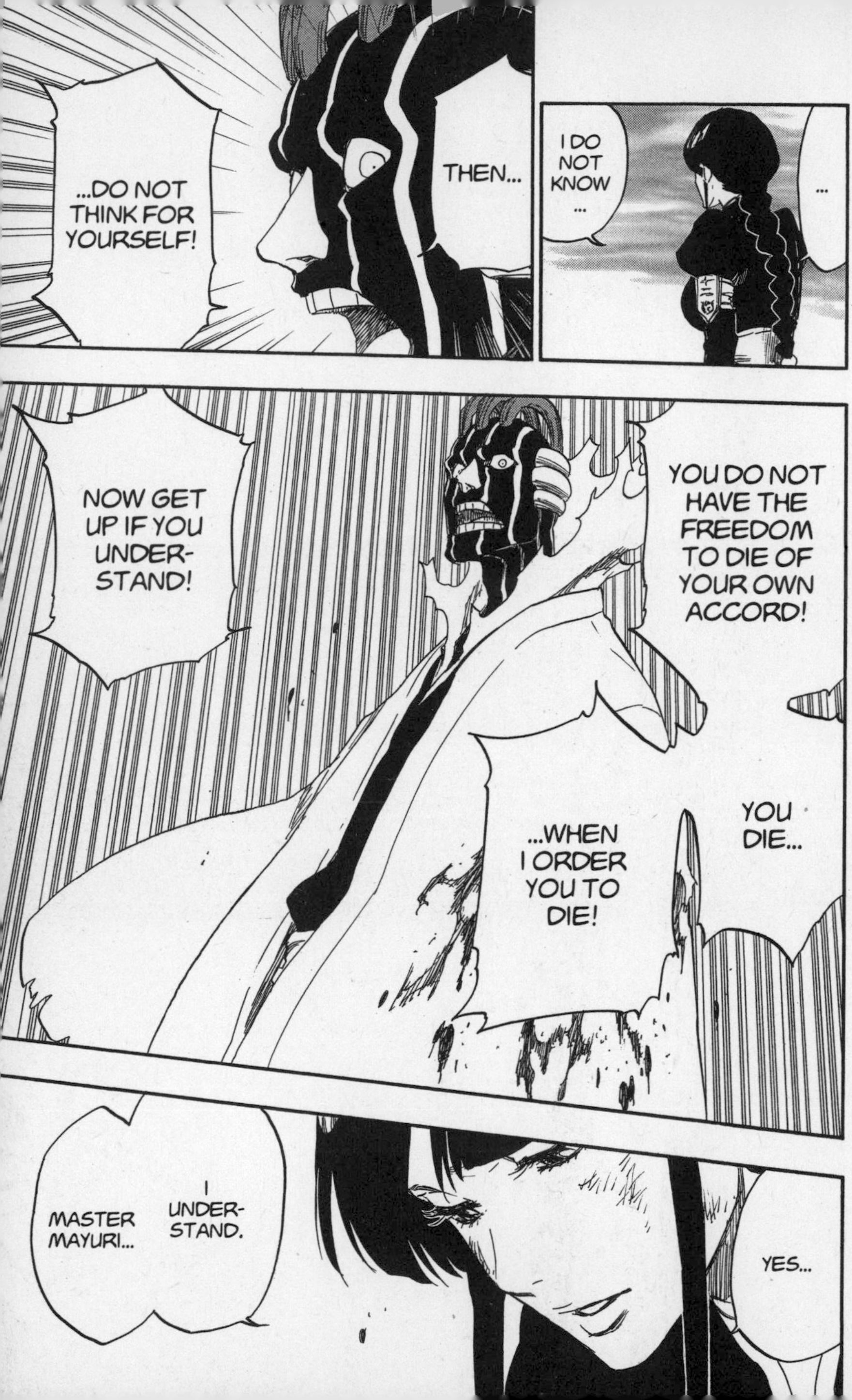
...
I DO NOT KNOW ...
THEN...
...DO NOT THINK FOR YOURSELF!
YOU DO NOT HAVE THE FREEDOM TO DIE OF YOUR OWN ACCORD!
YOU DIE...
...WHEN I ORDER YOU TO DIE!
NOW GET UP IF YOU UNDER-STAND!
YES...
I UNDER-STAND.
MASTER MAYURI...

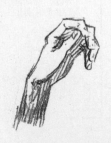

641. BABY, HOLD YOUR HAND 4 (WHEN I AM SLEEPING)

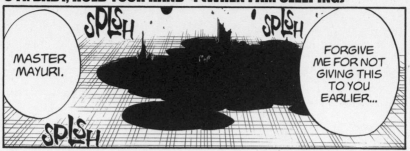

SPLSH
FORGIVE ME FOR NOT GIVING THIS TO YOU EARLIER...
SPLSH
MASTER MAYURI.
SPLSH
HOJIKU-ZAI. (FLESH-HEALING MEDICINE)
I STEPPED IN...
...TO GET THIS TO YOU.

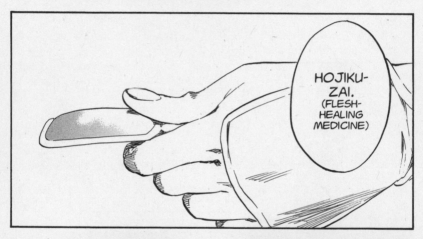

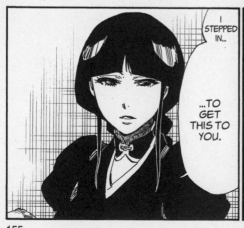

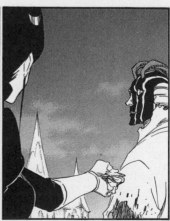

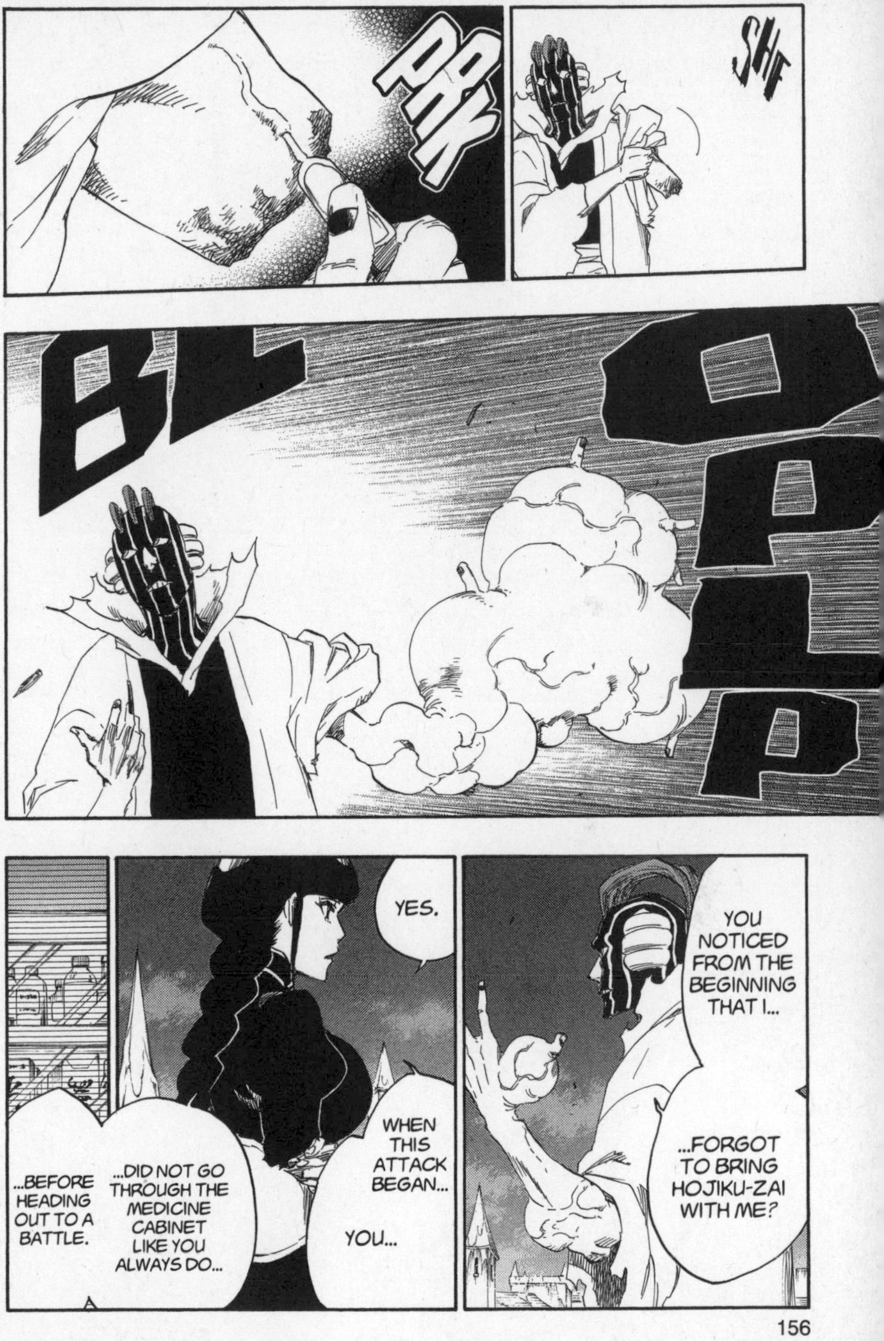
SHF
PAK
BLOOP
YOU NOTICED FROM THE BEGINNING THAT I...
...FORGOT TO BRING HOJIKU-ZAI WITH ME?
YES.
WHEN THIS ATTACK BEGAN... YOU...
...DID NOT GO THROUGH THE MEDICINE CABINET LIKE YOU ALWAYS DO...
...BEFORE HEADING OUT TO A BATTLE.

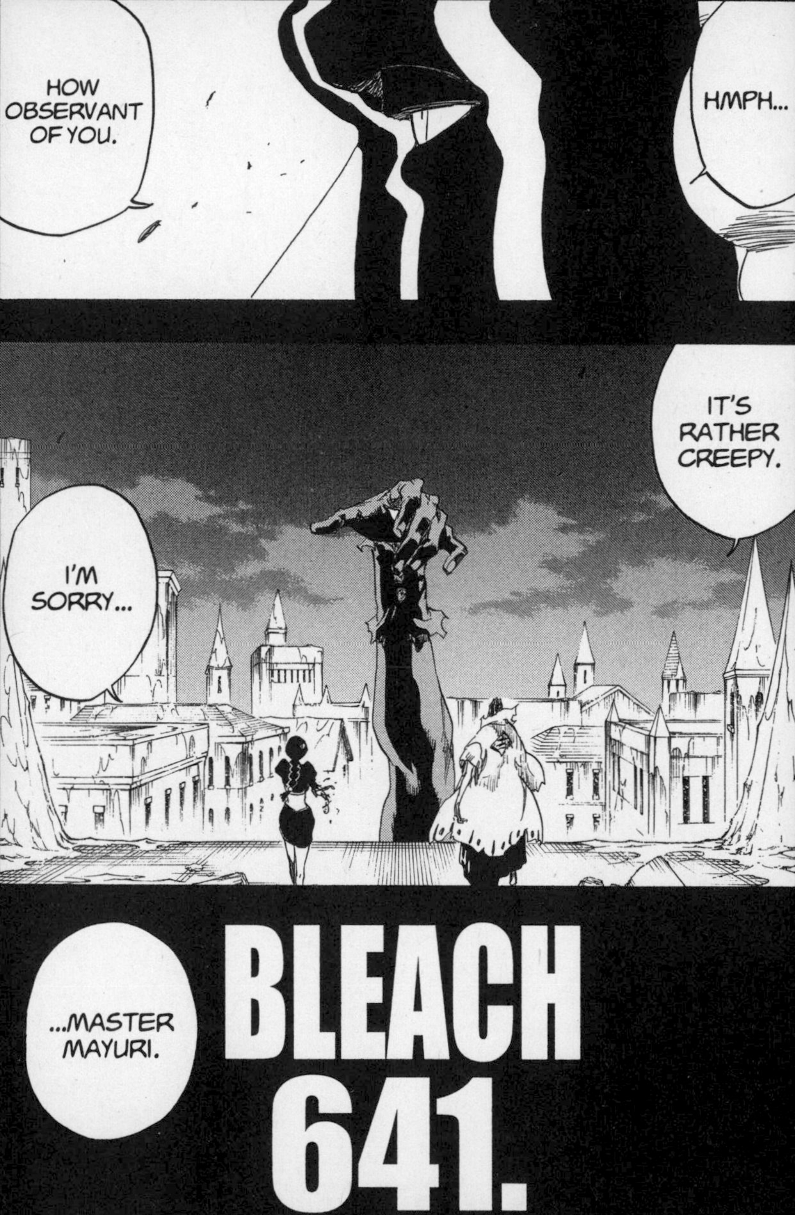
HMPH...
HOW OBSERVANT OF YOU.
IT'S RATHER CREEPY.
I'M SORRY...
...MASTER MAYURI.
BLEACH 641.

BABY, HOLD YOUR HAND 4

[When I am sleeping]

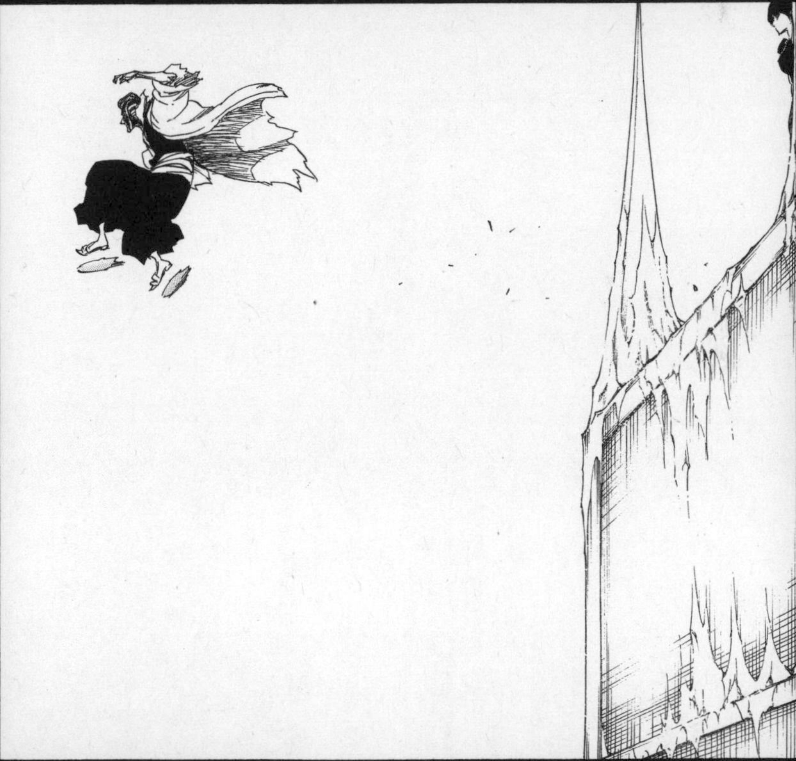

READ THIS WAY

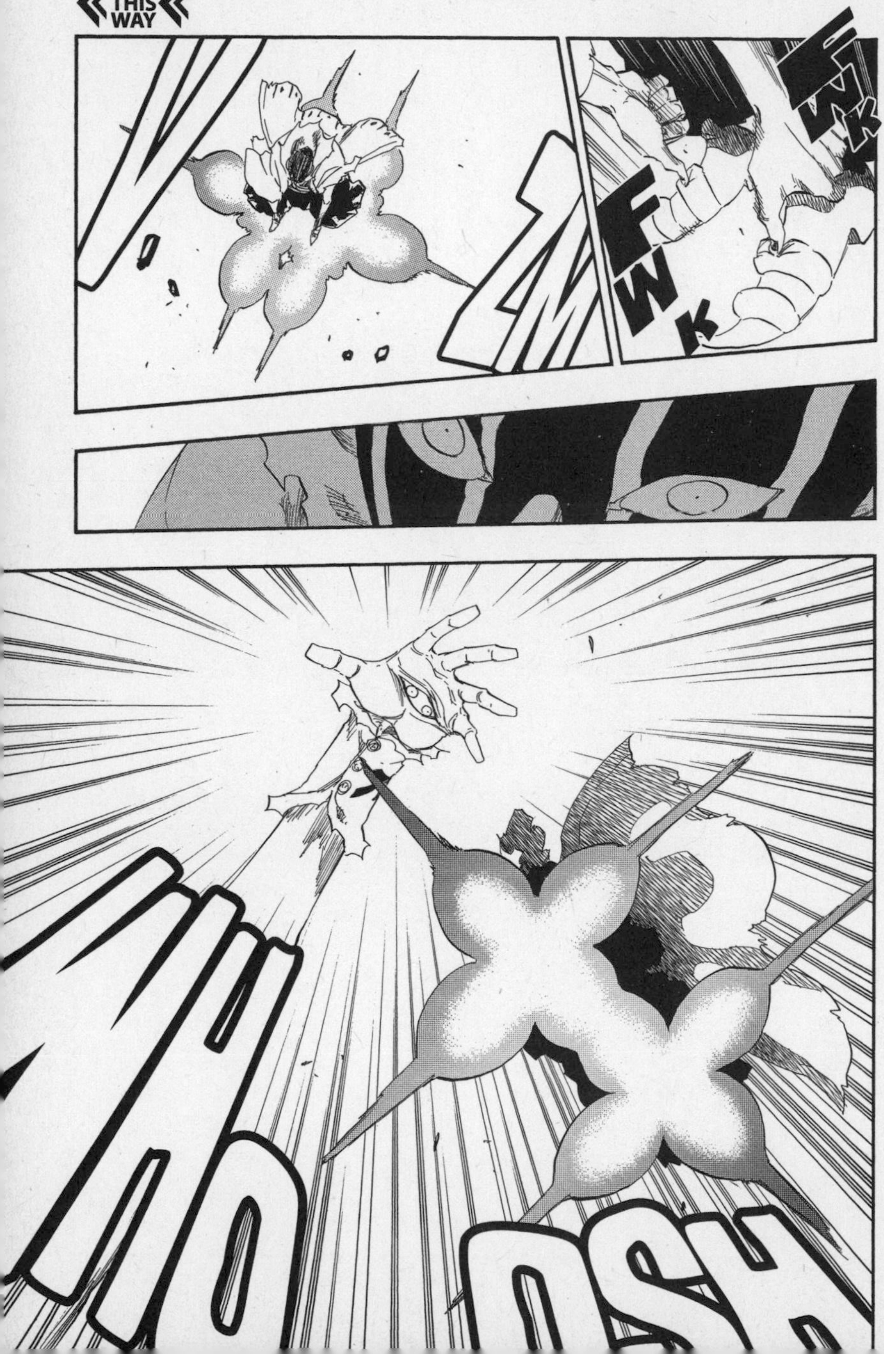
FWK
FWK
ZM
WHOOSH

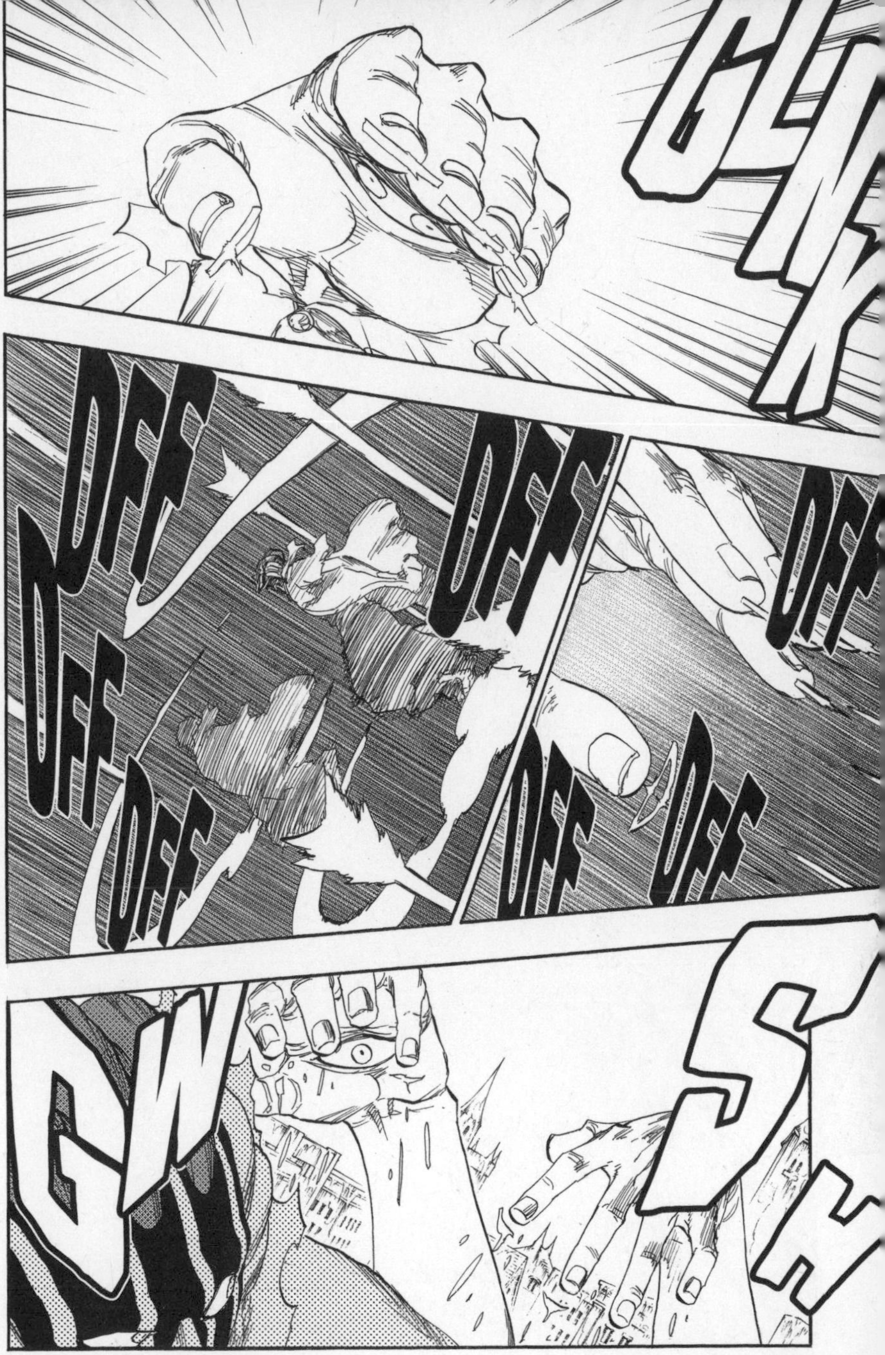
DFF
DFF
DFF
DFF
DFF
DFF
DFF
DFF
DFF

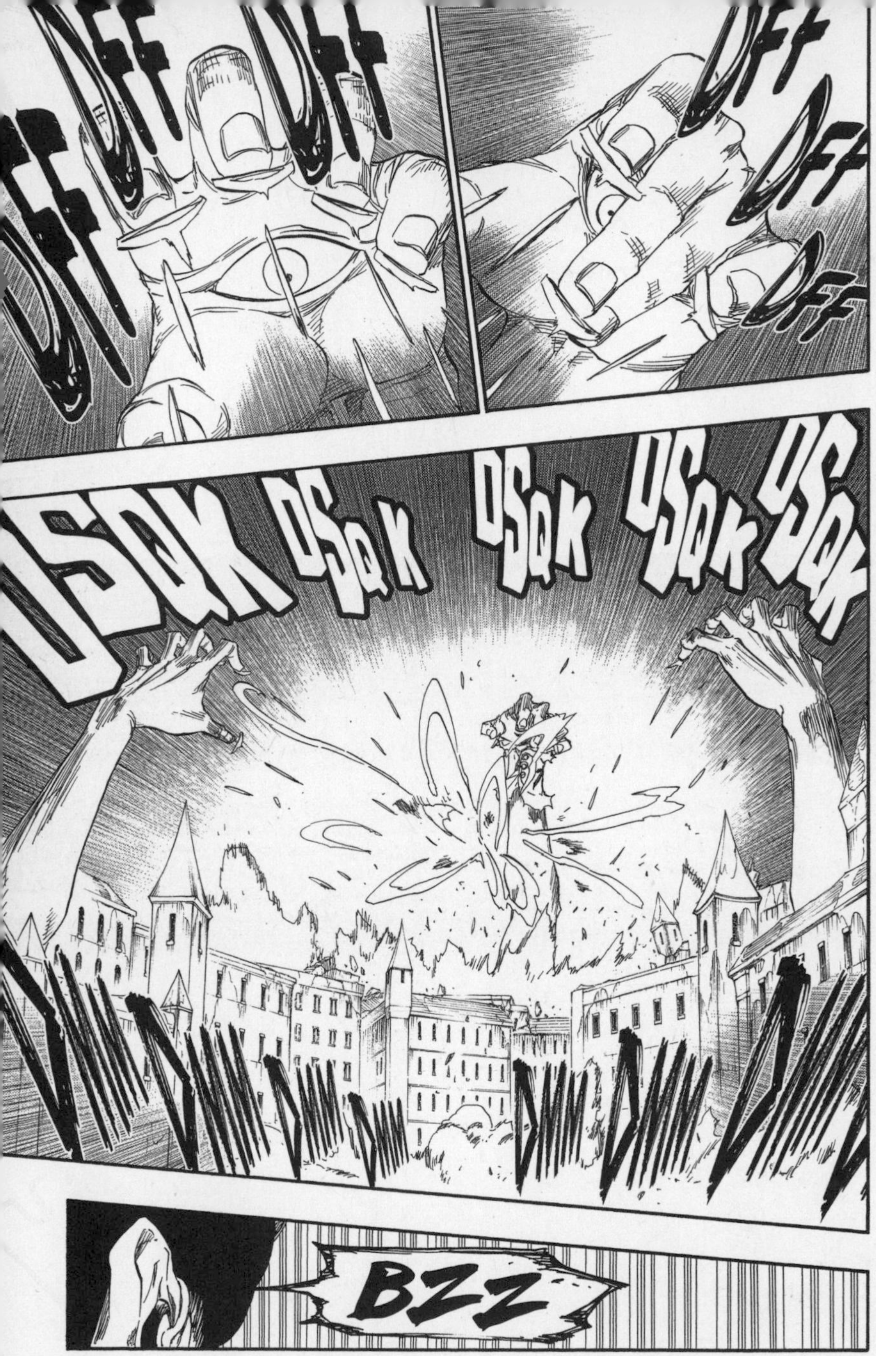
DFF DFF DFF
DFF DFF DFF DFF
DSQK DSQK DSQK DSQK DSQK
DMM DMM DMM DMM DMM DMM DMM DMM DMM
BZZ

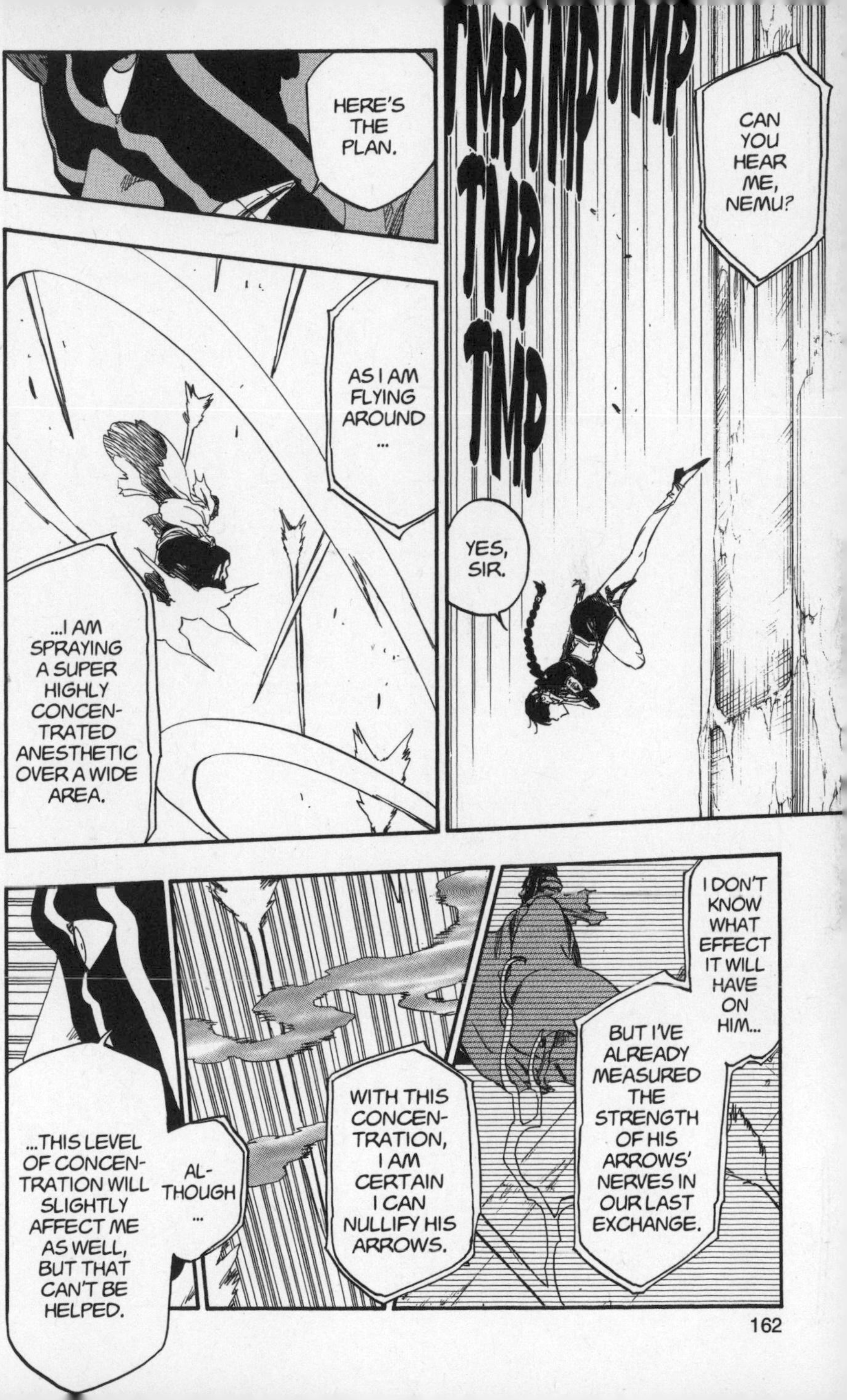
CAN YOU HEAR ME, NEMU?
TMP TMP TMP
TMP
TMP
TMP
YES, SIR.
HERE'S THE PLAN.
AS I AM FLYING AROUND ...
...I AM SPRAYING A SUPER HIGHLY CONCENTRATED ANESTHETIC OVER A WIDE AREA.
I DON'T KNOW WHAT EFFECT IT WILL HAVE ON HIM...
BUT I'VE ALREADY MEASURED THE STRENGTH OF HIS ARROWS' NERVES IN OUR LAST EXCHANGE.
WITH THIS CONCENTRATION, I AM CERTAIN I CAN NULLIFY HIS ARROWS.
AL-THOUGH ...
...THIS LEVEL OF CONCENTRATION WILL SLIGHTLY AFFECT ME AS WELL, BUT THAT CAN'T BE HELPED.

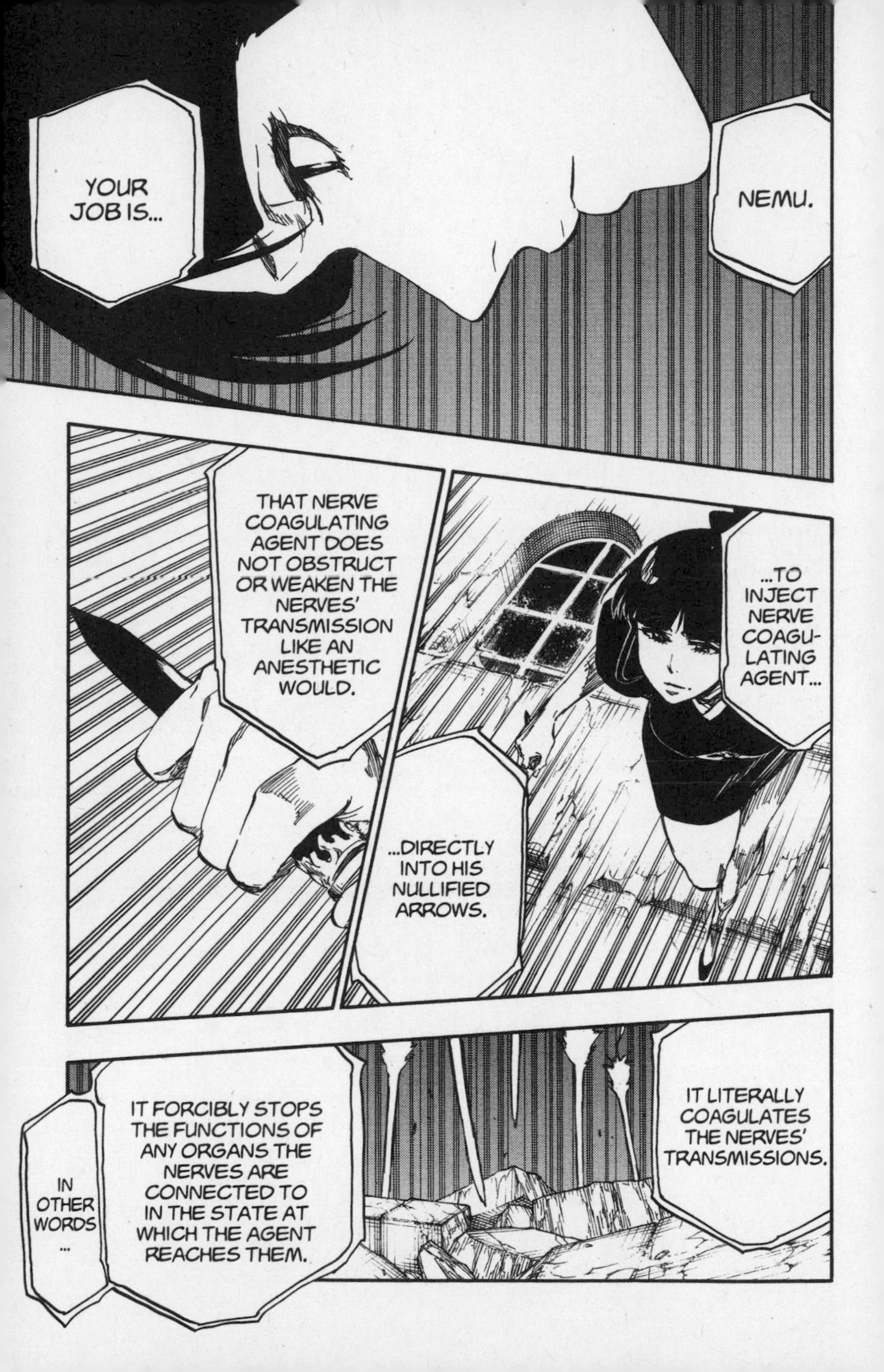
NEMU.
YOUR JOB IS...
...TO INJECT NERVE COAGU-LATING AGENT...
...DIRECTLY INTO HIS NULLIFIED ARROWS.
THAT NERVE COAGULATING AGENT DOES NOT OBSTRUCT OR WEAKEN THE NERVES' TRANSMISSION LIKE AN ANESTHETIC WOULD.
IT LITERALLY COAGULATES THE NERVES' TRANSMISSIONS.
IT FORCIBLY STOPS THE FUNCTIONS OF ANY ORGANS THE NERVES ARE CONNECTED TO IN THE STATE AT WHICH THE AGENT REACHES THEM.
IN OTHER WORDS...

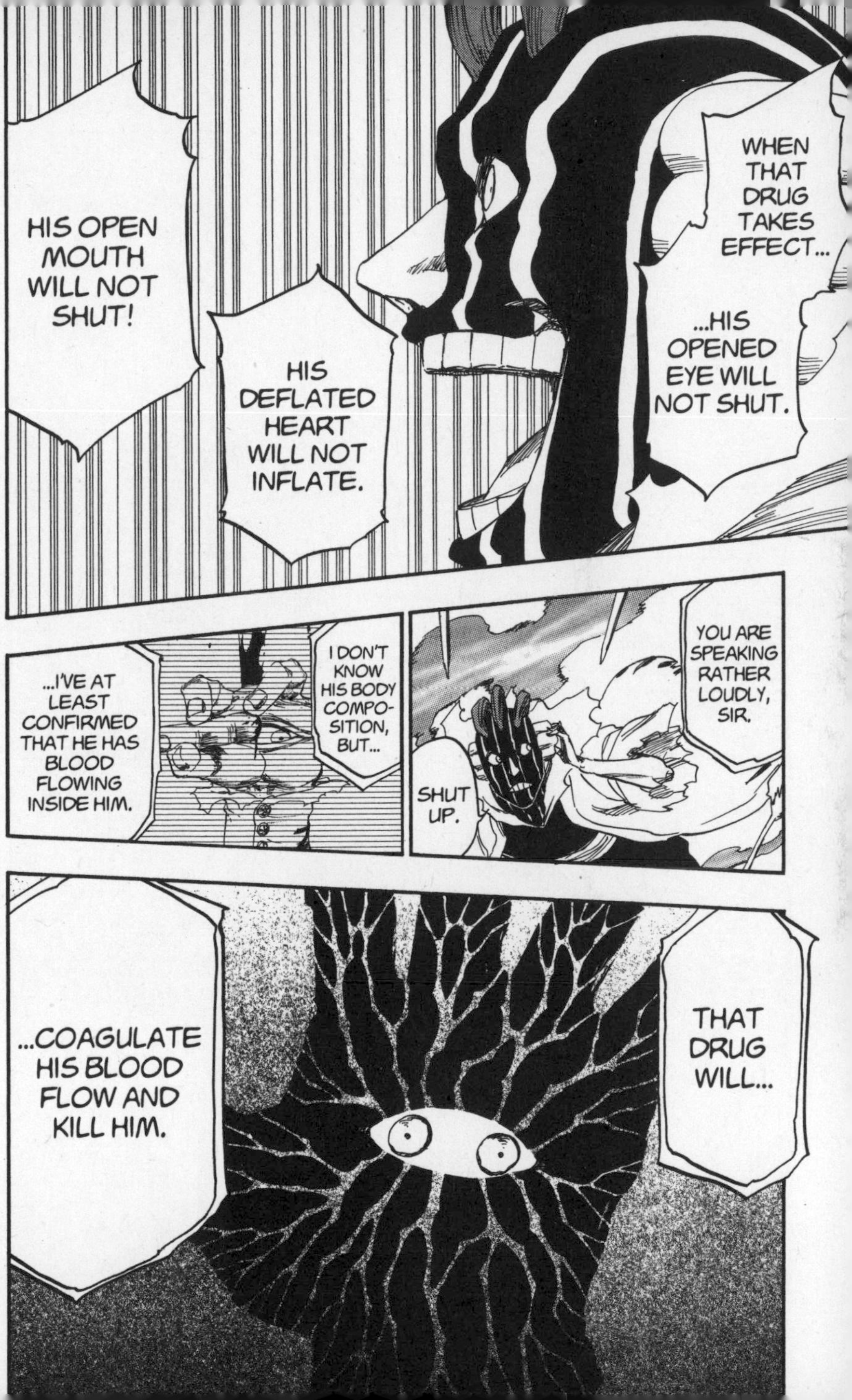
WHEN THAT DRUG TAKES EFFECT...
...HIS OPENED EYE WILL NOT SHUT.
HIS DEFLATED HEART WILL NOT INFLATE.
HIS OPEN MOUTH WILL NOT SHUT!
YOU ARE SPEAKING RATHER LOUDLY, SIR.
SHUT UP.
I DON'T KNOW HIS BODY COMPO-SITION, BUT...
...I'VE AT LEAST CONFIRMED THAT HE HAS BLOOD FLOWING INSIDE HIM.
THAT DRUG WILL...
...COAGULATE HIS BLOOD FLOW AND KILL HIM.

READ THIS WAY

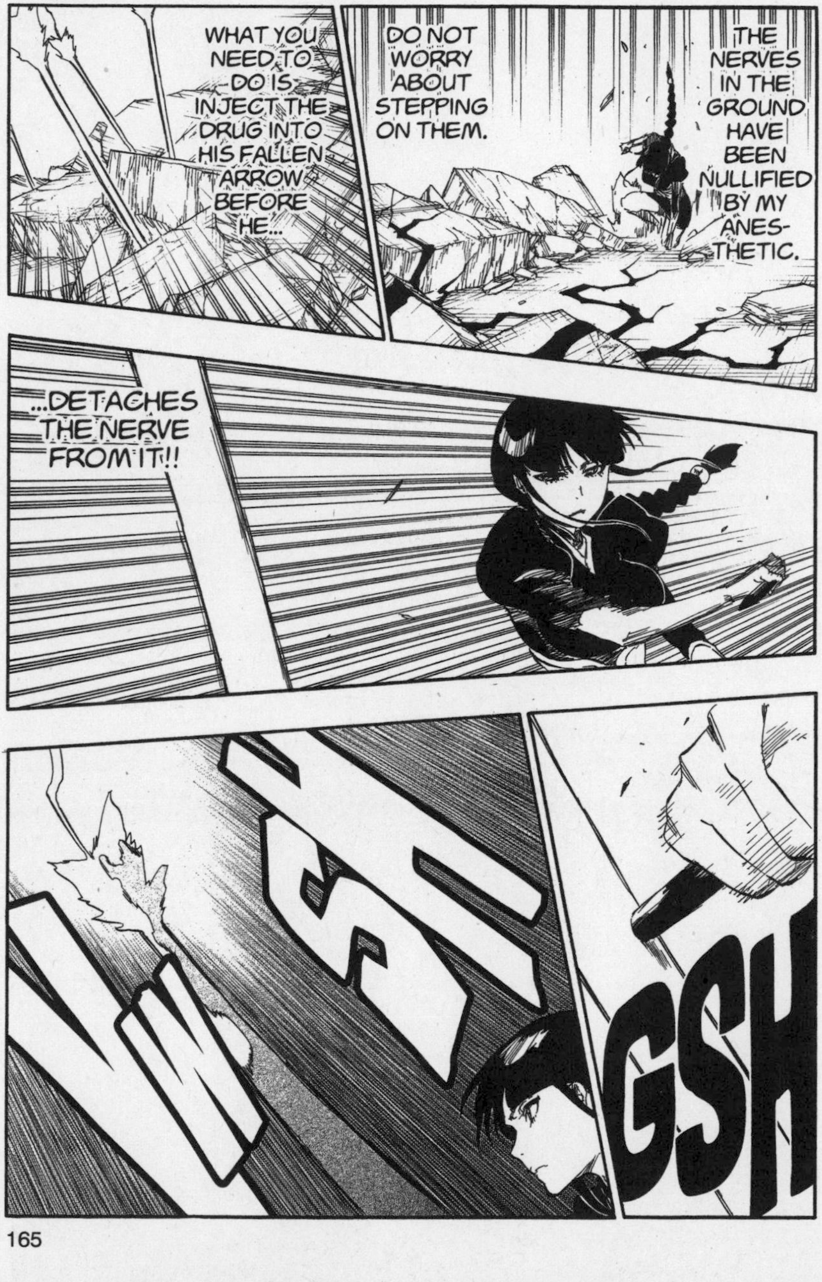
THE NERVES IN THE GROUND HAVE BEEN NULLIFIED BY MY ANES-THETIC.
DO NOT WORRY ABOUT STEPPING ON THEM.
WHAT YOU NEED TO DO IS INJECT THE DRUG INTO HIS FALLEN ARROW BEFORE HE...
...DETACHES THE NERVE FROM IT!!
GSH

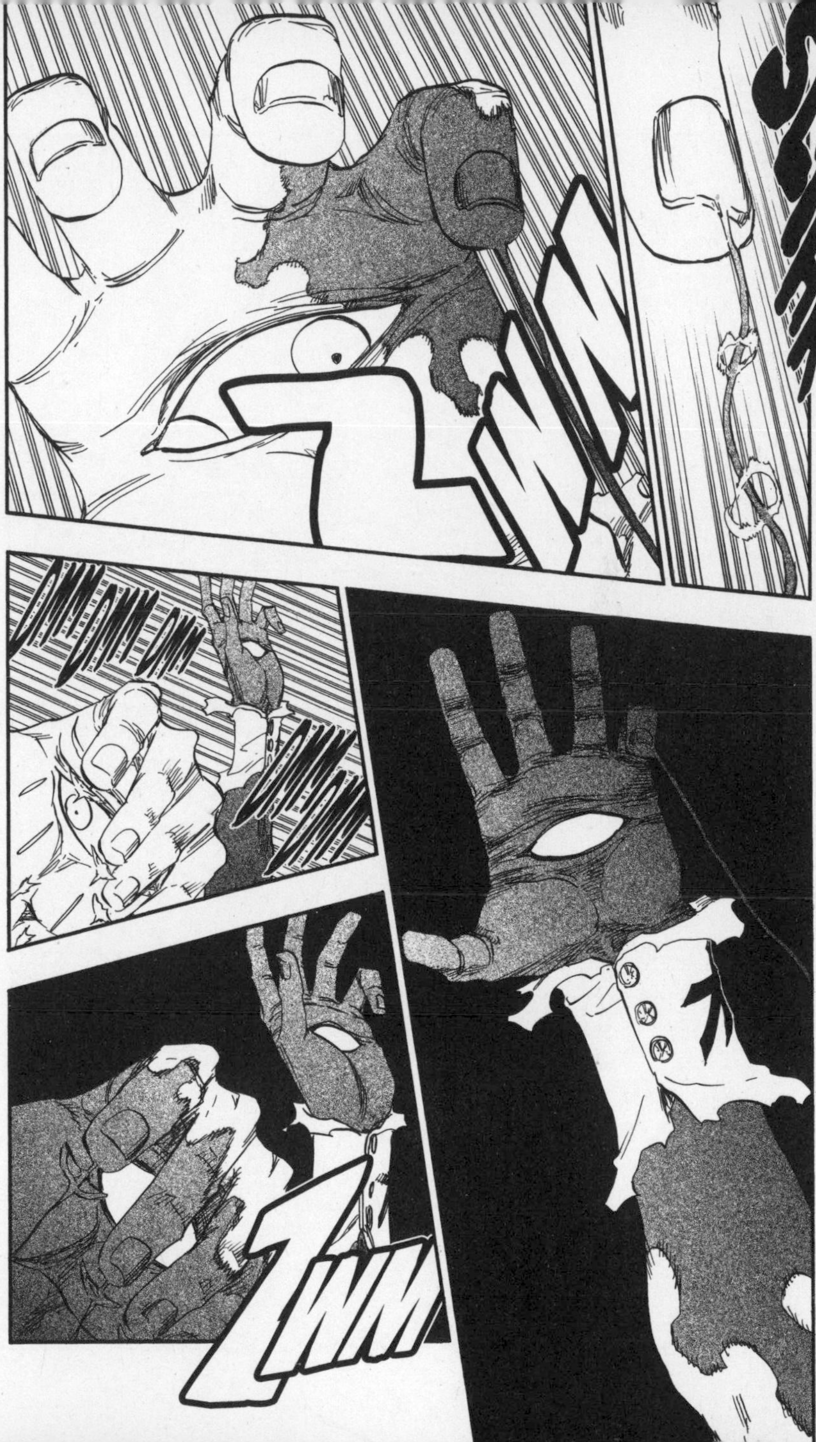
ZINN
ZINN

READ THIS WAY

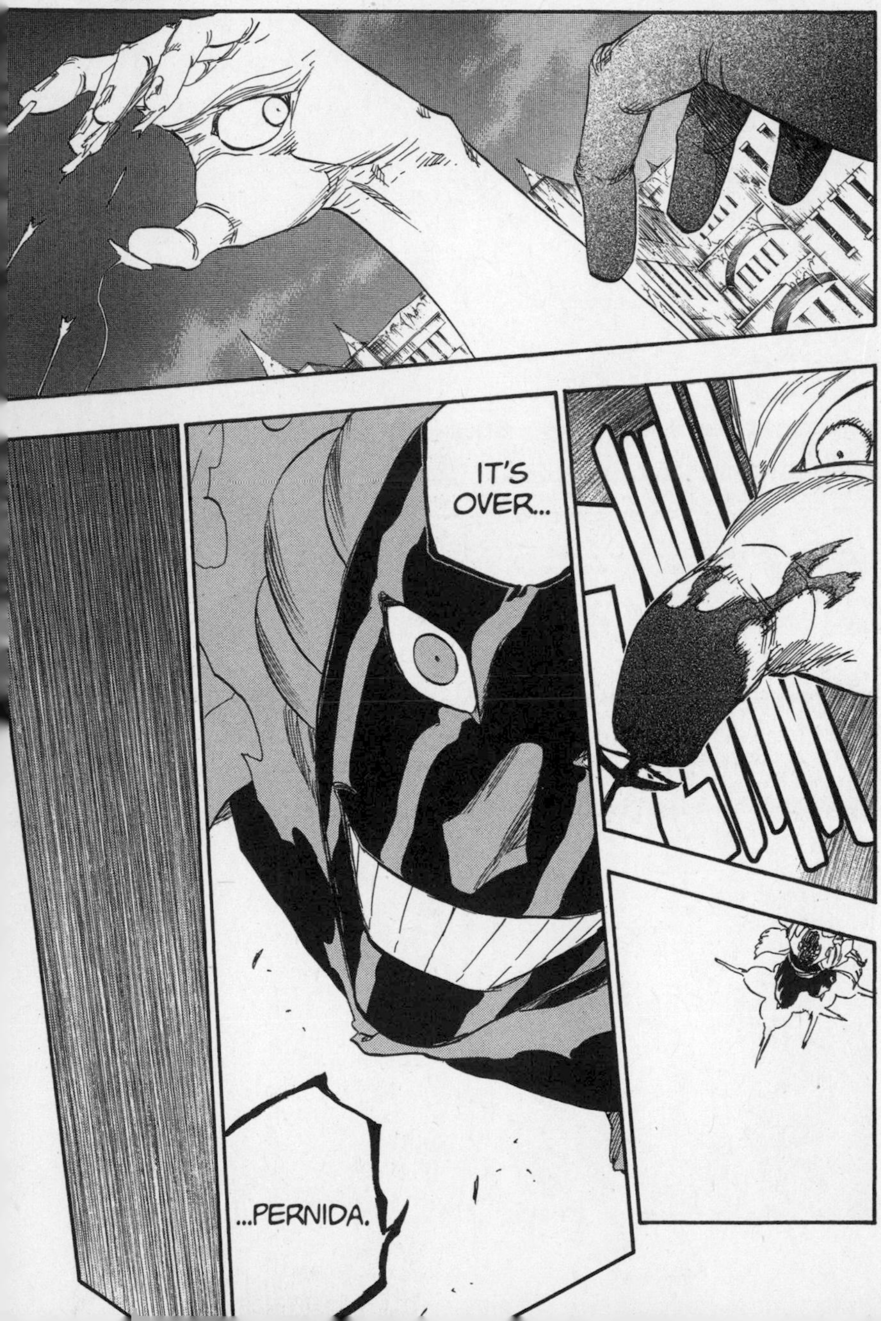
IT'S OVER...
...PERNIDA.

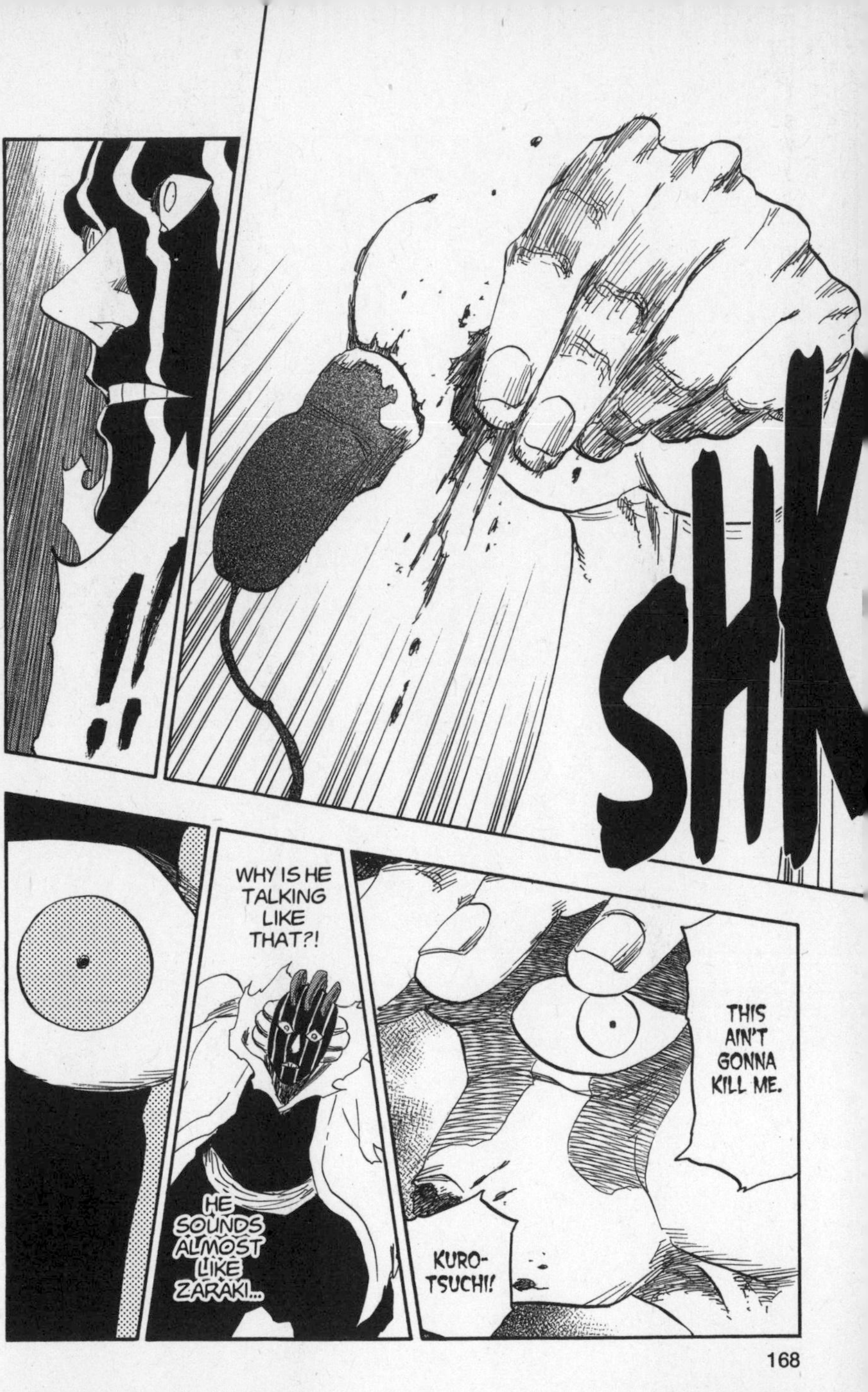
SHK
!!
THIS AIN'T GONNA KILL ME.
KURO-TSUCHI!
WHY IS HE TALKING LIKE THAT?!
HE SOUNDS ALMOST LIKE ZARAKI...

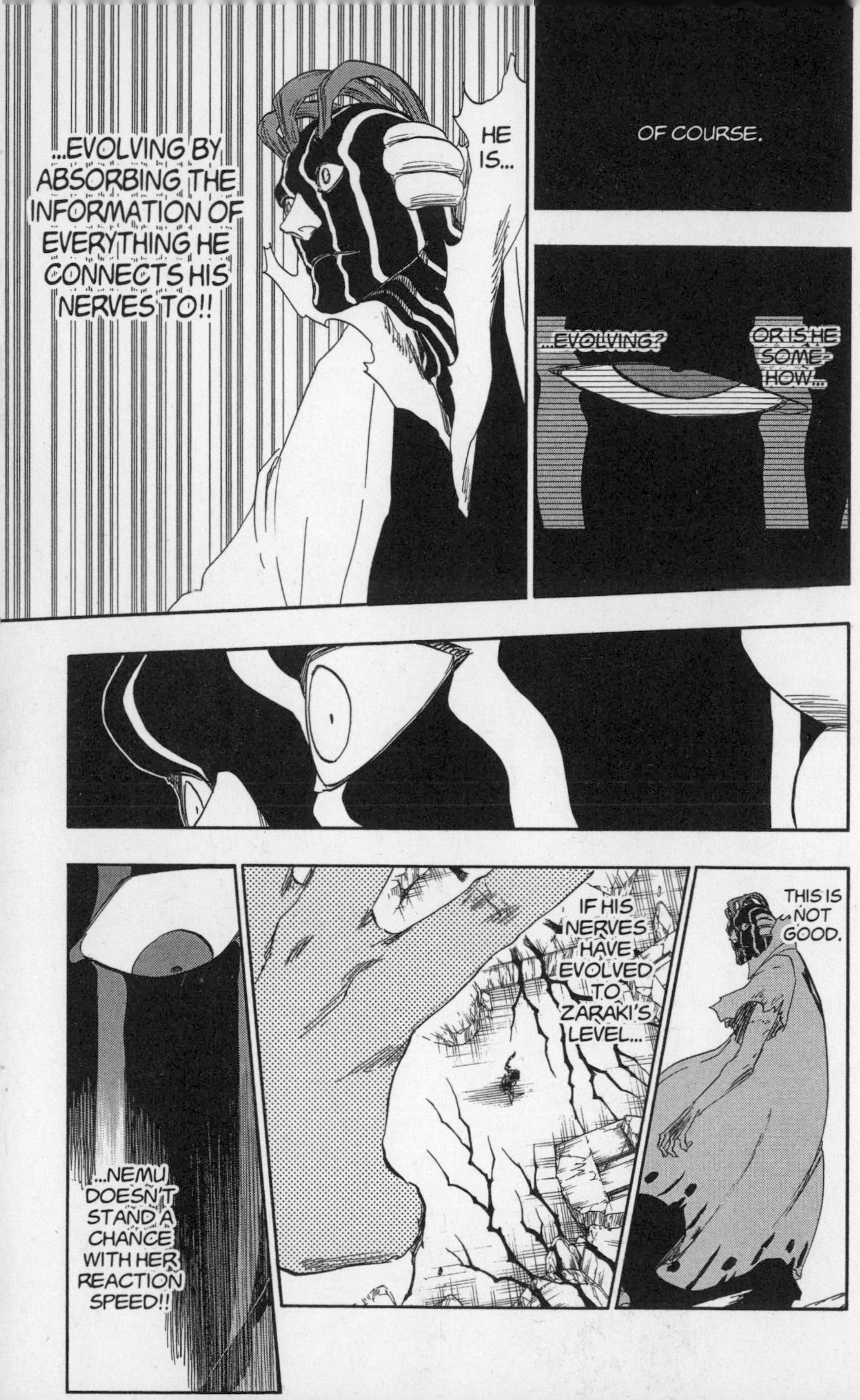
OF COURSE.
OR IS HE SOMEHOW...
...EVOLVING?
HE IS...
...EVOLVING BY ABSORBING THE INFORMATION OF EVERYTHING HE CONNECTS HIS NERVES TO!!
THIS IS NOT GOOD.
IF HIS NERVES HAVE EVOLVED TO ZARAKI'S LEVEL...
...NEMU DOESN'T STAND A CHANCE WITH HER REACTION SPEED!!

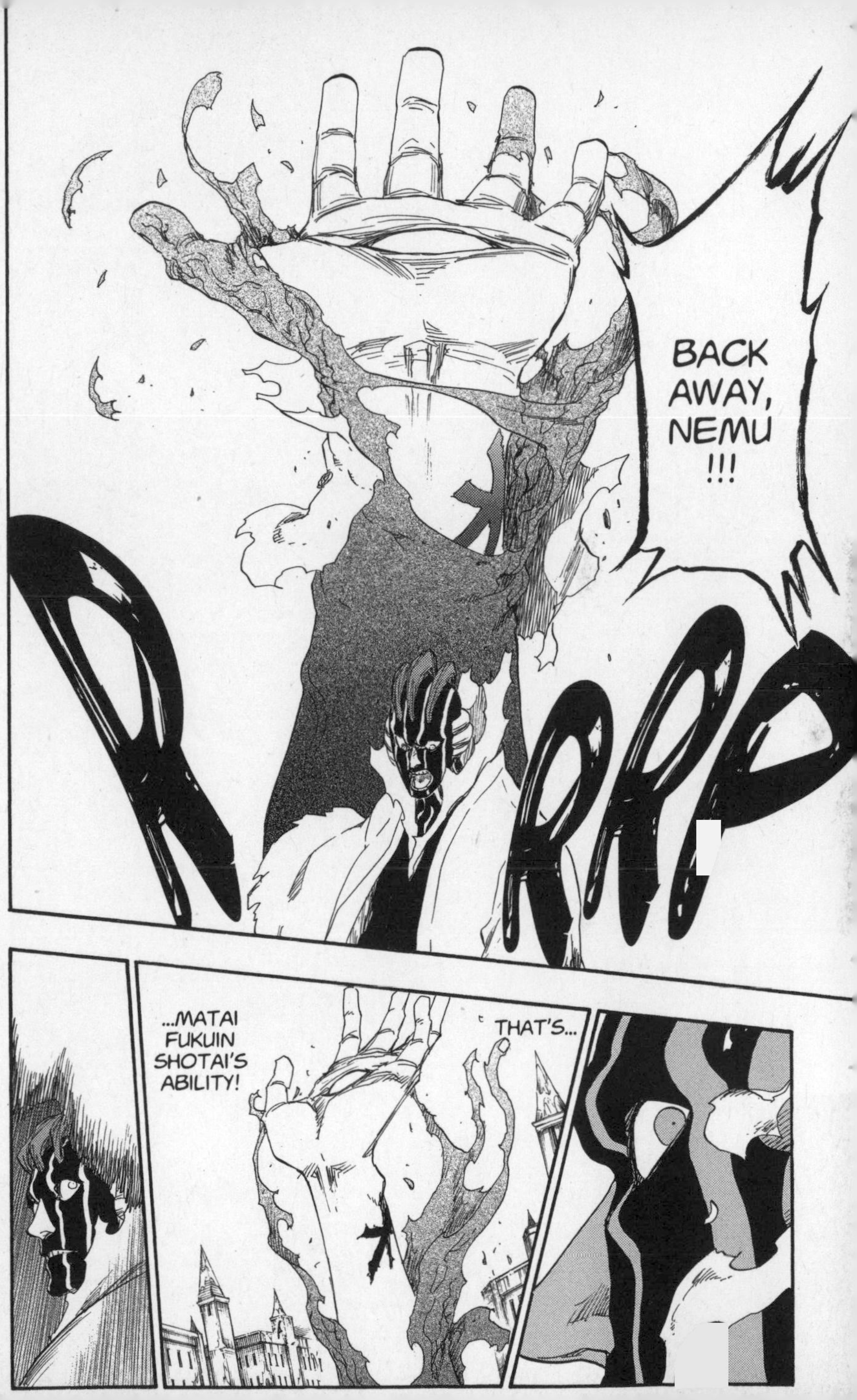
BACK AWAY, NEMU!!!
THAT'S...
...MATAI FUKUIN SHOTAI'S ABILITY!

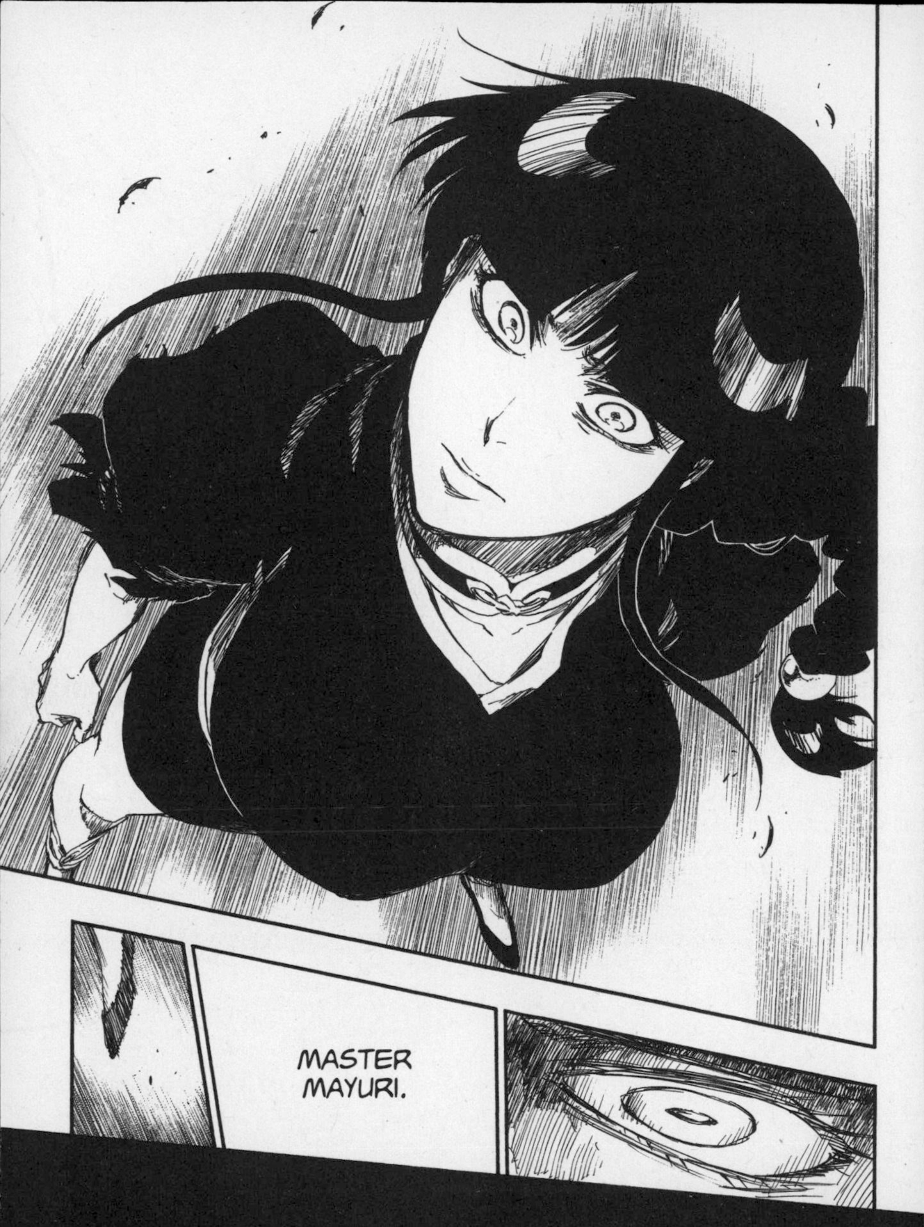
MASTER
MAYURI.

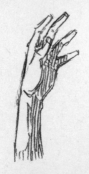

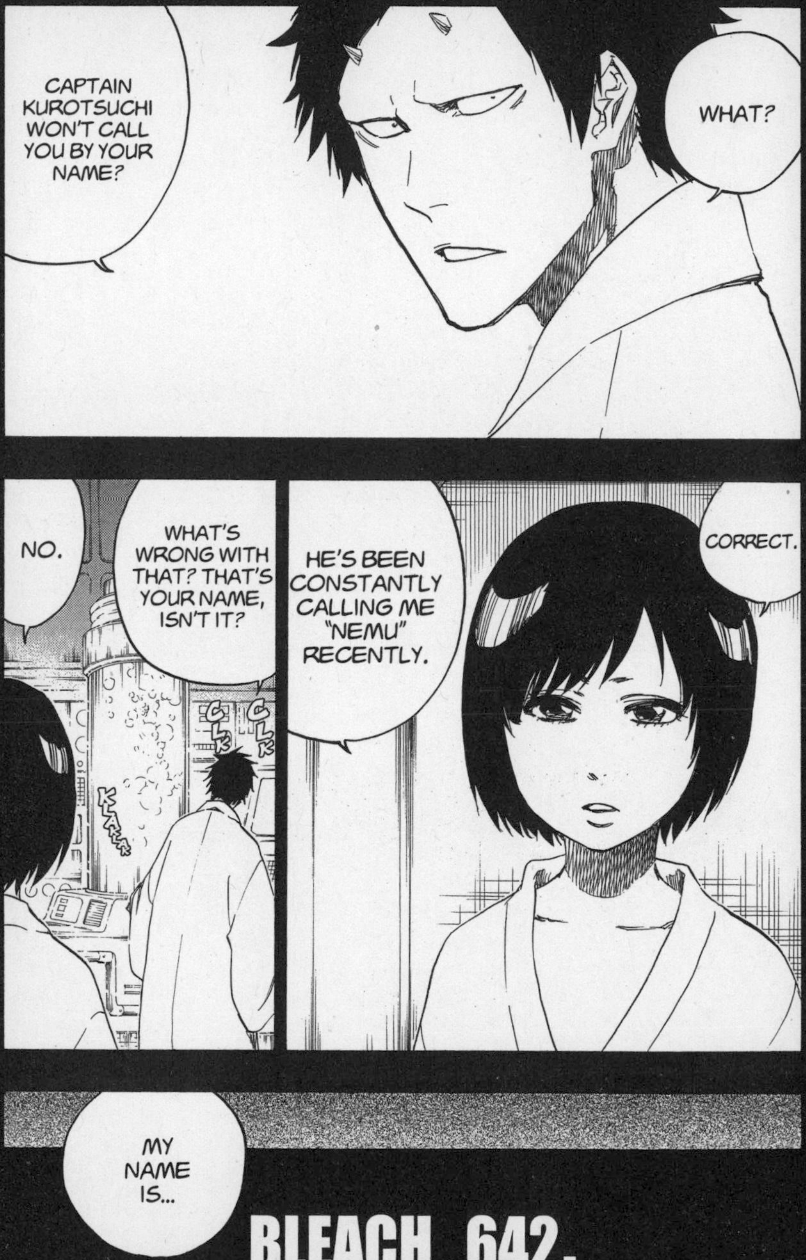
WHAT?
CAPTAIN KUROTSUCHI WON'T CALL YOU BY YOUR NAME?
CORRECT.
HE'S BEEN CONSTANTLY CALLING ME "NEMU" RECENTLY.
WHAT'S WRONG WITH THAT? THAT'S YOUR NAME, ISN'T IT?
NO.
CLK
CLK
KLAK
MY NAME IS...
BLEACH 642.

BABY, HOLD YOUR HAND 5 [Eyes Are Open]

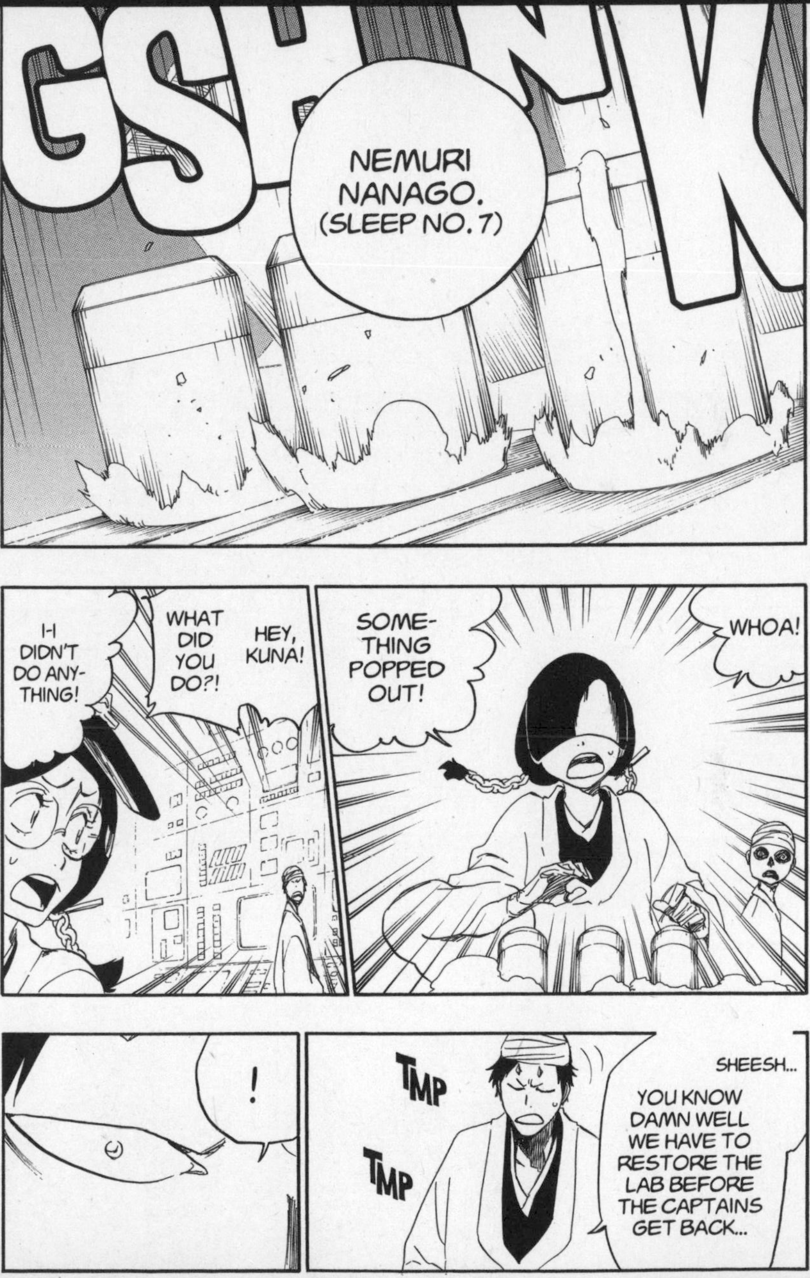
NEMURI NANAGO. (SLEEP NO. 7)
WHOA!
SOME-THING POPPED OUT!
HEY, KUNA!
WHAT DID YOU DO?!
I-I DIDN'T DO ANY-THING!
TMP
TMP
SHEESH...
YOU KNOW DAMN WELL WE HAVE TO RESTORE THE LAB BEFORE THE CAPTAINS GET BACK...
!

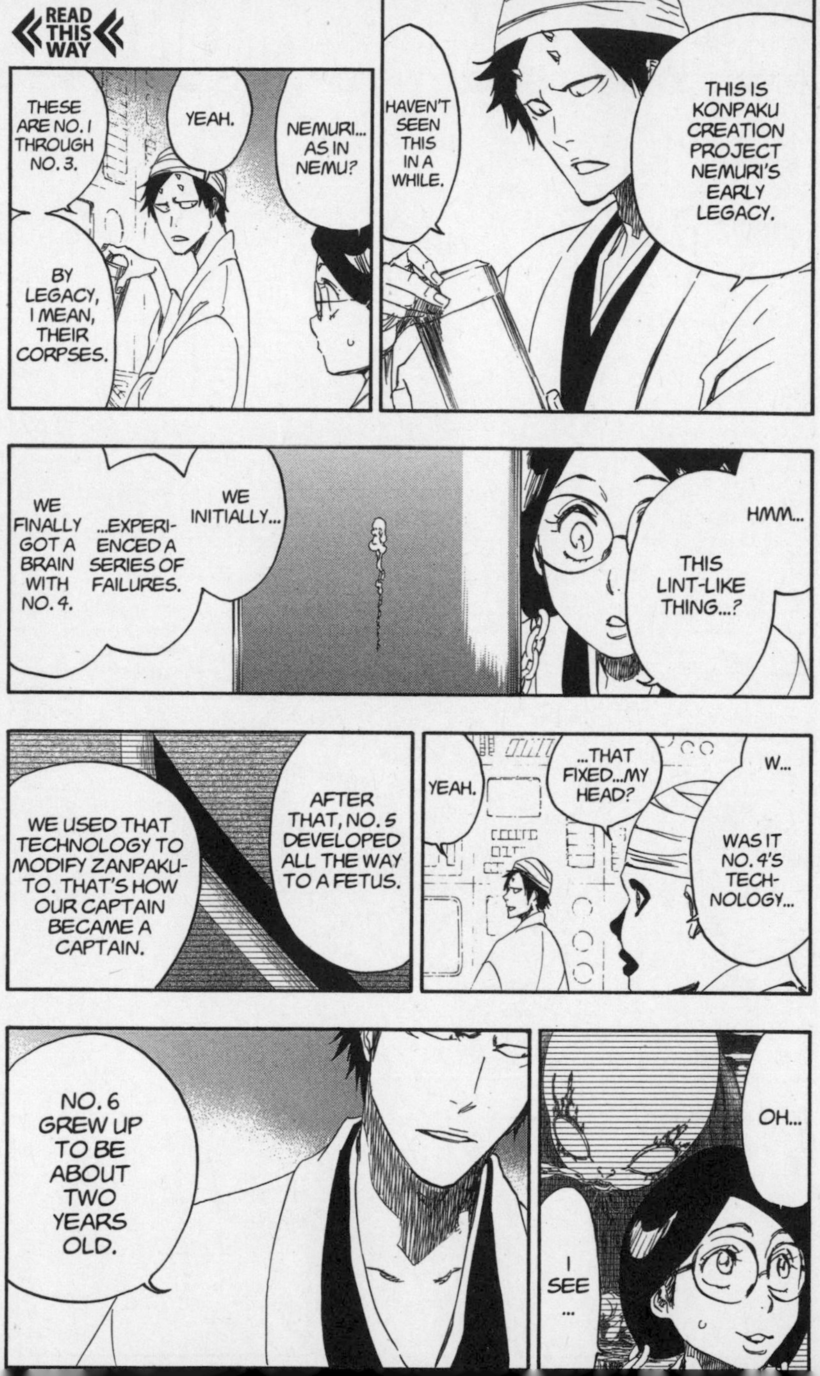
READ THIS WAY
THIS IS KONPAKU CREATION PROJECT NEMURI'S EARLY LEGACY.
HAVEN'T SEEN THIS IN A WHILE.
NEMURI... AS IN NEMU?
YEAH.
THESE ARE NO. 1 THROUGH NO. 3.
BY LEGACY, I MEAN, THEIR CORPSES.
HMM...
THIS LINT-LIKE THING...?
WE INITIALLY...
...EXPERIENCED A SERIES OF FAILURES.
WE FINALLY GOT A BRAIN WITH NO. 4.
W...
WAS IT NO. 4'S TECHNOLOGY...
...THAT FIXED...MY HEAD?
YEAH.
AFTER THAT, NO. 5 DEVELOPED ALL THE WAY TO A FETUS.
WE USED THAT TECHNOLOGY TO MODIFY ZANPAKU-TO. THAT'S HOW OUR CAPTAIN BECAME A CAPTAIN.
OH...
I SEE...
NO. 6 GREW UP TO BE ABOUT TWO YEARS OLD.

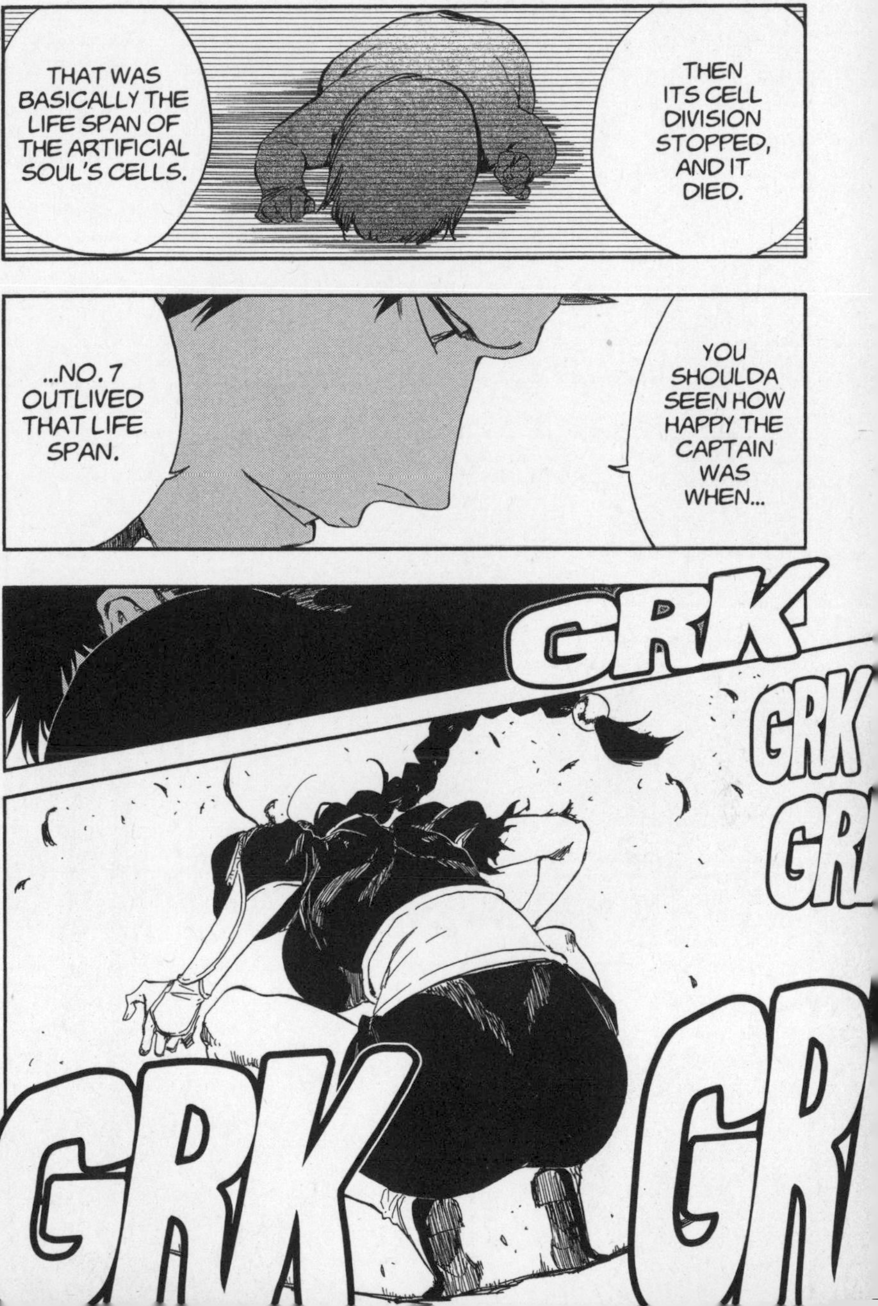
THEN ITS CELL DIVISION STOPPED, AND IT DIED.
THAT WAS BASICALLY THE LIFE SPAN OF THE ARTIFICIAL SOUL'S CELLS.
YOU SHOULDA SEEN HOW HAPPY THE CAPTAIN WAS WHEN...
...NO. 7 OUTLIVED THAT LIFE SPAN.
GRK
GRK
GRK

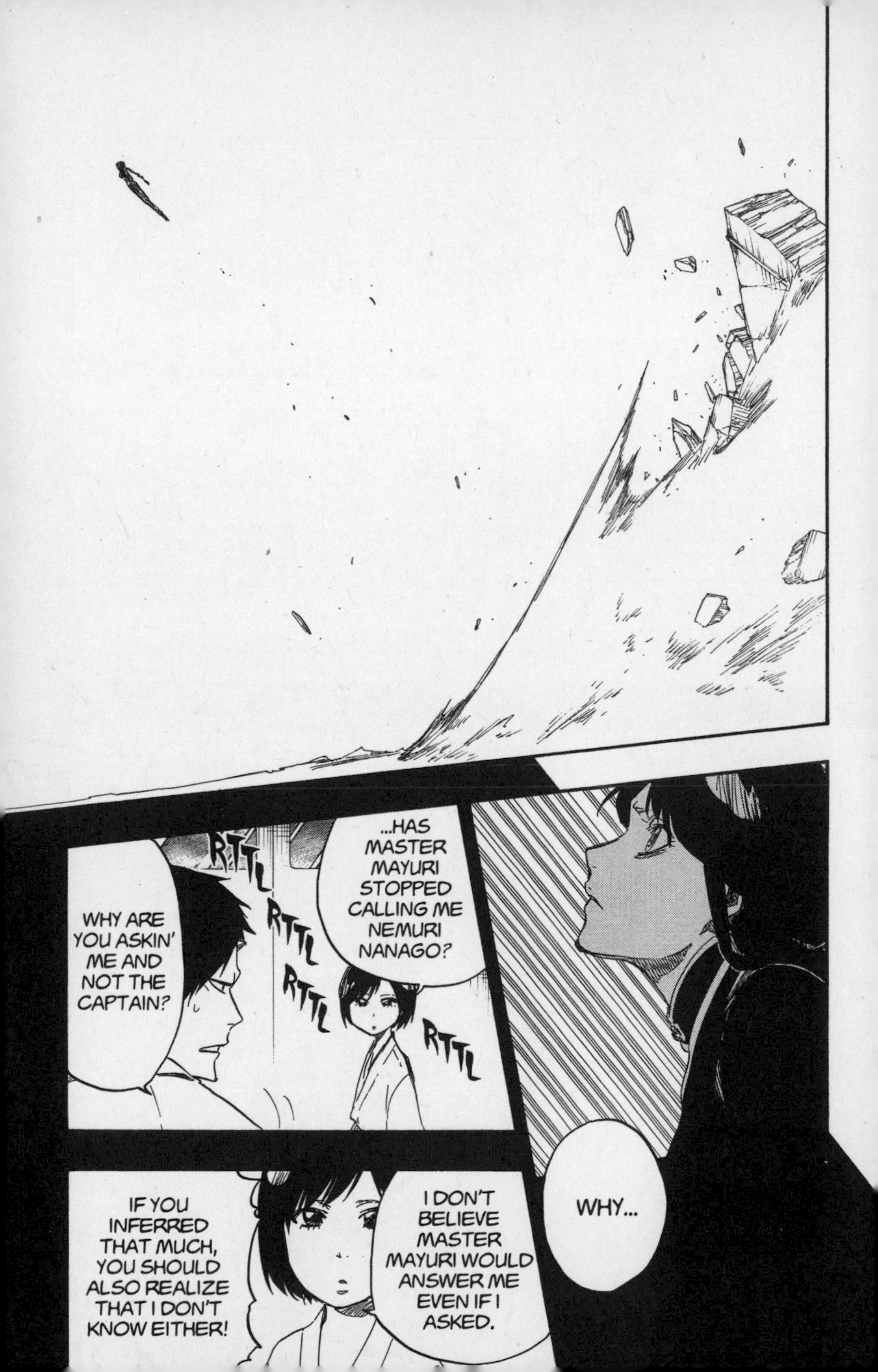
WHY...
...HAS MASTER MAYURI STOPPED CALLING ME NEMURI NANAGO?
RTTL
RTTL
RTTL
RTTL
WHY ARE YOU ASKIN' ME AND NOT THE CAPTAIN?
I DON'T BELIEVE MASTER MAYURI WOULD ANSWER ME EVEN IF I ASKED.
IF YOU INFERRED THAT MUCH, YOU SHOULD ALSO REALIZE THAT I DON'T KNOW EITHER!

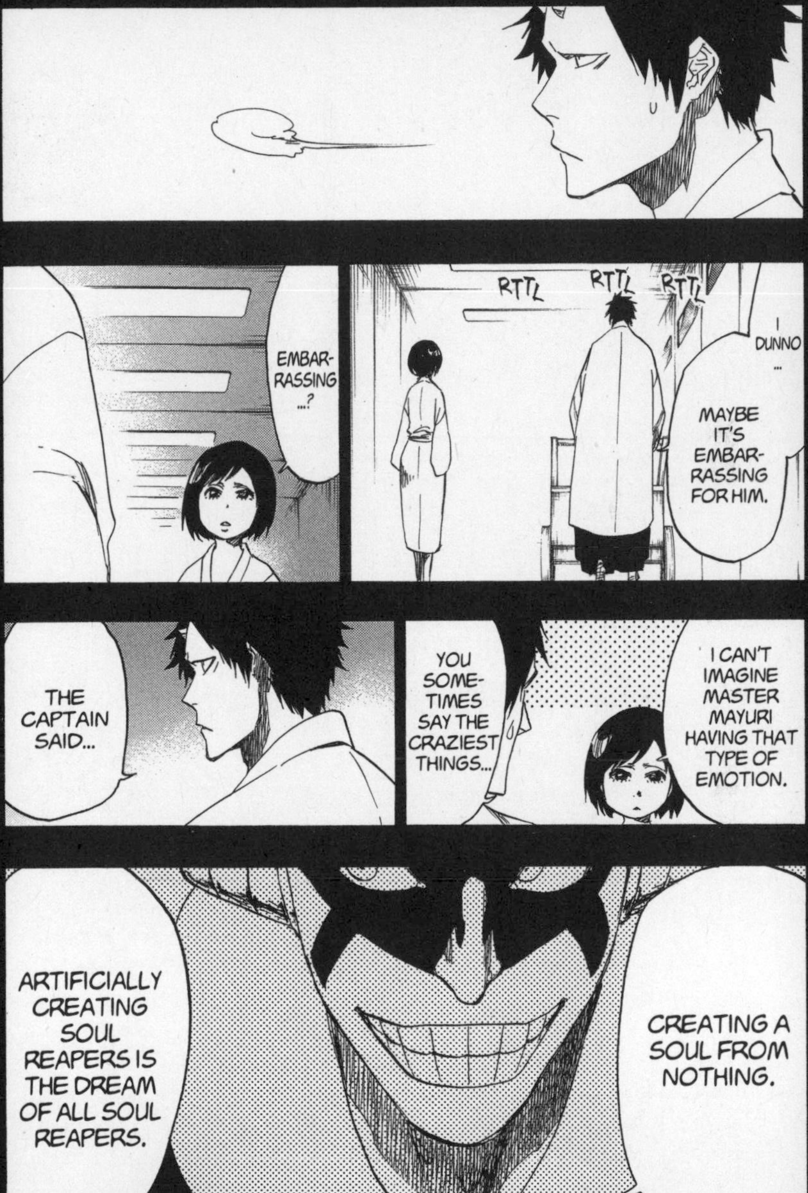
RTTL
RTTL
RTTL
I DUNNO ...
MAYBE IT'S EMBARRASSING FOR HIM.
EMBARRASSING ...?
I CAN'T IMAGINE MASTER MAYURI HAVING THAT TYPE OF EMOTION.
YOU SOMETIMES SAY THE CRAZIEST THINGS...
THE CAPTAIN SAID...
CREATING A SOUL FROM NOTHING.
ARTIFICIALLY CREATING SOUL REAPERS IS THE DREAM OF ALL SOUL REAPERS.

READ THIS WAY

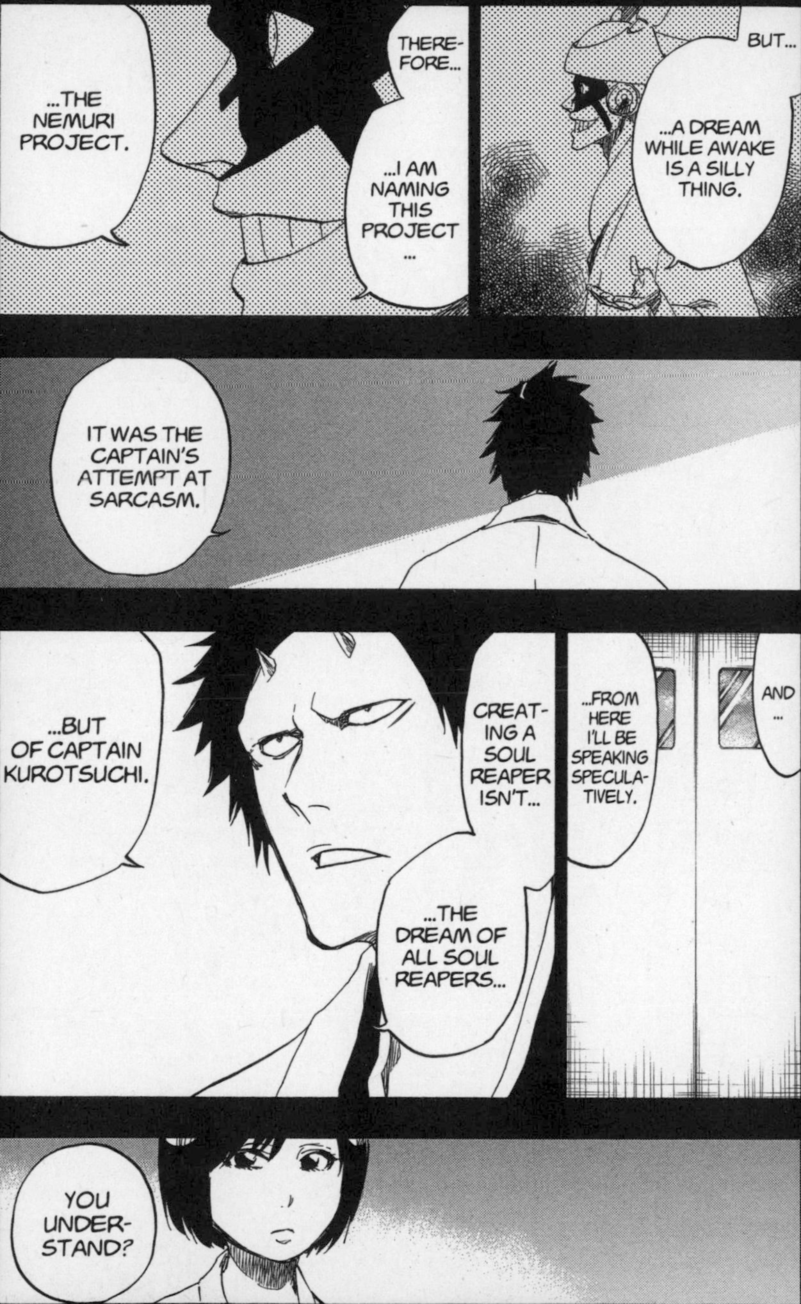
BUT...
...A DREAM WHILE AWAKE IS A SILLY THING.
THEREFORE...
...I AM NAMING THIS PROJECT...
...THE NEMURI PROJECT.
IT WAS THE CAPTAIN'S ATTEMPT AT SARCASM.
AND...
...FROM HERE I'LL BE SPEAKING SPECULATIVELY.
CREATING A SOUL REAPER ISN'T...
...THE DREAM OF ALL SOUL REAPERS...
...BUT OF CAPTAIN KUROTSUCHI.
YOU UNDERSTAND?

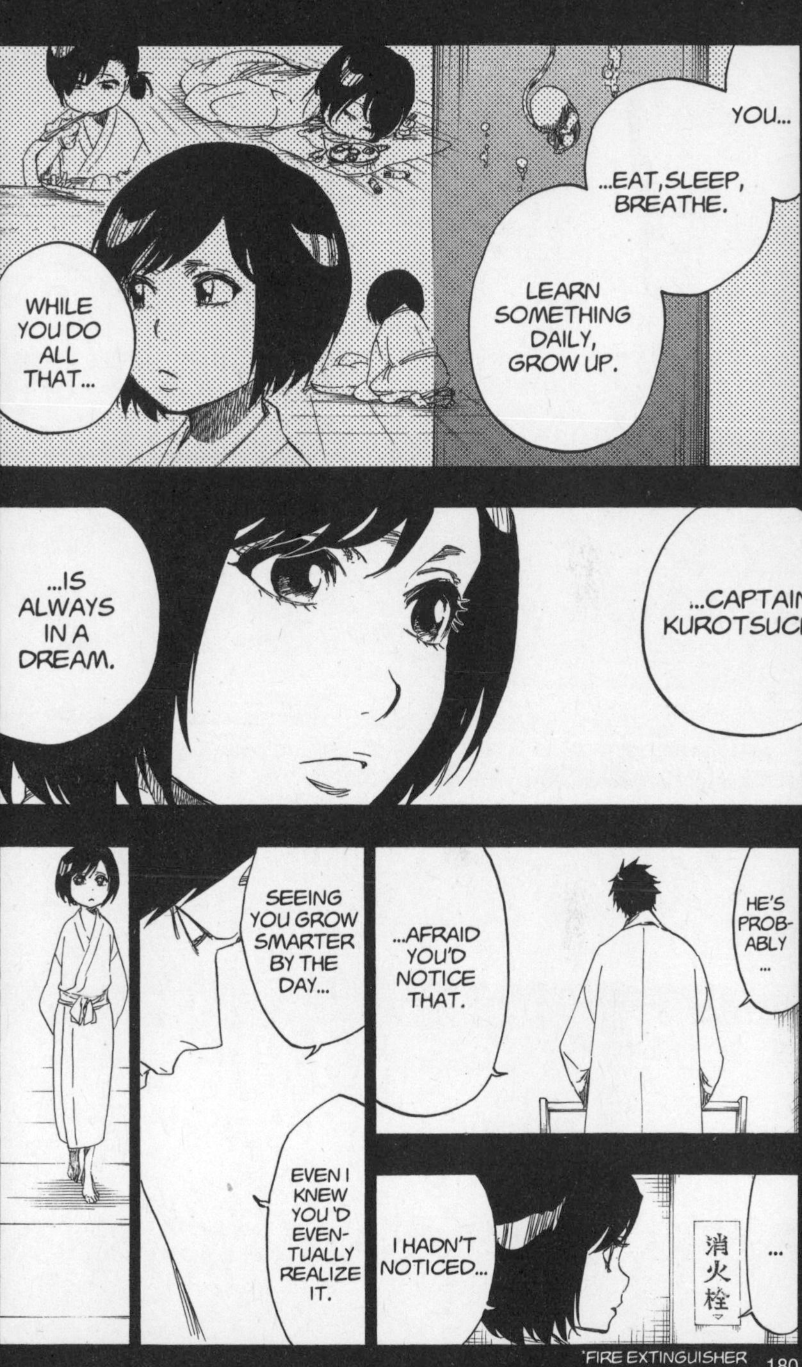
YOU...
...EAT, SLEEP, BREATHE.
LEARN SOMETHING DAILY, GROW UP.
WHILE YOU DO ALL THAT...
...CAPTAIN KUROTSUCHI...
...IS ALWAYS IN A DREAM.
HE'S PROBABLY ...
...AFRAID YOU'D NOTICE THAT.
...
消火栓
I HADN'T NOTICED...
SEEING YOU GROW SMARTER BY THE DAY...
EVEN I KNEW YOU'D EVENTUALLY REALIZE IT.

*FIRE EXTINGUISHER

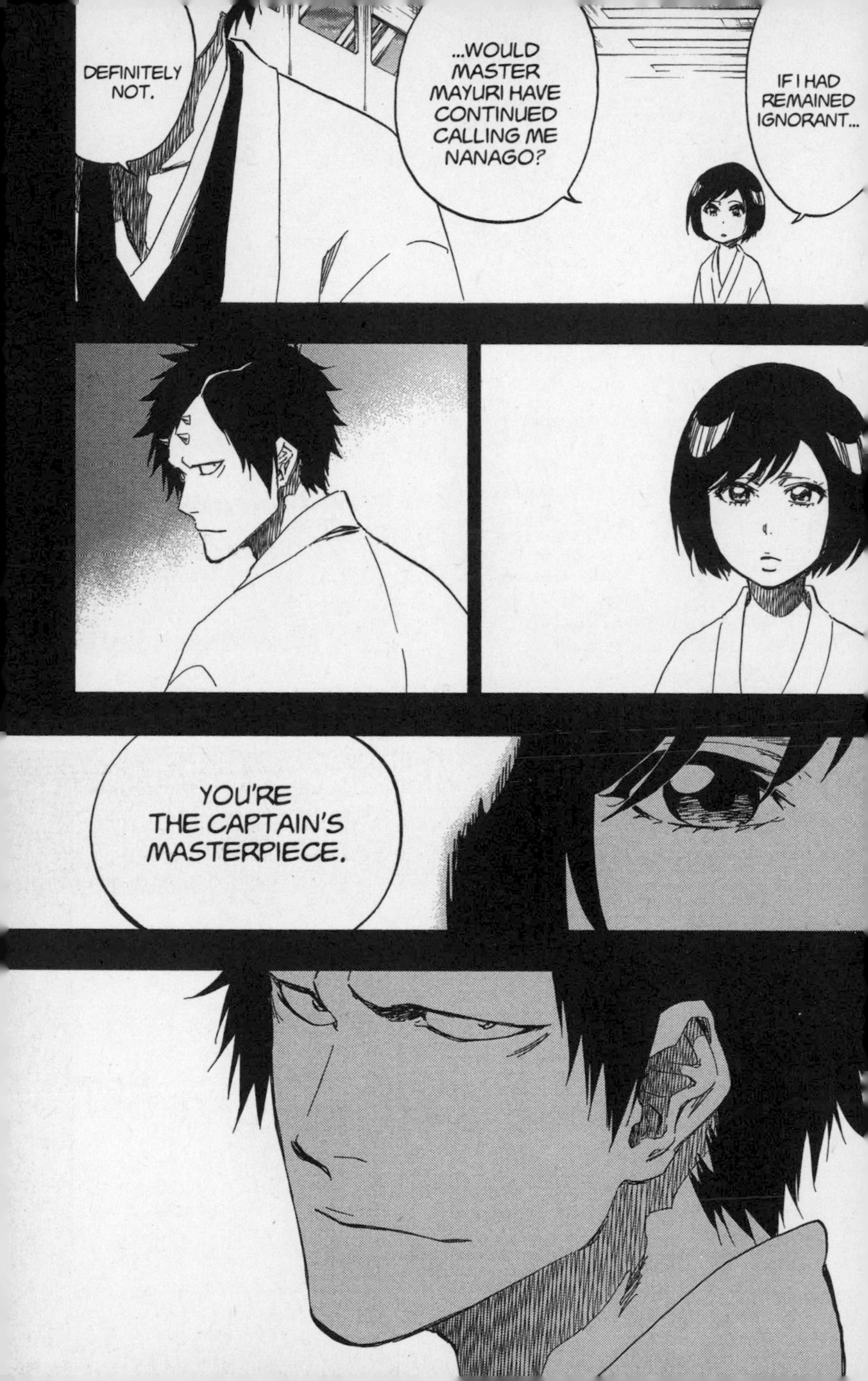
IF I HAD REMAINED IGNORANT...
...WOULD MASTER MAYURI HAVE CONTINUED CALLING ME NANAGO?
DEFINITELY NOT.
YOU'RE THE CAPTAIN'S MASTERPIECE.

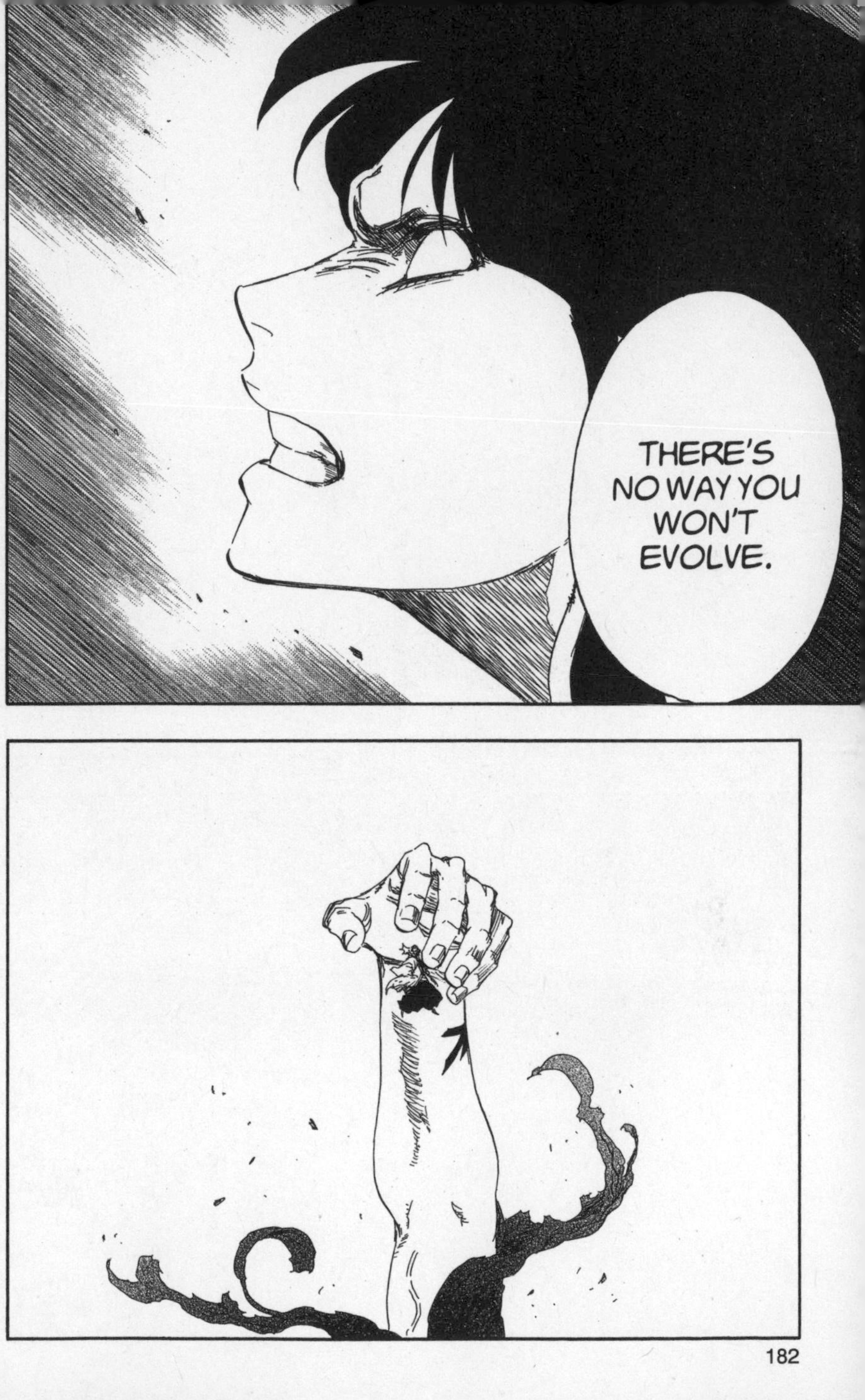
THERE'S NO WAY YOU WON'T EVOLVE.

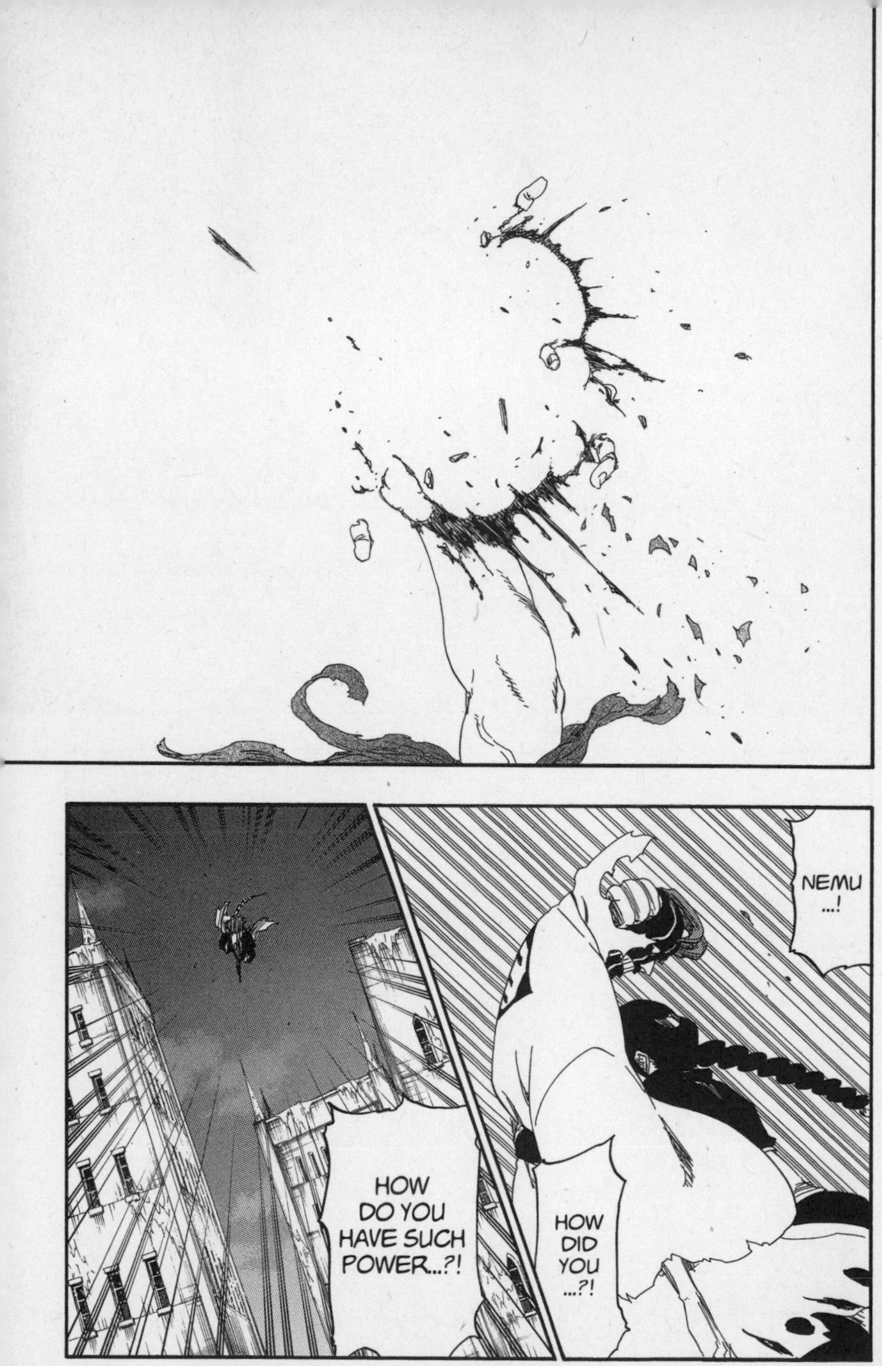
NEMU ...!
HOW DID YOU ...?!
HOW DO YOU HAVE SUCH POWER...?!

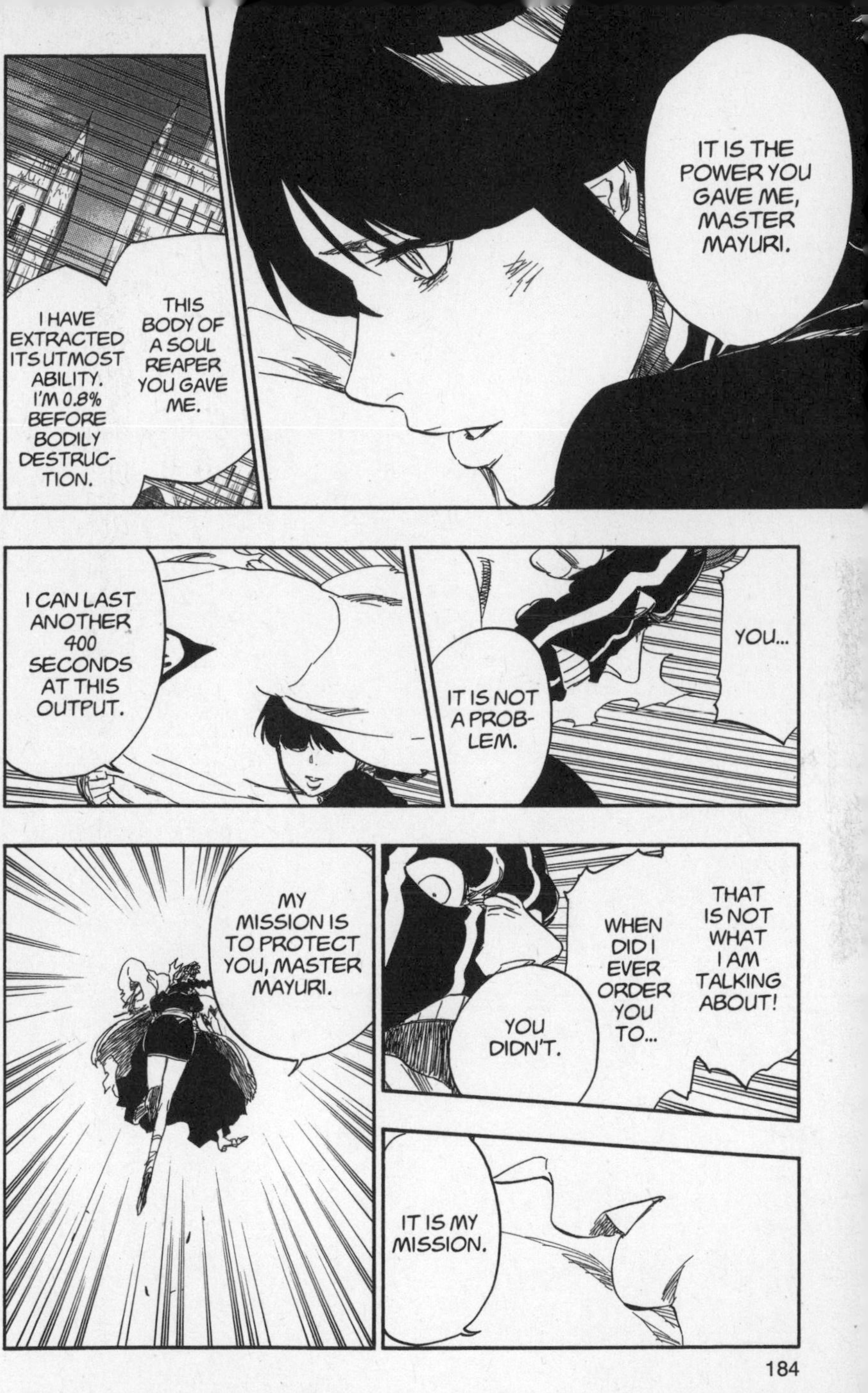
IT IS THE POWER YOU GAVE ME, MASTER MAYURI.
THIS BODY OF A SOUL REAPER YOU GAVE ME.
I HAVE EXTRACTED ITS UTMOST ABILITY. I'M 0.8% BEFORE BODILY DESTRUC-TION.
YOU...
IT IS NOT A PROB-LEM.
I CAN LAST ANOTHER 400 SECONDS AT THIS OUTPUT.
THAT IS NOT WHAT I AM TALKING ABOUT!
WHEN DID I EVER ORDER YOU TO...
YOU DIDN'T.
IT IS MY MISSION.
MY MISSION IS TO PROTECT YOU, MASTER MAYURI.

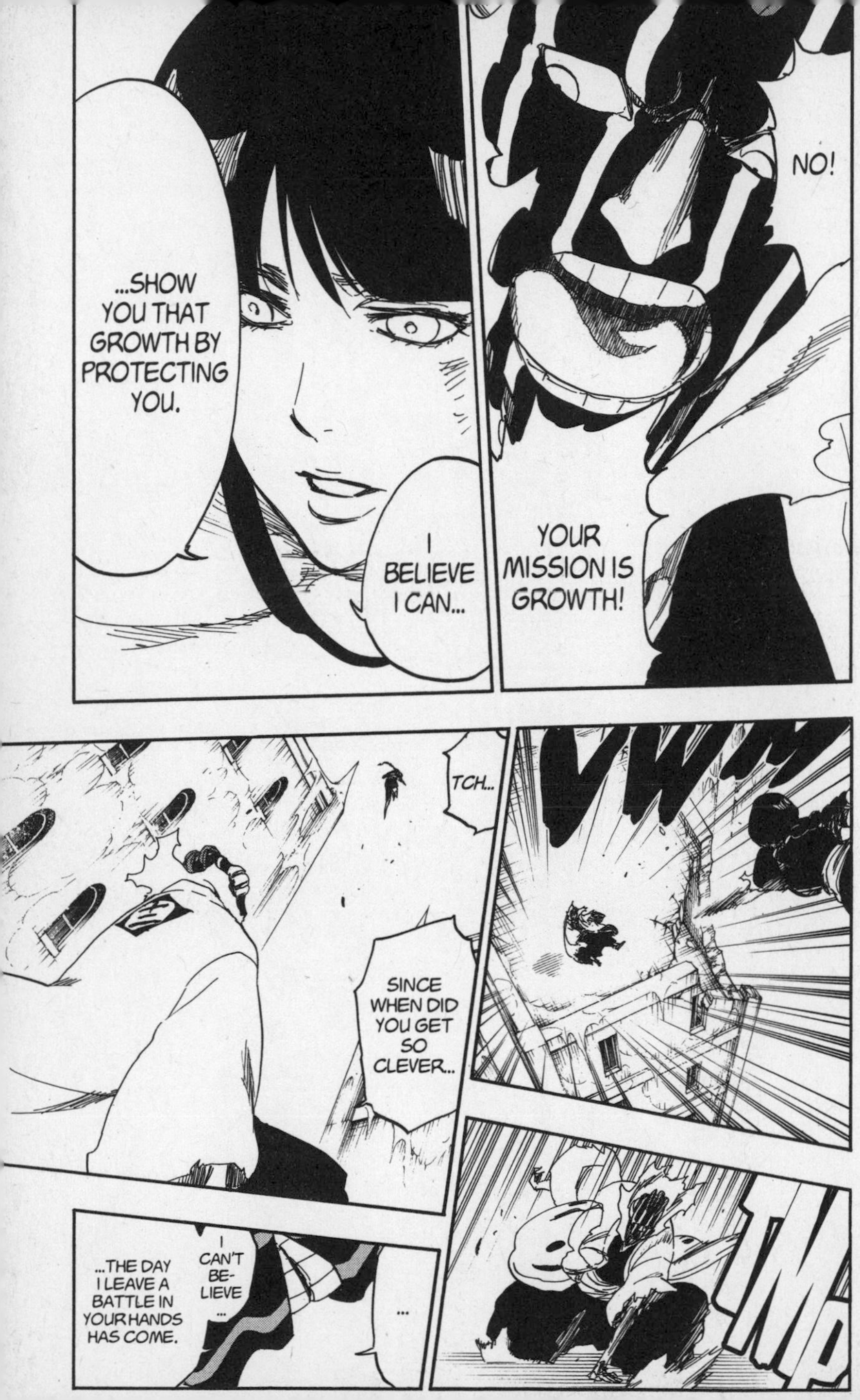
NO!
YOUR MISSION IS GROWTH!
I BELIEVE I CAN...
...SHOW YOU THAT GROWTH BY PROTECTING YOU.
TCH...
SINCE WHEN DID YOU GET SO CLEVER...
...
I CAN'T BE-LIEVE ...
...THE DAY I LEAVE A BATTLE IN YOUR HANDS HAS COME.

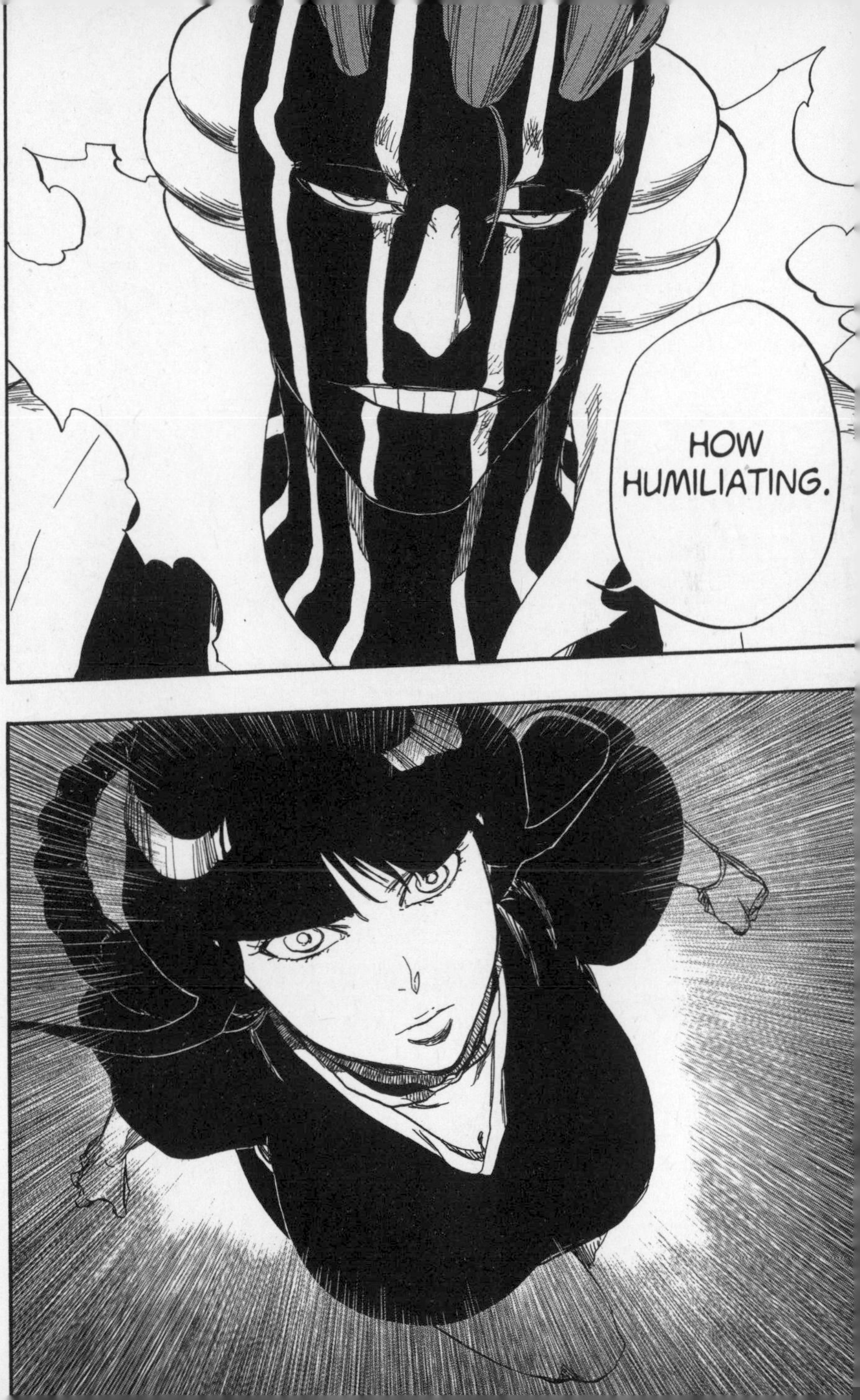
HOW HUMILIATING.

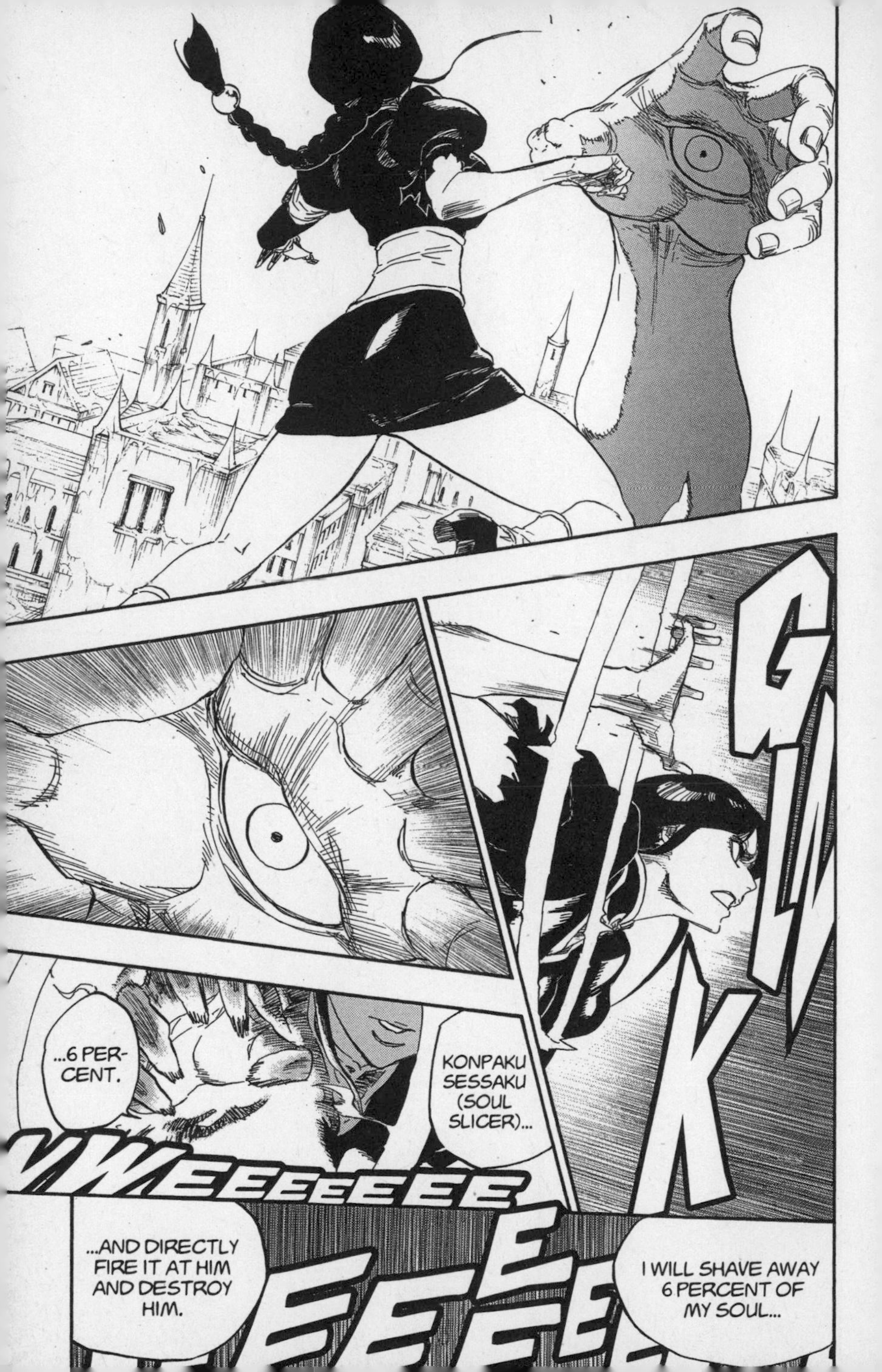
GNK
I WILL SHAVE AWAY 6 PERCENT OF MY SOUL...
...AND DIRECTLY FIRE IT AT HIM AND DESTROY HIM.
KONPAKU SESSAKU (SOUL SLICER)...
...6 PER-CENT.
WEEEEEEEE

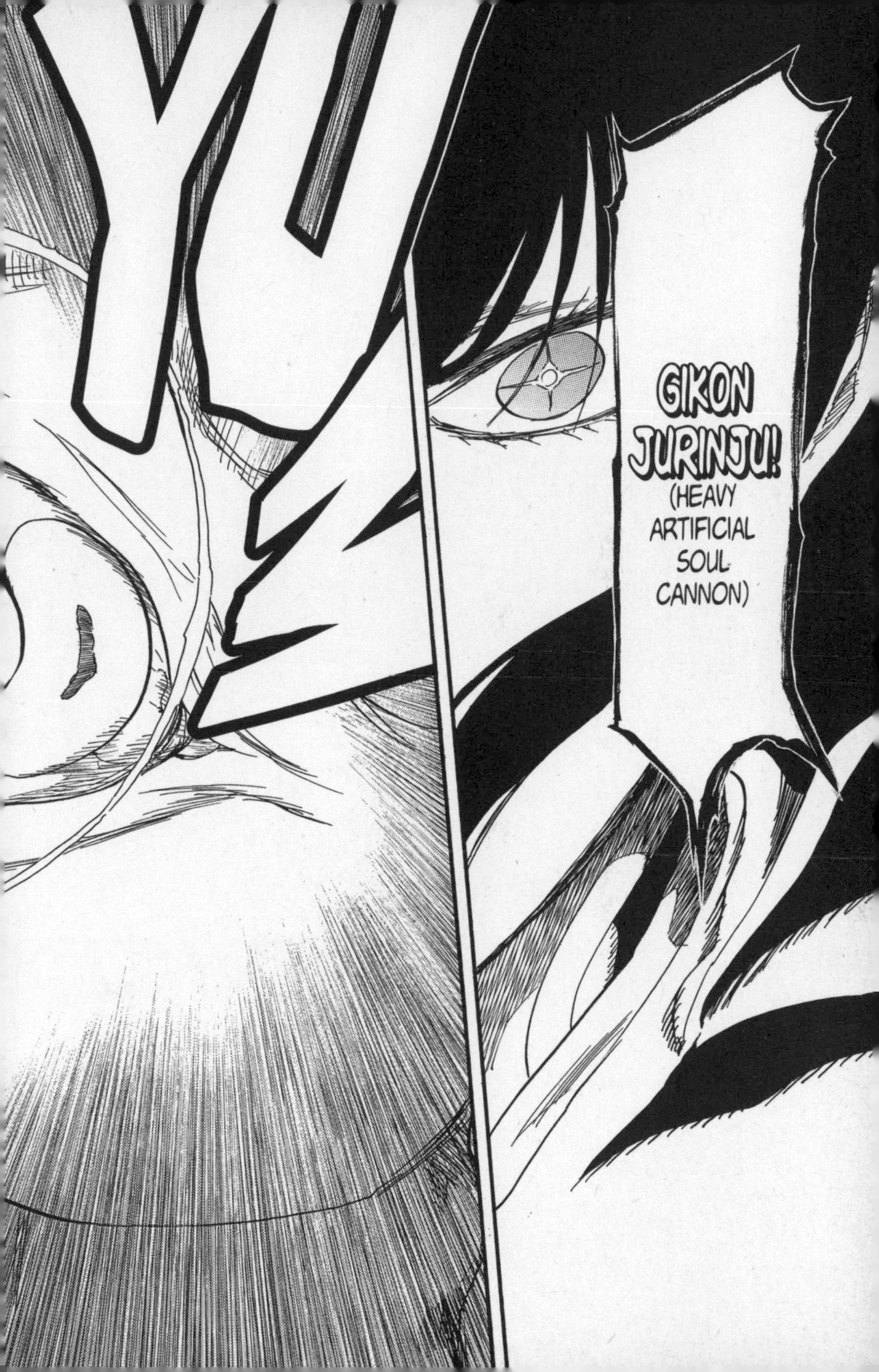
GIKON JURINJU!
(HEAVY ARTIFICIAL SOUL CANNON)

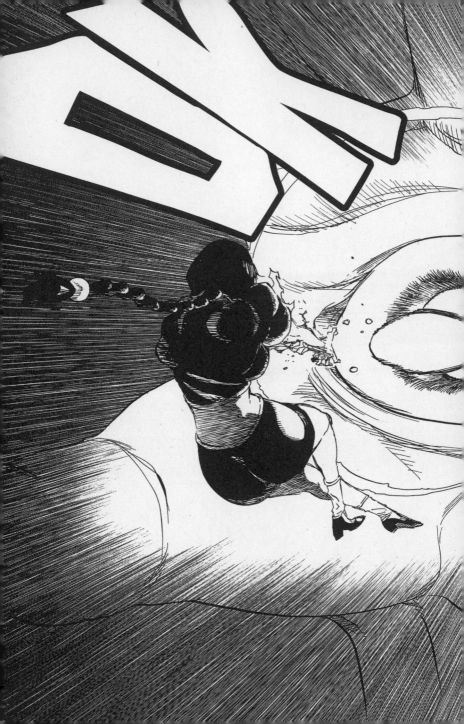

CONTINUED IN BLEACH 71

BLEACH.
untold stories
520.5
walk under
two letters

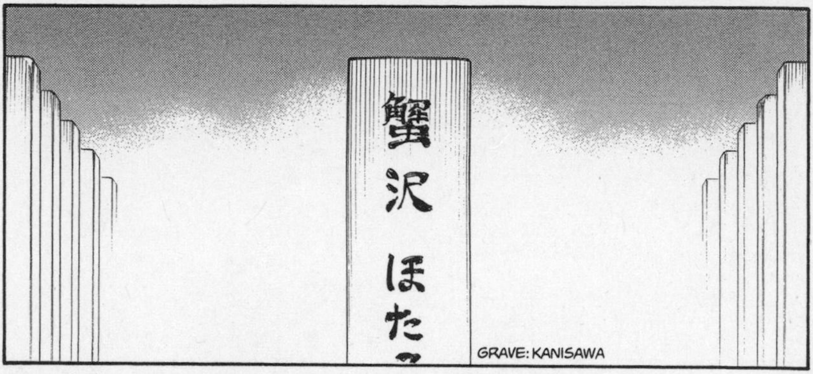
蟹沢 ほた
GRAVE: KANISAWA

bleach 520.5

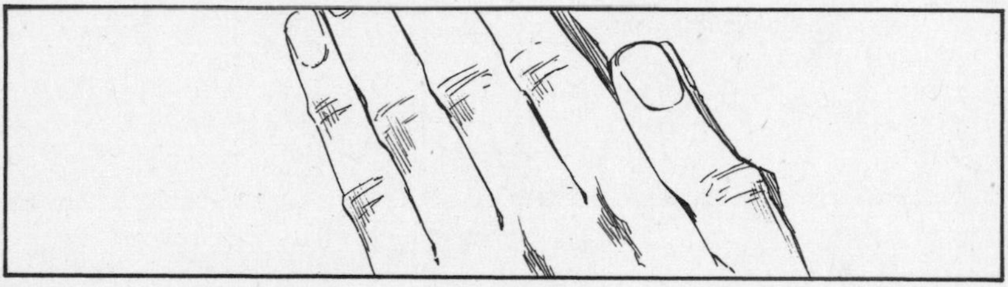

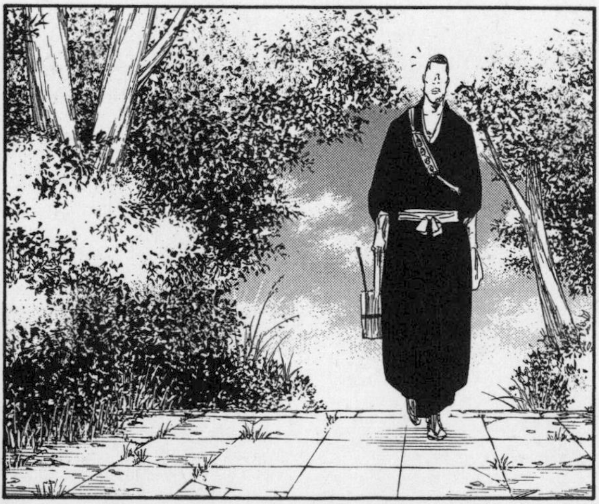

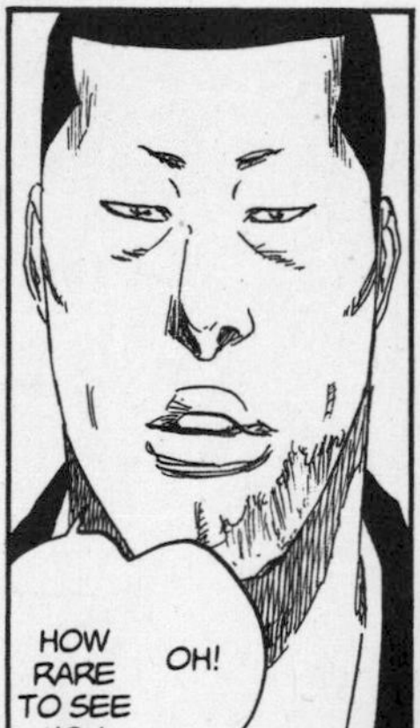
OH!
HOW RARE TO SEE YOU HERE.

walk under two letters

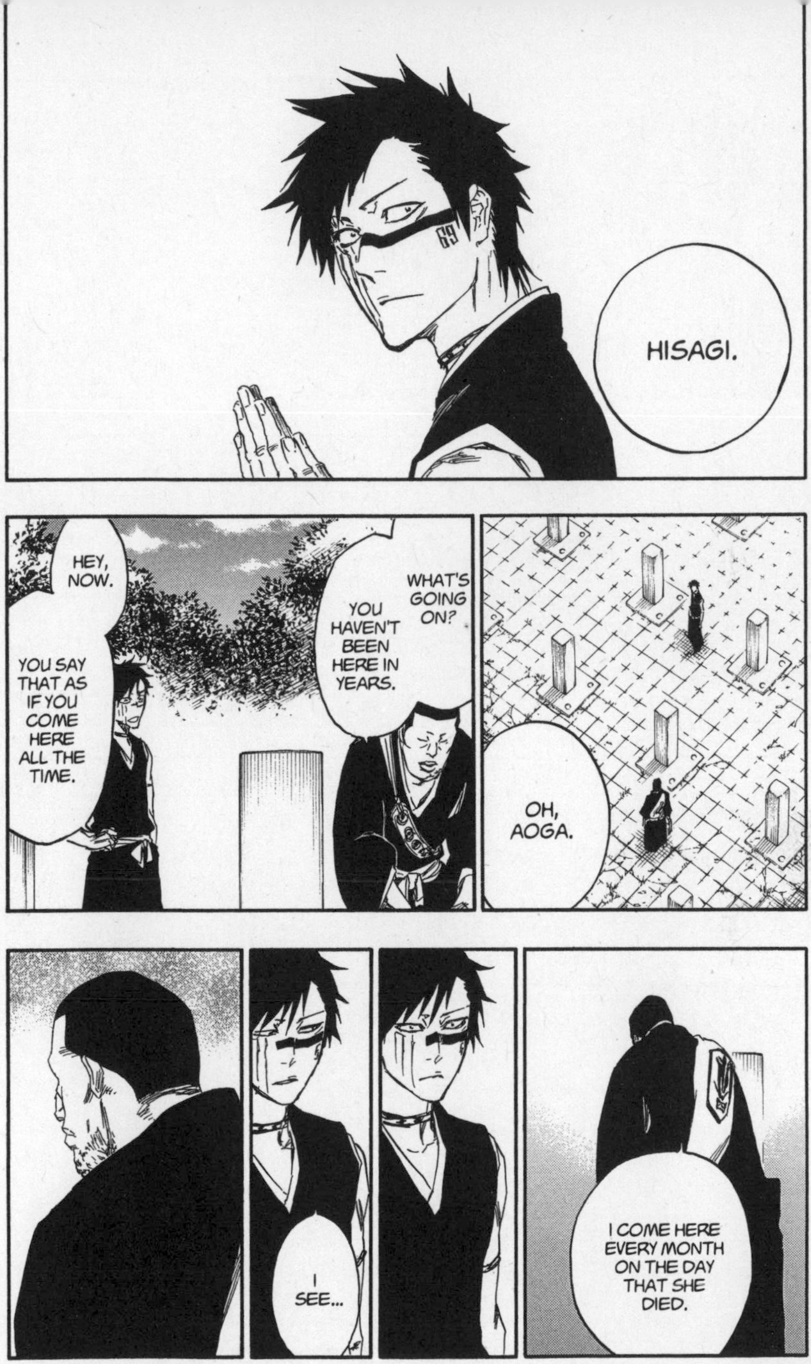
HISAGI.
OH, AOGA.
WHAT'S GOING ON?
YOU HAVEN'T BEEN HERE IN YEARS.
HEY, NOW.
YOU SAY THAT AS IF YOU COME HERE ALL THE TIME.
I COME HERE EVERY MONTH ON THE DAY THAT SHE DIED.
I SEE...

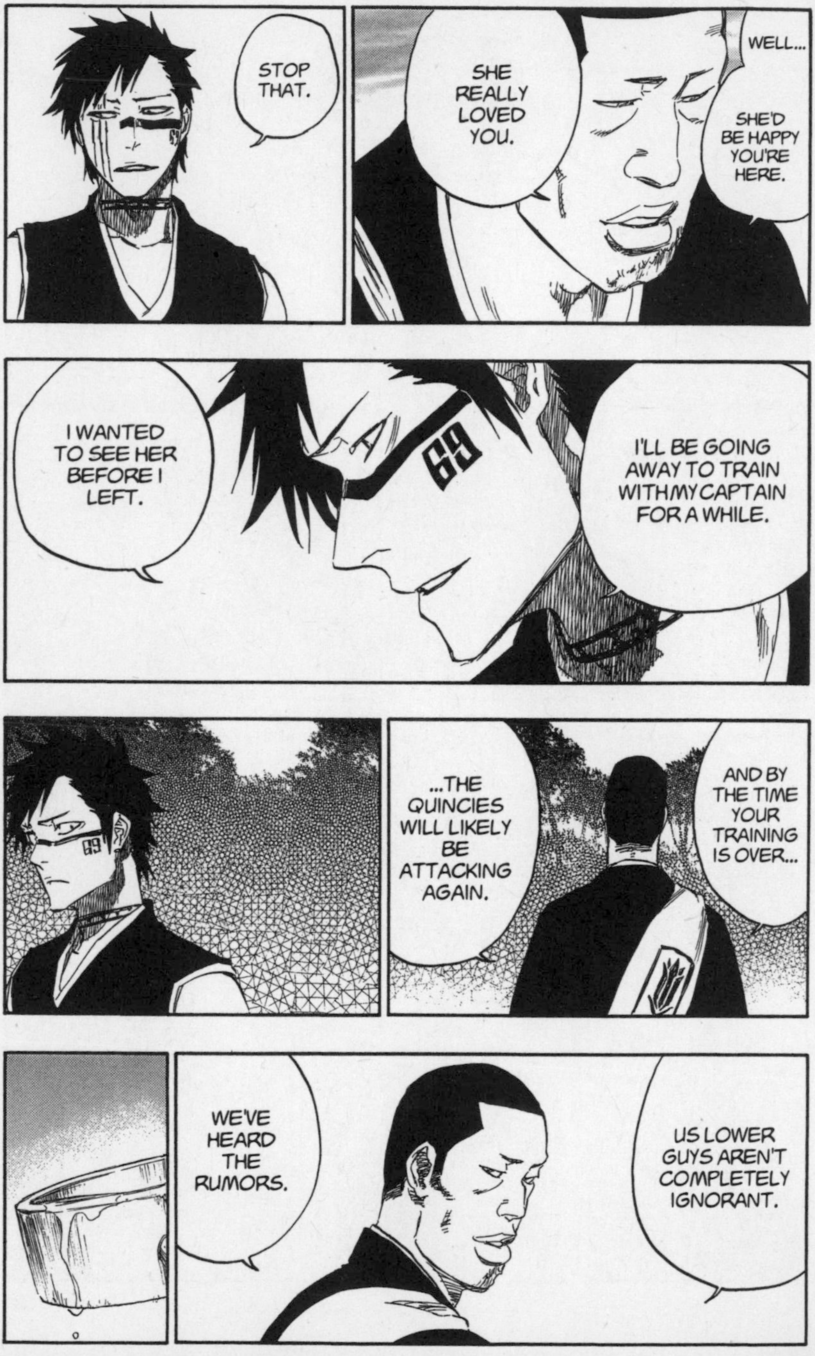
WELL...
SHE'D BE HAPPY YOU'RE HERE.
SHE REALLY LOVED YOU.
STOP THAT.
I'LL BE GOING AWAY TO TRAIN WITH MY CAPTAIN FOR A WHILE.
I WANTED TO SEE HER BEFORE I LEFT.
AND BY THE TIME YOUR TRAINING IS OVER...
...THE QUINCIES WILL LIKELY BE ATTACKING AGAIN.
US LOWER GUYS AREN'T COMPLETELY IGNORANT.
WE'VE HEARD THE RUMORS.

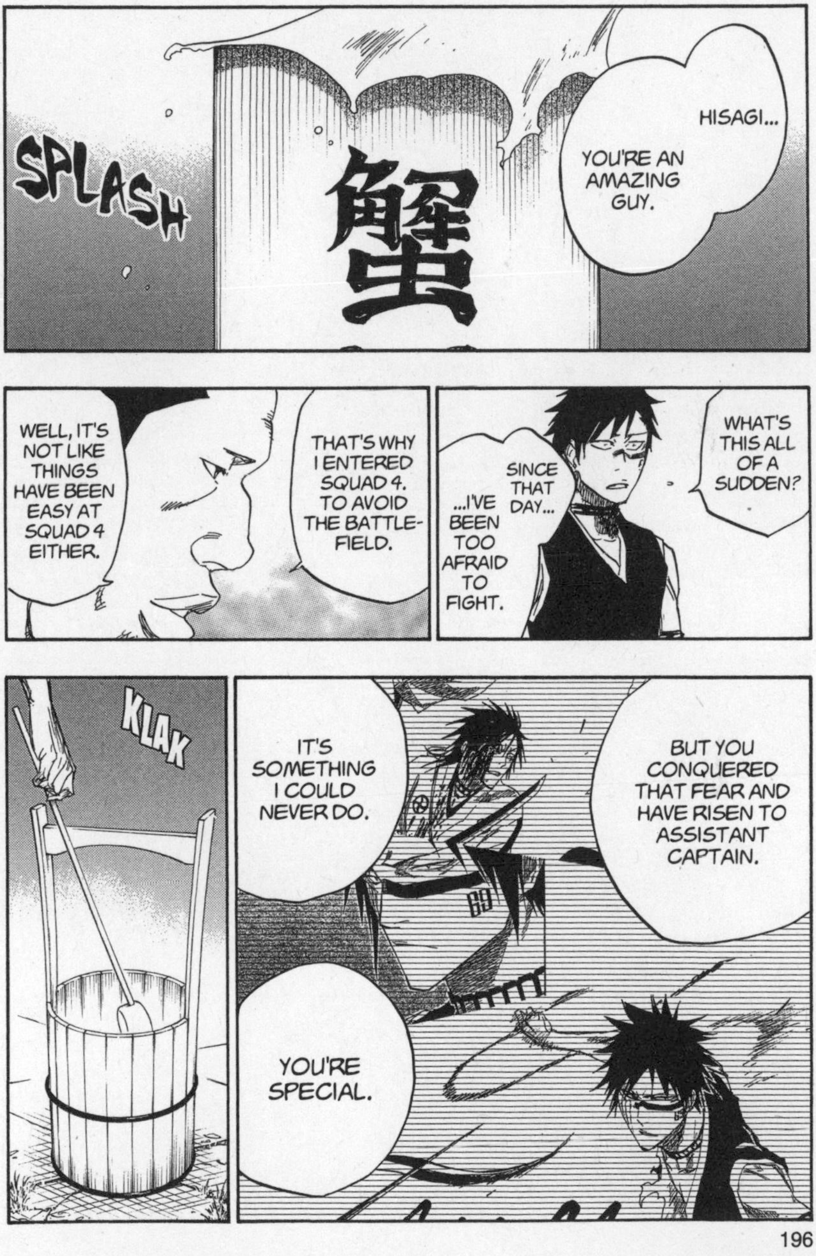
HISAGI...
YOU'RE AN AMAZING GUY.
蟹
SPLASH
WHAT'S THIS ALL OF A SUDDEN?
SINCE THAT DAY...
...I'VE BEEN TOO AFRAID TO FIGHT.
THAT'S WHY I ENTERED SQUAD 4. TO AVOID THE BATTLEFIELD.
WELL, IT'S NOT LIKE THINGS HAVE BEEN EASY AT SQUAD 4 EITHER.
BUT YOU CONQUERED THAT FEAR AND HAVE RISEN TO ASSISTANT CAPTAIN.
IT'S SOMETHING I COULD NEVER DO.
YOU'RE SPECIAL.
KLAK

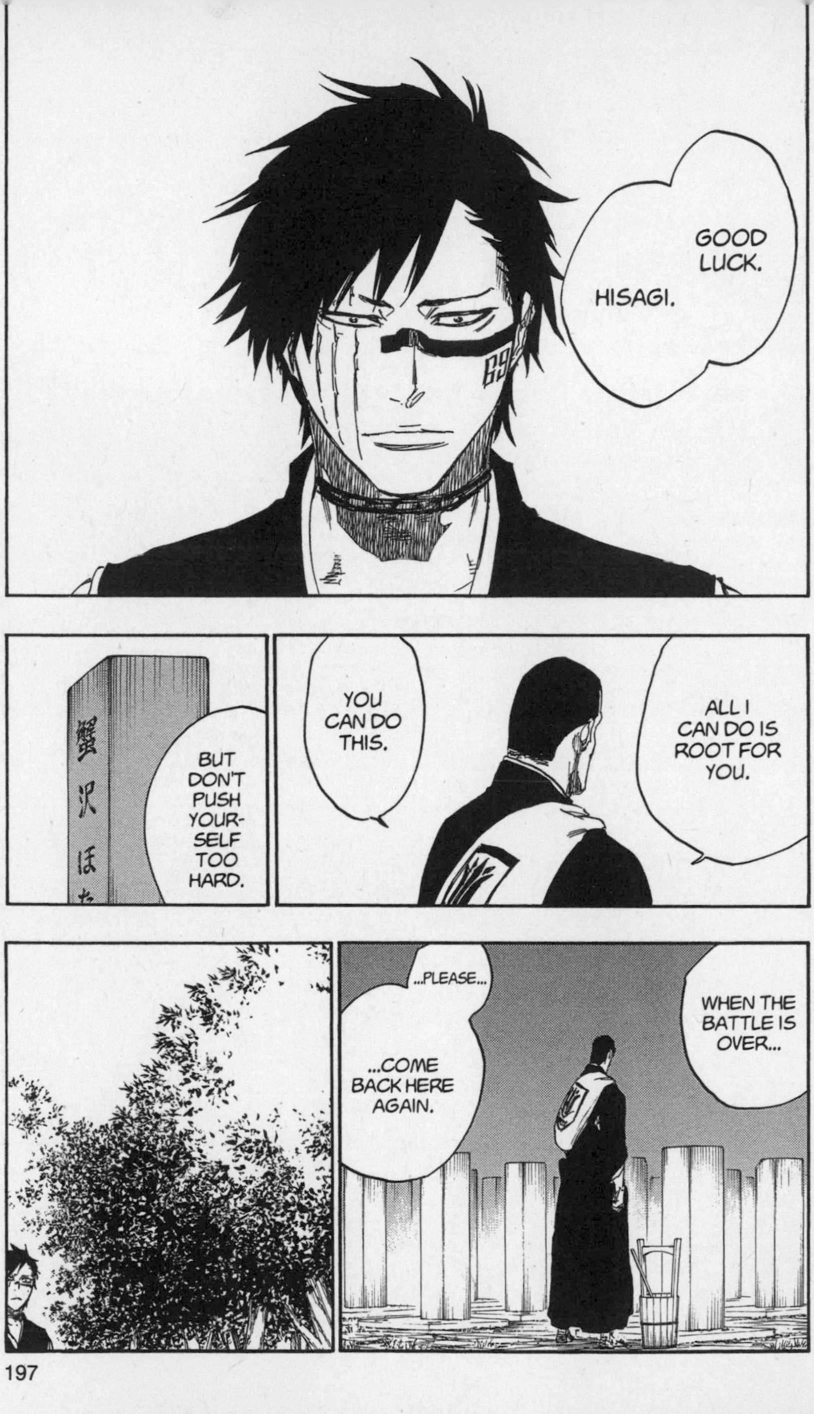
GOOD LUCK.
HISAGI.
ALL I CAN DO IS ROOT FOR YOU.
YOU CAN DO THIS.
蟹沢ほ
BUT DON'T PUSH YOUR-SELF TOO HARD.
WHEN THE BATTLE IS OVER...
...PLEASE...
...COME BACK HERE AGAIN.

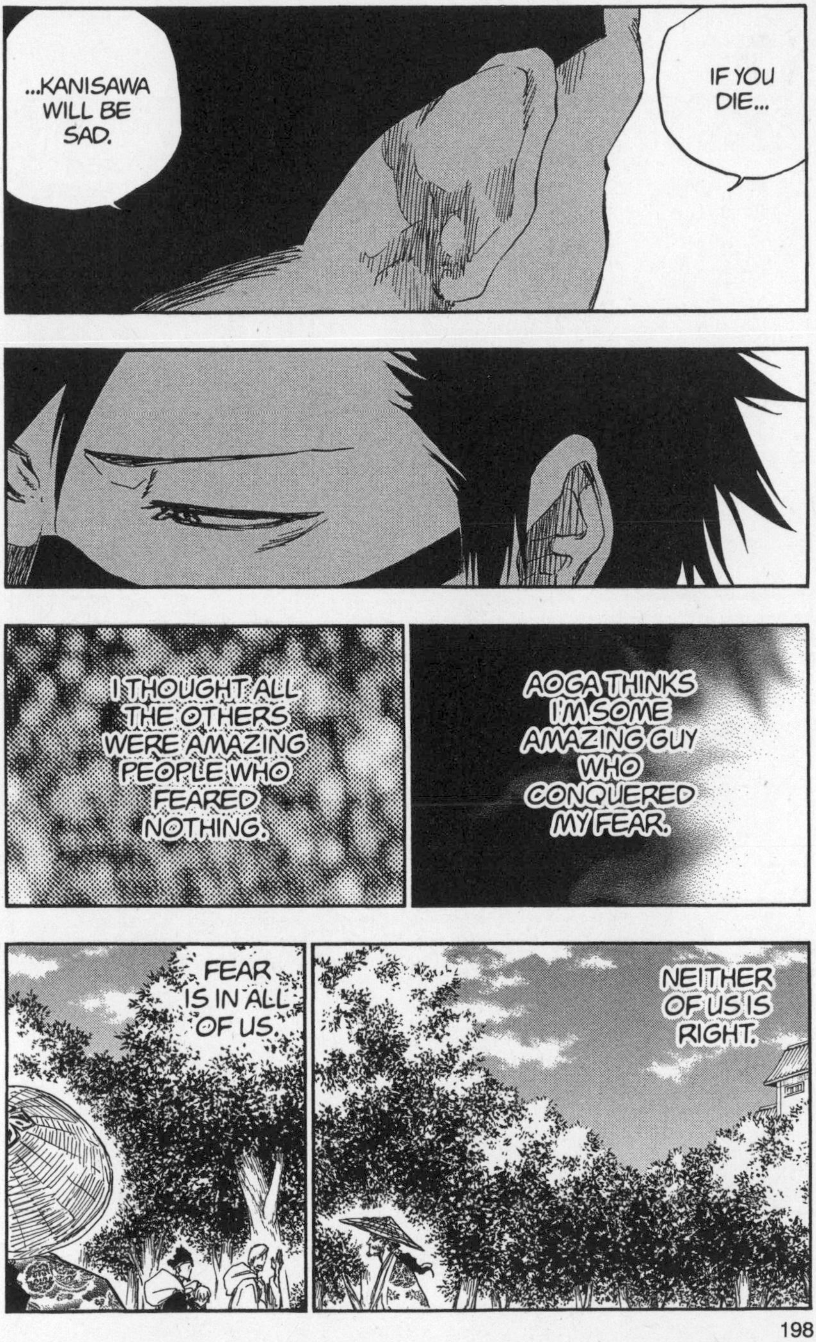
IF YOU DIE...
...KANISAWA WILL BE SAD.
AOGA THINKS I'M SOME AMAZING GUY WHO CONQUERED MY FEAR.
I THOUGHT ALL THE OTHERS WERE AMAZING PEOPLE WHO FEARED NOTHING.
NEITHER OF US IS RIGHT.
FEAR IS IN ALL OF US.

READ THIS WAY

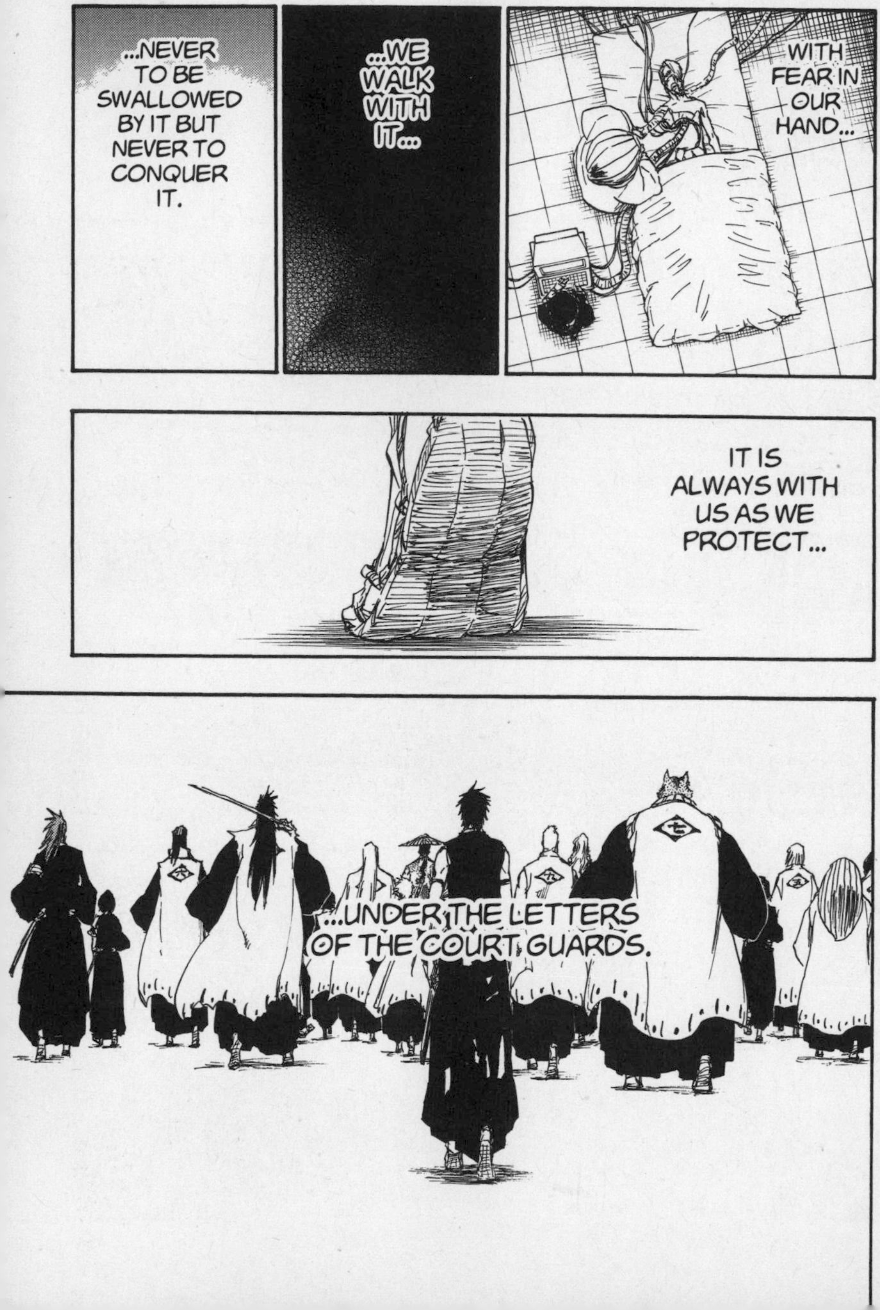
WITH FEAR IN OUR HAND...
...WE WALK WITH IT...
...NEVER TO BE SWALLOWED BY IT BUT NEVER TO CONQUER IT.
IT IS ALWAYS WITH US AS WE PROTECT...
...UNDER THE LETTERS OF THE COURT GUARDS.

You're Reading in the Wrong Direction!!

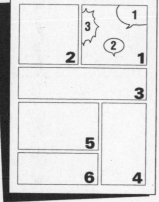

Whoops! Guess what? You're starting at the wrong end of the comic!

…It's true! In keeping with the original Japanese format, **Bleach** is meant to be read from right to left, starting in the upper-right corner.

Unlike English, which is read from left to right, Japanese is read from right to left, meaning that action, sound effects and word-balloon order are completely reversed… something which can make readers unfamiliar with Japanese feel pretty backwards themselves. For this reason, manga or Japanese comics published in the U.S. in English have sometimes been published "flopped"—that is, printed in exact reverse order, as though seen from the other side of a mirror.

By flopping pages, U.S. publishers can avoid confusing readers, but the compromise is not without its downside. For one thing, a character in a flopped manga series who once wore in the original Japanese version a T-shirt emblazoned with "M A Y" (as in "the merry month of") now wears one which reads "Y A M"! Additionally, many manga creators in Japan are themselves unhappy with the process, as some feel the mirror-imaging of their art skews their original intentions.

We are proud to bring you Tite Kubo's **Bleach** in the original unflopped format. For now, though, turn to the other side of the book and let the adventure begin…!

—Editor

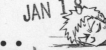

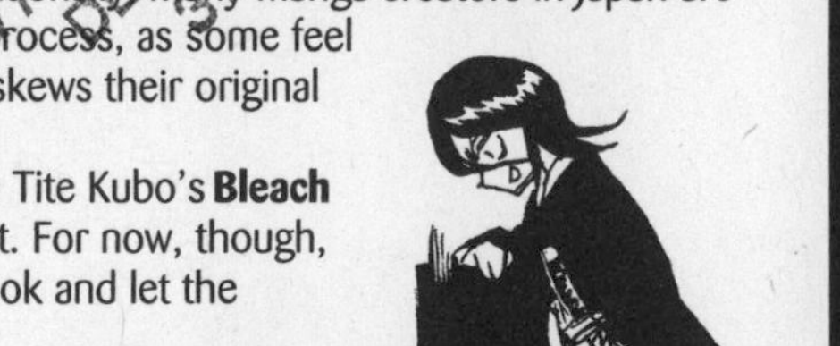